D0073000

Blood and Treasure

TEXAS A&M UNIVERSITY MILITARY HISTORY SERIES

41

BLOOD

& TREASURE

Confederate Empire in the Southwest

By

DONALD S. FRAZIER

Texas A&M University Press · *College Station*

txr

Library of Congress Cataloging-in-Publication Data

Frazier, Donald S. (Shaw), 1965–
    Blood and treasure : Confederate Empire in the Southwest / Donald
S. Frazier. — 1st ed.
        p.   cm. — (Texas A&M University military history series ; no.
41)
    ISBN 0-89096-639-7 (alk. paper)
    1. Southwest, New—History—Civil War, 1861–1865—Campaigns.
2. United States—History—Civil War, 1861–1865—Campaigns. 3. New
Mexico—History—Civil War, 1861–1865. 4. Arizona—History—Civil
War, 1861–1865. I. Title.   II. Series: Texas A & M University military
history series ; 41.
E470.9.F73   1995
973.7'464—dc20   94-39221
                                                      CIP

For my wife, friend,
and soulmate,
Susan,
who made it
all possible,
and to
Dad,
who loved to
"wind them up
and watch them go."

Contents

Illustrations

Maps

Preface

This work is certainly not the first telling of the Confederate invasion of New Mexico. Indeed, it builds upon a foundation that has been added to and refined for several decades. The first comprehensive exploration of the topic came in the early 1960s, from the able pen of the late Martin Hardwick Hall. A generation and a half later, Robert Kirby retold the tale. Others, most recently Alvin Josephy, have placed the campaign in the context of the war in the Far West. Don Alberts and Jerry Thompson have added to these surveys and the synthesis with specialized studies and with edited primary sources that have enriched the tale. By and large, the critical spade work had been done long before this most recent entry saw light.

The goal of this book is to build upon these earlier endeavors but also to add a sense of historical and continental context. From the blending of works of antebellum specialists, those interested in American imperialism, the chroniclers of the campaign, and traditional military history, a rich synthesis emerges. This work focuses, more closely than earlier ones, on the personalities, the participants, the military process, and the role of the campaign in the fight for southern independence. It is an attempt to bind together somewhat divergent lines of scholarship into one cohesive seam.

With such a large amount of research available, the bulk of the investigation for this book was aimed at uncovering new materials and reevaluating prior interpretations. Fortune and interested parties provided a wealth of new accounts on the campaign, each of which illuminated the story in amazing ways. This book then gives these tales the exposure they deserve, more richly embroidering a fascinating saga.

This work, like most scholarship, is indeed a collaborative effort. First, Don Alberts of Albuquerque and Jerry Thompson of Laredo introduced me to the sources and sites of the Confederate invasion of New Mexico. The staffs of the Eugene C. Barker Texas History Center, Special Collections at Louisiana State University, the Historic New Orleans Collection, the Texas State Library, Hill College Confederate Research Center, the Smith County Archives, the Fort Worth Public Library, Special Collections at the United States Military Academy, and the Southwestern Branch of the United States Archives immensely facilitated the task of finding new sources. Others, from all over the country, sent additional sources and materials. A special thanks goes to Mike Hewatt for a variety of contributions.

A wide array of people read and commented on the work. My boon companion on the fields of New Mexico, Erwin Bullock of Arlington, provided insights and asked critical questions that helped the book along. Richard B. Winders and James Bain, also of Arlington, likewise helped to knock off some of the rough edges. Larry McNay and Gil Vollmering also had a part. Alberts and Thompson read the work in its preliminary stages and offered much in the way of refining. Mike Parrish of Austin took an interest in the work early on and encouraged me to have it published. Capt. Tyree Smith and especially Lt. Col. Conrad Crane, both of West Point, gave portions of the work a critical military review which increased its value. Thanks to all for their help. Any errors that remain are mine alone.

Texas Christian University, while I was there, brought together some of the finest men and women I will ever know; they helped me immeasurably. Marvin Schultz, a fellow traveller, first suggested the thesis of my book during the course of a seminar. Robert Maberry, Jr., demanded that I cast my tale in terms of the human condition. Robert Pace was a long-lost brother, Jeff Pilcher a noble friend; both greatly helped me along the way. Ty Cashion read the work critically and provided a host of suggestions, while Dallas Cothrum and David Coffey encouraged me to "spin a good yarn." Margaret Farmer, the linchpin of the history department, was an enthusiastic supporter at critical times in my career. I also want to thank Juliett George and Lawrence LeBarge. Members of my dissertation committee, including Spencer Tucker, Don Worcester, and Ken Stevens, did their duty in making me defend my thesis while fine-tuning my communication skills. There was also an absolute army of undergraduates in several American history surveys that learned to do census work as a result of this project, and I sincerely thank them all for their efforts. Tori Gouge, whom I coerced into reading the manuscript, also helped.

This work is also a collaborative effort in terms of family support. Susan, my wife of seven years and friend for thirteen, supported me through graduate school and served as the sole source of true stability in my life while this task was completed. R. Mack Frazier and Robert P. Frazier, both older brothers, served as readers and cheerleaders for this project. Ed Frazier and brothers-in-law Alan Cochrum and Steve Eckersley also made useful comments. A huge amount of moral support came from my in-laws, Jack and Pat Buckley, who also suffered through the manuscript. Jimmie Faye Frazier, my mother, Tim Frazier, yet another brother, and my sisters Jennifer Cochrum and Beth Eckersley supported my decision to quit a decent job in industry to pursue graduate degrees. Thanks to all for all that you have done.

Two men—my father, James B. Frazier, and my mentor, Grady McWhiney—deserve special recognition. Dad introduced me to historical research. On a hot summer day in Macon, Georgia, he showed me the pathos of a cemetery containing dead from the War for Southern Independence. These men, like me, were Texans, and a long way from home. He taught me how to research them, their lives, and times. He died when this work was barely under way, but he would have been profoundly interested. He gets the credit for starting me down this road. McWhiney took me in from the outside, taught me his craft, and shielded me from some of the absolute nonsense involved in this profession. To him, training a student was not enough. He considered all of his students his children and nurtured and protected us all like a good father. Every day I am increasingly grateful for a man like McWhiney who so ably guarded his brood. I would never have made it without him.

Blood and Treasure

CHAPTER 1

Texans, Southerners, and Dreams of Empire

The South shook itself free of the Puritans and the Devil!
—*Charleston Mercury,* December 7, 1860

In 1885, sixty-six-year-old Trevanion Theodore Teel, aging and gray, sent the editors of *The Century* magazine an article for their "Battles and Leaders of the Civil War" series. His short article, "Sibley's New Mexican Campaign—Its Objects and the Causes of its Failure," sketched the Confederacy's brief but disastrous attempt at empire in 1861. "The object of his campaign was explained in detail by Gen. H. H. Sibley to the writer," Teel recounted. "President Davis had authorized him to enlist three regiments in Texas," and to form an army augmented by recruits from New Mexico, California, Arizona, and Colorado. His ultimate goal was the conquest of California. "If the Confederates succeeded in occupying California, New Mexico, and Arizona, negotiations to secure Chihuahua, Sonora, and Lower California, either by purchase or by conquest, would be opened. Sibley thought that he would have little difficulty in consummating the ends so devoutly wished by the Confederate Government."[1]

The country had changed much in the twenty years since the end of the war, but Teel, at his home in San Antonio and still the old Rebel artillerist at heart, remembered: He had suffered through heat and cold; he still saw his naive young gunners struggling to become men. The war had extinguished the dream of Southern independence, but his memories lived on—even as those stirring events of the 1860s were forgotten by a younger, more forward-looking generation of Americans.

By 1885, Sibley's invasion of New Mexico—Teel's campaign— had faded into merely a footnote in Civil War history, scarcely more than a quixotic misadventure. Things had been different in 1861, though. Confederate leaders knew the time had come to braid together two related threads of history. The South had long coveted the western territories and Mexico. Texas, in reality an extension of the South, also wanted these lands. Both powers—one a state and former republic, the other a nation composed of newly sovereign states—used the liberating mechanism of secession to claim what each considered rightfully its own.

The origins of Southern imperial ambitions are old, their roots deep. Americans, especially Southerners, had long manifested a penchant for expansion. Pushing inland from coastal enclaves, they carved an empire from the wilderness.

Eventually this outward momentum of the nation became concentrated on expansion to the west—although Americans attempted to push north and south, the path of least resistance seemed always to lead to the sparsely settled west. The drive for expansion continued even when impractical. During the Revolution and War of 1812, American attempts to take Canada had failed miserably. Expansionists had better luck against adjacent areas tentatively held by Spain and, later, by the nations descended from its colonial empire.

Southerners, with proximity to Hispanic domains, naturally became skilled expansionists. Land-hungry agrarians with a talent for things military, they were the principal agents and proponents of an ever-expanding American empire. Southerners gloried in this role and, throughout the first seventy years of American history, could be found in the forefront of national expansion. The Missouri Compromise of 1820 also fueled Southern ambition. With little territory then in the Union reserved for slavery as a result of this legislation, any expansion of the peculiar institution would, by law, come from south of 36°30' latitude. After 1821, this meant Mexico.

By the 1850s, sectional differences within the nation had undermined American expansionism. The slavery question, among other issues, eventually infected and deflected the American mission of continental domination. Bitter disputes over the newly acquired territories, whether they would be slave or free, blunted American expansionism and frustrated would-be imperialists. This sense of frustration was naturally felt most acutely in the South. The political impasse eventually led to the sectionalization of imperialism. According to historian Robert May, the Southern dream of empire, denied it by the North, helped fuel the drive for secession in 1860.[2]

The dissolution of the Union and resulting civil war changed the underlying principles, but not the essential nature, of America's expansionist tendencies—a Southern empire would, of course, be for slave owners. When Confederate authorities authorized a military campaign into the American Southwest in 1861, it was not an aberration in Southern war aims nor a sideshow to more important events in Virginia. The Confederate invasion of New Mexico was the heir of Manifest Destiny, filibustering, and the American drive for expansion. Expansion from coast to coast was required, for the same reasons that the United States had built its empire in the 1840s and 1850s, if the new Confederate nation was to succeed as a dynamic, progressive country. Building a Confederate Empire from the rubble of the Union was a basic goal of Southern independence, not an afterthought.[3]

Texans, the instrument of Confederate imperialism, wore the mantle comfortably. The state had a long history of nationalism, or, more accurately, localism. Lone Star soldiers and politicians had always been ardent expansionists. The state had also compiled an impressive résumé of imperialistic military adventures, and its fighting men were leaders or partisans in most of the more notorious attempts at armed expansion. The creation of empires suited the Texas temperament.

Texas was, after all, born in battle. The spirit of revolution, the promise of glory, and bounties of free land had attracted an adventurous breed of men to the young republic. Mostly from the Deep South came a mix of outcasts, drifters, and professional adventurers along with respectable, civic-minded men and ambitious planters. All came to build their dreams, and many tended to support

Territory Claimed
at Various Times
by The Republic of Texas

- - - Modern State Boundaries

San Francisco

Santa Fe

Albuquerque

Santa Fe County

Tucson

Worth County

REPUBLIC OF TEXAS

El Paso del Norte

El Paso County

Presidio County

Austin

San Antonio

Guaymas

Chihuahua

IMPERIAL TEXAS

REPUBLIC OF MEXICO

military solutions to most problems of state. In the 1830s and early 1840s, war in Texas was a reality, and men who savored combat splashed across the Red and Sabine Rivers in ever growing numbers. Their successes in "Rangering Companies" against Mexicans and Comanches led the Texan leadership to indulge in dreams far in excess of the republic's actual ability to accomplish.[4]

Texan imperialism blossomed with independence as the vision of a vast Texan empire took shape. With tenuous historical justification, leaders claimed the Rio Grande from source to mouth as the national border. This included Santa Fe, the great El Dorado at the foot of the mountains, as the rightful plunder and possession of the new nation. Other proposals urged Texas lawmakers to acquire, through purchase or by force, large tracts of northern Mexico from the Gulf to the Sea of Cortez. Texan claims expanded as the United States maneuvered the Texas boundary to meet its own territorial ambitions. In an effort to place an American claim on the Pacific coast, Pres. Andrew Jackson urged Texas to claim California.[5] Capturing the spirit, the bellicose Columbia *Telegraph and Texas Register* boasted, in 1837, that "The army of Texas will display its victorious banner west of the Rio Grande, and when once its conquering march shall have commenced, . . . the roar of the Texan rifles shall mingle in unison with the thunders of the Pacific."[6]

Early faith in this destiny led Texans to establish their national capital, Austin, on the frontier and away from the established centers of population. Expansionist Texan Pres. Mirabeau B. Lamar, who extravagantly predicted an empire from sea to sea, boasted that the rustic log cabin settlement would serve as the "seat of future empire."[7] The men charged with locating the capital concurred, anticipating the time when "a great thoroughfare shall be established from Santa Fe to our seaports, and another from the Red River to Matamoros, which two routes must always of necessity intersect each other at this point."[8]

Texans persuaded themselves that their claim on eastern New Mexico was legitimate, and volunteers were eager to establish control of the region. In 1837, the inhabitants of Río Arriba, or northern New Mexico, revolted, sending an encouraging, if mistaken, signal to the Republic of Texas.[9] As a result, starting in 1841, Texan forces made three separate attempts to invade, control, and coerce Santa Fe into the dominion, each meeting with bitter failure. These reversals, however, did nothing to dampen the Texans' claim to New Mexico east of the Rio Grande.[10]

Ultimately, in 1845, the United States and Texas annexed each other, a move destined to fulfill both nations' expansionist goals while further trampling the national honor of Mexico. The United States continued its westward drive while Texas, under the aegis of the American military, expected at last to achieve control over Santa Fe—a feat it had failed to accomplish on its own. Mexico refused to let Texas, which it still considered a province in rebellion, be swallowed up by the United States. War followed. By 1848, however, Mexico's armies had been scattered and defeated, and Americans occupied a third of its territory. The Treaty of Guadalupe-Hidalgo, which concluded the war, left the United States in possession of this vast area.

For the United States, however, this gain proved to be its undoing. Acquisition of this "Mexican Cession" gravely aggravated sectional issues plaguing the United States. Southerners were determined to maintain the balance of power in national politics by extending slavery westward into the new territories. Abolitionists were equally determined to exclude the peculiar institution from them. To expansionists, the consequence of this growing national deadlock was obvious—internecine political conflict would curtail the acquisition of any new territory in the future.[11]

Meanwhile, the State of Texas took steps to establish its jurisdiction over eastern New Mexico according to its own agenda. On March 15, 1848, the state legislature created Santa Fe County, encompassing most of the territory between the Rio Grande and the Pecos River, and sent Spruce M. Baird of Nacogdoches as county judge and the state's representative. He arrived in Santa Fe on May 24, but found his efforts blocked by U.S. military officers. The people of New Mexico, too, were hostile, preferring separate territorial status to union with Texas. Frustrated, Baird abandoned his mission and returned to Austin. Texans felt betrayed.[12]

By 1849, the impasse between the Lone Star State and the United States over the future of New Mexico had reached a crisis point: New Mexico, under the protection of the U.S. Army, was taking steps to organize its own government, blatantly ignoring Texan claims to part of the region. Texas Gov. Peter H. Bell urged his legislature to dispatch troops to back Texas' claims.[13] Texan settlers, mostly veterans armed with land bounties granted for service in the Texas Revolution and Mexican War, already claimed headrights along the eastern bank of the Rio Grande in the Mesilla Valley. The state owed a debt to these men, and should support them—they would lose everything if New Mexico succeeded in its plans.[14] Even so, the more moderate legislature rejected Bell's request for an invasion. Instead, the lawmakers continued optimistically planning for eventual Texan control; they reduced Santa Fe County by creating three additional counties: Worth, El Paso, and Presidio. On January 15, 1850, Robert S. Neighbors, veteran frontiersman and Indian agent, received orders to proceed to the Trans-Pecos region and to organize the new counties, whether New Mexicans liked it or not.[15]

Neighbors met with mixed success. The citizens of El Paso County reacted enthusiastically to Texan overtures but Indians in Presidio County made organization attempts there too dangerous. The people of Worth and Santa Fe counties resisted. Civil officials appointed by the U.S. Army refused to surrender their authority and they opposed Texan claims. Neighbors found pro-Texas sentiment among many of the inhabitants, but the political obstacles raised by U.S. officials and their appointees proved insurmountable. The commissioner returned to Texas, but left recently returned Judge Baird in Albuquerque to represent the state's interests.[16]

Neighbors' reports brought renewed storms of protest in the Lone Star State. Mass meetings across the state in June, July, and August all clamored for armed intervention. "We must protect our rights by that last resort of an injured people—the force of arms," trumpeted the *Austin State Gazette*.[17] Other papers claimed that hundreds of volunteers were eager to march on New Mexico. Some citizens decried the duplicity of the U.S. government. Benjamin Rush Wallace wrote Sen. Thomas Rusk an angry letter stating, "Jesus could be composed under insult, but the people of Texas are of a different breed: they will not submit to a government that divests them of what they prize higher than they do the Union itself."[18] Southerners expressed their support for Texas in the national media. "The first Federal gun that shall be fired against the people of Texas . . . will be the signal for freemen from Delaware to the Rio Grande to rally to the rescue," Sen. Alexander Stephens of Georgia wrote in the *National Intelligencer* on July 4, 1850. "The cause of Texas, in such a conflict, will be the cause of the entire South!"[19]

In August, war fever reached its highest pitch. Governor Bell again urged the Texas legislature to raise an army and invade New Mexico. Pres. Zachary Taylor responded by dispatching hundreds of additional U.S. regulars to Santa Fe. On August 5, the Texas senate debated a bill that authorized raising three thousand mounted volunteers to suppress the "rebellion" in Worth and Santa Fe counties. Patriotic citizens fired cannon in the streets of Austin, adding to the martial excitement gripping the state. War between Texas and the United States loomed.[20]

The death of President Taylor, the actions of the U.S. Congress, and the Compromise of 1850 defused the situation, and citizens of Texas relaxed. The demise of the president evoked little remorse in Texas. On September 7, the *Clarksville Northern Standard* wrote, "We did not put our paper in mourning, for the simple fact that we, and the community in which we live feel no sorrow, and did not regard [Taylor's] death as a National calamity."[21] Henry Clay's compromise, long opposed by the late president, now gained support. It called on Texas to trade the two "rebellious" counties for federal assumption of the state debt. Texas officials wisely advocated this measure to their constituents. Governor Bell convened the legislature, which put the U.S. proposal before the people. The citizens of Texas, although spoiling for a fight, knew the odds against them and approved the referendum by a decided majority. The crisis had passed—the western boundary of Texas was adjusted —but angry emotions still smoldered.[22]

For the South, other unsettled problems caused by the acquisition of the western territories were equally acute in 1850. The discovery of gold in California the previous year, and the resulting surge in its population, had enabled that territory to petition for statehood as a free state. This infuriated Southerners. Free Soil advocates wanted New Mexico as a western barrier to the extension of slavery, and so it had become. And now California.

Some disgruntled Southerners suggested disunion as the only practical solution. Pro-slavery partisans convened the Nashville Convention, marking a crucial milestone in the development of Southern nationalism. Spurred on by John C. Calhoun and other extremists, delegates from all the slave states gathered to consider national trends. They argued over the merits of Henry Clay's resolutions embodied in the Omnibus Bill, with the majority opposed to them. On June 10, the convention resolved to keep intact the Missouri Compromise of 1820 and to extend the line separating free soil from slave to the Pacific Ocean. Secessionists used the meeting to broaden separatist support, but failed to induce Texas and the Upper South to join the Lower South in such a radical stand. For Texans, defense of the frontier, among other things, necessitated strong ties to the federal government. Even so, a strong, radical, pro-slavery element in the state, encouraged by events in Nashville, coalesced and would ultimately shape future events.[23] Although the meeting failed to cement a total coalition of the slave states, secessionists had laid the foundation for it.[24]

Despite the militant posturing in the South, Stephen Douglas's Compromise of 1850 passed and temporarily averted a clash between North and South. Bitter feelings lingered: Among other grievances, Southerners now felt surrounded.

In 1853, a move by the Franklin Pierce administration briefly resurrected hope in the South, only to exacerbate further the sectional impasse. In July, the president authorized U.S. envoy James Gadsden of South Carolina to purchase a portion of Mexican territory for a southern, all-weather transcontinental railroad route. Southerners rejoiced. In the ensuing treaty, signed on December 30, 1853, Mexico sold a Tennessee-sized area known as the Gadsden Purchase.[25] Instead of becoming a new territory with predictably Southern allegiances, the region was quickly tacked onto New Mexico, neatly avoiding further controversy over the extension of slavery. Southern imperialists had sustained another injury.[26]

Americans living in the purchase area, mostly native Southerners and Texans, were equally unhappy about being joined to New Mexico Territory. Santa Fe, the territorial capital, was far removed from the Mesilla Valley, Tucson, and the mining region of Pinos Altos; and the territorial government was unresponsive to the needs of its more remote citizens. The citizens of the region demanded separate territorial status and self-determination. The U.S. Congress received several memorials on this subject, but the political climate was such that the creation of yet another territory, which would again raise the issue of slavery, was out of the question.[27]

The land acquired in the Gadsden Purchase, informally known as Arizona, was a rough and dangerous place rich in silver ore but populated by a desperate breed of men inured to sudden violence by Indians, bandits, and desperadoes. A U.S. official noted forty-seven graves of white men in the Tucson cemetery, only two of whom had died of natural causes. Fugitives made up a sizable portion of the population. "The Vigilance Committee of San Francisco did more to populate the new territory than the silver mines," wrote one traveler. "Tucson became the headquarters of vice, dissipation, and crime. . . . It was literally a paradise of devils."[28] Apaches made the trip to Santa Fe perilous, for the refuge afforded them by the proximity of Mexico allowed them to strike in Arizona often and with impunity. No capitalists would hazard an investment in mining or in building a southern transcontinental railroad until the Apaches were brought to heel. Mesilla, in contrast, boasted a more stable society. Noted for its fertile land, rich farms, and attractive prostitutes, this town claimed just over a hundred Anglo and Celtic inhabitants among four thousand Hispanics.[29]

With slavery blocked in the western territories, the only remaining outlet for slavery was in renewed foreign conquests. Behind Cuba, Mexico remained the great object of fascination for Southerners and many Americans. These expansionists saw in Mexico's extensive, yet sparsely settled, territory an escape from sectional difficulties. During the Mexican War, some Americans advocated annexing all of Mexico, to no avail. Even so, it remained the principal target for filibustering expeditions from the United States. Starting in 1851, raids into that nation occurred on an almost annual basis. Little evidence links these marauders to any sectional orientation or ideology—most seemed to have pursued personal gain. Some attempts took the form of military and financial support for Mexican revolutionaries like Santiago Vidaurri or José Carvajal. Other filibusters followed the more conventional method of outright conquest.[30]

Texans, as expected, especially supported acquisition of Mexico by whatever means. After annexation, bandits and revolutionaries could be curbed; fugitive slaves could be pursued into the interior. One citizen of the Lone Star State urged Sen. Stephen Douglas of Illinois to support such a move. "Permit me to suggest the idea of . . . annexing Mexico," the Texan had written. This act would "confer a favor on many Texans, and the South generally." A possible alternative, and one supported by such notables as Sam Houston, was a Texan invasion of Mexico independent of the United States.[31]

Although involved in restraining filibusters, Southern officers in the United States Army were not immune to the lure of conquest. In 1860, Maj. James Longstreet, army paymaster at Albuquerque, New Mexico Territory, along with "one or two friends," advocated an invasion of Chihuahua. Offering to lead a volunteer regiment into Mexico, the South Carolina native pointed out that northern Mexico would provide additional slave states. "Once we got a foot hold in Chihuahua[,] Sonora, which is more important, will very soon follow."[32] Also serving in New Mexico at the time were Capt. (Bvt. Maj.) Henry Sibley and Lt. Col. William Wing Loring, two men who would figure largely in the 1861 Confederate campaign in the American Southwest and with whom Longstreet was undoubtedly acquainted.

What developed, then, during the decade of the 1850s, was a distinctly Southern vision of Manifest Destiny. Southerners correctly saw their Northern opponents as hostile to slavery and despaired of ever making peace with them. Filibustering, openly discouraged by American officials, had proved ineffective, and by the end of the decade, Southern expansionists were convinced that new territory could be obtained only if the South seceded. Only then would Mexico and Central America fall "like ripe fruit" to a Southern nation. An empire composed of the existing American slave states, Mexico, Cuba, and California could be built. This vision soon had many adherents, including Jefferson Davis of Mississippi and William Samford of Alabama.[33]

The Knights of the Golden Circle, or KGC, epitomized the complete sectionalization of Manifest Destiny. Organized by George Bickley in 1855, this secret military society's goal was securing Mexico and the Caribbean basin as parts of a slave empire. The Knights took their name from their plan for establishing an imperial capital at Havana, Cuba, and extending their realm in a "Golden Circle" through the upper South, along the Gulf of Mexico, the Spanish Main, and across the Caribbean.[34] In a proclamation to his "knights," Bickley reveled in the superiority of Americans and exhorted them to "Let our Railroads and telegraph lines reach from Canada to Patagonia. Let our ships carry our manufactures to the inmost recesses of the continent. Let our cities rise on the Amazon as they have on the Mississippi." By 1859, this organization had become a powerful subversive force in many parts of the South.[35]

The KGC was a product of fears, ambitions, and frustrations that had plagued the South since the 1830s. Dedicated to the extension of slavery, this organization also epitomized the sectionalization of Manifest Destiny, the Monroe Doctrine, and states' rights theory. Relying heavily on the theme of tropical expansion, it claimed support from related nativist groups and secession advocates while providing a weapon against perceived abolitionist tyranny. The KGC also provided an outlet for that breed of restless, adventurous men who clamored for imperialism in the 1850s.[36]

The KGC had its strongest support in Texas. Thousands of recruits manned at least thirty-two castles in twenty-seven counties. Even Sam Houston, a longtime advocate of a protectorate over Mexico, reportedly joined. A jingoistic Dallas editor wrote, "Let these Texans range on the Mexican Frontier and infuse some of the Anglo-Saxon ideas of progressiveness into the stupid, leaden souls of the people—and then the world will notice a change."[37] The KGC moved its headquarters to San Antonio, and most of the more powerful castles within the organization operated in Texas.[38]

Texas, like the rest of the South, was in turmoil. The KGC added new members daily—castles quickly ran out of the necessary forms for inducting candidates. The effusive Bickley bragged on his castles: "They are in a working and flourishing condition, and constitute . . . a class of citizens on whom the public can rely in any emergency." Knights organized mass meetings and torchlight parades, adding to the growing hysteria. A KGC officer from Owensville in Robertson County reported, "Our ladies are today making the Lone Star flag, and . . . it will wave over the Court House. Our town . . . was enlivened by squad drills, . . . [a] blue cockade with the Lone Star in the centre, glistening upon the caps of the mustermen."[39] Bickley gloried in the role his "army" would serve. "Thank God," he wrote on November 15, 1860, "the KGC organization is now in the hands of the people of the South." The KGC was actually in the hands of Texans, as the group seems to have faded in the rest of the nation by 1860.[40]

As talk of secession became common, the political climate in the West encouraged Southern imperialists. Congressional representatives from Washington, Oregon, and Utah openly sided with the South. Oregon's charismatic and popular senator, Joseph Lane, ran for vice president on John C. Breckinridge's 1860 proslavery Democratic ticket.[41] Members of the California congressional delegation, including Senators Milton S. Latham and William M. Gwin, openly supported the cause of the South. Other congressmen urged the creation of a "Republic of the Pacific" out of the territories along the western slope of the Sierra Nevadas. Partisans defiantly raised the Bear Flag, the symbol of California nationalism during the Mexican War, in communities throughout the southern part of the state.[42] Meanwhile, Southern propaganda also blanketed the rest of California. Supporters claimed an improbable eighteen thousand Knights of the Golden Circle along the Pacific shore. Others pointed to the January 15, 1861, appointment of Texan Albert Sidney Johnston to command of the Army of the Pacific as the Buchanan administration's move to expedite the surrender of public stores in California upon that state's secession. In addition, an estimated thirty thousand Californians claimed Southern sympathy if not nativity.[43]

Another factor favoring Southerners was that Hispanics in the Southwest seemed receptive to secession overtures. Even if not genuinely cooperative, they were at least indifferent. In Arizona, this questionable loyalty led Federal officers to distrust Hispanics. Unionists in California reported that Confederate agents were busily converting the Spanish-speaking population there to the cause of secession, and feared the outcome. "When once a revolution commences the masses of the native population will act," Capt. Winfield Scott Hancock warned his department headquarters. "If they act, it will most likely be against the government."[44]

Ultimately, the growing national tension led to an eruption. The election of Abraham Lincoln on November 6, 1860, aggravated the angry mood of the South and its supporters. In Charleston, South Carolina, mobs milled in the streets, eager for more news and defiant over the prospect of Republican rule. Secessionists raised "Palmetto Flags" and talked openly of forming a Southern Confederacy. "The tea has been thrown overboard, the revolution of 1860 has been initiated," trumpeted the *Charleston Mercury* the following day.[45] On November 10, the state legislature ordered a convention to meet in Columbia on December 17 to consider secession. Other Deep South states precipitously followed South Carolina's lead. Even in faraway San Francisco and Taos, secessionists raised the Palmetto Flag and other banners of rebellion in obvious sympathy with South Carolina.[46]

The time for Southern unity had come. Despite its earlier reluctance, Texas enthusiastically linked its fate to the South, enabling the American empire, under Confederate auspices, to continue its course. Many Texans, following the lead of pro-South radicals, believed the federal government had betrayed the state; federal rejection of the state's claims to New Mexico after the Mexican War had been an affront to Texan honor and ambition. Secondly, they argued, U.S. soldiers had failed to protect the frontier against Indian attack, and this task could be handled more effectively by Rangers. Lastly, the sectional Republican Party had defiled the true mission of America—expansion—and Texas imperialists sought like minds to stay the course. In supporting the South, Texas would fulfill its own imperial destiny.[47]

A rebellious South was jubilant over the prospect of achieving the destiny the North had long denied it. When the South "shook itself free of the Puritans and the Devil," an anonymous writer for the *Charleston Mercury* asserted, Chihuahua and all the "Gulf country" would be added to the Confederacy. The *Macon Daily Telegraph* predicted similar glory. "Then will the proudest nations of the earth come to woo and worship at the shrine of our imperial Confederacy."[48]

The decade of the 1850s had borne bitter fruit, and the impasse caused by slavery, states' rights, culture, and imperial ambition had finally sundered the nation. The majority of Southerners had been gradually alienated from the Union over these issues. One by one, Southern states formally seceded. Once out of the Union, they were certain, the march to empire could proceed.[49]

Texas, too, found itself sucked into the vortex of secession. A mood of hysteria gripped the state when rumors of an impending slave revolt, complete with suspicious cases of arson, stirred many citizens into a frenzy against "Black Republicans" and abolitionists. Several abolitionist preachers as well as blacks died at the hands of North Texas lynch mobs. Radicals, screaming the rhetoric of a united South and resistance to Northern tyranny, drowned out the voices of reason. The average citizen, amid the frenzy over "rights" and "tyranny," found his actual situation unchanged, with nothing but an assumed threat coming from the election of Lincoln. Confusion reigned. An anonymous editorial described the public's dilemma: "At breakfast a man says, 'I am for secession emphatically'; . . . at noon, 'I would willingly go for secession, unless the Black Republicans recede from their position'; . . . at supper, 'The condition of the country is truly alarming, and I candidly confess my inability to fathom events that are to come'; at night, 'Speak of that matter no more, fore d——n if I know where we are going, what is going to be done, what ought to be done, or what I am in favor of doing.'"[50] This indecision paralyzed the public; secessionists and radicals presented the only unified front.

In San Antonio, mass meetings brought vocal and often violent crowds into the streets. R. H. Williams, a thirty-year-old Englishman, witnessed one such rally at Alamo Plaza. From atop a platform in front of the Menger Hotel, a secessionist speaker harangued the crowd to "defend their cherished institutions from the intolerable arrogance of the North." Listeners responded enthusiastically. "Revolver shots were fired in the air," remembered Williams, "whilst through the square rang frantic yells of 'down with the Yankees; to hell with the Abolitionists.'" A unionist spoke next, but the crowd shouted him down. "As soon as the 'Boys' realized his drift, six-shooters in hand, and with one wild yell, they stormed the platform and swept it clear of friend and foes," wrote Williams. "Then the shooting grew unpleasantly promiscuous."[51]

Williams was already a veteran of the sectional struggle. In Kansas, he had served with the "border ruffians" from Missouri. The violent scene in the Alamo Plaza convinced the Englishman he should renew his support of the South, and he joined the KGC. "Ostensibly formed to protect Southern rights," he remembered, "its real object was to bring about Secession, and all its weight was thrown into that movement." The Knights initiated Williams into the castle at Castroville, near his cattle ranch on the San Antonio–to–El Paso stage road where it crossed Medio Creek in western Bexar County. By joining, Williams wrote, he had committed himself as a "strong partisan of the Southern cause."[52]

The secession convention of the State of Texas met on January 28 and immediately began organizing for its task. Secession leaders authorized and organized committees to conduct the convention's business. The next day, a resolution supporting secession reached the floor, and the Committee on Federal Relations began drafting the document. During the week, representatives from South Carolina, Georgia, and Tennessee addressed the convention, strengthening its resolve for secession.

The convention completed the secession of Texas and moved to effect separation from the Union. On February 1, after debating the wording of the ordinance, the delegates overwhelmingly adopted the measure 166 to 8. The convention then organized a general election, slated for February 23, to ratify its action. Before adjourning on February 5, the convention voted to send a delegation to Montgomery to meet with the organizers of the new Southern Confederacy.[53]

At the same time, the other seceded states had moved to link their fates. On February 4, 1861, delegates met at Montgomery to form a provisional government. They framed an imperialistic constitution that guaranteed slavery in any "new territory" acquired. The meeting then elected Jefferson Davis, a hero of the Mexican War, as president. Before the end of the week, representatives from Texas arrived, promising the imminent secession of their state and its intention to join the Confederacy.[54]

The Texas secessionists had also taken steps to secure control of Arizona and New Mexico for the Confederacy. Delegate William Read Scurry of DeWitt County introduced a resolution to appoint commissioners to deal with the territorial governments on the Confederacy's behalf. Simeon Hart and his colleague Philemon T. Herbert received instructions to represent Texas and left on their mission. Hart, a well-known and respected leader in the El Paso area, was a good choice. Since 1822, he had traded between Chihuahua and Santa Fe, eventually establishing Hart's Mills across the river from El Paso del Norte. Growing rich from government contracts with nearby Forts Bliss and Fillmore, Hart employed a large portion of the Hispanic population in the region. Many people relied on Hart; many people owed him favors, and many people owed him loyalty.[55]

Thirty-five-year-old Phil Herbert, a native of Alabama, also had his share of fame and celebrity status. Trained as a lawyer, he immigrated to Texas in 1845, but followed the gold rush to California. In 1856, while a Democratic congressman from that state, Herbert shot the Irish headwaiter at Willard's Hotel in Washington for refusing to serve the Southerner breakfast after the posted time. This incident served as a cause célèbre in that election year, as abolitionists used it to illustrate what they considered contemptible "slaveholder's doctrine and slavedriver's law."[56] It proved, so they claimed, that Southerners would instantly and violently retaliate against any breach of etiquette by someone deemed to be in a subservient role. This, the abolitionists argued, was evidence of the evil heart of the slave holder. Frederick Law Olmsted, making reference to the incident, scribbled a letter to the editor of the *New York Daily Times* decrying the "ruffianism" rampant in the country.[57]

In the South, Herbert became the unwitting paragon of what could be considered correct manly deportment. Southern newspapers inflamed the affair, confirming abolitionist suspicions, by congratulating Herbert on his good judgment in teaching the upstart, a mere servant and Irish at that, a deadly lesson. Although acquitted of murder in court, Herbert soon left Congress and was living notoriously in Tucson and El Paso when he answered the call of secession.[58]

Reacting to turmoil in the territories, Southerners and Texans anticipated that the West would soon come into the secessionist fold. The sectional stalemate of the rest of the nation translated into political action in the southern towns of Tucson, Mesilla, and Pinos Altos. Frustrated and angry over being ignored by Congress and the army, delegates to a convention in Tucson declared the Territory of Arizona separate and apart from New Mexico, and appointed several former Texans, including filibuster Granville Oury, to high positions. The U.S. Congress refused to recognize the new territory's existence; even so, Arizona had become an established fact in the minds of the few thousand Anglo and Celtic Americans living in the region, and a delegation traveled east to meet with the Confederates.[59]

The rest of New Mexico, which just ten years before had violently opposed the Texan claims to part of its territory, also seemed politically inclined toward the South. According to U.S. officers stationed at Albuquerque, New Mexicans had embraced the "spirit of revolution." For the previous four years, Buchanan's administration had favored Southerners as appointees to the territorial government. The efforts of these officials, coupled with outspoken

Southern partisans and capitalists who sought a stable system of labor, had resulted in New Mexico passing a slave code in 1859, even though the region could claim less than a dozen slaves. This change in course was mostly a result of the leadership of Miguel A. Otero. In 1855, he had easily won election as the territorial delegate to Congress; in 1857, he narrowly returned in that capacity after defeating former Texan Spruce M. Baird in a bitter election. While in Congress, Otero cultivated Southern friends. In New Mexico, three Southerners—Territorial Sec. Alexander M. Jackson, Gov. Abraham Rencher, and *Santa Fe Gazette* editor Samuel Yost—encouraged his alignment with the slave states.[60]

Most Southerners knew that the North would not let the South go peacefully, and many new Confederates expected—even welcomed—a fight. Militarily, Texas and the territories faced the most vexing problem of all the seceding parties. Nineteen federal forts, organized in three lines, protected the Texas frontier. Some ten others dotted the New Mexican and Arizona landscapes. Three regiments of federal troops, numbering about fifteen hundred men, secured government property in the state. Not only did this threat have to be removed from Texas, but the frontier would have to be defended once the regulars had gone. The first action needed to secure legitimacy for the secession convention and the resolutions it had so boldly adopted was to seize federal property at San Antonio, namely the arsenal with its cache of muskets, cannon, and ammunition.

Accordingly, the twenty-two-man Committee of Public Safety, which held absolute power in military matters, began its task of securing control of the state. In a secret meeting, the committee empowered a four-man commission to negotiate with Gen. David E. Twiggs, commander of the Federal Department of Texas, for the surrender of federal property in the state. As a further precaution, however, the committee appointed Texas Ranger Ben McCulloch as a colonel of cavalry to raise a force to back up the commissioners' demands with military muscle.[61]

The February 6 meeting between the Texans and Twiggs went poorly. Twiggs, a Georgian, had definite Southern sympathies, but he took his duty to the army seriously. He refused to surrender the arsenal prior to March 2—the date of election returns on the secession referendum. The general's determination caused a serious problem for the commissioners, for federal authorities were likely to replace Twiggs with a less sympathetic officer prior to this date. Unless the Texans consummated the turnover quickly, a serious military confrontation would probably occur between the U.S. regulars and state troops. The commissioners continued working out details of the surrender with Twiggs, but urged McCulloch to hurry his command to San Antonio. By February 15, the situation at the arsenal had grown decidedly tense.

With troops gathering and the secession ordinance before the voters, Texas was on the verge of exciting events. Secession and the Confederacy offered the state many new avenues for expansion and the promise of economic boom times. Texas could achieve a satisfactory solution to the question of its western boundary by aligning with Arizona and New Mexico, both politically and economically. Texan armies could also develop client states in Mexico, with possibilities of later annexation. Texas would then become the thoroughfare of empire. James Reily, soon to become a colonel in the Confederate Army and a key player in Sibley's New Mexico campaign, was adamant on this point. "We must have Sonora and Chihuahua," he wrote. "With Sonora and Chihuahua we gain Southern California, and by a railroad to Guaymas render our State of Texas the great highway of nations."[62]

In the ensuing War for Southern Independence, the new Confederacy continued to uphold the old American justifications for expansion. National security required that the Confederacy's western and southern flanks be secured. Commerce would benefit from the raw materials of Mexico and the American Southwest, as well as from ports on the Pacific Coast. And there remained the perceived need to uplift the indolent societies of Hispanic America, even against their wishes.[63] Empire and Manifest Destiny had been a national mission since colonial days, and now Southerners, employing the instrument of secession, sought to restore the nation to its historic course and to carry forward the standard of empire that the North had abandoned. Southerners, through the Confederacy, would revive the American dream of empire.

The Confederacy regarded the western territories as its natural birthright. The inability to secure Southern traditions in this region had, in fact, contributed to the secession crisis and the War Between the States. When the rift between North and South had been finalized in secession, the Confederacy moved to enforce its claim. Many Southerners had viewed Mexico as rightful plunder—a paradise on earth to be rescued from indolent inhabitants and granted the benefits of the superior American civilization. For more than thirty years prior to Sibley's campaign, Southern writers, statesmen, and warriors had urged the occupation and development of the American Southwest and parts, if not all, of Mexico. In 1861, the time and conditions for a Southern empire had arrived.

CHAPTER 2

Beginnings of Empire

I have sold myself to Jef[f] Davis for twelve months.
—Pvt. Egbert Treadwell, Palestine, Texas

The night wind of February 15, 1861, blew cold on hundreds of men and horses preparing to carry out the edict of the Texas Committee of Public Safety. Ben McCulloch, pursuant to orders, had collected 400 volunteers to ride with him that night into San Antonio. These soldiers, their rank signified by makeshift red insignia on their sleeves, were in deadly earnest. As McCulloch's men broke camps on Salado Creek, more riders arrived. Six castles of the Knights of the Golden Circle, numbering about 150 men, reinforced the state troops. Citizens from Medina and Atascosa Counties also arrived. Grimly, the army moved toward the city, prepared to storm the Federal arsenal. Among the horsemen rode Capt. Trevanion Teel of the Charles Bickley Castle, KGC; Sgt. R. H. Williams of the Castroville Castle, KGC; and another better-known figure on the Texas frontier, John Robert Baylor.[1]

The six-foot-three, 230-pound, blue-eyed Baylor was a consummate adventurer. The secession crisis had created significant opportunities for ambitious men, and Baylor acted quickly. In December, 1860, he and his brother George had ridden across Texas organizing a "buffalo hunt"—a thin disguise for assembling

John Robert Baylor, lieutenant colonel of the 2nd Texas Mounted Rifles and governor of Arizona. From an 1861 oil painting on display at the Alamo. Courtesy of Alamo Collection, Daughters of the Republic of Texas, San Antonio.

well-armed volunteers. In January, Baylor attended the secession convention as an "observer." When the Texas Committee of Public Safety called for McCulloch to assemble a force for state service, Baylor and his "hunters" eagerly answered the call.[2]

For Baylor, the actions of February 15 were the fruition of a long-held fascination with Texas. In 1836, as a fourteen-year-old schoolboy, he and his older brother Henry launched an "invasion" of Texas. After slipping away from their southern Ohio academy, the brothers climbed into a small boat on the northern bank of the Ohio

River and rowed hard for Kentucky across the difficult current. Upon arriving, the weary pair discussed their upcoming adventure while gobbling down dinner. Texas was in revolt against Mexico, and the boys eagerly anticipated joining an older sibling who was already there. A gentleman sitting at an adjacent table heard the plans; he persuaded the boys to return to school and paid their fare on a steamboat to Cincinnati. When the disappointed young adventurers returned to school, the headmaster mockingly introduced them as "General . . . Baylor and his army returned from the conquest of Mexico."[3]

The Baylor brothers saw nothing shameful about their mission. These young schoolboys, in the spirit of their times, had abandoned their studies to find adventure and participate in the expansion of the United States. To young Americans of the 1830s, imperialism was a natural impulse, based on decades of practice. Texas was just the next logical step in redeeming the West from Mexico.

In 1840, with his education completed, Baylor did travel to Fayette County, Texas, and immediately took part in a number of campaigns against the Comanches. Two years later, he joined the ill-fated command of Nicholas Dawson that marched against the Mexican forces under Adrian Woll at San Antonio. By chance, the loss of his horse and a rain-swollen stream prevented Baylor from joining Dawson on September 18, in the fateful Battle of the Salado in which the small Texan army was soundly defeated and massacred by a larger Mexican force.[4]

After his adventure in soldiering, Baylor left the state in search of more peaceful employment, but trouble followed him. In July, 1843, he took a position teaching Indian children at the Creek reservation in Indian Territory. He had successfully established himself as an educator before the end of his first year, and his prospects looked bright. In the summer of 1844, however, Baylor became a fugitive with a $750 reward for his capture in connection with the murder of an American merchant.[5]

Returning to Texas, the twenty-two-year-old Baylor sought refuge with friends in Marshall and began to pursue a more stable, domestic existence. While in East Texas, he met, courted, and married sixteen-year-old Emily Hanna. By 1845, the couple had left Marshall and returned to Fayette County, buying a farm near

LaGrange. For the next five years, Baylor pursued farming and stock-raising while his family grew. He would eventually father seven sons and three daughters.[6]

In 1851, Baylor began his political career. Elected to the state legislature that year, he left his farm and moved to Austin, where he made several influential contacts and began reading law. Two years later, he passed the bar exam. In 1854, the State of Texas organized a reservation for various bands of Southern Comanches near Fort Belknap, and Baylor accepted the position of Indian agent to that tribe in 1855, working under the direction of Robert S. Neighbors. Initially confident that Comanches could be "civilized," he planned to move his family near the reservation on the Clear Fork of the Brazos River by 1857.[7]

Those who knew Baylor either loved him or hated him. Both quick to anger and prone to violence, he also had endearing qualities as a talented fiddle player, stump orator, and humorous storyteller. "He could not abide a coward, liar, or thief, and was a terror to evil-doers," remembered George Wythe Baylor, his younger brother. "Anyone he liked was the best fellow in the world, and anyone he disliked was the damndest rascal living. Such a man always has warm friends and bitter enemies and [he] had his quota of each."[8]

Baylor had trouble as Indian agent. He interacted extensively with the reservation Comanches, accompanying them on buffalo hunts and visiting their homes; on occasion he even allowed the Indians to camp outside the reservation boundaries. His latitude with his wards led to abuse, for some reservation Comanches joined war parties from north of the Red River, and Baylor was powerless to stop them. It was soon apparent to Neighbors that Baylor had lost control of the reservation Comanches.[9]

By 1857, because of Baylor's ineptitude and the irregularities in his conduct of state business, the Commissioner of Indian Affairs dismissed him as Indian agent. In December, 1855, Baylor had been implicated in a question of conflict of interest for working on behalf of a San Antonio firm seeking reservation contracts. Baylor also left his post without permission on several occasions. After the government finally fired Baylor on March 14, 1857, his ledgers came under scrutiny. "J. R. Baylor was . . . dismissed from service . . .

for having a 'good time of it' during the eighteen months he was in service," wrote Neighbors. "This his own accounts will show whenever anyone chooses to investigate."[10]

This disgrace changed Baylor. His dismissal, coupled with what he considered Comanche duplicity, embittered Baylor against all Indians, and those who worked in their behalf. After moving his family to a ranch in Parker County, he began organizing opposition to the reservations. He led one attack on the reservation tribes, but killed only one old couple. As the political figurehead in the conflict, Baylor was copublisher of *The White Man*, a racist Weatherford newspaper committed to the destruction of the reservation Indians. For the next three years Baylor organized frontier ranger companies, killed Indians, bred cattle, and raised his ten children. It was also during this period that he began agitating for secession and joined the Knights of the Golden Circle. In February, 1861, he left his family again, this time drawing his pistols for the cause of secession and eventually finding himself on the banks of the Salado on that fateful, chilly night.[11]

McCulloch's four-hundred-man army clattered into San Antonio in the early morning darkness of February 16, 1861. A ninety-man detachment dismounted and took up positions around the Federal arsenal, while the main body approached on horseback. "We of the rank and file fully expected a sharp tussle," R. H. Williams, the Englishman-turned-cattleman, wrote. With good discipline, the Texans advanced in columns through the streets of the sleeping town. "Our commander," he continued, "played the game as though it were in earnest."[12]

Another participant in the march on the arsenal was twenty-two-year-old Morgan Wolfe Merrick, a sergeant in a San Antonio KGC castle. A native of New York, Merrick had moved with his parents to San Antonio in 1851. As a teenager, he had adventured in Mexico, participating as a mercenary in Santiago Vidaurri's army during the War of the Reforma. Sometime after returning to Texas, he joined the KGC, enlisting near his home in San Antonio. On the night of February 15, 1861, his company executed its first military assignment for the state.[13]

Merrick's castle aided McCulloch's column after it entered town from the east. Having gathered at their meeting hall, members received their assignments. In addition to the regular routine of guard duty, a volunteer squad, including Merrick, left for the arsenal complex at the Alamo. There they were to "keep an eye on the U.S. soldiers' quarters and note their movements."[14] Taking a position atop the flat roof of a nearby house, Merrick waited anxiously for the Texan army to enforce the surrender ultimatum.

Behind the stone walls of the Federal complex—composed of the Arsenal, Ordnance Building, the Alamo, San Antonio Barracks, and the Commissary Depot—U.S. regulars prepared for the expected attack. From his perch, Merrick noted two howitzers placed to sweep the courtyard with canister. Sentinels walked their beats nearby. In all, nearly 150 veteran troops held the grounds of the San Antonio Barracks. Inside the arsenal, a dozen pieces of artillery, more than 800 rifled muskets, and hundreds of pounds of powder and lead lay stacked. According to Merrick, everything "looked very much like business."[15]

Merrick had a good vantage point from which to view the ensuing drama. He first noticed shadowy figures moving along the roofs near the arsenal yard. After determining that they were other Texans taking up positions, the vigilant sergeant relaxed and sought some relief from the cold. "I had left my coat in the [meeting] hall and, being out all night, I felt chilly," he wrote. Taking a seat atop a chimney, he watched as dawn broke and the Federal garrison began to stir, then he moved to the edge of the roof to observe the goings-on below. An enlisted Irish cook who saw the shivering Merrick peering down at him, offered the Texan a cup of coffee. After tossing up a rock attached to a string, the cook tied the loose end to a steaming tin cup. "I pulled up the coffee, [and] as I did, he threw up a loaf of bread," wrote Merrick. "My God," he added, "shoot a man that treats you like that?"[16]

The tense situation continued into the morning. While the volunteers were taking their positions around the facility, civilian delegates approached General Twiggs and requested the surrender of all Federal property in San Antonio to the State. By daybreak, while McCulloch awaited the negotiated surrender of government property within the arsenal, his force had grown substantially. Volunteer companies from neighboring counties had arrived, ready to storm the arsenal if necessary. Armed Texans lined the streets surrounding the arsenal. Merrick, having finished his breakfast, re-joined his KGC company as it assembled in a nearby street. At mid-morning, the troops received orders to disperse, and Sergeant Merrick returned with his unit to the meeting hall. General Twiggs had surrendered.[17]

The Texan army noisily celebrated its victory. "After a bit of a spree in the town to celebrate our bloodless, but glorious victory," wrote Williams, "we were marched back to camp and there dis-missed, each to his own abode." Colonel McCulloch gladly released his men, writing the president of the Committee of Public Safety, "I instantly informed the forces under my command . . . of their being no necessity for their remaining away from their ploughs and peaceful avocations."[18] Amid the euphoria, Merrick, who lived near the Alamo, volunteered to guard the newly won prizes. As the U.S. regulars marched away, Merrick and twelve other Knights of the Golden Circle took their places.[19]

The Texan commissioners next saw to the occupation of the re-maining Federal posts in Texas. The terms of Twiggs' surrender called for the evacuation of all U.S. property by the various garri-sons. The U.S. Navy would then evacuate the soldiers, along with their arms and baggage. Col. Henry E. McCulloch, Ben's brother, acted for the state on the northwest frontier, while Col. John S. "Rip" Ford secured the Rio Grande Valley installations. Volunteer squads, mostly from KGC companies, received the surrender of the forts along the San Antonio–to–El Paso stage road. Owing to lack of transportation, the evacuations proceeded slowly.[20]

The February 28 election returns of the secession referendum endorsed the actions of the convention by a three-to-one margin; the people of Texas had voted to secede. Only 18 of the 122 coun-ties rejected the measure. The secession convention reconvened in March to finalize the proceedings, and on March 5, adopted an ordinance uniting Texas to the Confederate States of America. Governor Houston, although reluctantly accepting the reality of secession, hoped to keep Texas independent and refused to take the oath of allegiance to the Confederacy. The legislature promptly declared his position vacant and elevated Lt. Gov. Edward Clark to the post.[21]

The protection of the state's long western frontier presented a serious problem to the new governor. Clark immediately ordered the creation of two regiments of mounted riflemen for frontier duty. The newly formed state military board posted notices in newspapers while recruiters traveled across the state, organizing companies to rendezvous at San Antonio. Col. Henry McCulloch, appointed to command the First Texas Mounted Rifles, built his regiment around the men whom he had led in seizing the northwest forts. The balance were volunteers from Bexar, Travis, Gonzales, and surrounding counties. Colonel Ford commanded the Second Texas Mounted Rifles, aided by his second in command, the newly appointed Lieutenant Colonel Baylor. This regiment, recruited from farther afield, took more time to complete.[22]

The new state regiments followed the Texan military tradition. Each man supplied his own horse, saddle, harness, and tack, and brought his personal weapons from home. Uniforms consisted of civilian attire or loose battle shirts of flannel or twill. The units were to pursue the traditional Texan military missions of frontier patrol and Indian control, and the short enlistments resembled those of the old ranger companies or of the Texan volunteers during the days of the Republic and Mexican War. Training was a low priority. Officers placed more emphasis on native ability than on discipline. Pay would come from Austin, for they served the state.

This reliance on what historian Tom Cutrer calls the "frontier military tradition" evolved from fundamental tenets of the South's unique character. The society that produced these aspiring soldiers valued the role of the individual. Power, from that of a sergeant to that of the president, issued from the individuals composing the group; the individual, knowingly and willingly, allowed his will to be subordinate to the greater good. Southerners granted this sort of permission sparingly, and even then, grudgingly. Relationships of power remained chronically fragile in such an organization.[23]

What resulted, then, was an army of individuals where unity was tenuous and jurisdiction jealously guarded. Discipline, in the classic military sense, would be bad. The young men that answered the call to arms were eager warriors and considered themselves to be talented fighters, but the society that produced them predisposed them to be mediocre soldiers. Only when constant drill hammered away their native individualism would they be of service to their nation. This was to be a bitter lesson.

Even so, these individuals claimed the cause of the Southern nation to be their own and unified their efforts in its behalf. Southerners, in a strange contradiction, reserved the right to fight among themselves. They resented, however, having outsiders meddle in their affairs. The threat of emancipation, the rise of the Republican party, and a host of imagined threats all unified these volunteers to the cause of their state, and secondarily to the cause of the South. Power, in their minds, was best expressed as local sovereignty. Men boasted of their hometowns, then their states, and only lastly of their region—the South. These were the warriors who answered the recruiter's call.[24]

The first of the companies for the Second Texas Mounted Rifles came from the East Texas counties of Houston, Nacogdoches, Cherokee, and Anderson. One volunteer was thirty-two-year-old Methodist preacher William J. Joyce. "I could not afford to hide behind my profession when the country called for defenders," he wrote. He characterized his comrades as "nearly all . . . very young men."[25]

Meanwhile, secession agitation in the western territories greatly encouraged Confederate and Texas officials. Estimates of 16,000 Southern supporters in California and 7,500 secessionists in Colorado boosted Rebel planners. Partisans had already flown a "rattlesnake flag" in Denver. In addition, leading Federal officers in the region, who had resigned their commissions to join the Confederate army, reported a grand opportunity for seizing the western territories for the new Southern nation. Perhaps the most convincing argument for Rebel intervention in the West, however, came from the citizens of Tucson, Pinos Altos, and Mesilla in the Gadsden Purchase region of New Mexico Territory.[26]

Arizona, which had much in common with Texas, used the secession crisis to affect long overdue changes. Many Arizonans hailed from the Lone Star State, for miners and ranchers who had departed Texas for California had returned to work the mines at Pinos Altos and Tubac, or to farm in the Mesilla Valley of the Rio Grande. This region had a separate identity from the rest of New Mexico, and citizens had made several attempts to get the Gadsden Purchase lands organized as a separate territory within the Union. The bulk of the population were Hispanics who seemed as indifferent to this new change of allegiance as they had been to becoming Americans in 1854. Rebel flags soon appeared in the town squares at Tucson and Mesilla, and a few "minuteman" companies of Arizona cavalry began mustering for service against Indians while awaiting news from the East. Messages from Arizona soon arrived in San Antonio asking for assistance. Federal officials considered Arizona politically unstable and an expected casualty of the crisis; they vowed to maintain control of New Mexico at all hazards.[27]

One observer in the American West was Henry Clay Smith. Born Heinrich Schmitt in Germany, he had come to the United States in 1851, when only fifteen, settling with his two sisters in Peru, Ohio. After a year of odd jobs aboard ships sailing Lake Erie, the young immigrant Americanized his name to Henry Clay Smith and headed for Missouri and the promise of the frontier. By 1854, Smith was at Westport, and took a job with a freight outfit heading down the Santa Fe Trail for New Mexico. Eventually the train made stops as faraway as Tucson in the recently obtained Gadsden Purchase, introducing the German to that rugged region. In 1856, the young wanderer worked as a surveyor in Nebraska, and then later as a deck hand on a Missouri River steamboat. In 1857, Smith turned twenty-one and joined an army ox train as a "bullwacker," working his way to Fort Laramie, where he joined a group of Mormons and accompanied them to Salt Lake City.[28]

Smith's travels were far from over. In 1858, the German-born adventurer pushed farther west and worked for a few months in San Bernardino, California, before heading to the Gila River region to prospect for gold. Unsuccessful, he changed vocations again, taking a job as a hay hauler with the Butterfield Overland Mail. Two years later, Smith took a job driving cattle out of Sonora to Tucson. In 1859, miners found gold and silver near Pinos Altos, and the restless German joined the rush to stake claims. He was still there when civil war came to his adopted country.[29]

Secession caused deep divisions and chaos even in this remote region of the West. "Rumors of war came thick and fast," wrote Smith, now a sergeant in a Pinos Altos minuteman company. "Our camp was divided and everybody talked war. The whole camp was in an uproar, some in favor of Uncle Sam and some in favor of Jeff

Davis, and most in favor of no war at all. The majority of the men, being of southern birth . . . got all hot-headed and made threats to those that were not inclined that way."[30]

Similarly, the mining camps of Colorado hosted bitter contests between would-be Rebels and zealous Unionists. In 1859, while prospectors chiseled away in Pinos Altos, some 100,000 additional gold seekers flooded into Colorado hoping to secure a large strike in the Rocky Mountains. Thousands of these newcomers included men of Southern birth and, by 1861, a third of the territory's people held Confederate sympathies. In Georgia Gulch, west of Denver, the news reached the miners via two Union recruiters. Having arrived to receive enlistments, the two officers informed the denizens of the mountain valley that war had indeed arrived. "We . . . found the unhappy war spirit on the increase and men enlisting liberally under the Stars and Stripes," wrote Daniel Conner, a Southerner. "The war spirit began to disclose its natural and latent cussedness. Rebel and Federal friends became Rebel and Federal enemies."[31]

Born in Bardstown, Kentucky, in 1837, Conner had heard of the Colorado gold discoveries in 1858, while visiting relatives in Missouri. The following spring, he joined a party heading west. The twenty-two-year-old fortune seeker arrived in Denver and went with his party into the front range of the Rocky Mountains. Conner spent the next few seasons vainly searching the valleys and slopes of the South Park. By the spring of 1861, Conner was living near Georgia Gulch, near the Swan River.[32]

As the news of secession traveled through the mountains, earnest partisans of both the Union and Rebel causes soon turned to gunplay. One duel ended with a Union man shot through the body. To further antagonize Northerners, a Southerner emptied both barrels of a shotgun at the U.S. flag flying above the recruiting office, blasting it to tatters. Two other duelists also decided to settle the national question between themselves. Each gunman agreed to sit across from the other at a table, a loaded revolver in their right hands while clutching each end of a cloth with their left. "All was now deathly silent," Conner wrote. Both leveled their weapons across the table; upon the given signal, both men fired at point blank range and fell. A doctor quickly examined the fallen parties. Both displayed a red mark on the chest, but no bullet hole. "Now those who were in on the trick burst into uncontrollable laughter," Conner remembered. "They had duped both the principals and the doctor by charging the pistols with powder only. As for the two duelists, . . . they were a brace of the funniest and most foolish-looking specimens in that camp." Soon enough, however, Conner would be embroiled in more sobering aspects of the nation's conflict.[33]

Texan commissioners Simeon Hart and Phil Herbert had also been busy in the West, but their labors had brought mixed results. Herbert reached Mesilla in early March, 1861, with a letter from the Texas convention to arouse pro-Confederate sentiment in Arizona. Aided by prominent citizens like James Magoffin of Franklin and Sylvester Mowry of Tucson, Herbert spoke at a secession meeting at Mesilla on March 16. After stirring speeches, many vehemently linking the destiny of Arizona with that of the South, the meeting adopted resolutions joining the territory to the Confederacy. The following week a militia company that formed in Mesilla received a hand-stitched Confederate flag from Dolores and Guadalupe Van Pattern, daughters of a local merchant. Similarly, a meeting on March 23 in Tucson endorsed secession. At the same time, Hart attempted to kindle secessionist flames in New Mexico. A business and political leader in the region since 1822, Hart relied on his many contacts to aid him in his mission. Working mainly through correspondence, he reported strong Southern sentiment around Santa Fe and Albuquerque, but added that a large Rebel military force would be required in the region before its citizens would respond.[34]

Other Southern partisans had also been active in both New Mexico and Arizona. Maj. Isaac Lynde, commander of Fort McLane near Pinos Altos, wrote his superiors of a plot by local miners to attack the fort. He also reported the treachery of the principal wagon master, William Kirk, who had seized the government wagon train and sold it in Mexico. Department commander Col. William Wing Loring wrote to army headquarters about secessionists' plans to take the supply depot at Albuquerque. Throughout his department, he complained, citizens refused to sell the government goods and services on credit. The Union's hold on New Mexico seemed to be deteriorating.[35]

In addition to Herbert and Hart, the secessionist movement in

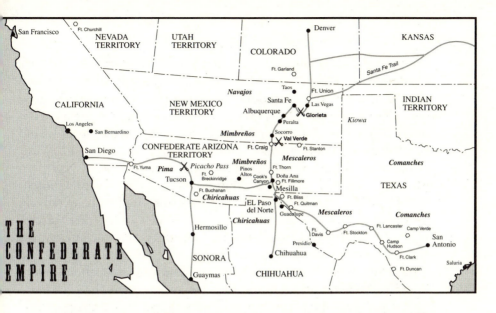

Arizona centered on Mowry, Magoffin, and editor Robert P. Kelly of the *Mesilla Times*. Magoffin, a merchant on the Chihuahua trail since 1828, had built a substantial house and estate near the village of Franklin, part of future El Paso, not so humbly naming his place "Magoffinsville." Like Hart, he had made his fortune largely through government contracts, with Fort Bliss located on his leased property since 1854. Mowry, an ex-Army officer, owned and operated the Patagonia mine near Tubac. A man of substantial wealth, he controlled the political scene in western Arizona. Kelly, a Virginian by birth, made his newspaper the mouthpiece of the secessionists.[36]

For the Union, the situation in New Mexico was cause for concern. The leadership of the territory included many Southerners of questionable loyalties. Since 1851, all five of the territory's governors had been Southerners, as were half the secretaries, judges, and military commanders of the department. The non-Hispanic population was also mostly Southern. Strong economic ties existed between Santa Fe and Missouri; New Mexico might follow the lead of that state. The loyalty of the territory would be bitterly contested in the coming months, but early indications gave great hope to the South.[37]

In the minds of some Rebel leaders, the domination of the western territories was vital to Texas and to the South. Texas would be the origin and principal beneficiary of all transportation routes heading toward the Pacific. The vivid dream of trade routes crossing the southern plains would become a reality. The South faced encirclement by the U.S. Navy and by Union-held territory; conquest of the Far West would break that grip. Pacific ports would be difficult to blockade and would provide privateer bases. Western mineral wealth would aid the Confederate treasury. Northern Mexico, if added, would compound the benefits to the Confederacy.[38] "Then . . . there would be plenty of room for the extension of slavery, which would greatly strengthen the Confederate States," Capt. Trevanion Teel, KGC, wrote.[39] Besides economic vitality, the conquest of the western territories would also lend military and diplomatic credibility to the Southern claim of independence and help in convincing France and England to intervene.[40]

In a revolutionary time when leaders dreamed big, the potential of success in the far West was staggering. First, however, the Rebels had to accomplish two vital, no-compromise steps: Arizona had to be maintained as a Confederate Territory, and New Mexico had to be redeemed from the Union. Only then could the dreams of empire proceed.

In early March, as the pace of rebellion quickened, Texas Knights of the Golden Circle became actively engaged in the transferring of Federal property. The castles were ordered to hold the forts until state troops could garrison them. Among others, Captain Teel's company divided into squads and headed for various posts along the stage road. Teel, with fifteen privates, took charge of Fort Duncan. Sergeant Merrick and twelve others occupied Fort Davis. By mid-March Williams was again in the saddle in the service of the state. Capt. James Paul's Castroville KGC company had instructions to receive the surrender of Camp Verde on the Medina River. "It seemed rather a large order," the Englishman Williams wrote, "but the 'Boys' were in high spirits and eager for a fight. Before daybreak our small bugler had roused the camp, and by sun-up we had drunk our coffee and were off on our long ride." The surrender went smoothly, and Williams, now orderly sergeant, gave receipts for all transferred property, including eighty camels. "They were of little trouble to us as far as the females were concerned, . . . but some of the males were the mischief, especially an old gentleman they christened 'the major.' He . . . bit and fought like a demon."[41]

This peaceful transfer of Federal property to the Southern states turned violent on April 12, 1861, when Confederate forces under Gen. Pierre Gustave Toutant Beauregard fired on Fort Sumter in the harbor at Charleston, changing the status of the retiring U.S. regulars still in Texas. On the national scene, the long, tense showdown was over, replaced by open warfare between North and South. In Texas, the regulars had almost completed their evacuation—only the garrisons of the far western posts had yet to arrive on the coast—but with the outbreak of hostilities, the rules had changed. The men could no longer be allowed to leave the state peacefully, and state officials made plans for their capture.[42]

The recruiting of state regiments continued accordingly. In Harrison County, volunteers had begun enlisting at the beginning of April. As spaces were limited, the enrolling officer placed a quota on each of the surrounding counties. Ten days later, the company was full. "There was a perfect rush to enlist," wrote William Williston Heartsill of Marshall. The belief among these East Texans was that "the company would be ordered immediately from Austin to Galveston" to take part in the cataclysmic battles expected in the East.[43]

Heartsill and the rest of the inexperienced volunteers presented a rowdy but patriotic appearance as they made the transition from civilians to soldiers. The troops adopted the name W. P. Lane Rangers after a local resident who earned fame in the early days of Texas. On April 19, the company prepared for the long ride to San Antonio. The men elected Sam J. Richardson, leader of the Marshall KGC castle, as captain, then spent the balance of the day and night drinking and celebrating. The next morning, the unit accepted a flag made by the ladies of Marshall and departed for San Antonio.[44]

A native of Tennessee, Heartsill had come to Texas in 1859 to work as a clerk and jumped at the chance to serve his new state despite his lack of martial experience. "An old Texas Ranger would rather think us a Caravan, crossing the desert, with a tremendous stock of merchandise, than a regularly organized company," Heartsill wrote in his diary. To the saddle of his horse "Pet," the young private strapped a "coffee pot, tin cup, 20 lbs ham, 200

bisquits, 5 lbs ground coffee, 5 lbs sugar, one large pound cake, . . .
6 shirts, 6 prs socks, 3 prs drawers, 2 prs pants, 2 jackets, 1 pr heavy
mud boots, one Colt's revolver, one small dirk, four blankets, [and]
sixty feet of rope. . . . When I tell you that I am not an exception,
you can imagine how we are packed up."[45]

By mid-month Confederate Col. Earl Van Dorn, recently arrived
to command the Department of Texas, moved quickly to force the
unconditional surrender of the remaining U.S. regulars. On April
17, with the aid of "cottonclad" steamers, Texas troops surprised
and captured the largest concentration of Federal troops, 500 men,
as they attempted to board steamers at Saluria and Indianola. After disarming and paroling the prisoners, Van Dorn ordered all
available state troops to assemble in San Antonio. The remaining
Federal column, 347 men of the Eighth U.S. Infantry from Forts
Bliss, Quitman, and Davis, was marching unaware toward San
Antonio.[46]

Van Dorn arrived in San Antonio the last week of April and
prepared to confront Union Lt. Col. Isaac D. Reeve and his professionals. Williams and the Castroville Knights were sent from
Camp Verde to intercept the regulars. After locating the Federal
column, Williams and his companions followed at a distance. Near
his own ranch on Medio Creek, Williams rode ahead to report to
Confederate authorities. "I had another good look at the troops I
had been shadowing for so long," he remembered. "They were as
fine and soldierly looking a body of men as ever I saw. If they meant
fighting, I was sure they could whip any force Van Dorn could bring
against them, though they had a poor chance of getting out of the
state."[47]

Heartsill and his East Texas companions arrived in San Antonio
just as news of the Federals' approach reached town. Many of the
eager volunteers, unarmed and without orders, rode hastily out of
town hoping to join Van Dorn and participate in the upcoming
showdown a few miles to the west. "The Rangers can stand the
suspense no longer," wrote Heartsill, "and arms or no arms they
are bound to have a share in the glories of the day."[48]

On the evening of May 8, 1861, Reeve prepared for a fight by
placing his men on a hill near San Lucas Springs. Using his wagons
as a barricade, the Federal officer fortified a ranch house and out-

buildings. The 347 nervous regulars took positions in the midnight darkness, expecting to be attacked at any moment. At nine o'clock the following morning, two Texan officers approached Reeve's line with a flag of truce.[49]

Van Dorn demanded that the Federals surrender, claiming he had sufficient force with which to enforce his demand, although Reeve remained skeptical. The Texans then moved their army over the crest of an adjacent hill and into full view of the entrenched Federals. A ragged but determined array, the thirteen hundred state troops under Col. Henry McCulloch presented three lines of infantry flanked by more than eight hundred mounted troops supported by six field pieces. Included in the array were five companies of the First Texas Mounted Rifles and a squadron of the Second Texas under Lieutenant Colonel Baylor. As evidence of their sincerity, the Texans allowed one of Reeve's staff officers to inspect their army. Convinced that the Rebels could enforce their demand, Reeve surrendered. The regulars became prisoners of war, and the Texan volunteers escorted them to San Antonio the following day.[50]

With the threat from the U.S. garrisons ended, Confederate officials in Texas faced a threefold problem. The first and most immediate was the need for a force to replace the U.S. regulars in checking the Indians who roamed the western part of the state. Second, troops needed to occupy the nineteen abandoned U.S. forts and secure their public property. Third, secessionists in the western territories looked to Texas for aid in their quest for disunion.[51]

By mid-May Texan officials had moved to alleviate some of the state's vexing military problems. After the victory at San Lucas Springs, both the First and Second Mounted Rifles transferred to Confederate service and took their places at the frontier installations. With the Confederate government now paying the bills, Rebel officers mustered out the volunteer caretaker garrisons at the forts, replacing them with Confederate troops. McCulloch's regiment occupied forts from the Indian Territory to Central Texas. Ford took four of his companies to the lower Rio Grande, while the remaining six stayed in the vicinity of San Antonio under Baylor.[52]

The men under Baylor's command came from various backgrounds and had their own reasons for serving in the ranks of the Second Texas Mounted Rifles—some hated Yankees; others hated

Indians; yet most joined for adventure. They hailed from places like Harrison, Upshur, Austin, Lavaca, Harris, Cherokee, Nacogdoches, Anderson, and Bexar Counties. The communities of Palestine, Rusk, Marshall, Houston, and San Antonio contributed many enthusiastic young recruits. From Bexar County came thirty-seven Hispanic volunteers. Some of the contributing counties had high slave populations, while others contained but few. Baylor brought his black servant Bower with him, while his second in command, Edwin Waller, was attended by his slave Simon. Most of the counties grew large quantities of cotton, but Lavaca and Bexar were home to immense herds of cattle. Twenty-three-year-old Nacogdoches Pvt. Charles Taylor, his twenty-two-year-old brother Milam, along with twenty-six-year-old Palestine Pvt. Egbert Treadwell, were representative of the bulk of Baylor's troops. Soldiers in Company A, Second Texas, these men thought garrison life along the frontier, with a few Indian skirmishes, awaited them. Enlisted into state service on May 17, these men were shocked when they were transferred to Confederate service six days later. "I have sold myself to Jef Davis for twelve months," lamented Treadwell in a letter to an uncle. In the coming days these men would find their destiny in the West.[53]

As Texas gathered its forces, the military situation in New Mexico Territory gave state officials cause for worry. Nearly two thousand Union veterans, representing fifteen companies of infantry, ten companies of mounted rifles, and four companies of dragoons, remained in the area. Nine principal forts that provided defensive positions and supply bases to the Union troops were spread over the area. The scattered companies of U.S. regulars began concentrating at the strongest forts—Fillmore, Craig, and Union—and began adding earthworks. The population centers of the territory, and the nuclei of secessionist sentiment, each had a U.S. garrison within a day's march. Until Rebel forces eliminated these troops, Arizona was just a fanciful desire. These Federals also jeopardized Fort Bliss, as yet unoccupied by Texan forces. Vital supplies, weapons, and ammunition included in Twiggs's surrender were at stake.[54]

Van Dorn intended to continue his streak of successes against U.S. troops in the Southwest. With Texas clear of Union troops, he knew he had to work fast to secure his captures and to prevent a Federal incursion from New Mexico. Fearful of Fort Bliss being recaptured, Van Dorn ordered six companies of the Second Texas Mounted Rifles to leave San Antonio immediately. They took cannon from the forts along the way to provide the necessary ordnance for an artillery battery. Once Confederates secured the posts and their public stores, the department commander contemplated another coup in keeping with his earlier Texas successes. "Within a short distance of . . . Fort Bliss there are several hundred United States troops," he wrote to Colonel Ford on May 27. "If the Union troops could be surprised, they could be easily taken."[55]

Secessionists in the El Paso area had already begun organizing military units for what they considered the inevitable campaign. Bethel Coopwood, a flamboyant thirty-three-year-old frontiersman from California, raised a sixty-nine-man-unit he called the "San Elizario Spy Company." One observer described the band as being composed of "comparatively reckless, but intelligent and well-behaved young men."[56] Most of these drifters and adventurers had previously infested southern California and the environs of Franklin. The soldiers recruited in Arizona were veterans of frontier life, in contrast to the green recruits from Texas. One of Coopwood's troopers, 2d Cpl. Silas W. Merchant, had been a wanderer most of his life. Raised near Mount Pleasant, Texas, Merchant lived in El Paso del Norte at the start of the war. Although in his early twenties when he enlisted, Merchant was described as "seasoned to frontier life, and ripe for any adventure, however daring or desperate."[57]

Twenty-six-year-old Cuban émigré Enrique B. D'Hamel also joined Coopwood's company. A veteran frontiersman, he had come to the United States in 1858 as stevedore, prospector, and adventurer. By 1860, he was broke, alone, and unemployed as he wandered down the Rio Grande toward Mesilla. He soon had a job as a manager at Hart's Mill, but he resigned after a few months to enlist. "Mr. Hart tried to persuade me to hold my job," D'Hamel said, "but I was too headstrong to listen to the wise advice of an older man." The men of the San Elizario Spy Company learned to drill from a recently deserted regular sergeant, who liberally berated his inexperienced charges. "We seemed to make very poor progress," D'Hamel wrote in a postwar memoir. "The drillmaster . . . would get out of patience with me on account of my over-

Corp. Enrique D'Hamel, San Elizario Spy Company. Carte de visite photograph taken in Havana, Cuba, on October 20, 1864. At the time, D'Hamel was a member of the 33rd Texas Cavalry. Courtesy of Lawrence T. Jones III collection, Austin, Texas.

stepping. As I seemed a hopeless task, they decided to give me no more marching lessons."[58]

The men in this outfit made themselves known to the U.S. garrisons along the Rio Grande as expert horse thieves. On June 15, Coopwood's troopers raided Fort Fillmore, carrying off nearly two hundred horses and mules. Magoffin, to divert suspicion, offered a reward for the raiders' apprehension; the Federal authorities knew better. Hart, acting Confederate Quartermaster in the area, purchased the animals by giving Coopwood and his men certificates and government notes.[59]

Colonel Ford, busy in the Rio Grande valley, ordered his second in command Baylor to carry out Van Dorn's orders. Baylor sent his companies F and H to occupy the closer frontier posts.[60] The move of Texas troops to El Paso County was a grand opportunity for Baylor. Disaffected and unsuccessful in state politics, especially after his violent and mercurial tenure as Indian agent, he saw an opportunity to restore his reputation. Campaigning in the Far West also promised military glory against U.S. regulars garrisoning the frontier forts. By advancing to Fort Bliss and then into the Mesilla Valley of Confederate Arizona, Baylor would be leading a substantial group of armed Texans into a region long claimed by the state. In a postbellum settlement, this action might help extend Texas' western border. Campaigning in the territories would also allow Baylor to further his war against the Indians, a race he seems to have genuinely hated.[61]

Baylor, his officers, and his men began their expedition by mid-June. Some troopers now carried high-quality Springfield and Harper's Ferry rifles captured from the Alamo arsenal, supplementing an odd assortment of shotguns and fowling pieces. The men of companies A, B, D, and E, Second Texas Mounted Rifles, rode a few days apart down the El Paso road. Captain Teel, his KGC company serving as an artillery battery, volunteered his men for the expedition.[62] The immediate goals appeared simple: occupation of abandoned military posts and securing government property. The political goal of establishing Confederate Arizona, however, had given the expedition the feel of a drive for empire.[63]

For Sergeant Merrick and the Texans at Fort Davis, Baylor's campaign promised action and an end to a tedious tour of garrison duty. Having lived at the posts since April 25, Capt. Samuel W. McAllister's squad of state troops had grown to forty-five men— the increase coming mainly from U.S. deserters. For months, however, the command had suffered from lack of supplies and from boredom. "We see from the papers that there is some prospect of troops being sent to New Mex. and Arazona," Merrick wrote. "But when? We will sure get away from here then."[64]

Secessionists maintained a cautious optimism about their chances of success in New Mexico and Arizona despite the sizable Union garrisons there. That department was in chaos; many of the high-ranking officers had resigned, and soldiers, worried about the government's ability to pay them, had begun deserting. The Navajos and Apaches continued their raids and depredations. Transportation in the department was scarce. The sectional crisis had made itself felt in the ranks of the officer corps in the western garrisons. In New Mexico, several line officers of Southern birth resigned, including Dabney Maury of Virginia, Joseph Wheeler of Georgia, and Henry C. McNeill of Texas. A number of field grade officers—among them James Longstreet of South Carolina and department commander William Wing Loring of North Carolina—did likewise. Even the commander of the Army of the Pacific, Texan Albert Sidney Johnston, quit the army in California. The resignation of these officers had been distressing for Unionists, but for the future of western territories, the defection of Henry Hopkins Sibley, an impressive-looking dragoon captain, would have the most profound effect.[65]

A native of Natchitoches, Louisiana, Sibley had made the military his life. West Point had been difficult for him—he had to repeat one year—and graduated a mediocre thirty-first in the forty-five-man class of 1838. His first assignment with the Second Dragoons led him to Florida, where he fought Seminoles for three years. Promoted from brevet to regular second lieutenant, Sibley joined the regimental staff as adjutant, spending the next few years alternately on recruiting duty in New York or at Forts Jesup, Louisiana, and Washita, Indian Territory. While in Manhattan, the debonair Louisianan married. Lieutenant Sibley served in Gen. Zachary Taylor's Army of Observation in 1845, as that force moved into Texas following annexation. Charismatic, Sibley again received orders for recruiting detail in New York. Two years later, with the Mexican War well advanced, Sibley rejoined the Second Dragoons as a captain and company commander at the siege of Vera Cruz. He displayed gallantry and heroism in Mexico and in the skirmish at Medellín, Sibley received a brevet to major. Afterward, his command participated in the march to Mexico City, including the various battles of that campaign. After the war, Capt. (Bvt. Maj.) Sibley returned to recruiting duty.[66]

Brig. Gen. Henry Hopkins Sibley, circa 1861. Courtesy of Massachusetts Commandery, Military Order of the Loyal Legion and the U.S. Military History Institute, Carlisle Barracks, Pennsylvania.

In the 1850s, Sibley returned to active campaigning against various foes of the nation on the Great Plains and in the territories. He served at various posts in northwest Texas for the next five years, and for a time was post commander at Fort Phantom Hill. In 1855, this energetic officer received orders to move his command to Kansas, where Sibley attempted to pacify free soil and slavery guerrillas who plundered the countryside. In 1857, he led his men in the Mormon expedition under Col. Albert Sidney Johnston, an officer Sibley admired so greatly that he named a son after him. After peace was restored in Utah, Sibley and his men moved to various posts in northern New Mexico where, in 1860, they fought the Navajos.[67]

During the secession crisis, Sibley faced a dilemma familiar to other officers in New Mexico. His native state of Louisiana had seceded, and some of his officers had already left for their homes in the South. Still, Sibley felt a loyalty to the Union and his men, some of whom had served with him for almost a decade. His New York–born wife, too, was a Unionist, and urged loyalty to the government. Sibley, carefully weighing his options, seemed swayed by the arguments of his superior, Col. William Wing Loring, who was planning to leave shortly for his home in North Carolina. For the last few months, both Sibley and Loring had anticipated the national rupture and had discussed what the implications might be. Opportunities for rapid advancement awaited those heading south, and that appealed to Sibley's ambition. Finally, in late April, he resigned his commission. Sibley even plotted to take his men with him, but eventually changed his mind; on May 31, 1861, he bid his veterans farewell and left for Texas. His colleague and peer, Maj. Isaac Lynde of the Seventh U.S., had suspected Sibley's loyalties all along.[68]

Sibley hoped to return to New Mexico as conqueror. As his stage rumbled south, the adventurous officer was already making plans for securing the territory and his reputation in a lightning campaign across the desert. As he passed U.S. soldiers on his journey, he reportedly leaned from his conveyance and yelled to them, "Boys, if you only knew it, I am the worst enemy you have."[69] On June 12, upon arriving at Hart's Mill at El Paso, he wrote a cryptic message concerning his plans to his colleague Loring. "Movements are in contemplation from this direction which I am not at liberty to disclose," he wrote. "You will arrive here in time . . . to hear everything." But Sibley still fretted over leaving his faithful veterans—some of whom he had led in Mexico, on the Great Plains, and in Utah—behind. "I regret now more than ever the sickly sentimentality . . . by which I was overruled in my desire to bring my whole command with me," he wrote. "I wish I had my part to do over again; no such peace scruples should deter me from doing what I consider a bounden duty to my friends and my cause." Sibley's dreaming fostered other delusions. The rocky, sun-baked environs of Franklin appeared to him as a vision of his beloved South. "The very Southern verdure and foliage," he wrote to Loring, "filled us with enthusiasm and home feeling."[70]

The grand schemer wasted little time in putting his plan in motion. Sibley knew of Baylor's approach—the first stage of empire had already begun—and he was anxious to be off. He met several times with Hart, Herbert, and Magoffin, initiating alliances and friendships that he would rely on in the days to come. The last week of June, he boarded a coach and left for San Antonio.[71]

In early July, as Sibley's stage rattled east across western Texas, he met hundreds of determined riders heading in the opposite direction. Amid the clouds of dust and the jingling of bridles, the horsemen passed the coach—rifles, muskets, and shotguns slung on their saddles. Near Fort Clark, Sibley must have seen their leader, Lieutenant Colonel Baylor, riding in a coach on the same road, but heading for El Paso. He was an impressive looking man, balding yet sporting a dark beard flecked with gray, his defiant eyes a piercing blue. Unknown to these two at the time, the distinguished looking soldier and the blue-eyed warrior would profoundly affect each other's lives. Lieutenant Colonel Baylor continued on, joining his men at Hart's Mill, while Sibley arrived in San Antonio. The twin threads of Texas and Southern imperialism, cultivated over the past few decades and embodied in these two men, would soon be woven together. A few days later Sibley, accompanied by former Lt. Henry C. McNeill of the Regiment of Mounted Rifles, left for Richmond, Virginia, the new seat of the Confederate Government, to fix their roles in an uncertain future.[72]

CHAPTER 3

The First Blow

*I have taken possession of the Territory, I trust a force sufficient
to occupy and hold it will be sent by the government. . . .*
—Lt. Col. John Robert Baylor, Second Texas Mounted Rifles

For Texas and the Confederacy, Lt. Col. John Robert Baylor was
indeed the advance agent of empire. As June, 1861, ended, his two
hundred troops galloped into Franklin. Nearly seven hundred miles
now separated them from any contact with, or interference from,
the rest of the state. The fate of the coming enterprise lay entirely
with him and his men. By July 1, they had secured Fort Bliss, one
of the official goals of the expedition. Simeon Hart and James
Magoffin in receiving the surrender of the fort on behalf of the
Confederacy, now turned over the keys and a year's supply of fodder and provisions to Baylor. From this base of operations, the
ambitious lieutenant colonel began marshaling his men for the next
and most critical aspect of his mission. Arizona—and his own destiny—beckoned a few miles up the Rio Grande.[1]

Meanwhile, some three thousand miles away, the standard of
Southern imperialism had also been raised. Henry Hopkins Sibley
had volunteered to serve as its bearer. His credentials as West Point
graduate, Mexican War veteran, and man of vision had gained him
easy access to the inner circle in Richmond. After a few interviews,
Sibley left the Confederate capital with the three wreathed stars of

BATTLEGROUND OF EMPIRE

Santa Fe Trail

Ft. Union

Santa Fe

Las Vegas

Galisteo

Albuquerque

San Antonio

Los Padillas

Peralta

Los Lunas

Rio Puerco

Manzano

NEW MEXICO

Polvadera

Socorro

ARIZONA

Fort Craig

Ft. Stanton

Alamosa

Jornada del Muerte

Pecos River

Pinos Altos

Fort Thorn

Doña Ana

Picacho

Las Cruces

Mesilla

To Tucson

San Tomas

Ft. Fillmore

Franklin

Ft. Bliss

El Paso

Isleta

TEXAS

CHIHUAHUA

Socorro

San Elizario

Guadalupe

Fort Quitman

Rio Grande

To San Antonio

To Chihuahua City

Ft. Davis

a Confederate brigadier general and an open-ended letter authorizing the campaign in the Far West. Officially tasked with driving the Federal troops from New Mexico while "securing all the arms, supplies, and materials of war," Sibley also received permission to raise two regiments of cavalry, a battery of howitzers, and "other such forces as you may deem necessary." Confederate and state officials in Texas were expected to throw open the arsenal doors and to allow the brigadier his pick of weapons. Once his army conquered New Mexico, Sibley was to "organize a military government within the Territory." While the steamy days of July hung heavy in Virginia, hundreds of boxcars rattled into Richmond, full of volunteers eager to repel the imminent invasion. Sibley, on the other hand, boarded a recently vacated coach and traveled on the empty train as it returned to the West. His instructions, though limited to the conquest of New Mexico, gave him great latitude for pursuing his dream.[2]

While Sibley's train swayed its way across the South, Baylor molded a small army along the banks of the Rio Grande. He counted just 350 men in his command after dropping off garrisons at the Texas Trans-Pecos forts but replacing the losses with recruits from the El Paso area. Local units, some raised to fight Indians, others recruited for the coming campaign, rode into town to offer their services. Capt. Trevanion Teel's KGC company, now armed with four six-pounder field guns, renewed its service as an artillery battery. Another organization, the mostly Hispanic Mesilla Brass Band, enlisted to provide martial music for Baylor's army. His final cadre included two companies of the Second Texas Mounted Rifles and detachments from two more, along with Capt. Bethel Coopwood's Spy Company and the adventurous denizens of the surrounding scrub.[3]

The newcomers from East Texas liked their new surroundings. "Well, Pa, I am very well pleased with this place," Milam Taylor wrote to his father in Nacogdoches. "It is the prettiest place I have seen since I left home." The local people also seemed pleasant. "The Mexicans came around this morning with eggs and apples, and we swap coffee, soap, and bacon for them," he added. "We had a very good dinner." Brother Charles echoed the sentiments about their new environs. "Fort Bliss is a very pretty place," he wrote, "fine shade trees and it is all sowed down with pretty grass, called Spanish clover; it is a very fine feed for horses. I believe it grows all time of the year. I will try to get some seed . . . and send you some."[4]

Baylor drilled and trained his men in the ways of the military, preparing them for imminent action. Soldiers received captured U.S. uniforms of shell jackets, kersey trousers, and kepis.[5] Commissary agents at Hart's Mill near Fort Bliss stockpiled feed and fodder for the horses. Charles, still shocked at being sent West, seemed confounded and impressed with his new military pursuits. "We drill regular about three or four hours a day," he wrote his father. "We are all improving very fast. We have a splendid brass band and a dress parade every evening at four o'clock. Some people say we are Texas Rangers; I don't think we are. I think we may be called Texas Regulars."[6] This newly implemented discipline naturally caused some hard feelings among the independent-minded volunteers. Charles complained bitterly. "Nary time did I think when I left home that I would be stuck in an old fort and treated as an old Irish regular," he wrote his father. "One of us can't cross the river without a written pass, and after nine o'clock at night, if one of us is caught over the guard line we are taken up and put in the guard house and remain there until next morning. This may be all good enough . . . if a soldier is informed what laws and regulations he is to abide by before he is mustered into the service."[7]

Another Nacogdoches man, Cpl. Charles Shanks, decried the unexpected changes occurring in many of the men and boys from home. Officers had turned into martinets. "There is a great deal of dissatisfaction in our company, owing to the treatment of our Captain towards us. He treats us more like slaves than anything else," Shanks wrote. "Regimentals have maken a surley dictator in place of a kind captain. There are a hundred . . . things to make his men hate and despise him." Shanks feared a mutiny. "There is every prospect for a row or resistance upon the part of the majority of the company, . . . and I am afraid they will be too hasty. There never was a company that got along better in the world than ours until since we arrived here, and the tyranny and oppression commenced."[8]

The deportment of his comrades also horrified the moralistic Shanks, who tattled to the home folks in a letter. One soldier, he said, had been "drinking a good deal since he arrived here. We keep him quiet all we can, but we can [do] but little with him." Another comrade from his company also stayed drunk much of the time, and he had lost his rank while in the guard house. This soldier was guilty of even more reprehensible crimes. "He has taken letters out of the [post office] . . . broken them open and read them," Shanks wrote in astonishment. "We found them here in his saddle bags[.] We found letters that were sent to be mailed. We held a council and decided that the proper way for us to act was to inform the Captain. We done so."[9]

Liquor, as a source of distraction for the young men, often led to tragic results. One drunken trooper shot a comrade during a whiskey-induced rage. A military court promptly found the offender guilty and sentenced him to death. Rev. William J. Joyce of Palestine went to visit the condemned in his cell at Fort Bliss. "His first words as I walked in," the preacher remembered, "were 'O what will my mother say. Sir I am to die before two o'clock tomorrow. I am a murderer and a drunkard. Is there no mercy for an unprepared and sinful wretch?'"[10]

His answer came the next day. Joyce had tried to comfort the man with appropriate scriptures, but the sentence remained. The following afternoon the preacher accompanied the man and watched as a guard led him to a chair facing a firing squad. The condemned "gave the boys a few words of warning against intemperance, and sat down," Joyce reported. "He asked the priviledge of looking at his comrades, at the moment of firing. Colonel Baylor gently denied him, and bandaged his eyes. A few minutes later he was in the hands of a Merciful God."[11]

As the restless men waited anxiously for some sort of action, homesickness eroded the men's morale. "This place is about one thousand miles from Palestine," Egbert Treadwell wrote his uncle. "We had a long and fatiguing journey and both men and horses got very tired of the trip. The country we traveled over . . . was very poor, very broken, and some parts desolate of water, grass, timber and everything else save rattlesnakes and prairie dogs."[12] Corporal Shanks, also feeling especially forsaken, commented on prewar promises the folks back home had made. "We get no news here. Some of our friends promised to send us a paper from home now and then, but never a paper have we received—forgotten us, perhaps."[13]

Anxiety born of the anticipation of combat also plagued the men. "We are all getting pretty tired of being confined to a fort," Shanks wrote in a letter to Nacogdoches, "and long to go into action, although some of us may never come out of it alive." One group of young rowdies visited the Mexican town of El Paso to relieve their tension, and caused a riot. Shanks apparently could not understand the natives' indignation over his compatriots' breach of peace. Bewildered, he wrote home, "The Mexicans across the river are trying to get mad at us for whipping and hanging one of them (for only a short time) for stealing pistols."[14]

Soldiers' rations did little to ease the mood. Hundreds of pounds of condemned government hardtack fell into Rebels hands at Forts Quitman and Davis; the men ate it for lack of any alternative. Reverend Joyce described the food as "crackers about four inches square and a half inch thick, and as hard as bread ever got to be. We began on the wormy, mouldy stuff . . . our eyes looking straight forward . . . and when from sore tongues we could eat no longer, we swelled the hard tack in water, and then we could pull it apart in broad flakes, with plenty of black headed worms half inch long to encourage us."[15]

While these East Texans became inured to the less glamorous side of army life, other recruits—mostly local frontiersmen and miners—joined the Rebel ranks. A Mesilla company, the "Arizona Rangers," arrived. Augmenting these Southern partisans were at least twenty-two deserters from the U.S. forces at Fort Fillmore who enlisted in the Confederate army. Sergeant Merrick's company, now veterans of nearly three months on the Indian frontier, finally received orders to move to Fort Bliss. Glad for the change of scenery, he and his comrades, under the command of Capt. S. W. McAllister, rode out of Fort Davis on July 8, after being relieved by a twenty-five-man detachment of Company D, Second Texas. Merrick and the other would-be warriors reached their new quarters at Magoffinsville on July 16. While Southern armies gathered at Manassas, Virginia to defend Confederate independence, other soldiers gathered in West Texas to begin an offensive, the first steps of the Confederate empire.[16]

As the Rebels organized around Fort Bliss, Union Col. Edward R. S. Canby, the recently appointed commander of the Department of New Mexico, rearranged his command and prepared for war. Nearly forty-five companies of regulars occupied the various forts in the department, but the U.S. government had ordered them east. To replace them, Canby raised New Mexico volunteers and militia. He then evacuated the majority of the forts in the region, concentrating his men at central points. Troops left Fort McLane on July 3, and Fort Breckinridge on July 10; the garrison at Fort Buchanan received its orders and vacated that post on July 23. Behind each of these columns trailed refugees, afraid to face the Apaches alone. Spirals of smoke also dotted the countryside as troops torched flour mills, warehouses, and wheat fields to keep them out of Rebel hands. Thirteen regular companies reported to Fort Craig, eleven to Fort Fillmore, and five to Fort Union, while an additional ten companies, including Sibley's former command of Company I, Second Dragoons, marched for Missouri.[17]

For both armies, hostile Indians constituted an additional military threat. While various Apache bands had long been a nuisance for white settlers in the area, Baylor and his Confederates unwittingly arrived just in time to take the initial brunt of a full-blown war. An incident with U.S. troops the preceding February had driven these natives to war, which they prosecuted with a fury never before encountered in the region. These guerrillas most often operated in bands ranging in strength from 10 to 40 warriors. On occasion, several such parties might combine for large-scale attacks. West of the Rio Grande, roughly 150 Mimbreños under Mangas Coloradas roamed along the headwaters of the Gila, especially around Pinos Altos. Some 150 Chiricahua, under Cochise, plagued the miners at Tubac and travelers on the road between Tucson and Mesilla. An additional 500 warriors from various lesser bands roamed between the Gila and the Colorado, and would occasionally join in raids. East of the river, Chiefs Espejo, Nicolás, and Antonio led 200 Mescalero warriors of the Davis and White Mountain bands across the desolate mountains of far West Texas, eastern New Mexico, and eastern Confederate Arizona. Adept at ambush and cruel to captives, the Apaches, more than any other of America's indigenous peoples, specialized in stealing livestock. These warriors did not

Col. Richard Edward Sprigg Canby, circa 1863. Canby commanded the United States Department of New Mexico and defended the territory from Sibley's invasion. Courtesy of Library of Congress, Washington, D.C.

understand the white's conflict, but they did claim credit for forcing the retreat of U.S. forces from the various forts; they were now determined to build upon their perceived success and drive the remaining white men from their land.[18]

The precipitous withdrawal of U.S. troops from the outlying posts was devastating to those settlers who had come to rely on Federal military protection. Panic rippled from ranch to ranch. Felix Grundy Ake, a native of Tennessee and Texas Revolution veteran, had moved his family to near Tucson, intending to purchase and raise cattle with money he made in the California Gold Rush. His teenage son, Jeff, remembered the day when the army left. "The Captain told us that we had just three days to get out, if we wanted to move with them." The settlers were invited to take away any government stores they wanted, but were urged to leave the area. "We couldn't get ready that quick." To the Akes, evacuation meant the loss of hundreds of cattle as well as their home. As scheduled, the army withdrew, leaving the bewildered and yet-unprepared homesteaders to their fate.[19]

The situation at the exposed Pinos Altos mining camps also became desperate after U.S. regulars abandoned nearby Fort McLane and the Indians made travel in the region perilous. Supply trains carrying provisions for the camps could not get through. "Chuck was so scarce that people began to suffer," Henry Clay Smith wrote. Abandoning their picks and shovels, he and other minutemen rode off to fight the Indians and to find regular meals.[20]

In mid-July Smith and twenty other minutemen rode escort for an eight-wagon train operated by Roy Bean, but ran into trouble near the empty buildings of Fort McLane. Seventy-five Apaches descended upon the train while the miners hastily circled the wagons. The Indians retreated to the fort, where they kept up a harassing fire on the miners throughout the night. An uneasy stalemate ensued, in which the miners and teamsters suffered from thirst and cold while hoping for help to arrive from the mines. The Apaches made several feints, but never closed in on the wagons. After a two-day standoff, a fifty-man party of Hispanic farmers from the El Paso region, along with twenty more minutemen from Pinos Altos, arrived to relieve Bean, Smith, and the others. The Indians, finding themselves outnumbered, set fire to Fort McLane and disappeared into the mountains.[21]

While the old war between red men and whites intensified, the new war between soldiers in Federal blue and Confederate homespun erupted along the Rio Grande. Maj. Edwin Waller, accompanied by Coopwood's Spy Company, left Fort Bliss on July 21 to determine the strength of Fort Fillmore. Based on his report, Lieutenant Colonel Baylor prepared to seize the initiative before the Federals organized an attack of their own. Under cover of darkness, he led 258 men from Fort Bliss toward Fort Fillmore on

July 23, launching the Confederacy's first offensive of the war. Arriving the next night, the Rebels took positions between the post and the garrison's only water supply at the Rio Grande and waited in ambush for the coming dawn. A Rebel deserter spoiled the surprise, however, informing the sleeping Federals of Baylor's trap. His plan aborted, the lieutenant colonel withdrew his men across the Rio Grande, capturing a small Union detachment at San Tomás. At noon, Baylor's army entered Mesilla amid the "Vivas and hurrahs" of its citizens.[22]

There, additional reinforcements—Sergeant Smith and the men of the Pinos Altos minuteman company—also arrived to a warm reception. These frontiersmen, however, were not yet convinced to side with the Confederacy. To impress these reluctant Rebels, Major Waller assembled the entire battalion to hear the impassioned speeches of local leaders. Afterward, the miners enjoyed the run of the town. "The high cockelorums invited us to a grand fandango that night and you bet it was a dandy," Smith remembered. "Whiskey, mescal, and champaign were as free as water. . . . The Señoritas came out in their best harness and, talk about love, every son of us fell in love and came very near ending our war propensities." The entertainment worked: Capt. Tom Mastin mustered in his minuteman company as the "Arizona Guards" of the Confederate States Army. Although agreeing to fight U.S. regulars, the principal mission of this unit would be keeping the road to Tucson and the mines at Pinos Altos free of Indian attacks.[23]

Other units also organized, but they never formally attached themselves to Baylor's command. One such unit, Roy Bean's "Free Rovers," numbered a few dozen men. Locals, who knew this group's propensity for pillaging, simply called them the "Forty Thieves."[24]

On July 25, the Federals moved to dislodge the Confederates from Mesilla. Leaving a small force to hold the fort, Maj. Isaac Lynde and 380 U.S. regulars marched to the village and immediately demanded its surrender. Baylor's reply was brief: "If you wish the town and my forces, come and take them!" Lynde ordered his troops into skirmish line while his mountain howitzers began bombarding Mesilla. Heavy sand and dense corn fields impeded the regulars' advance, while three companies of the U.S. Regiment of Mounted Rifles under Capt. C. H. McNally trotted beyond the infantry and prepared to charge the Rebels.[25]

This show of Federal power did not overawe Baylor's Texans and Arizonans. Behind stout adobe walls, the volunteers from Palestine and Nacogdoches, San Antonio and Rusk, Franklin and Pinos Altos, waited until the enemy horsemen cantered into range of their shotguns, muskets, and rifles. Private Treadwell noticed that even the townsmen were prepared to repel the attackers. "The citizens posted themselves on the tops of the houses on the principal streets to render their assistance," he wrote his cousin in Palestine. Federal artillerymen covered the advance with a pair of mountain howitzers. "They . . . commenced firing bombs and grape at us and into the town," Treadwell added. "Fortunately they never done any injury to a soul." As the Union attack gained momentum, Baylor ordered a few men with rifles to pick off the officers. The first bullet cut away McNally's saber; the second and third hit him in the chest and exited his neck. Fifty impatient Rebels then added their fire, sending buckshot and bullets ripping through the Federal ranks, killing one of the mounted rifles and wounding four others. Another volley followed, and the riders retreated. The firing then became general. "We were in a very curious position," Treadwell, who had never seen combat before, remembered. "The bombs and the grape whistled over our heads." Two Union gunners fell, compelling their artillery to withdraw, followed by the infantry. Lynde reformed his command, but decided to return to Fort Fillmore as Confederate cheers echoed from Mesilla. The Rebels cautiously pursued. "Our orders were not to push them too fast," Sergeant Smith wrote, "as we might run into an ambush in the bottoms of the Rio Grande." This first clash between the two armies had killed three and wounded nine Federals, while the Texans had six men seriously wounded and twenty horses killed.[26]

The next day, Baylor resumed his offensive. After waiting all afternoon for the Federals to attack, scouts reported that Lynde was building earthworks around Fort Fillmore. About sunset, Baylor ordered Captain Teel's artillery, accompanied by McAllister's State Troops, to move up from Fort Bliss, while the balance of the command rode toward the Federal post and prepared to attack. The Federals, meanwhile, had dug trenches around the fort and had tied ropes between posts to serve as cavalry obstacles. While Baylor and the bulk of his army prepared for battle, other members of his command scoured the area for horses.[27]

The casualties among the mounts during the skirmish at Mesilla had caused concern. During the day, Smith and the rest of the Arizona Guards received permission to replace their animals and procure additional horses. "The Mexicans, after finding this out, hid out the good horses," the sergeant remembered, but a party from the company found them at the town of Chamborino, near Hart's Mill. "We expected to buy, if possible, and if not get horses any way we could. The Mexicans suspicioned our purpose and didn't care to talk horse, and they asked exorbitant prices for what they did want to sell." Foiled, the miners changed their target to the horse herd at Fort Fillmore.[28]

That evening, while the rest of Baylor's army moved into position, twenty-five men from the Arizona Guards launched their horse-stealing expedition with the aid of a pro-Southern sergeant in the Union horse detail. After contacting their man near the Rio Grande, the Rebels divided into two groups. One detachment crept quietly into the herd, while the other took positions to cover the regulars as they played cards. "They could not see us coming as the game at that time was very interesting," Smith remembered. When the signal came, the Confederates sprang from the river bank on the unsuspecting Federals. "They all jumped up and at the command to drop their arms, they did so quick and started laughing." The raiders quickly gathered their prisoners and horses and rode away. The Arizona Guards had taken eighty-five cavalry horses and twenty-six mules; the raiders got to choose their personal mounts. "I picked Lieutenant McNally's horse—the same he was riding at the first fight," Smith recalled. "You bet he was a dandy."[29]

The loss of these animals, most of Fort Fillmore's transportation, crushed Major Lynde, setting up an even worse blunder. Correctly fearing that Baylor would attack the next morning, the Federal officer ordered the fort abandoned, intending to march to Fort Stanton, the closest U.S. garrison. Soldiers hastily destroyed supplies and ammunition and their wives and children prepared for the evacuation. Just before dawn, the troops marched out, setting fires as they left. When the Texans arrived that morning, Baylor ordered Teel's and McAllister's newly arrived companies to fight the fires and garrison the post while the rest of his army pursued Lynde and his demoralized regulars.[30]

The Union veterans suffered a disaster that long, hot day. "Well we crowded on in full chase after the brave birds, and about 30 miles from Mesilla we overtook stragglers of the infantry and disarmed them in squads," Pvt. Milam Taylor of the Second Texas wrote. The entire Union force had disintegrated as the midday New Mexico sun sapped its fighting spirit. Several Union soldiers had filled their canteens with "medicinal whiskey" abandoned at the fort, and were now begging for water. "Stragglers of the enemy were seen along the roadside almost dead from fatigue and thirst and hunger," added Private Treadwell of Palestine. Guns, cartridge boxes, canteens, clothing, and blankets littered the road. The retreating Federal column included 108 women and children—wives and families of soldiers—and Treadwell encountered dozens of these helpless victims suffering along the route. It "was a pitiful sight," he wrote. "Husbands and fathers was scared so bad that they ran off and left them."[31]

The entire Federal column, five hundred men and three howitzers, lost their fight against the desert and the pursuing Texans. As Baylor and his cavalry approached the main body of Union infantry near San Augustín Springs, desperate regulars formed lines of battle on several occasions only to collapse into milling mobs. The Texans took no chances but continued on in good order in a series of short charges. Finally, Lynde, with his remaining one hundred men, surrendered the entire command unconditionally. Baylor accomplished what had seemed impossible. "Our own force, good, bad, and indifferent, consisted all told of about 280 long eared, ragged Texans," remembered Private D'Hamel of Coopwood's company. "When Lynd's soldiers found they had to surrender to a mob of ragged Texans, they were ready to mutiny."[32]

The capture of Lynde's command allowed Baylor to refit his entire command from the spoils. Rebels collected hundreds of Springfield rifles and accoutrements from the dispirited Unionists. "This proved to be a Godsend as it gave us a number of the most modern rifles," wrote Private D'Hamel. "We also found plenty of ammunition among the stores captured." The Texans also seized the colors of the Seventh U.S. Infantry and more than nine thousand dollars in treasury notes. "Our command returned to Mesilla," D'Hamel added, "where we enjoyed a well-earned rest and for the first time in six months had real coffee with sugar."[33]

Meanwhile, after extinguishing fires at Fort Fillmore, Sergeant Merrick and the others in Teel's and McAllister's companies took stock of the situation. "They had left the place in a topsyturvey state," he wrote. "The [Quartermasters Department] was a confusion of boxes, barrels, paper, etc. At the hospital they had thrown the bedding in a pile and emptied and broken bottles of medicine over them, had pulled or turned over the shelving in the dispensary into the middle of the floor, making a fine mess." The men cleaned up the buildings and made themselves at home. "We began fixing up bunks, etc., to make ourselves comfortable," Merrick added. "This is a nice clean post and airy quarters."[34]

That evening, July 27, 1861, Baylor's men received further good news. Scouts had located a party of ex-U.S. officers who were offering their service to the Confederacy, one of whom was former Col. Albert Sidney Johnston. Arriving the next day, Baylor immediately offered his command to the well-known soldier. Although eager to get on to Richmond, Johnston agreed to command the Texan army while he rested in town, allowing Baylor to begin the political organization of Confederate Arizona.[35]

On August 1, Baylor took possession of the region for the Confederate States and declared martial law. "The social and political condition of Arizona being little short of general anarchy, and the people being literally destitute of law, order, and protection, the said Territory . . . is hereby declared temporarily organized as a military government," he proclaimed. Baylor then installed himself as governor, with his capital at Mesilla. His government, he decreed, would consist of executive and judicial branches. Next, he made "the appointments to fill offices necessary to enforce the laws," naming eleven men as judges or officers of the court. Baylor declared all of New Mexico territory between the thirty-fourth parallel and the Mexican border as Arizona, but later added the whole region south of 36° 30' latitude, theoretically eliminating New Mexico Territory. He also claimed the Colorado River to its mouth as his western border—an act that incorporated several thousand square miles of Mexico. The ambitious governor then authorized the raising of four additional cavalry companies which, combined with the three already in existence, would form a battalion for local defense. Baylor also worked diligently to restore mail service to the region and to make the road to Tucson safe for travelers.[36]

The citizens of western Arizona responded by taking political action of their own. On August 5, the residents of Tucson elected Granville "Grant" Oury to represent the territory in Richmond, for the most part ignoring Baylor's government. Politician, brother to San Jacinto hero William Oury, and would-be filibuster during Henry Crabb's raid on Sonora, Grant Oury left for Richmond immediately to press for recognition of the territory and to achieve immediate admittance to the Confederacy.[37]

While Baylor and citizens wrangled to organize the territory, fighting in the region continued against three enemies: Apaches, spies, and Union troops. The road from Franklin to Fort Davis was literally strewn with the remains of wagons, stage coaches, and animals that had once belonged to mail contractors. Crude graves, too, marked the route. Mescaleros had plagued the area for years, but now their attacks had almost closed the road completely. West of the Rio Grande, Cochise and Mangas Coloradas had established their summer headquarters around Cook's Peak and preyed upon anyone taking the road to Tucson. Other enemies of Confederate Arizona included a Unionist spy ring operating in the vicinity of Franklin and Mesilla. Baylor's every movement seemed to be known by the enemy, and he ruthlessly planned to hunt the agents down. And always, the threat of Federal troops loomed close by.[38]

The Arizona Guards and Coopwood's spies found themselves active as both scouts and Indian fighters. News had arrived from Tucson that the Apaches had raided the stage line near Stein's Peak. The Butterfield Overland Mail Company was evacuating the area as a result of the war and was removing its property, including a large herd of mules and horses. The manager of the line, people feared, had been abducted in the raid. The Rebels headed west toward Pinos Altos to rescue the missing executive, and in a few days, made a grisly discovery. Apaches had killed and mutilated five men, most of whom had died in the Indians' first volley from ambush. "Not a man escaped," Smith wrote. "Former chums of ours in the mines . . . were hung up by the heels to a cedar tree and burned."

After burying the bodies, the Confederates continued their search for the manager, but never found him. In their search, however, the scouts did locate a column of U.S. regulars—the garrison of Fort Buchanan.[39]

While some of the Rebel cavalrymen maintained surveillance of the Federal column, couriers hastened to Mesilla with the news. Colonel Johnston would now command his first Confederate army in the field. The approaching Union column, 250 regulars, had burned the post and was heading toward the Federal point of concentration at Fort Craig. To cut them off, Johnston moved his four hundred Rebels into position near the village of Picacho and prepared an ambush. Located a few miles west of Mesilla, this point offered the best route to the Rio Grande, and locals considered it the only possible path the wagon encumbered enemy could take. On the night of August 6, a Federal courier advised the regulars of the events that had transpired over the last fortnight. He then advised them of an alternate route while urging vigilance. After burning their vehicles and extra supplies, the unburdened Union troops escaped the trap and, by forced marches, made it to Fort Craig safely. The next day, the unsuccessful Johnston resigned his Arizona command and continued his journey east, taking with him Capt. George Wythe Baylor, the lieutenant colonel's brother, as aide-de-camp.[40]

Not only was his first command a failure, but Johnston had earlier disappointed Southern planners and dreamers in another, more grievous way. He had been—like General Twiggs in Texas—in a position to surrender California to the secessionists. Not only did he distance himself from the Rebels on the Pacific Coast, he offered neither aid nor advice. His background indicated he was a perfect imperialist for he had fought in Texas during the revolution and had served as that state's secretary of war. He had led troops in Mexico and in the later campaign against the Mormons. He and Henry Sibley were friends. Everything about Johnston indicated that he would be a key to the Southern empire by delivering California. Instead, he had quietly resigned and, in reality, fled. His destiny, it seemed, lay elsewhere.[41]

Even though Johnston had not delivered California to the Confederacy, Baylor's successes had encouraged secessionists on the

Pacific coast. Gen. Edwin Sumner, who had replaced Johnston in California, reported scores of rebellious gatherings, and he desperately gathered troops from his department to oppose the secessionists. "There is a strong Union feeling with the majority of the people of this state, but the secessionists are much the most active and zealous party," he wrote to Washington. "I have no doubt there is some deep scheme to draw California into the secession movement."[42] Rebel companies gathered at San Bernardino, others demonstrated at Santa Barbara, and some would-be Confederate privateers fitted out in Pacific ports. Other partisans collected arms and munitions, including artillery. In response, U.S. regulars gathered to protect the Federal arsenal at Benicia Barracks, and Sumner began organizing volunteer regiments in the state.[43] Concern over Rebel machinations and the security of California worried even the venerable Winfield Scott, commander in chief of the U.S. Army. As early as June, General Scott, through his Adj. Lt. Col. E. D. Townsend, wrote Sumner that the army and navy should frustrate rebel plans for "annexing Lower California to the so-called Confederacy."[44]

The Union army was now mostly expelled from Confederate Arizona, but Baylor's soldiers continued to feel Apache wrath during the hot days of August. The once-peaceful Davis Mountain Mescaleros had turned violent. Baylor, with the aid of Magoffin, had negotiated a peace treaty with Chief Nicolás of the Davis Mountain Mescaleros, but the Indian had promptly broken the accord by firing into the Fort Davis beef herd, killing several animals. On August 5, the warrior and an estimated one hundred followers attacked the ranch of Manuel Musquiz, just six miles southeast of Fort Davis, killing three herders and stealing a large number of horses and cattle. Second Lt. Reuban E. Mays, seven men of Company D, Second Texas, and four civilians pursued the Apaches into the Big Bend region. On August 10, the Texans overtook the raiders and recaptured nearly one hundred horses. The following day, as the troops returned to Fort Davis, the twenty-six-year-old lieutenant and his men blundered into a canyon where Nicolás and his warriors waited in ambush. Forewarned of the Indians' presence, the impetuous Texans galloped ahead; the Mescaleros quickly killed all but one. The lone survivor, a Hispanic herder who served as guide, hid in a cave until the Indians had left, and made his way to Presidio on the Rio Grande. When news of the massacre reached Fort Davis, Lt. William P. White went to retrieve the remains and search for survivors.[45]

Soldiers fell elsewhere in Baylor's area of operations, this time to White Mountain Mescaleros. Fort Stanton, which the Federals had abandoned after Lynde's surrender, now hosted a detachment of Texans. On August 29, four men left the post to scout for Indians in the Gallinas Mountains. Foolishly napping beside a picturesque spring, the unsuspecting men awoke to prepare breakfast. "While in the act of cooking . . . three Indians were seen running over an adjoining hill," Lt. John R. Pulliam of Company D, Second Texas, reported to Baylor. "The men immediately saddled their horses, and while in the act of doing so they were assailed by a shower of arrows." The outmatched Rebels took positions behind trees, but died one after the other. Finally, in desperation, the only surviving Texan leapt upon his horse and rode over a precipice—miraculously, he and his mount survived. Pulliam and fourteen Texans returned to the scene a few days later to bury the bodies of the fallen. A week later, Apaches attacked the village of Placitas, ten miles south of Fort Stanton. Pulliam and fifteen men galloped to the rescue, killing five Mescaleros in a running fight. In a driving rain, the soaked and exhausted squad returned to the fort. Unable to cope with the Indian raiders, the Texans abandoned Fort Stanton. Bloodied, the various detachments of Company D, Second Texas regrouped at Mesilla, leaving the West Texas forts to Company C.[46]

In mid-August, the Akes and other remaining whites living near abandoned Fort Buchanan formed a refugee column and also headed for Mesilla. In Tucson, dozens more joined, including Moses Carson, older brother of the famous mountain man Kit Carson. Sarah Borginis, known as "The Great Western" during the Mexican War and described as "the best whore in the West," also accompanied the party, as did Sam Houston, nephew of the famous Texan statesman. The entire party, some twenty-four men, seven women, sixteen children, and a half-dozen slaves, faced an uncertain destiny as their dozen wagons rolled east, trailed by hundreds of beeves and sheep. In Cook's Canyon, Cochise, leading an estimated two hundred warriors from various Chiricahua, Mimbreño, and Gileño bands, sprang an ambush. "We was going along, free and easy," Ake remembered. "Then, without no warning at all, the Indians come hellity-larrup, just swarming outen the rocks. There was a whole cloud of them."[47]

The surprised settlers tried desperately to organize a defense. One man fell dead immediately, two others lay wounded. Young Houston, with six others, bolted the ambush, leaving their comrades in jeopardy. The remaining settlers managed to circle most of their wagons but abandoned several, which the Apaches promptly looted. Scores of Indians swirled around the makeshift fort, exchanging shots with its defenders. After several minutes of intense fighting, the Apaches withdrew a short distance. Ten of their number lay dead. Behind the wagons, Ake surveyed a grisly scene among the settlers. "May and Redding was dead, that I could see; Pearl was a-laying under a wagon, shot and out of his head. . . . Old Cap'n Sharp had been shot in the ear with an arrow that come out the back of his head, but he busted off the shaft and pulled the head out through the back. Cotton was shot through the leg with a ramrod." Chancing that the Indians would not return to the attack, the refugees loaded the women, children, and wounded into wagons and made a dash out of the canyon to safety. "The Indians didn't foller," said Ake. "They might have been afraid, but I reckon the plunder was more interesting to them. We had only gone a little way when we looked back and saw the squaws already herding the stock away."[48]

When the survivors reached Pinos Altos, Captain Mastin's Arizona Guards gathered thirty men and, anticipating that the Indians would head for Mexico with their plunder, waited in the Florida Mountains to intercept them. Cochise and his followers had divided, however, and only eighty Chiricahuas blundered into the trap, promptly losing eight warriors killed. The Apaches abandoned their herd and scattered.[49] "With the help of the Confederates, we got our stock together," Ake said. "About half our sheep and cattle was saved." At the scene of the ambush, the white casualties had been scalped. Ake's family recovered the body of their bulldog, Jack. "Dad was pretty sad. . . . I'd rather lost a thousand dollars than that dog."[50]

With most of the western Apaches temporarily in Mexico, the Confederate government attempted to return order to West Texas and Confederate Arizona, including scheduled mail delivery. In August, Confederate postmaster John H. Reagan awarded George H. Giddings, a veteran frontiersman and mail contractor, Route 8075 with twice-weekly service between San Antonio, Mesilla, and, theoretically, California. His employees had served in the region for years, and the change of governments had affected them very little.[51] A passenger on the line described the drivers as "men who handled their reins and managed their teams with skill, whose eyes were ever alert for danger, whether by Indians or unavoidable accidents, who guard with true courage and bravery all that is consigned to their care."[52] Baylor, as governor and military commander of that vast, desolate stretch, was responsible for protecting the mail—a task he had far too few soldiers to accomplish.

After the May's massacre, Mescaleros regularly looted vehicles passing through western Texas but not with impunity. In late August, they waylaid James E. Terry and four companions carrying the mail on pack mules near the springs at Eighteen Mile Hole. Fifteen mounted Indians darted out from cover, while another group of warriors began the chase on foot. Abandoning the mules, Terry and his men rode hard for the cover of a nearby ridge. The Texans gained the height just hoof beats ahead of their pursuers and turned on the Apaches with rifle balls and buckshot. They blew apart one Mescalero and wounded several others. The warriors, their momentum spent, retreated, keeping up a long-range siege for the remainder of the day. Terry and the mail guard, discouraging the Apaches with well-placed shots from their Sharp's rifles, awoke the next morning to find the enemy and their parcels gone. Despite Baylor's, Gidding's, and Terry's best efforts, the mail to and from San Antonio arrived infrequently at best.[53]

Almost as bad as Indians, at least to Baylor, were spies. W. W. Mills, a resident of El Paso, had been in constant communication with both Lynde and Canby since Texas had seceded, and had carried numerous dispatches for the Union army. Shortly before the capture of Fort Fillmore, Mills traveled to El Paso, Mexico, attempting to contact U.S. diplomats and continue his career in espionage. Instead, he was ambushed by "a German named Kuhn, who . . . had a reputation of being a bad man," and troopers of Company E, Second Texas.[54] Mills saw the desperado near the main plaza, but attempted to avoid him. Instead, Kuhn rode his horse onto the sidewalk and grabbed the spy by the shoulder. "I looked up and saw that he had a pistol pointed at my breast," Mills wrote. "Half a dozen other horsemen appeared as though they had rizen out of the ground. One seized my pistol and ordered me to mount . . . and away we all went at a clattering gallop to the Texas side."[55]

This was not the only time Baylor violated Mexican neutrality by capturing suspected spies. Canby dispatched Lt. Donald C. Stith of the Fifth U.S. Infantry to Chihuahua to investigate the sale of a government wagon train that had been stolen a few months earlier from Fort McLane. In mid-July, fifteen Texans under Lt. W. C. Adams seized the officer some forty miles south of El Paso, at the village of Guadalupe. "I asked him by what authority he did so," Stith wrote his superiors. "He replied, 'By authority of the Southern Confederacy.'" Stith, like Mills, found himself awaiting trial in Texas.[56]

Once across the Rio Grande, captives received varying degrees of treatment. Mills went before Major Waller, who ordered him and Stith imprisoned at Fort Bliss. "A very close, hot and filthy guard house it was, filled with vermin and bad men," Mills remembered. The alleged spy languished in jail for a month, shackled and chained, before gaining limited freedom within the confines of Fort Bliss. The entire time he remained under threat of summary hanging if he violated this parole. After a few days of acting sincere, Mills bolted across the Rio Grande to Mexico and the eventual safety of Union lines. Stith, too, received parole, commenting that he had been treated with "the utmost kindness and consideration." As though to repay his good treatment, Stith defected to the Rebel cause, receiving a captain's commission and a staff position in San Antonio.[57]

Other citizens of Confederate Arizona also served as Union spies. As a postscript to Colonel Johnston's first command, Confederate officials discovered that Virgil Massie, a Hispanic teamster from the village of Picacho, had in fact been the man who alerted retreating Union troops from Fort Buchanan of the ambush, enabling them to escape safely. After Massie's cover was blown, Sergeant Smith and two other Arizona Guards hunted him, without success. "He was riding a newly shod horse and we had no trouble to follow it," Smith wrote. "We wanted him very bad."

Massie, however, managed to successfully escape to Fort Craig.[58]

Later in the year, the governor ordered the arrest of A. F. Wulff, a contractor living in Presidio del Norte. Lt. Emory Gibbons of Company C, Second Texas, and a detachment of nine men from Fort Davis rode to the Rio Grande opposite the town. Five of the soldiers, looking for entertainment, received permission to cross the river for the evening. After spending the night at a dance in town, the five Texans went to Wulff's residence at three o'clock in the morning, drew their pistols, and hammered at his door. When the startled man appeared, two soldiers barged into the house, seized Wulff by the hair, and forced him into the street as his screaming wife watched. Neighbors, awakened by the noise, scrambled out of their houses and pursued the Texans, as did a squad of Mexican militia. Three of the intruders quickly ran away, leaving the other two, who still held Wulff, to face the crowd. One Texan released the prisoner, turned, and fired at his pursuers, just fifteen yards away. Wulff pulled free of the remaining soldier as the Mexicans and Texans exchanged some fifty pistol shots, killing the two Confederates and one Mexican militiaman.[59]

Baylor, the spy hunter, also had agents of his own. These included William Kirk, former wagon master from Fort McLane, and José Maria Rivas of El Paso. Two others, John G. Phillips and J. F. Battaile, hailed from Santa Fe. Phillips, an Irishman with a quick temper, had owned a hotel in the New Mexican capital and had a reputation as a duelist and hothead.[60]

While elements of Baylor's army hunted Indians and spies, others under the command of Captain Coopwood continued skirmishing with the Federals along the Rio Grande; horse-stealing raids dominating the action. Baylor ordered Coopwood and his men to occupy an advanced post at Robledo, near the abandoned buildings of Fort Thorn and commanding the road to Fort Craig. On August 21, ten men from one of Canby's New Mexico volunteer regiments raided Coopwood's corral; the vigilant Texans, on a scout themselves, intercepted the raiders. Closing on the Federals, Coopwood's men opened fire, which the enemy returned before surrendering. Bullets struck only one man during the exchange—Enrique D'Hamel. The unfortunate Cuban émigré received a painful, though not fatal, wound. "I got a spent Springfield bullet in my left wrist, which went up my arm almost to the elbow," the Rebel remembered. He and the Union prisoners left Robledo for Fort Fillmore.[61]

After being in the region for just two months, Baylor was very familiar with the grave problems facing Arizona. Apaches had already killed more of his men than the Federals, and their constant raids threatened to exhaust his scant military resources. He knew he could not adequately protect the citizens of Arizona. Meanwhile, the Union garrison at Fort Craig continued to grow with the arrival of additional volunteers. Frustrated, Baylor wrote of his predicament to Col. Earl Van Dorn, the commander of the Department of Texas. "I would urge the importance of more men being sent to me," the governor argued. "I can't hold the United States troops in check and operate against the Indians with the limited number of men under my command."[62]

Even so, Baylor and his command had been very successful with their primary mission. His victories over the U.S. regulars in Confederate Arizona aroused great hopes in western secessionists. Richmond, too, applauded, and had moved to add his plunder to its realm. Baylor had never been so popular—with his men, his government, and his subjects—as he was in September, 1861. But his victories had also given pause to the United States government. At the outset of the secession crisis, Washington planners had placed little military importance on the western territories. Baylor's leadership and success as a warrior now drew the nation's attention to that remote region. The U.S. government had ordered Canby to eventually evacuate all U.S. regulars from the territory; the colonel had sent more than a thousand, but now that he knew how dangerous his opponents were, he refused to send more.[63]

Canby reinforced his cadre of regulars by raising auxiliary companies comprising both volunteer and militia units from among the local population in the vicinity of Federal forts. Later, he decided upon a more formal organization. These companies then became the nucleus of four volunteer regiments later augmented by various "independent" companies of militia. By the end of summer, these new troops, led by the likes of veteran scout Christopher "Kit" Carson and popular politician Nicolás Piño, were serving alongside the regulars. Capt. James "Paddy" Graydon, an Irish-born veteran of the U.S. Army, raised a company of spies and scouts. Federal

Col. Christopher "Kit" Carson, 1st New Mexico Infantry, from a carte de visite circa 1863. Courtesy of Lee Burke Collection, Dallas, Texas.

officials even suggested using other irregular troops—Kiowa Indians—to serve as guides and scouts. Recruiting continued while hundreds of additional men trickled into the U.S. forts. Canby also called for help from volunteers organizing in Colorado.[64]

Baylor had initiated the process of empire, but the task seemed on the verge of overwhelming him. Following Van Dorn's suggestion, he had eliminated the enemy outposts at Fort Fillmore by capturing its garrison. He had also organized Confederate Arizona Territory and had taken over as governor. Now, scores of problems plagued him. Cochise, Nicolás, and Mangas Coloradas were opponents on whom Baylor had not figured; on every side the mountain fastness offered these hardy guerrillas safe refuge. Their style of fighting differed greatly with that of his more familiar native opponents, the Comanches. Baylor inherited a bloody Indian war that had smoldered for years and had bested the United States' most talented soldiers. The Federal government, furthermore, at the urging of Colonel Canby, had refused to surrender the region without a fight. The process had at first appeared easy, but now it had become apparent that Baylor's eagerness to be the standard-bearer of Texan imperialism had landed him in difficulties he could not surmount. To Van Dorn in San Antonio, the self-proclaimed governor commented, "Now that I have taken possession of the Territory, I trust a force sufficient to occupy and hold it will be sent by the government, under some competent man." Unknown to Baylor at the time, the Confederacy had already found its man.[65]

CHAPTER 4

The Imperial Brigade

I like the appearance of "the old rascal" very much.
    —Pvt. William Randolph Howell, Plantersville, Texas

Subtly, the drive for empire was entering a new phase. Early gains had been made, and the instruments of empire—a military garrison and a government—were in place. The leaders of empire now had to build upon these foundations, but first the new government had to win the confidence of the governed. Not only did the courts have to function equitably; the military had to protect lives and property. Beyond that, Governor Baylor hoped to engineer secessionists movements in other western territories. All Confederate efforts thus far would be for naught if these goals were not achieved. The last four months of 1861 would be critical to the imperial dream. If Baylor succeeded, the march to empire could proceed. If he failed, the Confederacy would also fail as a progressive, dynamic, expanding state, and the lives and property of the those who had backed the Rebel cause would be in jeopardy. To succeed in these plans, Baylor needed troops.

The early months of 1861 had been equally hectic for Confederate military commanders in Texas. The continuing problem of protecting the frontier had claimed most of the standing military units in the state. The militia system, elsewhere in the Confederacy a reliable source of ready-made units, was in chaos. Texas had not only to supply men for garrison duty in the western forts but to send units out of state as part of its commitment to the Confederate government. Even so, Texas leaders maintained a commitment to the secessionists in the western territories and hoped to send troops to the West. All of these military organizations required arms, ammunition, clothing, and food before they could approach military efficiency. Coupled with an inexperienced and under-stocked quartermaster department, these needs resulted in critical shortages of war materiel. As the first summer of war passed, the state's military reserves dried up and the potential for future military call-ups looked bleak, even though thousands of men waited to join.[1]

Even with these problems, many Texans remained convinced that holding Arizona was vital and worth the expenditure of the state's scarce resources. Baylor and his small Texan army needed help, but the state alone could not save him. Regiments destined for Virginia, Missouri, and Tennessee had emptied arsenals and warehouses. Texas' financial reserves, never large, were drained to maintain these units in the field and to pay hundreds of debts once covered by the Federal government. While Texas struggled under the burdens inherent in secession, Baylor faced more fundamental issues—how to allocate his meager resources to defend Confederate Arizona against the twin threats of Apaches and Unionists. If relief did not reach Mesilla soon, the Confederacy would lose its only new territory, effectively stifling secessionist sentiment in the West. The Texans' ambition for a western empire would crumble.[2]

The salvation for Arizona had to come from Richmond, as Baylor realized when he wrote, "The vast mineral resources of Arizona, in addition to its affording an outlet to the Pacific, make its acquisition a matter of some importance to our Government."[3] Confederate planners knew of the West's potential, and lobbyists from Arizona and Texas had convinced the Richmond government that it, too, should allocate resources to secure the territories. But other matters more critical to the survival of the nation required immediate attention.

What the Confederacy needed was an able man who could build upon Baylor's success at a minimal cost to the government in men, materiel, and money. Baylor, unknown in the capital, presented more problems than solutions. Although so far successful against the

Federal regulars in New Mexico, he had no formal military training and he had a reputation for being unpredictable, violent, and hard to control. Jefferson Davis and his war leadership did not want more troublesome independent agents—they needed inexpensive and easy solutions, and a professional soldier who could lead an army of Texans to the rescue of Arizona. That man, they concluded, was Henry Hopkins Sibley.

Baylor had requested a "competent man," and Sibley's credentials convinced the Richmond government that he was. A West Pointer and a native of Louisiana, Sibley had emerged from the War with Mexico a hero and a friend of Albert Sidney Johnston. He also had a patent for the "Sibley Tent," a conical dwelling designed from Comanche tipis. This intelligent and scientific officer was also a convincing and a fairly charismatic man. Sibley's last assignment, and the most telling from the Confederate standpoint, was Fort Union, New Mexico Territory. Most importantly, Sibley offered a plan that embodied the fulfillment of long-cherished Southern dreams.[4]

After his decision to side with the Confederacy, Sibley had gone to Richmond to offer the government a plan based on his knowledge of the situation in New Mexico. He reasoned that because of a lack of Union strength and an abundance of sympathy for the Confederacy in the area a single brigade of well-mounted troops could easily seize the region in a self-sustained campaign. This belief was bolstered by Baylor's apparent success. Once Santa Fe had fallen, Sibley reasoned, the thousands of pro-South partisans in California would be willing to aid his command in conquering the West. The Stars and Bars would soon fly over San Francisco Bay; moreover, gold and silver from the Sierra Nevadas would finance the South's war for independence.[5] The next phase of his plan was even more ambitious. Once the American Southwest had fallen to the Confederacy, the northern Mexican states of Chihuahua, Sonora and Lower California could be acquired, by either lead or gold. Political chaos in Mexico at the time encouraged Southern imperialists and awakened filibuster dreams.[6]

Sibley established his headquarters in San Antonio in August, 1861, but soon ran into obstacles in raising his brigade. Commissioned a brigadier general by the Confederate government, he was authorized to enroll two regiments of cavalry and a battery of howitzers for duty in New Mexico. The task appeared simple, and Sibley anticipated getting his campaign underway within a few weeks. He believed that the state militia companies were merely waiting to be organized for the Confederacy. Upon arriving in Texas, however, he found the state militia system almost nonexistent. Units promised by Governor Clark, which on paper appeared fully recruited and ready to go, had in actuality been disbanded or were seriously under strength. General Sibley faced the unwelcome fact that he would have to build his brigade from scratch.[7] "At the very earliest day that it became apparent that the companies ordered out by the governor could not be relied on, I at once resorted to the people themselves," Sibley wrote to explain his delay. An experienced recruiter, he placed notices in newspapers as he did in his days with the Second Dragoons, this time calling for volunteers for the specific purpose of invading New Mexico. Dozens of letters from prospective company commanders soon arrived, and Sibley began making appointments. He assigned applicants the task of raising their own companies in exchange for their captain's bars. On paper he designated his new units the First and Second Regiments, Sibley's Brigade. In the state scheme of military organizations, however, they were known as the Fourth and Fifth Texas Mounted Volunteers. By the third week of August, Sibley was finally ready to begin building his command, but delays would later cost him dearly.[8]

In San Antonio, Sibley worked diligently through August to organize his staff. On it were influential Texans, including sons of well-known families or leading functionaries of the Texas secession convention. Lt. Tom Ochiltree, the twenty-one-year-old son of a prominent Lone Star politician, served initially as adjutant general of the brigade, later as Sibley's aide-de-camp. Alexander M. Jackson, the recently resigned secretary of New Mexico Territory, became assistant adjutant general. Sibley named William T. Brownrigg, secretary of the Committee of Public Safety, his chief of commissary and subsistence. Two of Magoffin's sons, Joseph and Samuel, received staff appointments, the former as a lieutenant under Brownrigg, and the latter as a volunteer aide-de-camp with the rank of major.[9]

Corp. John Henry, Company C, 5th Texas Mounted Volunteers, and wife.
A quarter-plate ambrotype taken in 1861. Courtesy of Lawrence T. Jones III
collection, Austin, Texas.

Sibley also made plans for supplying his army once it arrived in
Confederate Arizona. Josiah Crosby and Simeon Hart of El Paso
County became agents for caching food near Fort Bliss. Working
with Governor Baylor, the team authorized purchasing agents to
gather feed corn and flour for the army. Forts Davis, Quitman, and
Bliss became storage depots for Sibley's Brigade. To aid these men
in their procurement, Sibley sent officers to New Orleans to obtain

hard money for paying the Mexican and Arizonan vendors.[10]

Sibley's supply requirements seemed achievable. Hart and Crosby assigned purchasing agents to travel to Chihuahua and Sonora to buy corn, flour, salt, beef, soap, and beans. Once procured, these items would then be stored in Mexico until Sibley arrived with his army. In addition, Hart had increased production from his own mills, turning out some fifty thousand pounds of flour for Rebel use. In theory, arrangements remained in place to either purchase or produce all the food needed for the Confederate Army in that theater. "Be easy about your supplies," wrote Hart to the general. "We shall get all we want from Sonora—what this valley cannot furnish—until such time as you may be in full possession of New Mexico, and can avail yourself of its resources. . . . " The most important factor remained for Sibley to arrive with hard currency to affect the purchases.[11]

Next, Sibley organized the brigade leadership, relying on a mix of army veterans and dedicated imperialists to serve as field grade officers. James Reily, a politician, diplomat, and professional civil servant, became Sibley's second in command. He had been a major in the army of the Republic of Texas as well as a lawyer and an influential Whig. He bolted that party in 1855 because of its antislavery agitation, and had enthusiastically backed James Buchanan for the presidency. In return, Reily received the office of consul to Russia, which he resigned after a short time; by 1861, he was back in Houston. An ardent secessionist, Reily was known for his stump speeches. Sibley gave him command of the Fourth Texas Mounted Volunteers on August 20, 1861, intending to send him as diplomatic envoy to the Mexican states of Chihuahua and Sonora, in hope of obtaining support there for the campaign.[12]

The task of leading the Fourth through the campaign would fall to Reily's second in command, William Read "Dirty Shirt" Scurry, another notable Texan. A lawyer, Scurry had served as aide-de-camp to Gen. Thomas J. Rusk in the Republic of Texas Army and during the Mexican War he fought at Monterrey. After the war, he practiced law in various Texas counties, eventually serving as a delegate to the state secession convention in 1861. An orator and poet, Scurry campaigned hard for secession, riding feverishly through dozens of Texas towns, haranguing crowds, and earning his sobriquet, "Dirty

James Reily, colonel of the 4th Texas Mounted Volunteers, circa 1860.
During the campaign Reiley was on detached duty as a diplomat to the
governors of Chihuahua and Sonora. Courtesy of Archives Division,
Texas State Library, Austin.

Shirt," because of his road-grimed garments. Sibley commissioned
him lieutenant colonel on August 23, 1861.[13]

Forty-seven-year-old Tom Green, a popular Texan veteran of
many battles, also joined the new brigade. In 1836, he had first seen
combat at San Jacinto as a private of artillery; later he served the
Texas army in raids against Comanches and against the 1842

invasion of Mexican Gen. Rafael Vásquez. That same year Green also participated in the expedition of Gen. Alexander Somervell, choosing to return home with the bulk of that command instead of crossing the Rio Grande with the doomed Mier expedition. During the Mexican War Green fought at Monterrey as a captain under Col. John Coffee Hays of the First Texas Mounted Volunteers. After the war he returned to Texas, where he served as clerk of the state supreme court until the outbreak of the Civil War. One admirer described him as a "marked man in Texas, and in all her troubles, never failed in the hour of need to come to her assistance with that ardency and devotion which so strikingly marked his character." Sibley appointed him colonel of the Fifth Texas Mounted Volunteers on August 20, 1861.[14]

Of all the officers in the brigade, Green had the greatest reputation. His troops affectionately called him "Daddy." An admirer later described him as "Upright, modest, and with the simplicity of a child, danger seemed to be his element, and he rejoiced in combat. His men adored him, and would follow wherever he led. . . . The great Commonwealth . . . will never send forth a bolder warrior, a better citizen, nor a more upright man than Thomas Green."[15] He led by example and would often be seen in front of his troops in the coming days.

Henry C. McNeill, who had accompanied Sibley to Richmond, received the lieutenant colonelcy of the Fifth Texas Mounted Volunteers. A native of Natchez, Mississippi, McNeill had moved to Texas at an early age. After attending both the Kentucky Military Institute and the Western Military Institute, he moved on to West Point, appointed from his adopted state in 1853. McNeill graduated twenty-sixth in his class, described as "a gentleman of the highest honorable scruples, who would scorn to perform a mean act." His service was entirely in New Mexico with the regiment of mounted rifles, joining that unit on July 1, 1857, and earning promotion to the permanent rank of second lieutenant a few months later. He still served at that rank when he resigned his commission on May 12, 1861, at Fort Stanton. He met up with Sibley near Fort Bliss early the next month and had linked his fate to that of his superior officer.[16]

Another of Sibley's choices epitomized imperialism. Notorious

William Read Scurry, lieutenant colonel of the 4th Texas Mounted Volunteers. Courtesy of Archives Division, Texas State Library, Austin.

filibuster and soldier of fortune Samuel "Nicaragua" Lockridge became major of the Fifth Texas Mounted Volunteers. This Alabama native had killed a man on an Ohio River steamboat, had fled to Costa Rica about 1850, and six years later had fought for William Walker. Holding a colonel's commission and the posts of recruiting agent and master of transportation, he haunted New Orleans, enlisting adventurers for Walker. In 1858, Lockridge led a Texan relief expedition to Central America, where he moved up

Tom Green, colonel of the 5th Texas Mounted Volunteers, circa 1860.
Courtesy of Archives Division, Texas State Library, Austin.

the San Juan River against the Costa Ricans. The tall, gaunt Kentuckian was more brave than able, however, and Walker accused him of "pretension" when he refused to turn over the command of the expedition to more experienced soldiers.[17] Many of the rank and file echoed the sentiment, viewing Lockridge as a bully and a tyrant.[18] His subsequent failure in Nicaragua estranged him from his filibustering companions, and he deserted. Lockridge went to Mexico the following year, offering his services to Gen. Santiago

Vidaurri, the revolutionary leader of the Liberal party, who rejected him. After spending time in Brownsville, Texas, Lockridge drifted back to New Orleans, where he again crossed paths with Walker, whom he challenged to a duel, but without satisfaction. He also became active in the Knights of the Golden Circle. With the advent of secession, Lockridge linked his tempestuous fate to that of the Confederacy. One soldier in his regiment referred to the major as "the pride of the army" and "the worshipped idol of the old Fifth Texas."[19]

With brigade leadership in place, organizing and recruiting the companies of the invasion force proceeded rapidly. Unlike most regiments created to reinforce a particular "seat of war," Sibley's regiments were formed for a specific campaign and a specific purpose. Captains solicited commissions in exchange for recruiting companies from their home counties and neighboring communities. This "contracting" style differed from the usual procedure in which the rank and file elected their officers. Sibley's unique approach created difficulties later as the men resented leaders they did not elect.[20]

Competition for Texans, men to fill out the company rolls, was fierce. Militia units and volunteer companies had formed all over the state; three regiments of infantry had already been called to Virginia while others formed for Missouri and Tennessee. For Sibley's New Mexico project, individual soldiers had to be enticed away from their standing units or from their homes. In some cases, the reputation and charisma of the recruiting officers attracted recruits. The editor of the *Bellville Countrymen* described Jerome B. McCown of Hempstead, recruiting in the communities around his home, as "too well known to require any introduction at our hands." He added that McCown "is a whole-souled fellow, and will divide his bottom dollar with a soldier."[21] Some captain-designates, however, failed to win over enough men, and did not participate in the campaign as company commanders, if at all.[22]

Some overeager officers sometimes liquidated property and businesses at a sacrifice to advance their ambitions, benefiting enterprising Texans, such as the ubiquitous Englishman R. H. Williams of Bexar County. One summer evening, Dan Ragsdale, future commander of Company D, Fifth Texas Mounted Volunteers,

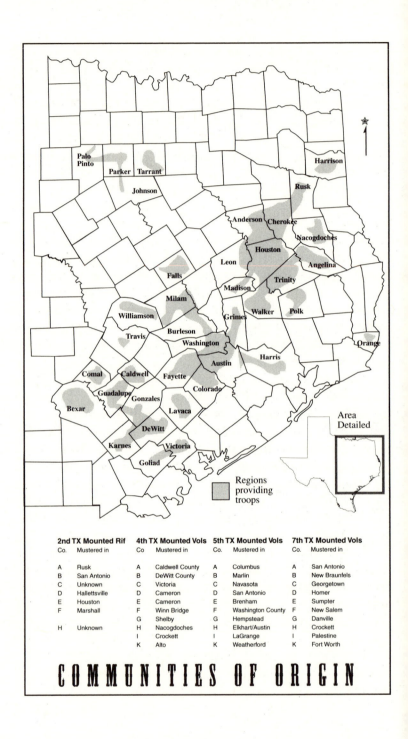

Palo Pinto
Parker Tarrant
Johnson
Harrison
Rusk
Anderson Cherokee
Nacogdoches
Houston
Leon
Angelina
Falls
Trinity
Madison
Milam
Walker
Polk
Williamson
Grimes
Travis
Burleson
Washington
Orange
Austin
Harris
Comal Caldwell
Fayette
Guadalupe
Colorado
Gonzales
Bexar
Lavaca
DeWitt
Karnes Victoria
Goliad

Area
Detailed

Regions
providing
troops

2nd TX Mounted Rif		4th TX Mounted Vols		5th TX Mounted Vols		7th TX Mounted Vols	
Co.	Mustered in	Co	Mustered in	Co.	Mustered in	Co.	Mustered in
A	Rusk	A	Caldwell County	A	Columbus	A	San Antonio
B	San Antonio	B	DeWitt County	B	Marlin	B	New Braunfels
C	Unknown	C	Victoria	C	Navasota	C	Georgetown
D	Hallettsville	D	Cameron	D	San Antonio	D	Homer
E	Houston	E	Cameron	E	Brenham	E	Sumpter
F	Marshall	F	Winn Bridge	F	Washington County	F	New Salem
		G	Shelby	G	Hempstead	G	Danville
H	Unknown	H	Nacogdoches	H	Elkhart/Austin	H	Crockett
		I	Crockett	I	LaGrange	I	Palestine
		K	Alto	K	Weatherford	K	Fort Worth

COMMUNITIES OF ORIGIN

appeared at his cabin door with a proposition. "The war-fever was strong on him," Williams wrote. "He was on his way to San Antonio to sell out 'lock, stock, and barrel,' and take a commission as a captain in the Confederate army, which had been promised him." Ragsdale's holdings included a ranch on the Frio River, two thousand head of cattle, four slaves, and a number of horses. "We paid him . . . $1,000 down, and I think he was quite as pleased to sell as we to buy," Williams remembered. "He . . . was keen to be off to the wars." On September 1, Ragsdale enrolled his unit, many of whom had served with him as rangers in the Texas Hill Country.[23]

John Samuel "Shrop" Shropshire, a twenty-eight-year-old Kentucky native and a member of the slaveholding aristocracy, also joined Sibley's brigade. Orphaned at an early age, he had been raised by an older brother and a wealthy aunt. After passing the bar exam, Shropshire followed his brother to Texas and, in 1855, established a law practice in Columbus, Colorado County. Over the next four years, the ambitious young man acquired land and wealth. In 1859, he further enhanced his status by marrying Caroline Tait of Alabama. In addition to large loans and money, Shropshire's wealthy in-laws gave him forty slave families. By 1860, he had amassed nearly thirty-eight thousand dollars in real estate and more than fifty thousand dollars in personal property, including sixty-two slaves and a thriving cotton plantation. The following year, he rejoiced at the birth of his first child, Charlie; he also accepted a commission in Sibley's Brigade. On August 17, this wealthy, sensitive, family man formally enrolled his "Colorado Cavalry" at Columbus. Mindful of the dangers he faced, Shropshire exhorted his "dear Carrie" to preserve her delicate health while he was away. "I may come back soon or it may be a long time, but when I do it would disturb me beyond measure to find you gone," the captain wrote. "If I should get killed, remember that Charlie alone depends upon you for protection and care. My love to you both."[24] One of his troops described the captain as "one of God's noblemen . . . his spirit so holy it would not stain the purest rill that sparkles among the bowers of bliss."[25]

Volunteers answered the recruiter's call from across the state. The bulk of the command came from South Central and East Texas. A small, but significant, element of the brigade hailed from frontier counties. The companies that arrived in San Antonio differed from many such units that mustered in the state. Men enlisted from regions instead of specific counties, with successful captains—proprietors combing important roads and byways in their quests for soldiers. Kinship groups and social circles responded, providing tight-knit groups of friends and families who volunteered to fight together.[26]

These troops composed the loose edges of the societies they represented. Nearly half cannot be identified in the 1860 census, suggesting a high degree of mobility. Of those who were enumerated, few pursued static occupations; only one in three is listed as a farmer. One carpenter turned soldier, for example, left a house in Colorado County only half-framed, prompting angry, but impotent, threats of a lawsuit. Few, besides officers, owned significant amounts of real estate. Slave ownership, too, was rare. Curiously, most of the communities supplying men to Sibley's Brigade were heavily engaged in cotton production, an industry requiring holdings in land and slaves and factoring against mobility. Yet the principal economic pursuit of these same regions was herding. A number of the men claimed "stock raising" as their profession, a fairly fluid vocation, while the balance claimed a trade, no occupation, or proclaimed themselves a "laborer."[27]

The men who volunteered to go to New Mexico apparently had few home ties and were subject to peer pressure. Most were young, the average age being twenty-four. Only one-quarter were married, even fewer had children. Of the unmarried men, the majority were elder sons, a mobile position within the family. Kinship ties undoubtedly influenced some to join, as cousins and brothers living in distant towns persuaded one another to join a company so they could serve together. Neighbors also joined, for the prospect of adventuring in New Mexico with old friends held great appeal.[28]

The officers of Sibley's Brigade knew what lay ahead; some of the enlisted men, however, seemed unsure exactly how and where the Confederacy would utilize them. As a result, Sibley drew an interesting assortment of men with widely varying sympathies and motivations. Some, knowing the western territories to be the goal, saw the destiny of their state and nation in the West, reflecting the imperialistic milieu of 1860s Texas. Others merely chose this opportunity to fight Yankees, regardless of the theater of operations. One such soldier from Angelina County made his predilections clear as he settled his affairs prior to leaving home: "I, William H. Cleaver . . . being about to submit my mortal body to the uncertainties of the present unholy war waged against the Confederate States of America under the auspices of the usurper and despot Abraham Lincoln do make ordain and establish my last will and testament. . . . "[29] Such men were true Rebels. Others enlisted with the idea that the brigade would seize New Mexico and then march to Missouri to aid the forces of Sterling Price. A number believed they would ultimately ride to Virginia. Others saw it as a grand gun-stealing mission aimed at the western forts.[30]

William Randolph Howell of Plantersville in Grimes County was an enthusiastic recruit for Sibley's Brigade. A native of South Carolina, he had come to Texas the previous year with his physician father, the family bringing with them that region's views on states' rights. Once in Texas, the nineteen-year-old Howell had clerked in a local store. Upon the advent of secession the following year, he quit his job to join the army. He had originally attempted to enlist in an infantry regiment destined for Hood's command in Virginia; illness had ended that ambition and doctors recommended mounted service instead. Accordingly, on August 19, he joined the "Grimes County Rangers" as a private when that company mustered in Navasota. After receiving a flag from the citizens of that town, the unit made its way to San Antonio.[31]

Twenty-one-year-old Henry C. Wright of Moscow, Polk County, also hastened to serve the Confederacy. His parents were English; he had been born in New York and grew up on Long Island. In 1855, the family had come to Texas. "It took but a very little while for my mind to grasp and appreciate the Southern ideas of the States' rights and the white man's supremacy," the soldier wrote in later years. "So when . . . the state voted for secession, I was among the first to volunteer." On September 9, this Northern-born warrior assembled with his friends and neighbors at Winn Bridge, halfway between Livingston and Moscow, to form the "Lone Star Rangers." The command then began its westward trek.[32]

In Victoria, the "Invincibles" also mustered for the coming

campaign, gathering recruits from all walks of life. Twenty-three-year-old Alfred B. Peticolas joined. An aspiring young lawyer, the well-educated adventurer had come to Texas from Virginia in 1859 to escape the memory of an unhappy love. Tall, handsome, and intelligent, he was soon popular with the rank and file, who would elect him as fifth sergeant. One of his closest companions, by contrast, was Ebeneezer Hanna, the eighth child of a poor farmer. A native of Arkansas, he was just sixteen when he enlisted, but he soon came to be known as a good observer and note taker. Hanna received the designation of "company historian." Among the troops, he was known for always having a pencil on hand.

The Victoria Invincibles were a cosmopolitan mix of men typical of the frontier population of Texas and portrayed the different personalities of a newly raised company. Peticolas described his comrade Gideon Egg, a native of Switzerland, as "a rapid talker and vehement in all of his actions. . . . He is kind in his disposition and possesses considerable quickness of perception." Meanwhile, he described another of his comrades, Irishman John Owens, as "a man of low stature and rugged countenance, with a decided partiality for whiskey, an enthusiastic admiration for everything Irish." Slavery and states' rights meant little to this soldier; instead he claimed he was striking against "aristocracy" as personified by Yankee arrogance. This Celt possessed "sufficient brogue and irish humor to render him interesting."[33]

There were a number of Germans in the Victoria Invincibles. Peticolas described his fellow soldier Gustavus Dietze as "a German of quiet and retiring disposition, of good manners and tolerable education, with high cheek bones and prominent nose, but rapid in action and words when roused." Another European, and a veteran of the Prussian Army, was John Schmidt. "The oracle of his mess," wrote Peticolas, "to whom it is impossible to apply for information but that he will attempt to give it." The know-it-all Schmidt discussed war, politics, and religion with equal authority. "He talks incessantly when started, and lays down his opinions to the Germans and Irish as one would enunciate an axiom in mathematics. He is the arbiter of all disputes amongst the Germans, and whether the question concerns an idiom of a language, the usage of a certain nation, the government of an Army, or the right way

to bake bread. . . . Add to this, he is fond of manufacturing facts."
In contrast, young Philip Meyer possessed a charming personality
that made him a favorite in the company. "He . . . has a deep scar
on his cheek . . . is a good singer, a first rate mimic, a great jester,
and has a great deal of pig-headedness when he determines upon
any given line of action. . . . He is free of speech and is quite interesting; . . . playful and full of life and fun."[34]

Other volunteers arrived from across the state. From Giddings,
in Fayette County, came twenty-one-year-old Pvt. William Henry
Smith. A native of Georgia, he had lived in Texas since 1856. He
rode to LaGrange to join the volunteers. Others fell in at Nacogdoches, including eighteen-year-old James Franklin Starr, scion of
a wealthy and influential East Texas family. In New Braunfels, where
eighteen-year-old Joseph Faust volunteered and in Cameron, Milam
County, thirty-one-year-old Robert Thomas Williams and his
twenty-three-year-old brother John joined their friends and neighbors for the coming campaign. Even in faraway Weatherford, fifty-
three-year-old S. L. R. Patton answered the recruiter's call by joining
the Parker County Rovers.[35]

Theophilus Noel, a twenty-one-year-old Michigan native, also
enlisted in Sibley's Brigade. After some experience as a newspaper
reporter, he had been in Texas since 1853, running a bookstore in
Richmond, Fort Bend County. During the excitement surrounding
secession, he had been forced out of business for selling *Harper's
New Monthly Magazine,* supposedly an abolitionist publication. To
prove his loyalty to the South, therefore, he joined the expedition
to capture the U.S. regulars at the mouth of the Rio Grande in April,
1861. In August, he had attached himself as scout and war reporter
to a company from Caldwell County.[36]

Other soldiers showed less ardor for the Confederate cause. A
number of recruits, after hearing of Baylor's near-bloodless victories, undoubtedly saw this campaign as being fairly safe, while others, many of Northern birth, used this opportunity to escape the
more odious duty of fighting countrymen in the East. Many Germans, whose support of secession had been lackluster, also joined
the command. Others undoubtedly joined for adventure and a
chance to travel. Edward Burrowes, a native of New Jersey, left his
cattle herds in Hays County for the war, believing that a campaign

in the West would be enjoyable and safe. "I love my country . . . but all the boys are going," he told his cousin shortly before departing. "I shall not be likely to fight New Jerseymen in New Mexico, [and] besides, it is a healthy country and I hope to have a fine trip and be back again before a great while." This cautious warrior enlisted in Austin as a private on October 5.[37]

The trip to San Antonio began an exciting adventure for the young recruits as they encountered both new sights and adversity. Private Wright of Polk County remembered Huntsville, Gonzales, and other towns that held warm receptions for his company. "Never can I forget the smiles that gave us welcome," he wrote, "[or] the music and feasting that entertained us, or the tearful faces that bade us farewell."[38] Private Smith had fond and humorous memories of Seguin. One youth, in order to impress the locals, attempted to mount his horse, while wearing huge, Mexican-style spurs. "The horse jumped over the courthouse fence [and] ran through the town," recalled Smith. After the excitement of the ensuing horse chase died down, and as the company left town, citizens lined up to send them off. "The ladies in mass waved . . . white handkerchiefs," he remembered. The soldiers returned the salute. "The volunteers [in turn] pulled off their hats and gave three lively cheers for the ladies."[39]

Private Howell noticed the war fever gripping the towns the Grimes County Rangers passed through. "Terry and Lubbock are getting several companies out here in these counties for their Virginia Regiment," he wrote his parents. "The whole country seems to be up to the fighting point." As a result, he soon fretted over arriving in San Antonio too late to receive weapons. "Two other companies have passed here on their way to join General Sibley," he added. "I am afraid so many companies have gone ahead of us that it will be doubtful about us getting Six Shooters, *but if I don't get one I know the way home and will go straight back.*"[40]

Heavy rains and accidents made the trip miserable for many aspiring soldiers. Howell, young and inexperienced, almost ended his military career prematurely as he headed west over well-traveled roads in Central Texas. During a storm near Gonzales, he rode his horse into a creek, but on the muddy bottom the animal tumbled and threw its rider. Drenched and hurting from the fall, Howell spent the night in a local house and was soon nursing a cold.[41]

S. L. R. Patton, much older than most of the men riding to the rendezvous, had lived in the state since the late 1830s and had served as an official for the Republic of Texas. As he journeyed, the newly elected sergeant was a keen observer on his trip from the northwest frontier to San Antonio. Rain fell in torrents. "After leaving Weatherford the 4th [of October] we reached Buchanan Saturday evening during a very heavy fall of rain and we took the Courthouse by storm piling into it bag and baggage, all promiscuously." Patton noted that secession sentiment grew as he rode on through towns like Waco, but felt a sense of apathy in the state capital. "The people are more patriotic as we get south, the ladies saluting us by waving of handkerchiefs frequently. We find the people of Austin a little more indifferent, perhaps the passing of companies is of too frequent occurrence to excite much attention." While housed in the land office there the veteran speculator took care of some business discussing the status of several of his own land claims. "I find the officers in this office very accommodating."[42]

Road and weather were every bit as inhospitable to Captain Shropshire as he made his way from Colorado County to San Antonio. After riding in rain for hours, he wrote his wife, his company was "the wettest set of poor devils you ever saw. I tell you soldiering so far has not been the most pleasant occupation I have followed." He added, "If I could . . . have been back at home with dry clothes, a good toddy on hand, and a lounge to be upon I would be the happiest man on earth. But these are no times to long for the comforts of home when the home itself is threatened."[43]

The brigade rendezvous, San Antonio, proved an exotic place for the naive young recruits. Sightseeing was a popular pastime. Howell, still suffering a stiff neck from his accident, marveled at what he saw. "I found San Antonio a much larger place than I expected to see," he wrote his parents. "It has the worst mixed population I have ever seen—Americans, Germans, Mexicans, & any sort of people you want to see." Howell also showed a prejudice against the alien culture he found in the city. "About half our company visited the Catholic Churches this morning for curiosity—there being two—one Mexican & 'one where the white folks' go to get their sins prayed off. I intend to hear the Baptists before I leave here."[44] Other soldiers counted the local girls as part of the city's attraction.[45]

Some of the officers and a few enlisted men brought their slaves with them to war. There may have been as many as fifty with the army when it left for New Mexico. Colonel Green, who owned ten slaves, brought at least one. Capt. Willis Lang, owner of seventy-four slaves in Falls County, brought a servant, as did Lt. Pleasant J. Oakes and Lt. Tom Wright. Captain Shropshire also took a slave to war. "Bob is a great Negro, a perfect scamp—yet I am attached to him, I can't tell why," the officer wrote to his wife. "When we brought our wagons he asked me if I was going to have a Mexican to drive us. It never occurred to him that he was a suitable person to perform the feat."[46] The father of eighteen-year-old Pvt. John Wafford of Victoria sent one of his four bondsmen to wait on his son during the campaign.[47]

Soon after arriving, the recruits became members of the Confederate army. "We . . . took an oath long as a 'fence rail,'" Howell wrote to his parents. Next, officers determined the value of the soldiers' horses and equipment for credit from the Confederate Government. "They were not very particular in the appraisement, I don't think," Howell continued, "from the way they appraised some horses." The officers then directed the newcomers to temporary lodgings where the troops also drew government fodder and rations before joining the rest of the brigade outside of town. "We are now camped in a lot in this city," Howell wrote, "at the expense of the Confederate Government and are allowanced like regulars." The new companies then went to the brigade camps along Salado Creek, a few miles east of the city. There the new troops learned battle-field maneuvers from Winfield Scott's *Tactics* and William J. Hardee's *Rifle and Light Infantry Tactics,* practicing infantry drill in the mornings and cavalry drill in the afternoon. The various commands also received their company letter and regimental designations.[48]

The regimental camps along Salado Creek soon resembled tent cities, laid out in infantry fashion about two miles apart, with the brigade mounts pastured near by. The various companies of the regiments formed "streets," fifteen feet wide, running roughly east and west, perpendicular to the stream. The noncommissioned officers bivouacked at the head of the street; the cook fires burned sixty feet further back. Sixty feet behind the "kitchens," the regimental officers formed rows of shelters running roughly north and south, perpendicular to and behind the enlisted lines. In the first row resided the company officers, followed by a sixty-foot interval to the regimental officers' row. Sibley and his staff lived and worked in San Antonio. Companies received letter designations depending on the expertise of their captain and the date of their enrollment. On the regimental front, from right to left, the companies received letters A, F, D, I, C, H, E, K, G, and B. This would be their order in battle, and assured the regiment of having experienced officers on both flanks and near the colors.[49]

Many of the new soldiers recorded their experiences, either in letters, diaries, or postwar memoirs. At Camp Sibley, the bivouac of the Fourth Texas Mounted Volunteers, Noel, who would later publish a brigade history, found himself on the first street as part of Company A. On the next street over was "Hank" Wright, who later wrote a memoir from his perspective in Company F. Three streets down, near the center of the regiment, "Alf" Peticolas and "Abe" Hanna began their diaries as part of Company C. On the next street, Lt. William Lee Alexander, former president of Nacogdoches College, and his friend, "Frank" Starr, both of Company H, began writing letters home. On the next street resided the Williams brothers in Company E, with "Tom" carefully recording the brigade activities in his notebook. Two streets down, Lt. Edward Robb, of Company K, also started a diary. On the next street, Lt. Julius Giesecke, a plainspoken and fastidious German in Company G, kept a journal from his perspective on the left of the regiment.[50]

The situation was similar at Camp Manassas, home of the Fifth Texas Mounted Volunteers, but fewer primary works have been discovered about them. William Lott Davidson of Company A, who would later write a history of the brigade, lived on the first regimental street while his captain, Shropshire, wrote letters from officer's row. Next to his tent was Lt. Benton Bell Seat of Company F, who composed a memoir in later years. William Henry Smith, writing in a leather-bound pocket diary, served as part of Company I near the right center. Private Howell, in the center with Company C, kept a detailed diary and wrote copious letters to the "home folks" at Plantersville. On the far left of the regiment, young Joseph Faust of the predominantly German Company B began a rich correspondence with friends in New Braunfels.[51]

While on the Salado, the routine of drill, marching, and inspection matured the raw troops. A bugler in each company announced the daily schedule, and regular guard duty obliged the men to become accustomed to the army. Officers attempted to make the men proud of their growing military competence, pronouncing several companies the "best" in various categories. Eighteen-year-old Frank Starr of Company H, Fourth Texas, wrote his famous father in Nacogdoches that, "I am told that our company is the best mounted and the best armed of any in the brigade." Other soldiers told similar stories. "This morning our company was praised by the Major as the best drilled company," boasted seventeen-year-old Faust. "Major Lockridge . . . pronounced us the best dressed and best looking company in the field," recalled trooper Henry Wright of Company F, Fourth Texas. Not surprisingly, Howell also claimed superiority for his company, "C" of the Fifth Regiment. "It has been remarked by many that our company is the finest, best looking company," he boasted, and "best mounted that has yet been mustered in."[52]

Officers also introduced the new soldiers to camp discipline by regularly posting guards and running the various camps strictly according to regulations. "We had a guard to stand at night, as well as in the day," remembered Noel. "Not, however, to keep the Indians off, but to break the greenhorns in and to teach them how it goes in war. The strictest guard that we ever had . . . was while we were camped . . . a thousand miles or more from the foe."[53] One novice caused a serious incident by falling asleep with a loaded weapon while on guard duty. "In some way, [he] caused the gun to fire, wounding one man in the arm and [another] in the arm and hip." Howell wrote in his diary. "Considerable excitement is caused by the accident."[54]

Sibley ordered the formation of two four-gun batteries of mountain howitzers, one to accompany each regiment. The weapons had been designed to be light and easily disassembled for transportation aboard pack mules. The tubes of these cannons were short, just thirty-two inches, and weighed only 220 pounds each. One hundred-pound ammunition chest carried eight rounds of three types of ammunition: one round of canister—a thin, iron casing containing dozens of projectiles for close range, antipersonnel use, one of hollow shell filled with gunpowder and detonated by a timed fuse, and six rounds of spherical case designed to burst in midair, scattering musket balls on the soldiers below. In addition, the chests contained all the necessary powder charges and fuses. While providing the fire power of artillery at a fraction of the weight and encumbrance of conventional guns, mountain howitzers had limitations. None of the weapons could fire solid shot; each had a maximum range of only one thousand yards with shell, just eight hundred yards with spherical case.[55]

The howitzer batteries also required men and animals. In all, each of Sibley's batteries consisted of twenty-two mules carrying four cannon tubes, four four-piece carriages, twenty-four ammunition chests, two tool chests, and some forty-eight rounds of ammunition per gun. Each battery was crewed by thirty-six men, each mounted. First Lt. John Reily, son of the Fourth Texas colonel, commanded that regiment's battery which included 1st Sgt. John E. Hart of Lockhart and Pvt. Frank Starr of Nacogdoches, who decided to try service with the artillery. To command the guns of the Fifth Texas, Sibley promoted Pvt. William Wood to the rank of "acting first lieutenant."[56]

The restless soldiers, tired of their camp routines, eagerly anticipated the upcoming campaign. "We will be detained here, perhaps 3 or 4 weeks," Howell wrote. "We are bound for Arizona and New Mexico sure enough. . . . Ho for the long march!! All [of the boys] seem certain of returning—most of them saying they were never born to be killed by a Yankee. Of course all hope so, but that is yet to be tried." At the Plaza Hotel in San Antonio, Howell had seen General Sibley, the man who would control his fate in the upcoming months. "He is a fine looking officer & is said to be a perfect gentleman as well as a fine drill officer," wrote the private. "I like the appearance of 'the old rascal' very much."[57]

From his offices at the hotel, "the old rascal" wrestled with the nightmare of obtaining equipment and transportation for his command. Since most of the arriving companies were short of weapons, Sibley desperately sought someone with authority to issue weapons and ammunition from the San Antonio arsenal. At the time, Gen. Paul O. Hébert, who replaced Van Dorn as department commander, was in Galveston with all of the responsible ordnance officers; no one in San Antonio had the power to release government stores. Sibley irately demanded action from the minor officials at the arsenal; they reluctantly complied.[58]

Lack of transportation also caused delay. Sibley, remembering his service in the Mexican and Mormon wars, insisted on having a well-supplied wagon train and endeavored to acquire the necessary vehicles. Eventually his brigade had more than three hundred wagons and some three thousand mules. Officers allowed each soldier to place fifteen pounds of personal gear in one of three company wagons. The quartermaster, brigade and regimental head quarters, and the medical corps also had wagons. Because the teamsters were Hispanics, the men nicknamed the brigade wagon train "Mexico." Twenty-three-year-old Bill Davidson of Colorado County, newly promoted from his company to quartermaster sergeant for the Fifth Texas, gave Sibley high marks for his organizational ability. "He deserves great credit for the manner in which he organized and equipped the brigade," Davidson wrote. "Here is where the talent and ability of the man lay. He knew every little thing in every little way that a brigade needed, and he procured it. It was the most complete and perfectly equipped brigade sent out by the Confederacy during the war."[59]

Despite Davidson's enthusiasm, the arms and equipment available for issue to the brigade varied greatly in quality and uniformity. Weapons included shotguns, hunting rifles, confiscated Federal smoothbore and rifled muskets, revolvers, single-shot saddle pistols, a scattering of swords, large knives, and even lances. Necessary accoutrements, including cartridge boxes and haversacks, were in short supply, but the arsenal provided a variety of tents, including a few conical "Sibleys." Issued clothing also varied greatly; some companies drew "a full military suit, coat, pants, drawers, pantaloon boots, [and] coats—broadcloth with brass buttons." Others relied on the charity of home folks. "In regards to boots," wrote Private Faust to his friend and former teacher in New Braunfels, "I could very well use a pair. Size six would please me very much. I believe that we will soon be paid . . . and

I could reimburse you. Please pardon my affrontery."[60]

While Baylor anxiously awaited succor from the east, Sibley called for yet another regiment to be raised for his brigade. This unit, the Seventh Texas Mounted Volunteers, would be used primarily to garrison conquered territory and the Mesilla Valley. Unlike the other two regiments, it did not include a howitzer battery. In general, this organization began with two excess companies that had failed to find a spot in the other units. One organization, Dr. Powhatan Jordan's Bexar County company, had enrolled for duty in early September, but there was no opening for the unit. Composed of rugged frontiersmen and many Texas Rangers, including Mier campaign veteran 1st Lt. Alfred Sturgis Thurmond, their talent and expertise seemed perfect for the upcoming campaign. Hesitant about revoking the commissions of men who had already raised commands, Sibley instead decided to incorporate them in his plan. This action also created positions and opportunities for Sibley's friends and allies. A new encampment, Camp Pickett, was planted on the banks of the Salado, two miles upstream from Camp Manassas.[61]

New York native and West Point graduate William Steele presented an impressive résumé. A professional soldier and acquaintance of Sibley's from the "old army," Steele received his Confederate commission on October 4, 1861, as colonel of the Seventh Texas Mounted Volunteers. He was also a dear friend of the Baylor family. After graduating in the bottom quarter of the academy class of 1840, he served with Sibley in the Second Dragoons against the Seminoles in Florida. During the Mexican War, Steele fought under both Zachary Taylor and Winfield Scott, receiving a brevet promotion to captain. Like Sibley, Steele spent his postwar career at various frontier posts in Texas, New Mexico, Kansas, Nebraska, and Missouri. He resigned from the U.S. Army at Fort Scott, Kansas, on May 30, 1861. During the upcoming campaign, Steele would command the rearguard and the garrison at Mesilla, leaving the battlefield leadership of his regiment to subordinates.[62]

The Seventh Texas would be led into combat by a seasoned Texian warrior. Steele's second in command, John Schuyler Sutton, was also a native New Yorker, but had come to Texas in 1836, a little too late to participate in the revolution. In 1839, Sutton

William Steele, colonel of the 7th Texas Mounted Volunteer, circa 1861. Courtesy of Eleanor S. Brockenbrough Library, Museum of the Confederacy, Richmond, Virginia.

received a commission in the Army of the Republic of Texas and led his company on the Santa Fe expedition two years later. Captured with the rest of the command in New Mexico, Sutton endured nine months in Mexican prisons. He returned to Texas in time to participate in the Somervell expedition in 1842 but, like Green, wisely refused to cross the Rio Grande to attack the town of Mier. During the Mexican War, Sutton fought at Monterrey. "In every expedition that was organized," wrote a Texas admirer, "he was always among the first to proffer his services." After the war, Sutton drifted west to San Francisco. He later returned to Texas, serving as a Ranger and holding a number of odd jobs until receiving his commission into the Confederate Army on October 6, 1861.[63]

The twenty-nine-year-old major of the Seventh Texas was Arthur Pendleton Bagby, Jr., technically another professional soldier. The wealthy son of an Alabama politician, Bagby had spent much of his youth in Washington, D.C.—exposed to great men and the stirring spirit of the times, yet never really a part. He received an at-large appointment to West Point, the usual road to greatness; his time there was not impressive. He graduated in 1852 near the bottom of his class and served in various mundane offices with the Eighth U.S. Infantry. After an unspectacular year, he resigned, returning to Alabama to be near his parents. Bagby became a lawyer but found his world again upset by the death of his beloved father in 1858. Restless and unsettled, Bagby moved to Gonzales, Texas, where he married and started a law practice. Upon secession, this untested warrior received major's stars. His father's reputation undoubtedly helped.[64]

Its officers chosen, Sibley's extra regiment slowly filled out. Demographically, the men of the Seventh Texas Mounted Volunteers resembled their sister regiments in Sibley's brigade. Recruited largely from East Texas counties, these companies had the similar proportions of farmers and stock raisers. The Seventh Texas also included Germans and frontiersmen in numbers similar to the other units. However, the companies necessary to complete the regiment were slow to arrive, and the process of organization slowed considerably.[65]

Unlike the other two regiments, only two important primary sources showing life in the Seventh Texas Mounted Volunteers have surfaced. One is a diary and letters written by Dr. Henry "Hal" Hunter of Palestine, a member of Company I and later regimental surgeon. The second is the reminiscences of Felix Robert Collard, a volunteer from Walker County, who served in Company G.[66]

Throughout most of October, Sibley and his reinforcements still remained idle in San Antonio. Last-minute details continued to harass the general as he worked to equip his men. His vision of what his brigade should be was never fully realized, however, and delays became increasingly pointless. Sergeant Davidson chaffed under what he considered constant dawdling. "After the organization was complete, and after everything was ready to start, we were kept lying around . . . for another six weeks," he wrote. "Several times orders were issued for us to take up the line of march and we prepared to do so, but the orders were as often countermanded. Contrary to . . . expectations, [we] had been compelled to lay around San Antonio for several weary, tedious, months." The brigade had now passed even Sibley's deadlines for departure.[67]

Sibley maintained his army's martial appearance. Dress parades were a frequent event. He staged ceremonies. His fifteen-year-old daughter, Helen Margaret Sibley, presented a Confederate flag to one of the three companies of lancers. Marching orders, though, still remained weeks away.[68]

CHAPTER 5

Empire Imperiled

Hurry up if you want a fight.
—Lt. Col. John Robert Baylor,
Governor, Arizona Territory

While the Confederate army gathered and trained in Texas, Governor Baylor of Arizona hatched his own plan for how the empire should proceed. Seven hundred miles from San Antonio, and with no knowledge of Sibley's specific intentions, Baylor planned to divide the task of expanding the empire more or less equally between him and the general. Western Arizona was the gateway to the Pacific, and Baylor planned to lead at least one thousand men to Tucson, where he could operate either against Sonora or California. The governor anticipated first using his men of the Second Texas in conjunction with the various Arizona companies, organized into a new battalion. In addition, Baylor believed that additional troops could be had from Texas. Meanwhile, Sibley would hold the Mesilla Valley and fight the Union garrisons of New Mexico Territory.

Baylor positioned himself politically to implement his plan. Maj. Edwin Waller, his second in command and willing subordinate, became "ex-officio" governor of Arizona, freeing Baylor to travel and recruit without leaving the territory leaderless. Waller, uninterested in the honor, quickly named Samuel J. Jones, a notorious proslavery veteran of "Bleeding Kansas," as the civilian governor. The fact that the highest political office in Arizona could be so easily manipulated is indicative of its dubious influence in the territory. Despite the political shell game, people continued to refer to Baylor as governor, and he continued to act nominally in that role.[1]

Baylor also endeavored to raise more troops for his imperial scheme. His proposed four-company "Arizona Battalion," commanded by newly appointed Lt. Col. Phil Herbert, was just the first of such units the governor anticipated leading. After building his original unit to regimental strength, he planned five additional six-company battalions, an "Arizona Brigade," to come galloping from Texas to the aid of Arizona. In Baylor's mind, he would eventually be a brigadier general at the head of some three thousand troops.[2]

Guaymas, Sonora, was the key to Baylor's plan. His first goal was to deny its use by the enemy. Rumors of a Union expedition landing at this port and marching overland through Sonora abounded. A Rebel force at Tucson could then counter this threat, or, if the rumors proved false, move against California troops coming up the Gila River. Federal spies confirmed a Rebel plan to establish a headquarters at the border town of Calabazas and to invade Mexico to secure a Pacific port. Once firmly in Confederate control, Guaymas would furnish a supply base through which supplies would flow to the Southern army in exchange for Texas cotton.[3]

Baylor's specific plans for western Arizona were also ambitious. With the aid of an accomplice, Tucson politician Palantine Robinson, Baylor planned to turn that town into a bastion of the Confederacy. First, all Union-held assets, including some lucrative mines, would be forfeited to the Confederate States. Second, the Apaches would be mercilessly attacked, pursued, and slaughtered, ending their depredations in the area for good. Third, Rebel agents working out of Baylor's headquarters would infiltrate California, organizing, arming, and leading the secessionists there. Simultaneously, the road between Guaymas and Tucson would be heavily patrolled to insure an uninterrupted line of food and bullets. With steady supplies, a strong forward base, and recruits swarming to the Rebel banner, Baylor would then complete the march to San Francisco by driving through Fort Yuma. Western Arizona was the true "highway to the Pacific."[4]

News from the other territories was encouraging to Baylor and the Confederacy. Travelers from California told amazing stories of revolution. Writing to his superiors in Texas, Baylor begged for the government to make arrangements to arm and mount the supposed secessionists on the Pacific coast. "I could now buy the best of horses for less than $50 per head," he reported, "and there are many Southern men who would sell them for Confederate bonds."[5] Rebel partisans under Daniel Showalter organized near Los Angeles and appeared to be ready to head east and join Baylor's army. Colorado secessionists, too, seemed to be gathering strength; rumors of secret mustering points for a Confederate regiment there circulated freely. The Mormons of Utah also seemed eager to oppose the Federal government, and there was even talk of secessionist plots in Oregon and Washington. Rumors of Rebel companies forming to take Fort Churchill in Nevada Territory, emulating Baylor's triumph against Fort Fillmore, also reached Mesilla.[6]

Baylor was also encouraged by the poor conditions of the Federal troops at Fort Craig. The Hispanic population of New Mexico Territory seemed apathetic toward, if not hostile to, the U.S. government. Recruits from the small villages made indifferent soldiers, and several companies of these mounted militia had already been captured or permanently routed. Near Fort Stanton, Rebel forces had surprised, disarmed, and paroled more than forty members of one New Mexico command. Recruits for the supposedly more reliable Federal volunteer regiments continued to trickle into Fort Craig, but never in large numbers. Baylor's growing confidence in the face of overwhelming Union strength led him to move his military headquarters from Mesilla to Doña Ana, some twenty miles upstream. He then ordered troops to establish a forward base of operations at Robledo, some seventy miles downstream from Fort Craig.[7]

All of these grandiose plans, of course, depended on Sibley. Baylor knew Sibley was coming, and he anticipated working with him on near equal terms. The addition of three Confederate regiments in the Mesilla Valley would keep the Federals in New Mexico occupied while Baylor operated farther west. For Baylor and his version of Confederate imperial ambitions, the only remaining question was when Sibley would arrive.

While waiting, Baylor busied himself with governing the territory.

The courts, the only governmental bodies in the territory beside the governor, struggled for legitimacy. Two judicial districts—one east of Apache Pass with headquarters at Mesilla, and the other west of the pass at Tucson—encompassed several district and probate court jurisdictions. The only place where Confederate law ever held sway, however, was in the probate district including Mesilla and Doña Ana. The various judges in this region went about their task conscientiously. First, a public accounting was made in which all officials reported on funds left after the transfer of power from the United States to the Confederacy. Less than thirty dollars turned up. To make up for the shortage of money, the judges levied taxes on public balls and fandangos as well as on pool and billiard tables. The next business involved thirty-five civil suits filed against residents with outstanding debts, most of whom had disappeared long before. Qualified jurors also were few. Other legal business included admitting lawyers to the bar, including Capt. Trevanion Teel of Baylor's artillery.[8]

To facilitate his schemes, Baylor made grudging allies of the local Hispanic population. At least ten percent of his command was Hispanic, and he appointed two Hispanics to territorial offices. He also commissioned others, including Don Pablo Milendres, a Captain Barela, and a Captain Garria to raise Spanish-speaking companies of three-month volunteers to fight Apaches. His gestures in ethnic matters paid dividends, as relations between the dissimilar cultures in Confederate Arizona remained peaceful until the end of the year. In addition, the Hispanic Apache hunters proved highly successful, inflicting severe defeats on the Indians on two different occasions. A delegation of local Hispanic leaders, no doubt at Baylor's suggestion, even wrote a note to Jefferson Davis in Spanish recommending that their governor and benefactor be promoted to brigadier general.[9]

For the time being, however, Baylor's army was in no condition to travel. Horses, used hard and poorly fed since they left Texas, remained weak, poorly shod, and short-winded. The health of Baylor's men, though, was the biggest concern. Smallpox had arrived in the region from northern Mexico. Other ailments—simply known as "camp fever"—also plagued the men. Company A of the Second Texas found itself crippled by invalids. In all, disease hospitalized nearly a dozen from this unit in October; another three dozen fell ill before the end of the year, most being confined to camp. Reverend Joyce attempted to alleviate some of the suffering of his hometown friends. "I hunted and killed many wild ducks to make soup for them. . . . I could not supply the demand. Poor fellows." On October 2, Charles Taylor of Nacogdoches wrote home complaining of "bad dysentery." His comrade, the upright and homesick Egbert Treadwell of Palestine, died of smallpox three months later. Six others eventually died.[10]

These myriad cases, along with many from other companies, filled the four hospitals at Doña Ana, Mesilla, and Forts Fillmore and Bliss, taxing the inadequate medical facilities. Sgt. Morgan Wolfe Merrick of McAllister's Company, Texas State Troops, received an appointment as hospital steward at Fort Fillmore. His first patient was a friend and messmate, Jack Iago, suffering from chronic diarrhea. A second patient, one of the paroled soldiers from the former U.S. garrison, arrived with a tightness in the chest. Doctors prescribed the crude cures of their day, "calomel and opium and an inunction with mercurial ointment." Smallpox packed the hospitals with patients. "The disease is spreading rapidly," Merrick wrote in his diary, listing forty-five cases at the various posts. Exposed daily to the epidemic, the steward also fell ill. He, and most of the others, recovered. Private Iago, however, did not—the tortured man cut his own wrists rather than face the continued agony of dysentery.[11]

Sharing the hospital space were a few wounded soldiers struggling to recover their health. Pvt. Enrique D'Hamel was near death from the bullet that hit him in the late-August skirmish with New Mexico volunteers. After arriving at the Fort Bliss hospital with a supposedly minor wound, his health had declined rapidly and he fell into a coma. "My eyes seemed glazed and no moisture was left on a looking glass when put to my mouth," D'Hamel recalled. Hospital stewards prepared to bury the dead man. "All that saved me from being interred was the interference of one of my chums. . . . He was half drunk and said I was not dead and would see to it that I was not buried until I stunk." For the next few days, D'Hamel's friend guarded him with a loaded pistol. A few weeks later, the recovered Cuban rejoined his command.[12]

Others in Baylor's army became involved in the local community. Reverend Joyce opened a school to teach English to the children of Mesilla. "Several Americans had married Mexican wives, and wanted their children taught. . . . I could speak but little Spanish . . . but I went ahead. Put them all in the blue-black speller and to learning the alphabet." After six-weeks time, the pupils had mastered the basics. "Two children of a Tennessean . . . were in school," he added. One of them, Guadalupe, "had large black eyes—a handsome girl she was—and I took occasion to say once in Spanish that I did not like small eyes." The young woman burst into laughter. "I had used the Spanish word that meant small in QUANTITY," the embarrassed instructor explained. "Oh no, . . . I wanted bushels."[13]

While Baylor labored to get his government established, a dispatch arrived from San Antonio urging action against the Federal forces. On September 22, the governor followed the directive by sending his trusted scout Capt. Bethel Coopwood, his own spy company, and 112 men from Companies B and E of the Second Texas toward Fort Craig on reconnaissance. Two days and thirty-five miles later, the Texans learned that Unionists from a New Mexico regiment had occupied the hamlet of Alamosa, some forty miles south of Fort Craig. Coopwood moved to block this unit's line of retreat by circling the town and approaching it from the north. Once in position, he waited for nightfall, then ordered his men to ride in line of battle toward the town.[14]

Coopwood's attack, early in the morning of September 25, overwhelmed the unsuspecting defenders. Union Capt. John H. Minks of the New Mexico Mounted Volunteers had spent a fitful night. He had received word of mounted troopers in the vicinity the previous day, but his scouts reported them to be friendly forces operating in the area. When a similar report reached him an hour later, he assumed that it too, referred to allies. He was wrong. At about 2:00 A.M., sentinels awakened Minks and told him of hearing sounds to the north. Minks ordered his men to their horses; instead of forming a defensive line, however, many of them slipped away in the dark, leaving the captain with only half of his command. Confusion reigned. At first, the Unionists thought they were under Apache attack. "At this moment a terrible Indian yell was heard from town," Minks reported. "I . . . was prepared to march to the rescue of the inhabitants, when we heard distinctly cavalry coming down on us, and a voice near our line hallooing out 'Here's their camp; give them hell!' I then knew they were Texans."[15]

The fight that followed was a house-to-house, nighttime melee. Scattered firing erupted from several parts of the town as New Mexico volunteers continued to steal away. Still, neither side knew much about its opponents' strength or intentions. Captain Minks determined to burn parts of the town to provide light and drive Coopwood's men from cover. He sent two of his soldiers with matches and dry wood to start a fire; a volley from the Rebels drove them back under cover. At dawn, Minks found himself in command of only ten men. At 8:00 A.M. on September 25, he reluctantly surrendered.[16]

The skirmish yielded promising results for the Texans. Captain Coopwood and his men secured a supply of weapons, three wagons loaded with fodder, and a number of horses and mules. Other soldiers rounded up some twenty-five Union stragglers whom they stripped of their government property and then released on parole. Four Federals lay dead and six had been wounded. All of the Texans remained unharmed, although four horses were killed. Captain Minks, 2d Lt. Metiaze Medina, and a sergeant accompanied the Rebels as prisoners and started down the river road toward Robledo.[17]

The Texans moved at a leisurely pace as they headed south, but were soon attacked by pursuing Federals. On the morning of September 27, as the Rebels prepared breakfast at a grove of trees called "E Company Grove," scouts reported Federals arriving from the north. "Rising to my feet, I saw the enemy," Coopwood reported. In the next ten minutes, one hundred men from the United States Regiment of Mounted Rifles, recently redesignated the Third U.S. Cavalry, moved to surround the Rebel camp. "None of the ordinary ceremonies of attack were performed," Coopwood wrote. "There being no misunderstanding, we at once commenced business."[18]

The opposing lines kept up a constant fire for the next four hours. The U.S. regulars formed an inverted V as they moved against the Texans, who formed a smaller but identical formation in the trees. The superior weapons of the Federal regulars began to tell as Rebels and their horses were hit. "We discovered that about thirty head of our mules and horses had been wounded in the legs," lamented the just recently recovered Corporal D'Hamel. "We killed the poor beasts, and formed breastworks of their dead bodies. . . ."[19] As bullets thudded into horse carcasses and tree trunks, the action increased in intensity. A U.S. bullet killed Lieutenant Medina, one of Coopwood's prisoners. "The poor fellow was tied to a large Alamo," D'Hamel remembered. "We thought [he was] out of range of rifle shot, but unfortunately a spent bullet hit him in the thigh and cut a large artery from which the poor man bled to death."[20] Eventually, the Federals' firing slackened as they exhausted their ammunition. By noon, the troopers of the Third Cavalry retired, taking four dead and a half-dozen wounded with them. Coopwood warily held his position throughout the day and the following night, then continued his retreat toward Mesilla. Federal bullets had killed two Texans and wounded eight others, as well as killing several dozen animals. Reverend Joyce performed the funeral for the Confederate casualties. "At their shallow grave, Captain Coopwood . . . with tears in his eyes . . . said 'Parson, I don't want the poor boys buried like dogs; get out the old Book and read and talk to us some.' He was a sympathetic . . . tender-hearted man."[21] Despite his losses and the fact that he had been surprised, Coopwood was proud of his troops. "I would say to you, sir, that I have not witnessed such a display of manly courage and perfect order during my experience in wars," he reported. "The officers and men . . . acted more like veterans than volunteers. I cannot with words express the esteem I had for all who were with me."[22]

At the same time, Baylor's prestige took a blow from another quarter as Cochise and Mangas Coloradas increased their raiding. These chiefs had gathered their bands in early September to avenge their defeat in the Florida Mountains at the hands of the Arizona Guards. At dawn on September 27, while Coopwood fought the Federals on the Rio Grande, nearly three hundred Chiricahua, Mimbreño, and allied Apaches attacked the various mining camps scattered around Pinos Altos.[23]

Sgt. Hank Smith and the Arizona Guards, having just escorted a wagon into the settlement the day before, helped the surprised miners make a disjointed defense. As the sound of shooting rolled up the various gulches toward the town center, Smith and three Arizona Guards scrambled to an isolated log cabin joining twenty men already there. "We began a cross fire . . . and . . . the Indians fell back . . . to the main camp," he wrote.[24] There the fighting became desperate, as Apaches set fire to buildings; combat became hand to hand. In town, Capt. Tom Mastin of the Guards and a few dozen men organized a makeshift defense. In desperation, miners Roy and Sam Bean rolled out a six-pounder cannon and fired a load of nails and buckshot at the surrounding hillsides. "After . . . we touched it off at the Indians," Smith remembered, "you bet it made them scatter."[25]

Gamely, the unwounded miners and Confederates pursued the retreating attackers. "We never gave them a chance to concentrate again," Smith wrote. "Most of the fighting was done from behind pine trees and log cabins on our part, the Indians dodging from place to place." Eventually, the frontiersmen returned to their camps to assess the damage.[26]

The hours-long battle at Pinos Altos had been costly for both sides. Captain Mastin, hit in the arm, died ten days later from blood poisoning. One private in the guards and three miners were dead; seven others lay wounded. Confederates and miners found ten dead Indians in town, figuring that some twenty others had been carried off either dead or wounded. Since the settlement was held, the Battle of Pinos Altos appeared a clear victory for the whites, but the majority of the settlers and miners in the region, apprehensive at the severity and audacity of the attack, abandoned their claims and headed for "civilization." The Indians, meanwhile, returned to their separate bands as Cochise led the Chiricahua to Mexico while Mangas Coloradas and his Mimbreños headed for the upper Gila.[27]

In the aftermath of the raid, Baylor received a petition from Pinos Altos that expressed the desperation felt in that settlement. Already the population had fallen from a prewar three hundred to about seventy. The petitioners wrote: "We are determined to defend this place to the last. If it is in your power to send a sufficient number of mounted men here that would pursue the Indians to their hiding places and make our roads safe again, this place would soon have a large population again, and would save a place . . . which at no distant day will become the most important of Arizona. . . . I am confident that you will do all in your power for our safety and protection in our dangerous position." Dispatches such as this intensified Baylor's hatred for Indians; he responded by sending the agreeable Major Waller and one hundred men to the settlement.[28]

At the same time, Capt. Peter Hardeman and twenty-five scouts attempted to pursue the dispersing Apaches. Riding north from Doña Ana through the Jornada del Muerte, the detachment circled west across the Rio Grande toward Fort Thorn. Here the Rebels sighted the tracks of Apaches, probably Mimbreños, driving a large flock of sheep into the mountains. Hardeman and his command gave chase, but they ran out of food and exhausted their horses without ever catching sight of their quarry. "I thought it prudent to abandon the chase," the captain wrote. "Which we did without having the pleasure of capturing the red rascals. . . ." This expedition, like most of the other Confederate attempts against the Indians, heightened frustrations as the Apaches vanished into the mountains with hundreds of head of stolen livestock.[29]

Other blows fell heavily against Confederate hopes for empire. Disturbing reports from the rest of the territories seemed to spell imminent disaster. Earlier hope for control of California dimmed as new reports arrived telling of five thousand volunteers for Federal service. Other reports claimed that Arizona would soon be invaded by U.S. troops marching overland from the Sonoran port of Guaymas. In addition, Colonel Canby had amassed twenty-five hundred men at Forts Craig and Union and expected more from Kansas. After an original burst of optimism, nothing had been heard from the Rebels in Nevada and Colorado. To compound the problem, the relentless Apaches continued to harass Confederate citizens near Tubac, Tucson, and Fort Davis. There was also a critical shortage of hard currency with which to purchase supplies; Mexicans and Arizonans were suspicious of Confederate script. As a result, commissary officers found caching food and fodder increasingly difficult. Baylor expected Sibley to alleviate that shortfall when he arrived with a supply of gold and silver coin. The other problems would disappear with the arrival of Texan reinforcements, but only if they hurried.[30]

These nagging rumors and chronic problems fostered doubt, causing Baylor ultimately to lose his nerve. On October 23, two of his spies, John G. Phillips and J. F. Battaile, reported that indeed Canby and his formidable army would move on Mesilla by November 1. In addition, converging columns would arrive from California, either via Guaymas or Fort Yuma, and from Fort Union. These Federal forces would meet at the Confederate capitol easily by mid-month, outnumbering the defenders nearly ten to one. His worst fears realized, Baylor panicked before even substantiating the questionable report.[31]

The governor hastily issued orders calculated to remove his precious army and supplies out of immediate danger. Baylor first ordered Judge Simeon Hart, acting chief of subsistence, to begin moving all food and fodder stored at Fort Bliss to Fort Quitman, seventy miles down the Rio Grande, or even all the way to Fort Davis. The governor also instructed the other large property owners at Franklin to move their goods over the river into Mexico, but not to create a disturbance. "Keep cool, for we have time," he urged. "Be calm, and do not create a panic. All will turn out right." The citizens of Mesilla reacted hysterically, many fleeing to Mexico. Robert Kelly, the vitriolic editor of the *Mesilla Times,* even dismantled his press, shipping it to El Paso del Norte while he hid his type. The frenzy soon began to perpetuate itself.[32]

Hart and Crosby, after carefully stockpiling supplies for Sibley's army for the last three months, hoped for the best. "You can imagine what an unsettled state the country hereabout is in," wrote Crosby in haste. "The merchants and most of the families . . . have 'pulled up stakes' and gone to the Mexican side. I for one shall stand my ground until the last moment, and will not cease to do all that I can for your command, at least so long as I may have it in my power to remain."[33] Hart added an equally distressing letter. "[Baylor's] command is in peril. I hope God in His goodness will so order things as not to make his retreat necessary from Arizona."[34]

On October 24, the day after receiving the news, Baylor appeared professional, calm, and even defiant at his headquarters in Doña Ana. "I shall just keep out of the way and let them fall to pieces of their own weight," he assured his friends. "I can get out of the way. . . . A little time is all we want. Besides, it only amounts to the inconvenience of moving, for when General Sibley gets with me we will return and get pay." Baylor continued on with a brave tone.

"You will hear of some tall guerrilla work before long," he promised. Anticipating that Sibley would soon have his army in motion, the governor dispatched a courier down the San Antonio stage road to intercept its advance elements. "I . . . will keep the enemy in check, if possible; but send up men as soon as possible, for they will be needed," his note read. "Hurry up if you want a fight."[35]

By October 25, Baylor's attitude had changed, his tone more excited. He first sent an angry note to his superiors in San Antonio. "I have petitioned time and again for reinforcements to prevent this disaster, to all of which a deaf ear has been turned," he protested. "I have only to add that the abandonment of the country will necessarily be attended to with a great sacrifice of property, and subject the friends of our cause to persecution and ruin. If it is the wish of the colonel commanding the department that Arizona should be abandoned, and I presume it is, he can congratulate himself upon the consummation of that event."[36] Baylor then vented his anxiety at his partner, Sibley. "I would respectfully urge that reinforcements be sent at once," he wrote. In his excited state he even began disparaging the local Hispanic population whom he had so carefully cultivated. "The Mexican population . . . will avail themselves of the first opportunity to rob us or join the enemy. Nothing but a strong force will keep them quiet. I would again urge that reinforcements cannot be too soon sent up."[37]

The galloping dispatch riders had an electric effect on the garrisons they passed on the road to San Antonio. The men of the western forts speculated over the implications of the threatened Union invasion. "You may soon expect to hear of a fight near Fort Davis," wrote William W. Heartsill of Company F, Second Texas Mounted Rifles while stationed at Fort Lancaster. "As to the result, you may as well publish it now, for if ever there was men that wished to fight, it is these Frontier Troops, for they have missed all the RACES of the season." His honor still bruised from being assigned garrison duty, Heartsill added, "When they get a chance, they will prove to the world that idleness is not what they wished for."[38]

He was destined for disappointment, however, for the great Union offensive was a farce. Because his spies reported rumor as fact, Baylor's reputation suffered greatly. In reality, the Californians were nowhere near, and Col. Edward R. S. Canby's army was suffering from a lack of supplies, transportation, and mounts almost as badly as the Rebels. A number of wagons arriving at Fort Craig had started a cycle of speculation that had eventually sent the Texans scurrying for cover. Scouts, dispatched to give warning of enemy movements, reported that the Federals remained immobile inside their forts. After a few days at Fort Bliss, Baylor sheepishly returned to Mesilla—the panic along the Rio Grande had passed. The mighty hero of Fort Fillmore, the savior of Arizona, had been swept away in the confusion, and now he was embarrassed. In addition, he was ill, making him surly. His reputation had clearly suffered. No one criticized him more than editor Kelly of the *Mesilla Times*. "Such a stampede never was witnessed, save at Manassas," he sarcastically railed. "Only, . . . we had a Manassas . . . without a fight or even a sight of the enemy."[39] Kelly insinuated that Baylor was a coward, inflaming an already bitter feud.[40]

The frustrated governor looked for a target—someone either to blame for, or to deflect attention from, his blunder. The press had inflamed the panic by printing news of the impending disaster, but Kelly enjoyed the protection of his celebrity status. News from Doña Ana, however, provided Baylor with a scapegoat—a butcher named Anton Brewer. A veteran of the Pinos Altos mines, Brewer had looted government property left behind during the retreat and had headed toward the mountains west of the Rio Grande with a wagon load of plunder. Baylor immediately ordered Sgt. Hank Smith, the German miner from Pinos Altos, and fifteen of the Arizona Guards to track the thief, arrest him, and bring him back to Mesilla for a trial and probable hanging.[41]

The Arizona Guards, however, were unwilling soldiers for the task. Brewer was well known among the ranks. Before the war, the butcher had supplied the miners with mutton and beef. During hard winters, he had even foraged for venison for the hungry camps. He had braved the Apaches in former days and had saved many prospectors from missing a meal. Sergeant Smith and his squad could not betray their friend. Brewer's wagon already had a three-day's head start; the detail from the Arizona Guards allowed him to get away. As they passed through Picacho, on the road to Pinos Altos, the lively strains of a fandango provided the posse a convenient distraction from pursuit. After dancing until midnight, the party pitched camp and abandoned their halfhearted chase. "Not being very anxious to overtake and bring back an old and true friend," Smith remembered, "we returned to Mesilla the next day and reported that Anton was beyond our reach and we returned without him." Baylor, having lost his sacrifice, hurled his rage against the troopers, busting Smith to private and putting the whole detachment in the guard house for a few days. Afterward, the luckless German was detailed as a clerk in Baylor's headquarters.[42]

The governor next acted to settle affairs with editor Kelly. Honor, and his regimental officers, dictated that Baylor confront the publisher and force a printed retraction. On Sunday, December 12, shortly after printing his most scathing article, Kelly met Baylor by chance on a deserted street in Mesilla. Most of the town's residents were indoors, having returned home after attending mass at the local church in celebration of the Feast of the Virgin of Guadalupe. Baylor, from inside the hospital building, had seen the editor strolling by a doorway. Grabbing a nearby rifle, the governor confronted Kelly. "Hold on, my lad," Baylor called. As the editor turned, Baylor swung the longarm. Kelly avoided the blow, but Baylor quickly tackled the man and pinned him to the ground. "You can't come [like] that on me, I am too much a man for your sort," the enraged governor screamed. Instinctively, Kelly reached for his knife. Baylor reacted by drawing his pistol with his left hand and cocking the weapon on his thigh. "You try to stab people, do you?" he raged. "Throw the knife down!" By now, a small crowd had gathered, and a voice from the crowd pleaded with Baylor, "Don't shoot him!" The governor, still weak from his illness, continued his attempt to break Kelly's hold on the knife. Unsuccessful, Baylor thrust his pistol into the editor's face, and pulled the trigger, sending a bullet crashing through the man's jaw and out his neck. Baylor stood up as the severely wounded Kelly convulsed on the ground. "Give him a chance for his life," the governor said, then turned to surrender himself to his second in command, Major Waller, fresh on the scene. Kelly lingered for two weeks, managing to pen one more acid editorial against his assailant before he died.[43]

In the resulting trial, Baylor was found innocent of murder. Waller convened a panel of all available officers from the garrison at

Mesilla and called witnesses to testify on particulars of the feud. "Hank" Smith, from his unsought clerk's position at Baylor's headquarters, had seen the entire fight. "I, and the adjutant's clerk, being the only witnesses to the killing, were summoned," he wrote. After they told their story, he added, "the court decided that Colonel Baylor was justified in doing what he did."[44]

The street fight and sham trial were just more humiliations plaguing Confederate Arizona. Citizens of the region, at first wildly enthusiastic about secession, had cooled to the prospect after what was considered shabby treatment by the Richmond government. Grant Oury, the elected delegate to Congress, had been coolly received by his political colleagues and, although seated, was given no official status. Since his arrival in early September, he had constantly lobbied for official territorial recognition but the subject was not raised on the floor of the House until November. The Texas delegation and Pres. Jefferson Davis backed the cause of Arizona, but to no avail against uninterested parties in the legislature.[45]

Oury was disgusted and felt betrayed. "I had thought and hoped," he wrote to politicians from Texas, "that the people of Arizona, loyal and devoted to the South, would receive that attention which common justice . . . would naturally accord them. I find that I have been incorrect in my conclusions." Frustrated, the delegate continued, "Arizona, fearless of consequences and acting upon principle, made her stand with the South . . . and assisted . . . in driving the minions of abolitionism from her soil. The same time that we have been knocking on her door for admission, the states of Missouri and Kentucky, where treason to your cause and to your institutions are the strongest elements . . . have been received with open arms, while we are neglected and refused." Baylor rewarded Oury's diligence by replacing him. The governor did not know the delegate personally, and disregarded the actions of the Tucson convention. Instead, Baylor elevated Marcus H. MacWillie, his attorney general and protégé, to the position of territorial congressional representative.[46]

Though cleared of charges, the governor was convicted in popular opinion of a variety of excesses. Baylor, a successful warrior but a political incompetent, had seemingly reached the nadir of his career in Arizona. The feud with Kelly, the retreat to Fort Bliss, and his dictatorial manner of government had done much to alienate Baylor's constituency. Citizens, outraged over Kelly's murder, demanded a civilian trial, but without success; martial law, which had also impressed thousands of dollars of personal property into Rebel service, was odious. Baylor had also subverted the will of the people by replacing the elected Oury with a political appointee. The governor had shamelessly manipulated the Hispanic population to accomplish his political machinations, earning additional resentment among the Anglo and Celtic population. And, despite his efforts, his government had not been able to protect the citizens from violent death; nearly one hundred had fallen to Apaches and desperadoes since secession. Some citizens openly advocated the governor's replacement. Major Waller, their suggested candidate for the post, could no longer take the strain—he had already been treated for "nerves" at the Fort Bliss hospital—and he made plans to abandon Baylor and return to Texas. By mid-December Baylor was obviously losing control.[47]

For the Confederate Empire, speed and decisive action were vital. Baylor's effectiveness as an administrator over the Confederacy's only western territory was rapidly waning. The empire needed new talent. Baylor had done all he could; he had hurried to Arizona at the suggestion of his commanding officer and had boldly captured Fort Fillmore; he had pursued the dream of empire by proclaiming, organizing, and administering the territory on his own authority; he had sincerely attempted to curb Indian depredations and to prevent the reconquest of Arizona by Federal troops, but all with mixed success. He had attempted this, all that could have been expected of him, with only a few hundred men. But Baylor's abilities had limits. It was now up to Sibley to break the stalemate and roll forward the borders of empire.

CHAPTER 6

Empire Rescued

New Mexico pertains to the Confederacy.
—Brig. Gen. Henry Hopkins Sibley

On October 23, 1861, the very day Baylor's spies had provided their erroneous reports, Sibley's Brigade finally started its march to Arizona amid great ceremony. " 'Orders to March,' " wrote Bill Davidson, "were the words that brought joy and gladness to the hearts of the members of Sibley's Brigade." At their camp along the Salado, the command assembled in a grand parade to listen to Sibley's orders. The brigade lined up with the Fourth Texas on the right, followed by Reily's Battery, the Fifth Texas, Wood's Battery in the center, and the Seventh Texas on the left. "Such a cheer as rent the air was never heard before along the Salado," Davidson added. "At last we were to have a chance to contribute our share in covering Confederate arms with glory."[1]

Pvt. Theophilus Noel, now a member of Company A, Fourth Texas, remembered well the brigade's departure. There was a slight autumn chill in the air as Colonel Reily formed his regiment in a square and addressed his men. "He told us . . . that a people, who in after years would prove grateful to us for our acts, expected much from us," Noel wrote. "After closing his remarks, he drew off his hat and . . . offered up to the High God . . . one of the most fervent and eloquent prayers that it has ever been my lot to hear. Everyone was moved to tears and solemn thoughts." Next, the Fourth Texas headed to San Antonio, the men singing a sentimental ballad, "The Texas Ranger," as they started their adventure. Spirits were buoyant.[2]

The excited warriors continued cheering as they passed in review in front of the venerable Alamo. R. H. Williams, English-born cattle rancher, sometime militiaman, and Knight of the Golden Circle, remembered the command with its "drums beating and flags flying, and every man, from the general downwards, confident of victory." In Alamo Plaza, the regiment assembled in a column of companies to receive a flag presented by the ladies of Nacogdoches. Next, the commanding general, mounted on a restless and prancing horse, addressed his command. "General Sibley, . . . in a few unguarded remarks, convinced all that he was no orator," commented Noel. "Yet in his speech, which was short, he displayed a great deal of originality and much determination. He told us that . . . he did not fear the result of the campaign with such men to follow him as . . . he had the honor . . . to command." The Fourth Texas then departed; the rest of the brigade followed Reily and his men during the ensuing weeks.[3]

The thousands of men and animals required a large amount of water on the march. The springs and waterholes of arid West Texas were small and filled slowly, requiring Sibley to divide his regiments into smaller groupings that marched a day apart. At Leon Creek, seven miles west of San Antonio, the Fourth Texas split into three groups. On November 9, the van—two companies and Reily's battery of mountain howitzers—under the command of Maj. Henry Raguet, started its trek. The center, four companies under Lt. Col. William Read Scurry, departed the next day. The remainder of the regiment, four companies composing the rear element, followed a day later under Colonel Reily. Beef herds and thirty wagons accompanied each regiment, extending the columns for miles.[4]

As the Fourth Texas made its way west toward Arizona, frantic horsemen galloped east with Governor Baylor's urgent requests for reinforcements. Sibley was packing up his headquarters at San Antonio's Plaza Hotel when the dispatches arrived. "I regard the probable advance of the Federal forces there as a movement decidedly to be desired by us," the general wrote confidently. "So soon as my force shall reach the field of action it must result in the destruction or capture of the enemy's forces." Sibley then moved to enhance his reputation with his superiors by claiming credit. "It is no doubt induced by the threatened attack of Lieutenant Colonel Baylor on Fort Craig, made by my orders. Not an hour shall be lost in pushing forward the whole force." The vain and crafty general also explained away his shortcomings and late start. "The delays heretofore encountered have been unavoidable."[5]

The delays had, however, been costly in terms of commissary and quartermaster expenditures. Each of the brigade's nearly four thousand animals consumed six to twelve pounds of feed a day, and most of Sibley's horses and mules had been in San Antonio for about sixty days. Thousands of soldiers had also consumed thousands of dollars worth of food while wearing out hundreds of dollars worth of clothing. Beef cattle, to be driven along with the regiments, became weak and thin from a lack of pasture.

Sibley's late start also cost the army favorable weather. Men, mules, and horses that had idled away the moderate days of September and October along the Salado would now, as autumn waned, be subjected to bitter cold. With each passing day, food became harder to find and grazing became difficult. Exposure also took its toll by increasing the number of camp diseases. Sibley, the horrors of the Mormon war undoubtedly still haunting him, had unwittingly embarked on a winter campaign of his own.

The Fifth Texas started its march that same week. As that unit passed through San Antonio, the ladies ushered them through in grand style with waving handkerchiefs. Pvt. William Henry Smith of Company I, composed of Col. Tom Green's neighbors from LaGrange, watched with pride as the colonel cantered along the column exclaiming, "I will bet on the Fayette County boys!"[6] Lt. Benton Bell Seat of Brenham took the opportunity to address his men. "I rode out in front of them and spoke briefly of the expedition and the necessity of obeying orders," he remembered. As he returned to the ranks, an older member of the company, astride a small mule, took his uninvited turn at inspiring the troops. "'Boys, I want to say good bye . . . for they is a good many of you I may never see any more,'" Seat recalled him saying. "'You'll soon be way up yonder where the wolves howl and the chickens never crow, and ye won't have mammy's apron strings to tie to.'"[7]

Like Reily's regiment, the Fifth Texas Mounted Volunteers divided into three elements for traveling. The lead element, under Maj. Samuel Lockridge, included two companies and the artillery. A day behind, Lt. Col. Henry McNeill shepherded the four companies composing the center, while Colonel Green and four more brought up the rear.[8]

Capt. John Shropshire, in the middle squadron of the Fifth Texas Mounted Volunteers, took steps to make his trip as enjoyable as possible with the help of his slave Bob. The wealthy captain rode one of his four horses while his servant drove his personal wagon loaded with baggage. "I believe I would like the life we are now living, if I did not want to be home so much," he wrote his wife. In the evenings, the slave prepared the captain's bed. "Bob has just made down my bed," Shropshire continued. "He first had it on the side of a hill with the head down. I have made him change ends."[9]

As units continued to depart, Sibley and his staff prepared to join the army on the road. On November 10, the brigade commander was on hand to review McNeill's command as it started on its way. "General Sibley was stationed on a hill in his carriage," wrote Private Smith in his diary. "The whole regiment shouldered arms and marched by in regular order." The gesture was returned. "The old Gen. pulled off his hat and gave them a general salute." On November 18, Sibley and his staff left the Plaza Hotel and joined the columns on their fateful adventure.[10]

Col. William Steele of the Seventh Texas Mounted Volunteers remained in charge at San Antonio and took measures to ready his command for the march. Most of his troops were still drawing equipment, and a few companies remained as yet unorganized. In addition, men from the other regiments left behind as sick or temporarily unfit to travel, had been assigned to his command. Anxious to have at least some of his troops underway for Arizona, Steele ordered Lt. Col. John Sutton to take the five most ready companies west on November 28. Steele and Maj. Arthur P. Bagby led four more companies out of San Antonio on December 15. Company K, serving as escort to the brigade paymaster, did not begin its journey until the following spring. Unlike the other regiments, little fanfare heralded the departure of the Seventh Texas.[11]

The brigade's route lay through some of the most inhospitable country in Texas; the gentle, rolling countryside west of San Antonio contrasted sharply with the rugged terrain north and west of San Felipe Springs. Near Uvalde, Pvt. William Howell of verdant Grimes County described the land as "pretty well timbered in places," but inhabited by "rattlesnakes . . . in abundance." Upon reaching the Rio Grande, the troops followed the Devil's River, crossing that stream several times within a few miles as the trail twisted through rocky canyons. The passage of hundreds of horses and men soon churned the powdery soil into billowing clouds of stifling dust. At Beaver Lake, a pond a few miles from Camp Hudson, the brigade turned northwest toward Fort Lancaster with orders to carry as much water as possible. Just past that post, the Pecos River provided refreshment for the troops and their mounts. After following that stream a few miles, the brigade crossed over into the rugged wilderness of far West Texas.[12]

The command then gradually made its way through the arid expanses of the Trans-Pecos; the men were relieved to reach the rare water holes in the region. Comanche Springs, one of the largest springs in the state, served the troops as they approached Fort Stockton. Leon Holes—very deep pools formed by the collapse of several underground caverns—provided ample water for the separate companies as they angled southwest along Limpia Creek to Fort Davis. From here, the trail led across dry, rugged landscape until it dropped into the valley of the Rio Grande near Fort Quitman. From that point to Fort Bliss there was no shortage of water for both men and horses.[13]

The brigade's march was slow. "Our daily travel was limited to the miles the beeves could be driven, and the distance the water holes were apart," Pvt. Henry Wright of Company F, Fourth Texas, remembered. "Sometimes we would not travel over 10 miles, and then again we would go thirty. We dragged our slow way onward, handicapped by the weakness of the cattle that we depended on for food, and the want of grass for our horses and mules." On numerous occasions the troops made dry camps at which the animals and men suffered greatly from thirst. Sometimes the long distances between water holes dictated bone-tiring night marches across the rugged plains. "It is well that we did not try to cross with great numbers,"

Wright added, "for at most of the watering places we would, in one night, exhaust the supply."[14]

Even so, the troops found that the New Mexico campaign offered excitement and adventure. Most of the men kept themselves entertained by pursuing new diversions. Even before the companies left San Antonio, the soldiers had engaged in sham battles. On the road, the men took great pleasure in hunting "Mexican hogs," described by Private Heartsill as "a grizzly, savage, one hundred and twenty pound institution." They also enjoyed catching trout and other fish in the numerous creeks they crossed. A number of the recruits, when nearing the Rio Grande, rode ahead like excited schoolboys to catch a glimpse of fabled Mexico.[15]

First Sgt. John E. Hart, with Reily's Battery at the head of Sibley's army, maintained a romantic, imperial attitude about the adventurous journey. Scribbling in his notebook as he rode, Hart described the hard-scrabble scenery as "truly grand, approaching the sublime." Near El Muerto Springs west of the Pecos, the artilleryman climbed atop one of the surrounding mesas. "I had the finest view I ever beheld. I could see the country around for 25 miles," he wrote. "The plain is beautifully diversified with mounds and mountains. I bethought myself standing upon the top of Mount Blanc with Europe lying before me . . . and here and there would rise the crude castle of some baron or knight." After riding down into the valley near Fort Quitman, Hart experienced a lifelong ambition. "Long I had the desire to see the Rio Grande," he recorded. "Its name was intimately associated with the war with Mexico. I felt a peculiar satisfaction in gazing upon the river celebrated by song, and the scene of so many bloody battles. No foreign land had my eyes ever witnessed and Mexico bore an important position in my mind, among the nations on this continent."[16]

The volunteers also followed familiar pastimes while on the march. Since the stage line was still operating, many soldiers wrote frequent letters home. Other men tended to their spiritual welfare, as preaching and Bible reading remained a part of the soldiers' weekly schedules. Mundane chores also had to be performed, such as wash day about every ten days or whenever a usable source of water permitted.[17]

Old vices from home, coupled with a few newly learned, followed the men. When a sutler arrived at Fort Davis, the troops sought entertainment in his liquor stock. Lt. Julius Giesecke, an upright German from Austin County of the Fourth Texas, wrote disapprovingly of his regimental commander's drinking. After passing Fort Davis, the officer recorded that "the Colonel stayed behind and tanked up considerably."[18] Another vice, gambling, prevailed among the soldiers. R. T. "Tom" Williams of Milam County and others spent much of their spare time on "wrestling and horse races."[19]

An erratic commissary gave reasons for complaint on the march, but the resourceful soldiers managed to keep themselves fed. Although Hispanic contractors drove large beef herds along with the units, the troops soon became tired of poor beef and "wormy crackers." In the more settled areas of their journey, the men quickly learned to rely on their own ingenuity for supplemental rations. At the little village of D'Hanis, just west of San Antonio, local women greeted the Confederate column with butter, eggs, chickens, and watermelons to sell. Near Castroville, a group of officers traded government coffee to an Alsatian immigrant for butter, cheese, and milk. As the brigade continued westward, the towns and their supplemental provisions disappeared, and Private Howell found himself "obliged to take anything that chanced along." In that spirit, he readily sampled hawk one morning at breakfast.[20] The forts that lay along the route were always a welcome sight as flour and feed corn could be obtained. At Fort Lancaster, Lieutenant Gieseke feasted on flapjacks.[21] At Fort Quitman, that resourceful German ground corn from the stables in his coffee grinder to make meal for bread.[22] At another post, Pvt. William Henry Smith dined on "sop and biscuits."[23] As the brigade passed through the Mexican settlements around Franklin, hungry soldiers took whatever they chanced to find. In one Hispanic home, Private Howell, tired of two months of poor government rations, happily gobbled "spare ribs and fried eggs for . . . supper and breakfast."[24] "Men are tough," added Wright, "and we pulled through, most of us laughing at our conditions and telling what we would do when we reached the land of plenty."[25]

Captain Shropshire, however, grew irritated as his troops constantly grumbled about their rations. "The men all complain of not having anything to eat, yet there is not a man in the camp, except 1 or 2 puny ones, but has fattened greatly."[26]

As the march dragged on, the men began to wear on one another's nerves; this friction often sparked violence. First Sgt. John Hart fought with an artilleryman in his battery. "No incidents during the day worthy of note," wrote the sergeant, "except a fight I had with a scapegoat . . . of our company. Though quite unwell, I give him a pretty good thrashing." Similarly, another soldier recorded the beating of one soldier, "knocking him senseless for a time." Some soldiers took personal differences more seriously. On December 18, two soldiers in the Fifth Texas started an argument that ultimately left an eighteen-year-old dead at the aptly named El Muerto Spring.[27]

Sibley's men certainly lacked discipline, but experienced and determined officers soon inured the troops to the dicta of military life. Offenders found extra duty, including chores like cutting wood. When three soldiers fell asleep on sentry duty, a court martial sentenced them to "close confinement upon bread and water for ten days." Insubordination was also a problem. Some recruits did not respect their officer's pronouncements, leading to a number of fist fights. One court martial sentenced a private to wear heavy irons for one month and to be tied to the hind end of a baggage wagon for striking his captain. All of these offenders, however, later had their punishment remitted as a gesture of clemency by their commanders.[28]

On occasion, the soldiers boldly snubbed their officers. Colonel Reily addressed the men of the Fourth Texas' leading element, expecting an enthusiastic response. After his speech, an obliging lieutenant "called out for three cheers for Col. Reily," wrote Sergeant Hart; none of the soldiers responded. An awkward silence followed. "After receiving his command in military style, we returned to our tents."[29]

Disease plagued the command on its march across Texas, and fresh graves marked the brigade's route. Hospitals at the forts along the way were filled with patients from Sibley's Brigade. Measles especially stalked the column, killing fifteen men from one company alone. Smallpox, already present in Arizona, posed a threat; regimental surgeons countered by vaccinating most of their men. Other volunteers fell ill on the march, far from even the relative comforts of the crude medical facilities. Routine camp diseases, especially dysentery, affected some troops. Pneumonia also appeared in the command. A fifty-nine-year-old private in Green's Regiment died of the disease when his unit reached Fort Quitman. Although few of the troops were diagnosed as having pneumonia during the march, many had acquired an unsettling, rattling cough.[30]

The large droves of cattle, brigade mounts, and draft animals that composed a critical part of the brigade, dwindled as the march progressed. Even before the army departed for the West, some soldiers had lost their mounts through carelessness. The herds and baggage trains were guarded, but not very well. Early in the trip, many of the Fifth Texas' beef cattle and work oxen wandered away. Brigade mounts, usually allowed to graze near camp, often disappeared. Comanche Indians, active between San Antonio and the Pecos, accounted for many of the lost horses. In the dark hours of New Year's Day, Colonel Green's slave stole his owner's mare and crossed the Rio Grande to freedom. By the time the brigade began to reassemble around Franklin, dozens of men were on foot.[31]

The lack of pasture for the animals, and the increasingly bad weather, also crippled the brigade. "The weather is beginning to tell heavily on our horses and teams," wrote Bill Davidson, "although the men have walked half the time in order to keep warm while facing those northers."[32] His company commander, Captain Shropshire, loved horses and worried about their health early in his journey. "If we have cold and rainy weather, our horses, having no corn, will become very much reduced, and I fear some of them will die," he wrote.[33] As the march progressed and the weather worsened, he complained bitterly over the loss of brigade mounts. "Our horses are growing thin . . . every day. My fine horse would not now be worth more than $100 at home. I hope we will not have a sleet, for it will play hell with the horses."[34]

Poor diet, bad weather, and increasing Indian raids turned Shropshire's fears into despair. "With stampeding and starving the majority will soon be afoot," he lamented.[35] After one long march he wrote of the pitiful condition of his animals: "Our mules and oxen broke down, having been 36 hours without water. Our horses are all in as good a condition as could be expected—all poor and some very poor."[36] At that rate, he added prophetically, "Our cavalry will be converted to infantry before we return. . . ."[37] Shropshire soon wished he had followed a friend's advice: "I wish now I had . . . bought a mule. A good mule out here would be a great stake."[38]

Sibley, with his staff and escort, traveled rapidly up the brigade line of march on the way to Fort Bliss. On November 23, the general passed Privates Howell and Smith in the middle squadron of the Fifth Texas on the Devil's River. Five days later, he was at Fort Lancaster, where he reviewed the garrison, the men turning out in their best uniforms and cantering across the parade ground to the general's commands. At one point, Sibley ordered the troops to the left; the mounted soldiers instead thundered noisily across the hard ground and trotted away from the fort and over an adjacent rise. "Gone to hell," the general reportedly muttered before continuing his journey. He held another review, with better results, on December 11. "General Sibley caught up with us, and we had a grand parade," wrote Lt. Giesecke. "[We had] many good promises made [to] us."[39]

The general and his escort finally arrived at Fort Bliss a few days ahead of the brigade on December 13, the day after Baylor's Mesilla street scuffle with editor Robert Kelly. With Sibley's arrival, the governor unexpectedly found himself further eclipsed. The next day, Sibley took command of all forces above Fort Quitman, declaring the creation of the Confederate Army of New Mexico. It included Baylor's troops, which removed the disgraced governor from any military command and stripped him of anything but nominal rank. Sibley did, however, confirm Baylor as the chief executive of the territory, a position for which the Indian fighter had the least talent. He was now a bureaucrat in charge of a would-be territory that had trouble collecting taxes, finding jurors, and protecting miners from Apaches. That same day, Baylor, perhaps remembering his earlier trouble as Indian agent on the upper Brazos, took steps to safeguard his position by sending a statement to the Confederate secretary of war accounting for all the funds he had received or had captured from the Federals up to that time.[40]

Sibley, now in command of all Confederate forces in the area, exercised his authority over the men formerly under Baylor and gained their support. He promoted Maj. Edwin Waller of the Second

Texas Mounted Rifles to lieutenant colonel and ordered him back to Texas to raise a battalion of cavalry for service in Arizona. That talented officer quickly complied, leaving the area aboard the next mail coach for San Antonio. Sibley then promoted the senior captain, Peter Hardeman, to Baylor's old post of lieutenant colonel in the regiment. Capt. Charles L. Pyron then became major.[41]

Even as Baylor's personal prospects dimmed, the future of his territory and his empire brightened as the hoped-for relief arrived. On December 17, the leading elements of Sibley's Brigade passed through San Elizario, Isleta, and Socorro and trotted into Franklin, making their bivouacs in the grassy, fertile Rio Grande Valley. The scattered companies of Reily's Fourth Texas Mounted Volunteers reunited and continued on to encampments just inside Arizona. Every few days units of a few hundred men continued to arrive. The leading elements of Colonel Green's regiment rode in the following week, but the Seventh Texas remained weeks behind.[42]

Sibley, having established his headquarters at Fort Bliss, prepared politically for the coming campaign by issuing a proclamation to the people of New Mexico. "By geographical position, by similarity of institutions, by commercial interests, and by future destinies New Mexico pertains to the Confederacy," the December 20 announcement read. "Upon the peaceful people of New Mexico the Confederate States wage no war. We come as friends, to re-establish a governmental connection agreeable and advantageous to them and to us; to liberate them from the yoke of military despotism . . . to insure and revere their religion, and to restore their civil and political liberties." Sibley carefully cast himself in the role of liberator.[43]

He also reassured the New Mexicans that the southern cause was just, and that victory and prosperity would follow the coming Rebel invasion. "The existing war is one most wickedly waged by the United States upon the Confederate States for the subjugation and oppression of the latter by force of arms," he proclaimed. "Victory has crowned the arms of the Confederate States wherever an encounter worthy of being called a battle has been joined. The army under my command is ample to seize and to maintain possession of New Mexico. . . . It is my purpose to accomplish this object without injury to the peaceful people of the country." Once he had driven the Federal army from the territory, he asserted, rule of law would return to New Mexico. "A government of your best men . . . will be inaugurated. Your religious, civil, and political rights and liberties will be . . . sacred and intact."[44]

The tone of the address invited cooperation on the part of the New Mexicans and was intended for a mostly Hispanic audience, many of whom had relatives serving in Canby's volunteer and militia regiments. "It is well known to me that many among you have been forced by intimidation . . . into the ranks of the foes. The day will soon arrive when you can safely . . . throw down your arms and disperse to your homes. . . ." Sibley's address included both a promise and a threat. "Follow . . . your peaceful avocations, and from my forces you have nothing to fear," Sibley wrote. "Your persons, your families, and your property shall be secure and safe. Those who co-operate with the enemy will be treated accordingly, and must be prepared to share their fate. Persist in [their] service, and you are lost."[45]

Despite Sibley's enthusiasm, Arizona was unfamiliar and strange to his Texans, and, upon inspection, many wondered if the territory was worth having. The midwinter scenery looked especially uninviting to the weary troops and many questioned their earlier dreams of empire. "I candidly confess—I would never have come this way had I imagined the country was so mean," wrote Captain Shropshire to his wife. "If I had the Yankees at my disposal I would give them this country and force them to live in it. Nations fight for principle—the U.S.A. spent millions of money to buy this country . . . and spent money and life to whip it from Mexico. Our people . . . got cheated."[46] Similarly, Private Smith asserted, "this country will be a tax to any government to which it may belong. It is one of the roughest countries that ever I saw or ever expect to see."[47]

In addition, the journey across Texas had been painfully slow and much more difficult than many had imagined possible. Men and beasts had suffered. "Mounted Volunteers on the march have a hard time at best," Captain Shropshire wrote. "Especially do they suffer when they march through a wilderness when a scarcity of everything of comfort prevails." A great many horses and mules, weak from inadequate food, poor grass, and overwork on bad roads, were nearly broken down. Rations for the troops were bad and lacked nutrition. The morale of the men was low. "I fear I will be tempted to desert yet—or do something else desperate," added Shropshire. "This is a hard lot for a man who has as good a home as I have."[48]

Sergeant Davidson, having just arrived at Franklin, looked forward to a little rest after his grueling journey. "We have marched 700 miles facing the north wind in the middle of winter, our teams are worn down until they can hardly walk and our horses are not much better," he wrote. "But we have plenty of corn now and can soon recruit them up, and we are in comfortable winter camps with everything comfortable around us. . . ." After arriving in town, he resigned as quartermaster sergeant and rejoined his friends as a private in Company A, Fifth Texas Mounted Volunteers.[49]

Christmas day found Sibley's Brigade strung out from Mesilla to Fort Lancaster, thousands of young men away from home in an alien setting with a cold front blowing through. Of those keeping journals or writing letters, most recorded pangs of homesickness. Sergeant Hart wrote sadly from his camp just north of Franklin. "Oh! What a flood of tender memories. What a vast avalanche of thoughts cover the mind of one who has tasted of the sweets and joys of friends and kind relatives, long ago." He added, "Today where am I? In the rude wilds of New Mexico, surrounded by a set of rude men demoralized . . . by the thousand vices of the camp." Eighty miles away, Shropshire wrote his wife from a windswept camp on the Rio Grande near Fort Quitman. "Christmas day, 1861, will be remembered a long time by this regiment, not a man of which . . . would not gladly be at home. I thought of you many times. . . . I could have enjoyed a dinner with you amazingly. . . ."[50] Fifty miles farther away, in the Davis Mountains, Private Howell lamented his bad luck to his diary. "Spend Christmas in guarding an ox train. Quite a difference in Christmas out here and Christmas back home."[51] In a nearby camp, Private Smith wished that he, too, was back home. "We made our breakfast on bisquit, coffee, and poor beef. The day is cold and cloudy, looks verry much like snow. I was on guard day and night. This day will be long remembered by me should I live to be an old man."[52]

Christmas was a day of contrasts at Fort Lancaster, which was ahead of the "blue norther" that was bringing such bitter weather further west. After four days of resting, Dr. Hal Hunter, now assistant surgeon of the Seventh Texas, used the day to continue the march, the soldiers leaving that post and covering fifteen miles before nightfall. Hunter made no mention of holiday festivities in his journal. Meanwhile, Private Heartsill and his comrades in the garrison spent the unusually warm day playing "town ball" and shooting coyotes.[53]

Christmas was also a day of violence. Several men from the Fifth Texas, encamped near Fort Bliss and Franklin, spent the day across the Rio Grande in El Paso. Davidson and five companions, reunited after the long march, looked forward to an enjoyable outing to celebrate the day amid cool but moderate weather. Twenty-eight-year-old Pvt. Seth Platner, a powerfully built man in Company F, also wandered the streets of the city. His timing, however, was unfortunate. In town, a woman called for the police after discovering an uninvited Texan entering a house; meanwhile authorities were seeking a suspect who reportedly shot another woman. The police, linking the two incidents, quickly responded, arriving on the scene at the same time Platner, who was reported drunk, unsuspectingly rounded the corner. The Mexicans called for the Texan to stop; unarmed and sensing danger, he ran instead.[54]

Gunfire quickly shattered the peace of Christmas morning as the policemen emptied their pistols at him. "We immediately proceeded in the direction of the firing," Davidson remembered, "and soon met the squad of police." Texans from other commands quickly formed an angry crowd around the twenty Mexican constables. Strapped across a burro was Platner, unconscious but still alive after being shot eighteen times. After following the Mexicans to the town jail, the Texans carefully laid their dying comrade on a mattress. Confederate officers soon arrived to investigate.[55]

According to Davidson, the shooting was a case of mistaken identity, and the Texans wanted vengeance. "The woman failed to identify Platner, but 'piensó' (thought) that the man in her house was smaller . . . ," he wrote. "In describing the man . . . she said he was 'Un muy chiqueto hombre. . . .'" After suffering through the night, Platner died. "The whole brigade was in a terrible state of excitement," Davidson wrote. Agitated soldiers threatened to burn El Paso. "But owing to the fact that the South, and especially Texas, was in no condition to raise a rumpus with Mexico, better counsel prevailed." After eating a few tamales, Davidson and his party returned to Franklin, irritated over their ruined holiday plans.[56]

The incident was only one of many clashes between Hispanics and the invading Texans, who cared little for the local culture. The adobe towns and alien customs amazed some of the young men from East and Central Texas, who reacted with a racist air of superiority. "The people here are in a very low state of civilization," wrote First Sergeant Hart. They use "the rudest implements I ever saw—cart wheels made of huge slabs of cottonwood trees, plows made of wood . . . houses made of mud with a few poles set upright. They bake in large mud ovens, oval shaped, . . . into which I saw several hogs enter."[57]

Sibley's Texans, almost from their first arrival in the area, antagonized the local population. Despite Sibley's proclamation promises that "persons . . . families . . . and property shall be secure and safe," his troops quickly made him a liar by ruining the Hispanic-owned farms of the Rio Grande Valley. "The wheat fields in the river valley were green and lovely, and were a great temptation to men with hungry horses," wrote Private Wright of the Fourth Texas. "Hundreds of horses were grazed on these fields. A reprimand followed, and perhaps a day or two on extra duty as a punishment, but that did not cover the damage to the poor Mexican." Neither did the soldiers respect homes and families. "When the weather turned cold, it was much more comfortable to sleep in a warm adobe house than in a tent," Wright remembered. "The owners rather objected to being crowded into one room, or being driven out altogether. This, with the appropriation of their donkeys and very often their wives and daughters worked up a feeling of hostility. . . . It is sad to think that the actions of a few thoughtless men can react to the detriment of the many."[58]

Davidson also remarked on the propensity for plunder that characterized Sibley's Brigade. A soldier would "march all day and ransack the whole country for ten miles around his camp at night," he wrote. Like most occupying armies, troops added local pigs, chickens, and turkeys to their camp fare. "Some even said," Davidson added, that we "did not stop at pigs chickens and turkeys but that bee-gums, sheep, goats, and even old ganders along [the] line of march stood no show."[59]

Union spies, working from Mexico, quickly noted the growing

tension between the Texan "liberators" and their hosts. "They have acted about El Paso in such a manner as to enrage the whole community against them," read one report. "They do just as they please, and you know what men off on a long trip please to do; females neither in nor out of their houses are safe. Blankets, onions, wine, and everything they can lay their hands on they carry off."[60]

The systematic pillaging of Arizona by Sibley's men also embittered the rapidly deteriorating relations between the general and the territory's governor, John Robert Baylor. The Confederate government, through the authority vested in General Sibley, had snubbed Baylor by stripping him of his troops and dismissing his plan for advancing the empire. All of the achievements made since the previous summer were rapidly coming undone. Baylor, not surprisingly, was furious. While traveling through Doña Ana, he had an informal conversation with Sgt. Morgan Wolfe Merrick, an orderly at the hospital. "He told me that . . . the good will of the people of the territory he had gained was being destroyed by Sibley's troops," Merrick recorded in his journal. "The higher authorities had not treated him fairly there was no doubt, and he was sensitive on that point, and I don't blame him."[61]

The governor still enjoyed the support of a few soldiers like Merrick. John Phillips, Baylor's fiery Irish spy, along with half a dozen of his colleagues, remained something of a secret service in the territory, and could be counted on to perform Baylor's more sensitive tasks. The Arizona Guards, serving in detachments from Mesilla to Pinos Altos, also remained allies. In the future, though, Baylor would rely on the crack company then being raised by Arizonan Sherod Hunter.

Confidently designated Company A, Baylor's Arizona Regiment, Hunter's men were veteran frontiersmen, well known in the territory for their dash and martial skill. Captain Hunter, a native of Tennessee, was a resident of the tiny, but thriving, ranching settlement of Mowry City in the Mimbres River Valley. He had gone to Mesilla at the beginning of the war and enrolled in George Frazer's Arizona Rangers, and was subsequently elected lieutenant. At the beginning of December, Baylor had authorized Hunter to raise his own command. The company remained incomplete upon Sibley's arrival, which kept it out of the general's immediate control.

Eventually, between fifty and seventy-five men enlisted in the unit, including Lt. James Tevis, a veteran of William Walker's Nicaraguan Army. Many of the rank and file transferred in from Bethel Coopwood's San Elizario Spy Company and from the Second Texas Mounted Rifles. The average age of these seasoned warriors was twenty-eight.[62]

With the aid of these men, Baylor planned his comeback. His scheme for invading Sonora and California could continue, he reasoned, but first he needed to travel to Richmond and secure the necessary credentials. The enlistments of his old command, the Second Texas Mounted Rifles, would expire in the spring, and most of them would return to Texas and away from Sibley's authority. He could then return with his reorganized regiment, and his proposed brigade, then pursue his ambitions. Confidently, he wrote his wife, expressing a desire to move his family to his Mesilla residence, complete with a garden, in the coming months.[63]

After establishing his headquarters at Fort Bliss, Sibley set up his personal residence in fine style while his men tented in the brisk wintry air in the surrounding fields. As the general moved his belongings into the lavish residence of James Magoffin, his men set up regimental camps. The Fourth Texas laid out company streets east of the Rio Grande in Arizona, less than a dozen miles north of the Texas border at Willow Bar and Cottonwood Station. Later, these troops moved to within a few miles of the territorial capital. The Fifth Texas Mounted Volunteers, its companies still arriving, encamped near Fort Bliss. Soon, the once-quiet towns of Franklin, El Paso, Mesilla, Doña Ana, and Las Cruces became haunts for these unsupervised soldiers as they sought food, shelter, and entertainment.[64]

The arrival of Sibley's army created a bonanza for the Apaches. Soon after the first troops from the Fourth Texas clattered into Franklin, hundreds of horses and mules began to disappear. At times, small parties of Mescaleros, Chiricahuas, and Mimbreños were content with stealing just a few; on other occasions, they drove herds numbering hundreds of animals into the surrounding mountains or across the river into Mexico. On at least one occasion the marauders also burned several wagons. By camouflaging themselves with oil, dirt, and grass, the raiders remained undetected at night, waiting for the pickets to walk to the farthest points of their beats. Then, the Indians slipped into the remuda, cut halters and ropes, and made off with the animals.[65]

The inexperienced newcomers had little experience in Indian fighting and rarely foiled the Apache marauders. Troops unsuccessfully pursued one group of White Mountain Mescaleros—driving 160 stolen horses and mules—as far as the Organ Mountains twenty miles to the east of Mesilla. Sentries occasionally killed a few warriors during these raids; the body of one such casualty was dissected by fascinated brigade surgeons. But despite the death of an occasional Indian, horses continued to disappear as long as the command remained in Apache territory.[66]

The first two weeks in January, 1862, Sibley prepared for his campaign by putting his command in shape for an offensive. First, he ordered a lightning raid on Alamosa, hoping to capture its garrison of New Mexico Volunteers and their supplies. Lieutenant Colonel Scurry and Companies A and F of his regiment left their camps near Mesilla on New Year's Day, and men from the Second Texas Mounted Rifles joined them en route. On the night of January 2, after a hard, sixty-mile ride, the three hundred Texans surrounded the village. At dawn, however, they found the town deserted—someone had warned the garrison of their approach. "Wind of the move had been received, and the 'birds had flown' to Fort Craig, and nothing but a few 'greezers' were left," wrote Theophilus Noel of the Fourth Texas. "Our boys [were] greatly disappointed, which was increased when . . . they were permitted to see the flour, sugar, rice, coffee, and beans scattered broadcast over the streets of the dirty looking place." The Texans returned weary and unsuccessful.[67]

Meanwhile, Sibley moved on diplomatic matters. "In view of the importance of establishing satisfactory relations with the adjacent Mexican states of Chihuahua and Sonora," Sibley wrote his superiors in Richmond, "I have ordered Colonel James Reily, Fourth Regiment Texas Mounted Volunteers, to proceed to the capitals of those States. . . ."[68] On January 2, Reily, with an escort of a dozen men, departed for Chihuahua City as a special ambassador to the governor of that Mexican state with a number of instructions. First, he was to ascertain if Gov. Louis Terrazas would allow Union troops to cross Chihuahuan territory, as had been reported. Next, he was to get an agreement permitting "hot pursuit" of Apaches into Mexico. Finally, he was to confirm the right of Confederate agents to buy supplies in Chihuahua. In his absence, Lt. Col. William Read Scurry commanded the regiment.[69]

From his Fort Bliss headquarters, Sibley ordered Lt. Tom Ochiltree of his staff to issue official congratulations to his troops for their trek from San Antonio. In General Order Number Two, Sibley praised the men, expressing "high appreciation of the patience, fortitude, and good conduct, with which, in spite of great deficiencies in their supplies, they have made a successful and rapid march of seven hundred miles in mid winter, and through a country entirely devoid of resources." The order concluded, stating that "he will never be disappointed in his early boast, that 'We could go anywhere, and do any thing.'"[70]

Other official business included the brigade's only execution. On January 9, most of the Fifth Texas Mounted Volunteers assembled at Fort Bliss to watch as soldiers escorted the condemned, Michael Behen, alias Tom Harvey, in front of the firing squad. The prisoner, convicted by a military court of murdering eighteen-year-old James Tobin at El Muerto Spring on the march from San Antonio, defiantly pinned a white piece of paper to his chest. According to Theophilus Noel, he "bid every man to aim at that, saying that he neither feared death nor cared to live." Eight soldiers, executing the court martial's sentence, put bullets through the murderer's heart.[71] William Howell, in his diary, remarked, "He met his fate very coolly and seemed to be very little agitated."[72]

Sibley, with both the Fourth and Fifth regiments finally on hand, again put his army in motion. He selected abandoned Fort Thorn, forty miles north of Mesilla, as a suitable forward position, and established a brigade depot and hospital there. Wagons began a continuous caravan to the post, stocking it with supplies from forts Fillmore and Bliss. Meanwhile, the Army of New Mexico broke camp and moved to its new bivouacs closer to the fort. By January 10, the last of Colonel Green's companies left Fort Bliss—the entire army was under way.

Sibley attended to last-minute business, which included the organization of a mounted escort for courier duty, before following his army. William Henry Smith of Company I, Fifth Texas, arrived at Fort Bliss on January 12 to take his place on the staff. "The General treated us all to a basket of champaigne," the proud trooper wrote. "After drinking it, [Lieutenant Thomas] Ochiltree gave us a speech." The headquarters of the Army of New Mexico moved the next day.[73]

The citizens of the Mesilla Valley were glad to see the Texans go. Despite Sibley's promises, the world as the citizens of Confederate Arizona knew it had changed dramatically during those last two weeks of 1861 and the first two of 1862. Into their midst had come an army, in reality an undisciplined, ravenous horde, causing hardship and grief on a scale unimagined. For months the residents of the towns along the Rio Grande had looked east, eagerly anticipating the arrival of Sibley's Texans. Now many hoped they would never return.

Even friendly armies are often rude guests, and Sibley's men had made nuisances of themselves. The arrival of the brigade added more than two thousand temporary residents who descended on the area like a human avalanche. Food, both purchased and stolen, became scarce, and prices rose. Contractors for the army, like flour mill owner Simeon Hart, increased their earnings while poor farmers and their families went hungry. Civil and property rights disappeared, and crime increased. To be sure, all of these things had occurred when Baylor arrived the previous summer, but on a much smaller scale. He had brought only three hundred men and had dispersed his fairly disciplined soldiers among the various settlements when not campaigning. The arrival of two regiments of undisciplined volunteers had made soldiers a common sight on the streets of the various villages. Baylor's Texans had been a curiosity; Sibley's liberators were a calamity.

CHAPTER 7

The Advance of Empire

This eternal delay is what is trying most on the men.
                                                            —Pvt. William Lott Davidson

For two weeks in January, 1862, Sibley's forces assembled near Fort Thorn, placing the Confederate Army of New Mexico some ninety miles south of the Federals at Fort Craig. The men of the Fourth Texas Mounted Volunteers, under Lieutenant Colonel Scurry, arrived first and set up camp two miles south of Fort Thorn by January 7.[1] First Sgt. John Hart, of Reily's Howitzer Battery, marveled at the mountain scenery along his route. "Lofty mountains covered with snow . . . presented a charming sight, a thing I never before witnessed," he wrote. "They shot up in turrets, white and glittering. . . . The dreams of my youth were realized," he added, "often I wished to gaze upon those mountains, the scene of so many wild and thrilling adventures." His unit passed east of the river, through nearly deserted Fort Fillmore, then Las Cruces and Doña Ana before fording the Rio Grande at San Diego Crossing.[2] The march was cold and dusty, and once past the last settlement, the countryside seemed empty and vast. "The country was practically given over to Indians for many miles," remembered Pvt. Henry Wright; "careful watching was at all times necessary to protect our stock."[3]

Upon arriving in camps near Fort Thorn, Sergeant Hart made a careful examination of the proposed brigade depot. "The buildings are large and good but I am told there never were many troops in it because of its unhealthy locality," he wrote ominously. "The old flag staff still remains to show the conqueror where once the proud flag of our country bathed its folds in the pure breeze of heaven."[4] Private Wright found the place desolate and spooky. "We found the gates closed but the fort empty," he wrote. "In the plaza were lying the carcasses of several fine fat beeves. They had been skinned and cut up into quarters . . . but we were afraid to eat them, for it was rumored that the Federals had poisoned and left them there as a trap. . . . I do not believe it was true, but we took no chances and left the meat untouched."[5]

Soon the abandoned post was filled with men and materiel. The adobe buildings bulged with "groceries" for the brigade, enough rations to last over a month. As the troops moved up the Rio Grande Valley, sutlers also arrived, selling preserved fruits, candy, raisins, tobacco, pipes and pipe stems, and other items to the eager soldiers.[6] "Be it said, to the credit of General Sibley, our grub is good," wrote Bill Davidson. "General Sibley will provide for his men if it can be done."[7] Additional supplies were expected to be taken from the enemy.

Colonel Green and the Fifth Texas followed on January 8, and took a week to make their way from Fort Bliss to Fort Thorn. The general reviewed the cheering troops as they passed through Franklin. This regiment followed the same dusty road through Fort Fillmore, but received a special reception at Las Cruces. "[We] are reviewed by Colonel Baylor," Private Howell recorded in his diary. "A Brass Band gives us some good music." The regiment then passed through the Robledo camps of Major Pyron's Battalion of the Second Texas Mounted Rifles, less Company A but augmented by two additional companies—the remnants of the San Elizario Spy Company and the Arizona Rangers. For some in Sibley's Brigade, this was the first opportunity to see the veterans of the Second Texas, many of whom were neighbors back home. "Here we were united with Baylor's regiment and Teel's Battery," remembered Davidson. "These are a glorious set of boys, I saw them last spring when they were organizing. . . ." By January 17, the last of the Fifth Texas arrived in their camps a few hundred yards from the post. For the first time since Fort Thorn's abandonment in March of 1859, the buildings bustled with martial activity.[8]

Sibley, as usual, followed his command up the Rio Grande road. Pvt. William Henry Smith, with the general's escort, commented on passing through Mesilla that, in contrast to the largely Hispanic Franklin, "it is a pretty white place." On January 19, the soldiers fed their horses "bountifully on corn and hay of the best quality" at Doña Ana. Here Smith also saw Governor Baylor as well as two old friends from Bastrop, Texas, serving in Company E, Second Texas Mounted Rifles. "I was verry proud to see them, indeed." The headquarters of the Army of New Mexico then resumed its journey, arriving at Fort Thorn on January 21. Sibley quickly moved with his staff into the relative warmth of the fort's buildings.[9]

His base firmly established, Sibley ordered additional drill and reconnaissance. Brigade officers reestablished camp routines and held skirmish drills. Although Sibley had concentrated his army, he still hesitated to begin the campaign without the lead battalion of the Seventh Texas, which was still en route from San Antonio. As a result, his men remained at the fort for the rest of the month.[10]

Sibley also made a new appointment to his staff. He promoted Capt. Trevanion Teel, Knight of the Golden Circle and battery commander, to major and chief of artillery for the Confederate Army of New Mexico. Teel's command included the howitzer batteries under Lt. John Reily and Lt. William Woods, as well as his old battery under Lieutenants Joseph H. McGinnis and Jordan H. Bennett. Sibley and Teel quickly became friends. Lt. Phil Fulcrod, an artillerymen under Woods, described his new chief as "energetic, noble-hearted, and gallant," adding that "he was one of General Sibley's friends and confidential advisors. He . . . helped to plan and [was] always ready to execute."[11]

While they waited, the men of the Army of New Mexico rested in camps, refitting from the quartermaster stocks at Fort Thorn. The troops gladly used their time off to supplement or upgrade their equipment. The condition of the army's clothing was poor. "Our shoes are all worn out," wrote Davidson. "Many of the men are completely bare-footed, a few are bare-headed." A number of troops were destitute, having lost most of what they owned when a prairie fire swept through their camp. Fortunately, the payroll arrived and the troops formed long lines outside the dwellings of the newly arrived sutlers at Fort Thorn as they spent their government script on pants and other clothing. Some of the Texans even managed to acquire new weapons from captured stores. One of the three lancer companies traded in their "spears" for guns, but ammunition remained scarce.[12]

With money left over, soldiers also bought up the rest of the sutlers' stocks, which consisted of "liquors of all brands." Imbibing soon spread through the command, and for a week after the traders arrived, inebriated soldiers could be seen stumbling around regimental streets as "drinking went on by the whole sale." General Sibley, it was rumored, was also well-acquainted with the bottle. His chronic illness, described as "renal colic" or chronic kidney stones, may have been aggravated by, or a reason for, his drinking; whatever the reason, it would cause him to turn over command of the Army of New Mexico to subordinates on several occasions.[13]

Some troops received extra duty as the brigade came to life, for many dismounted soldiers were assigned to the depot. Lt. Julius Giesecke lost his horse "Caspar" to marauding Indians. Unable to drill with his company, he was detailed as a guard at Fort Thorn. "Felt awfully bored," he scribbled in his diary. For the next seven days, the luckless German recorded the same or similar entries. The highlights of his week were when he traded for tobacco with men from another command and played a game of chess with another German. After being dismissed, he caught a wagon ride back to his camp.[14]

Courier duty had dire consequences for Pvt. William Henry Smith. For his first five days at Fort Thorn, he spent his time herding horses and listening to the rumors buzzing around headquarters. One day, however, he was ordered to carry dispatches to Mesilla with all available haste. Smith's roan mare galloped sixty miles down the Rio Grande Valley, delivering Smith in the territorial capital by nightfall. On the return trip the next day, the Texan pushed his mount beyond the limits of her endurance, for a few miles short of Fort Thorn, the horse collapsed and died. Five days later, Smith found himself heading back to his old company. "The Lieutenant in command told me that without a horse, I was of no use to him."[15]

The increasing cold and inclement weather bothered the men.

Often, wrote Lieutenant Giesecke, "dust [flew] so thick that it [was] impossible to see a horse fifty yards away."[16] Tents and bedding were scarce, and snow fell on a number of occasions. "The weather was very cold and some of the men were very insufficiently provided with clothes and blankets," Pvt. Hank Wright remembered. "As for myself, J. T. Poe and I chummed together, and each of us had two heavy blankets so, though we had no tent, we were warm at night. One time I waked up in the morning feeling too warm," Wright added, "but [upon] pushing the cover off my face, found 3 or 4 inches of snow had fallen in the night."[17]

While the brigade waited for orders to take the offensive, disease and disability ravaged the command. Company I, Fifth Texas Mounted Volunteers, camped close to the Fort Thorn hospital because, as Private Smith observed, "most of the men in [the] company are sick, dead, [or] discharged." "The small pox and measles have broken out among us," wrote Davidson, "and while both are in a mild form . . . many of our men are dying." The entire brigade had been vaccinated against smallpox, keeping losses low; pneumonia was the most feared killer. According to Davidson, pneumonia killed two out of three soldiers who contracted it. "This winter campaign is beginning to tell on the health of the men." As disillusioned soldiers buried their comrades, the muddy water of the Rio Grande received the blame for the sickness in camp—they may have been right. Fort Thorn had been abandoned by U.S. troops because of its unhealthy climate. Carelessness accounted for several other patients in the various hospitals. Bored soldiers, "practicing" with their pistols, accidentally shot themselves with their own weapons; the most common wounds were to the leg, foot, or hand.[18]

The most serious threat to the invasion was the poor condition of the brigade animals for the chronic lack of feed corn had weakened them. Vital in rebuilding the strength of the horses, high energy feed for the draft animals remained in critically short supply. A diet of poor grass kept the creatures alive, but barely. Many of the draft animals, as a result, became weak and useless, immobilizing dozens of the supply wagons Sibley had so carefully brought from San Antonio. This, in turn, caused a shortage of transportation for carrying vital food and ammunition forward with the army. This problem was partially compensated for by driving beef herds behind the command, but these animals were also in wretched condition. "Our beef cattle were so poor they could barely stagger along, and we could hardly eat the meat," remembered Private Wright of Company F, Fourth Texas. "But it was that or nothing, and that beat nothing a long ways."[19]

While waiting to march, many of the men lost enthusiasm for the campaign and wrestled with boredom. Around the campfires, Private Smith recorded, soldiers complained, "cursing the army, some cursing the Confederacy." Others cooked, played cards, went hunting, or read their Bibles. Idle time accentuated friction between the enlisted men and their company commanders, who had been appointed by Sibley instead of being elected by their volunteer commands. A number of the line officers resigned under pressure and returned home. The dozens of sick and dying men sapped morale. "The boys in the company are very much down in the mouth," Smith observed. "The Captain is disheartened at seeing so many men getting sick and dying."[20] Every week, the regimental camps moved a few miles to better grass, briefly breaking the monotony. Bill Davidson chaffed at the boredom and suffering caused by the army's continual delays. "We spend the day pulling grass for our horses and digging roots to build fires," he wrote.[21] "All this we can bear without a murmur, if they would just march us on. This eternal delay is what is trying most on the men."[22]

In the meantime, the soldiers waged a constant battle against lice. "I believe in my soul the things fatten on being boiled in water," Davidson wrote. "All the good it done was to make the eggs deposited in the shirt hatch out. We have tried every way we could to get clear of them . . . but the vermin get thicker." Eventually, the soldiers used the cooties for entertainment as contending troopers staged races by dropping especially healthy looking specimens onto heated tin plates and betting on which would exit the surface first.[23]

Meanwhile, back in the Mesilla Valley, Governor Baylor's informal secret service kept track of activities in the territory. John Phillips, Baylor's Irish spy and counterintelligence agent, became something of a fixture near the capital along with his colleagues from the gambling dens of Santa Fe; honest citizens gave them space. Capt. Sherod Hunter's company continued to grow, adding men mostly at the expense of other commands, including the San Elizario

Spy Company, Arizona Rangers, and the Second Texas Mounted Rifles. Detachments from the Arizona Guards patrolled for Indians while others followed leads concerning spies. After intercepting a pair of Hispanic field hands, officers discovered suspicious correspondence implicating two civilians as spies. The documents suggested, as many in Mesilla had suspected, that "traitors" had warned the Union garrison at Alamosa of Lieutenant Colonel Scurry's raid two weeks before.[24]

On January 19, Governor Baylor ordered a squad of soldiers from Captain Hunter's command to arrest the accused—Crittenden Marshall and Jake Applezoller—in Mesilla. These men, along with three others, were apprehended and thrown into the Doña Ana jail. The next day, Phillips ordered an Arizona sergeant to march the prisoners to a nearby grove. Here guards separated Marshall from the group, tied his hands, put a noose around his neck, and threw the rope over a cottonwood branch. On command, he was hoisted into the air to gasp, struggle and twitch in mid-air until unconscious. The process was repeated for Applezoller; when he passed out, the soldiers abruptly dropped him to the ground. Marshall died, but Applezoller rallied and lived to serve a long stay in the Doña Ana jail.[25]

Meanwhile James Magoffin, the influential merchant, volunteered two Indians in his employ from the village of Isleta to infiltrate Union lines and gather information. One Texan officer marveled at these curious new allies. "They are from an old and partially civilized tribe who up to within a few years ago kept a fire burning in their temple," he wrote. "They claim to be the only true descendants of Montizuma's tribe. They are as far advanced in the arts almost as we are."[26]

Throughout the rest of January, Union and Rebel patrols scouted and skirmished along the Rio Grande. Lt. Col. Henry McNeill and Capt. Dan Ragsdale's ranger company of the Fifth Texas company scouted toward Fort Craig on January 19, attempting to ascertain the intentions of the Federal forces there and the feasibility of a mounted assault on the post. "The Yanks sent them back as fast as they went," remembered Davidson. A few days later, the Unionists retaliated. "We have had two false night alarms in which the brigade was got under arms, thinking the Yanks were upon us,"

Davidson wrote. "They've been prowling around our camp, but then we've been prowling around theirs, too."[27] The tortured town of Alamosa, already the scene of two raids, became no-man's-land as Rebel and Federal forces clattered through it with increasing regularity.

Capt. John Samuel Shropshire of Company A, Fifth Texas, had an uneasy feeling about the reports coming from up the Rio Grande. "Our scouts have returned from Alamosa . . . bringing no news. . . except that the Mexicans have been ordered to move their families above Craig . . . which indicates to me that the enemy are prepared to receive us at that place," he wrote. "I have no doubt that we will whip them and look upon a fight . . . as our only salvation for if the enemy should retreat, [we] will have to follow them in winter to Fort Union. We will be worn out and our transportation entirely exhausted before we could overtake them."[28]

Shropshire's fears were well-founded for the Union Army in New Mexico was strong and ably led. Col. Edward R. S. Canby, commander of the Federal Department of New Mexico, had not been idle. After ascertaining the route that the Rebels would use to invade the territory, he collected most of the scattered Union forces in and around Fort Craig, one hundred miles south of Albuquerque, blocking any Confederate move north along the Rio Grande. Other detachments watched for Rebel advances along the Pecos River via Fort Stanton. To augment his twelve hundred regulars, Canby had formed several companies of six-month mounted militia and had started raising five regiments of New Mexico volunteer infantry. Gov. Henry Connelly, shamelessly capitalizing on racial fears, issued a proclamation in English and Spanish urging enlistments, claiming that the Texans would seek vengeance against the citizens of the territory for past misadventures. Even so, by February, only the First New Mexico Infantry, composed of Spanish-speaking natives commanded by the legendary mountain man Col. Christopher "Kit" Carson, approached any military efficiency. A company of Colorado "Pikes Peakers" under Capt. Theodore H. Dodd had also arrived to reinforce the Federals. Canby placed his hopes, though, on his artillery: two twenty-four-pounder howitzers in a battery under Capt. Robert Hall, and a mixed, six-gun battery under Capt. Alexander McRae. Canby then organized his ad hoc command into five battalion-sized columns to maneuver against the Confederates. As a further precaution, soldiers reinforced the adobe walls of the fort while others dug earthworks outside.[29]

The Confederates received good news during the last week of January, as Lt. Col. John Sutton and his five companies of the Seventh Texas Mounted Volunteers finished their march from San Antonio. On January 25, the battalion passed Fort Bliss, and rode through Franklin before making camp for the night. These curious newcomers, like their predecessors, took the opportunity to cross over to Mexican El Paso. "Drank some of the delicious native wine," noted surgeon "Hal" Hunter in his journal. Five days later, the troops camped near Las Cruces and visited the capital of Confederate Arizona across the river. "Mesilla is a very pretty town," Hunter noted. "The buildings, however, are characteristic of the country—doby—with one exception, a large two story brick building on the Plazza which is the capitol building. There are 8 or 10 white families, the rest Mexicans of low class." On February 3, the Texans crossed the Rio Grande and camped near Fort Thorn.[30]

Sibley reviewed his reinforcements the following day and liked what he saw. "The General said we were in [a] better plight, both men and horses, than any other that had come through," Dr. Hunter wrote. "Our horses looked better than those that had rested here a month."[31]

The next morning, Hunter inspected Fort Thorn with little enthusiasm for the facilities or its inhabitants. "It is very unhealthy," he noted, "so much so that for years it has been abandoned." On a subsequent visit, he met General Sibley but was not impressed. "Don't like our staff and General much. Too much drunkeness among them."[32]

On February 5, Col. James Reily arrived at Fort Thorn from Chihuahua with more agreeable news for Sibley. Gov. Luis Terrazas had received the colonel with great ceremony and had treated him well. In addition, he had forwarded some pleasant, though far from decisive, dispatches. The Mexican governor was vague about U.S. troops being allowed overland through his jurisdiction, although he privately reassured Reily that he "did not think" he would permit them passage across Chihuahua. Terrazas refused, however, to grant absolute permission for "hot pursuit" of Apaches into the state; again, Reily assured Sibley that enough diplomatic precedent existed to justify that action when necessary. Reily did receive permission for the Confederate government to purchase supplies, although Terrazas expressed concern over the inflationary effect this would have on the local economies. Reily had further news for Sibley: "Permit me to congratulate you, general, in having obtained the first official recognition of the Government of the Confederate States by any foreign power."[33]

On February 6, Colonel Reily was gone again, this time heading for Sonora on a mission that was of the greatest and most far-reaching importance for General Sibley, Governor Baylor, and the Confederate Empire: Reily was to seek permission for establishing a Confederate depot at Guaymas. To assure Reily's safety, Sibley had accepted Capt. Sherod Hunter's sixty-man company into the Confederate service, ordering them to escort the diplomat as far as Tucson.[34] From there, Reily would head south while Captain Hunter would secure western Arizona for the Confederacy and open communications with California. Governor Baylor seems to have regained his influence. With his Sonoran schemes receiving diplomatic sanction, Baylor's dream and ambitions seemed resurrected. Men loyal to him would accompany Reily every mile of the journey. In addition, because of Mexican diplomatic attitudes concerning "hot pursuit" of Apaches, Baylor finally had a chance to act upon a long-cherished desire. He would take the field again, leading the Arizona Guards in a pursuit to the death of the hated Apaches.[35]

In the first week of February 1862, all of the military forces in Confederate Arizona stood poised to expand the Confederate Empire. General Sibley, with his troops resting in camps at Fort Thorn, would soon send his force of twenty-five hundred against the Union stronghold of Fort Craig. Once in possession of that post, he would take Albuquerque and Santa Fe. By April, his victorious Texans would be in position to succor the secessionists in Colorado or to press overland to California. To keep the route to the Pacific open, Captain Hunter and sixty men prepared to make a hard winter march to Tucson to amass supplies there. In his care also was the true hope of the Confederacy—Colonel Reily and his diplomatic mission to Sonora. Company A of the Second Texas Mounted Rifles remained near Doña Ana, and Col. William Steele was just days away from Fort Bliss with another four hundred men of the Seventh Texas. Meanwhile, Governor Baylor would chastise the Apaches and Lieutenant Colonel Waller would organize reinforcements in Texas, who would possibly ride to the aid of the expanding Confederate empire. And, unknown to Sibley, Baylor maintained plans to bring in a brigade of his own. All of the elements for both Baylor's and Sibley's plans had fallen into place.

With supplies at Fort Thorn dwindling and bad weather increasing, Sibley finally launched his campaign. Dismounted soldiers from all four commands reported to Fort Thorn, where they were placed under command of Lt. Charles Linn and left in garrison. Major Pyron had already moved to occupy Alamosa, while on February 7, 1862, Colonel Green's regiment and Capt. Trevanion Teel's old battery of four six-pounders led the army's advance. Two days later, Lieutenant Colonel Sutton and the Seventh Texas followed. The Fourth Texas started the next morning.[36]

As news of the orders arrived, Captain Shropshire took his wife's picture from his breast pocket, gazed upon it, and took time to write one last letter home. "You expressed a hope . . . that I might return in the spring. I fear not . . . the war . . . to me now appears but just begun," he scribbled. "The deeds of heroism and acts of sacrifice will be but nothing to those that will yet [occur] before peace and quietude are restored to us." After giving instructions on practical matters including the sale of that year's cotton crop, he added a few tender lines. "But Darling, let us hope for the better and pray that we will soon be reunited. I am no soldier, and am [longing] for a release. My home with my wife and little one are more to me than all the flags and pomp and circumstance of the military. I would not forgo them to be generalisamo of the American continent." He then dreamed of their future together. "My mind has been idle and allowed to roam at will. Many are the fancy castles I have built you and I and our little ones. I have once been happy beyond my most vain expectations and can see no cause why I should not [be] again. Yours affectionately, Shrop."[37]

First Sergeant Hart, before leaving the vicinity of Fort Thorn for an uncertain future, added a closing entry to his journal before bundling it up and trusting it to the mail. "Its few pages I have filled with matter perhaps which may be interesting to no one save a participator in the scenes and incidents of travel," he wrote. "I have made my notes when I was on the line of march during the five minutes halt we generally had every two hours. Part of the time... I wrote my notes on my horse. . . . Dangers thick and imminent crowd upon us," he added, "but yet I fear not. So adieu, dear old book."[38]

As his columns lumbered up the Rio Grande, Sibley received some unsolicited reinforcements. Phillips and his cronies, with Baylor preparing to take the field on an Indian campaign and Hunter's command heading for Tucson, found themselves without a sponsor or local supporter in the Mesilla Valley. Eager for action, especially in the direction of Santa Fe, the ten ruffians formed themselves into an ad hoc company, assuming the colorful title of "The Brigands." From Mesilla, this group of drifters, gamblers, and desperadoes traveled to Fort Thorn, where Sibley, no doubt grudgingly, accepted them into service. On the trip up the Rio Grande, other ne'er-do-wells joined the party, including William D. Kirk, the infamous wagon thief from Fort McLane. On February 10, Confederate officers "hired" Phillips and his followers as civilian employees, assigning them to the quartermaster department as guides.[39]

Just as quickly, Sibley's men arrested Kirk. While Sibley was still in the U.S. Army in New Mexico, Kirk had been wagon master at Fort McLane. In March of 1861, he had stolen the wagons belonging to Maj. Isaac Lynde's command and had driven them to Chihuahua for sale. This incident had already caused a year of diplomatic wrangling and administrative headaches, and, in Sibley's opinion, Kirk's presence tarnished the reputation of the Confederate States. Sibley considered Kirk, one of Baylor's favorites, a common outlaw as his crime had occurred prior to the outbreak of hostilities between the Confederacy and the United States; it was not patriotism but simple banditry.[40]

Kirk and two accused collaborators were sentenced to be handed over to the Federals for justice. Sibley ordered Capt. Willis L. Robards, his chief of ordnance and aide-de-camp, to take an escort under a flag of truce and deliver the outlaws to Federal authorities at Fort Craig. This action may have been an elaborate ruse designed to get a good look at Union forces. More probably, though, Sibley intended it simply as a gesture to regain Confederate honor by refusing to protect criminals. Whatever his motivation, Robards never made it.[41]

As the prisoners and escort passed the Fifth Texas Mounted Volunteers on the road, Col. Green ordered Robards to stop. After hearing details of the mission, Green ordered Kirk released. This prompted a heated exchange between Robards and the colonel. According to Davidson, Green declared loudly that "he wished he might be shot and be damned a thousand times rather than see those men . . . turned over to the Federals." Green declared that "they could not carry those men to the enemy's camp until they whipped the Fifth regiment." Robards backed down. "Kirk . . . was a gallant soldier," added Davidson, "but the thread of his life hung upon the nerve of Tom Green in February 1862." Sibley, preoccupied with his campaign, did not pursue the issue further.[42]

As the army moved north, the poor condition of the brigade animals severely affected the command. The shortage of healthy mules caused half of the army's wagons to be left at Fort Thorn and Mesilla. All available transportation was used first for ammunition, then for food. As a result, the men marched on half-rations. Extraneous equipment, including company tents, extra shoes, and horse tack had been left behind. The troops readily improvised. "The boys are utilizing the hides of the beeves that are killed and all the horses that die in making sandals for themselves," Davidson wrote, "or shoes for their horses. We have been on half-rations . . . and yet the men are all in fine spirits, around the campfire, they crack their jokes and sing as merrily as if they were home."[43]

After the march started, the health of the commander of the Army of New Mexico steadily declined. His kidney disease had plagued him for years, and while whiskey softened the pain it also aggravated his condition. These vicious cycles accelerated until ultimately Sibley could not remain in his saddle, and retired to an ambulance. "I believe that General Sibley was a brave and gallant man and a true patriot," Davidson wrote in the officer's defense. "His health was such that he was not fit to command. The mind naturally becomes turned when disease and pain racks the body. [He] ought to have resigned. . . ."[44]

For the next few days, the army marched across the last year's battlegrounds while a cavalry screen kept the enemy at bay. At the swampy grove where Bethel Coopwood had fought the previous September, traces of breastworks and scattered horse skeletons were seen. In the bullet-scarred village of Alamosa, Private Howell noted "several Mexicans and hogs. . . ."[45] Lt. Col. Henry McNeill and Maj. Samuel Lockridge led three companies forward to drive away Union scouts. On the evening of February 12, the Texans returned with news of a Federal advance. The next morning, Green held a position near a small hill, fifteen miles from Fort Craig, as Northern cavalrymen rode forward in line. Green immediately sent couriers down the Rio Grande to hurry forward the rest of the army. The attack, however, never came. "This movement," wrote Lieutenant Fulcrod, "proved to be a ruse. . . ." That night, as a heavy snow fell, Green's men maintained their battle array as the Fourth and Seventh Texas hurried forward on a grueling, freezing night march, some troops traveling thirty-five miles. "Some were cursing the Yankees," wrote Henry Smith. "Others were almost praying for an attack."[46]

The following day, Green's men pushed onward toward Fort Craig, skirmishing with the enemy while their compatriots rested. Late in the afternoon, Rebel horsemen successfully cut off a twenty-one-man detachment of mounted New Mexico militiamen, forcing their surrender.[47] "The prisoners say they were forced to join them," wrote Dr. Hal Hunter. "They were told that the Texians were coming to murder all—both men, women, and children."[48]

From the New Mexican captives and his various scouts, Green determined that Fort Craig was too strong to be carried by assault, so he tried unsuccessfully to lure the garrison onto the plains. On February 15, the Texans moved to within five miles of the fort and deployed behind a low rise that ran east and west. Canby, better equipped but aware of the shortcomings of his newly levied troops, still refused to fight. That evening, the Texans moved to within a few thousand yards of the enemy stronghold.[49]

The next day, after a nighttime snowfall, the Confederates boldly prepared for a decisive battle. Five companies remained as a reserve while the remaining twenty-five rode to within a few hundred yards of the seemingly deserted adobe fort. After a few moments, the Stars and Stripes were unfurled from the post's flagpole and Union troops

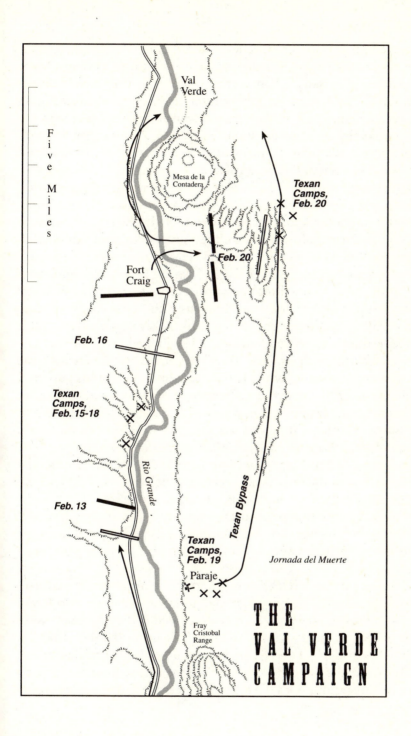

Val
Verde

Five Miles

Mesa de la
Contadera

Feb. 20

Fort
Craig

Feb. 20.

Feb. 16

Texan
Camps,
Feb. 15-18

Rio Grande

Feb. 13

Texan Bypass

Texan
Camps,
Feb. 19

Jornada del Muerte

Paraje

Fray
Cristobal
Range

THE
VAL VERDE
CAMPAIGN

Texan
Camps,
Feb. 20

deployed into the outer entrenchments. "Major Lockridge says he intends to make his wife a shimmy out of that flag," Private Smith scrawled in his diary. "If he can get a wife as easy as he can get that flag he will never sleep by himself any more."[50] Canby again refused to commit his volunteers to battle, but sent several companies of cavalry to skirmish with the Rebels. At this critical point, with combat looming, an inebriated Sibley turned over command to Colonel Green and retired to an ambulance.[51]

Green prepared to fight in earnest. Regimental surgeons took their posts, and Teel ordered the artillery forward. Almost immediately, the Texans found themselves on the defensive as New Mexican cavalrymen galloped toward their left flank. "Our boys fire on them, yell and wave their hats at Yankeedom, and beckon them on," wrote Private Howell of the Fifth Texas. The Federal horsemen closed to within a few hundred yards before turning away. Texan rifles dropped two riders. The Unionists returned a volley, sending minié balls whistling through the ranks. Private Davidson felt a shudder and then pitched forward. "They killed my mule today— over a half mile with a minnie rifle," he recorded. "The fellow was actually so far off that while I could see the smoke of his gun . . . I could not hear the report of it. This thing of shooting at each other is becoming a common thing now . . . and somebody is bound to get hurt." Confederates pursued the retreating enemy to within range of the troops at the fort, then prudently veered away. The sniping and skirmishing lasted most of the day. "Much to the disappointment of the men, who expected a fight, about 3 o'clock we were ordered back to our camp," Fulcrod remembered.[52] "Nothing done," wrote the irritated Dr. Hunter. "All a perfect farce."[53] Frustrated after several hours of anticipation, Green withdrew his men a few miles, then he consulted Sibley and considered alternatives.[54]

A council of war that evening charted the army's future course. Most agreed that a decisive fight had to be made; either Fort Craig had to be taken or Canby's army destroyed if the campaign were to proceed. A direct frontal assault was unthinkable, although Major Lockridge offered to lead one that night. Up to that point, no Texans had managed to slip behind the fort to interdict its lines of communications with the rest of the territory. The ground to the west favored the defense, and the Federals would be there first.

Another possibility was to bypass the fort to the east by crossing the Rio Grande, although the terrain was unknown. Once north of the Fort Craig, Sibley's army could pen Canby within its walls between a blocking force near Socorro and Colonel Steele's forces in the Mesilla Valley. The Texans, theoretically, would acquire supplies by interdicting those destined for the Federals. No matter what course was adopted, something had to be done quickly, for the Army of New Mexico was down to just a few days' rations.

The Texans spent the next two days exploring their options. Scouts waded the river and located a difficult, but safe, passage for the brigade herds and wagons. The terrain was rough and crossed by several deep sand-filled ravines, but it allowed access to the Val Verde fords, just north of Fort Craig. The command would have to traverse a dusty, waterless route for only one day. Elsewhere, Texans scattered Union patrols and pickets. On February 18, amid clouds of blowing sand, the soldiers in their camps prepared for hard fighting—artillerymen packed ammunition, while other troops cooked rations.[55]

While riding with his company, Pvt. Henry Wright remembered a peculiar incident that, under different circumstances, might have caused some excitement. "A young man who had been riding all day in one of these scouting parties, approached Mr. [John] Poe who he knew was a watchmaker and jeweler by trade. . . ." The soldier then produced a marble-sized lump of ore, which the craftsmen recognized as high quality gold. "He said he found it in a gully on the day's march . . . saying there was plenty more where he found this." After refusing to divulge the whereabouts of his discovery, the young man rejoined his company, promising that, when the war was over, he would come back and investigate. "We never heard from him again," Wright added. "I expect he was either killed or died. . . ."[56]

With supplies dwindling and morale ebbing, Green and the recovering Sibley knew they must move. The Confederates crossed the icy Rio Grande on February 19, at the tiny village of Paraje, then ascended the basaltic ledges above. Ridges of drifting sand impeded the soldiers' progress as they forced their way parallel to the river en route to the fords a few miles above Fort Craig. The next day, the brigade struggled northeast through trackless gullies filled with loose and shifting sand as they flanked the large, black Mesa de la Contadera—an ancient lava flow that overlooked the fort and river valley. Green and Sibley remained confident that the Federals would be forced to fight if their line of communications with the rest of the territory were threatened.[57]

At dusk, as the Confederates made their camps atop a crescent-shaped ridge overlooking Fort Craig, Federal troops crossed to the east side of the river and prepared to attack. As the Unionists pressed the Texan pickets, the Rebels deployed their artillery and unfurled their flags, while the brassy notes of "Dixie" were carried on the cold New Mexico wind. The Confederates had finally forced a battle. "They came out in splendid order, their guns shining like the spangles on the dress of a lord," Dr. Hunter wrote. The Federals, some two dozen companies of regulars and New Mexico volunteers in line of battle, fired two harmless volleys from nearly one thousand yards, followed by a few shots from their artillery. Lt. Col. John S. Sutton of the Seventh Texas Mounted Volunteers rode among his men, urging them to "think of their rights, and [to] remember the honor of Texas." The Southerners replied with a six-pounder, accompanied by a few lobbed shells from mountain howitzers, that sent echoes crashing against the surrounding hills. Texans cheered as a few enemy soldiers fell amid the bursts of fire, iron, and smoke. "Their men soon became restless, and Colonel Green directed us to play upon their volunteers," Lieutenant Fulcrod wrote. "Our fire soon became too hot for one of their regiments, and it broke and fled."[58] As the Federals regrouped, Major Lockridge led four hundred mounted men in a dash to the spur of a nearby ridge, providing the Texans with a covered position within a few hundred yards of the enemy line. "Thinking this a charge," Fulcrod added, "all of the efforts of the Federal officers to restore order failed and they withdrew."[59]

The night of February 20 was miserable for Sibley's army. Livestock losses among the Confederates, already critical, were heightened by their waterless jaunt. "Our mules were so completely exhausted that . . . they broke down and could go no further," Fulcrod wrote. That night, 150 thirst-crazed mules broke loose and stampeded for the river, effectively immobilizing nearly two dozen wagons. Artilleryman Frank Starr wrote dejectedly, "Our stock of mules was scant at first and by this loss we were badly crippled." The troops dined on dried beef and husbanded their few kegs of water. A volunteer detachment of a few men gathered canteens, slipped quietly into the darkness, and retrieved a few dozen quarts from the Rio Grande. Near the camp of the Seventh Texas, rifles flashed as pickets fired on enemy scouts.[60]

At the artillery park, an ailing General Sibley called on his friend Major Teel, confident that the Federals would not resist the Texan crossing at Val Verde. "[He] was quite sick all day and have spent much of the time in his ambulance," Fulcrod wrote. "He camped close to me and came over to where my battery was . . . and complained of being unwell." The lieutenant offered the general some water, and filled his canteen. "He did not think the enemy would meet us the next day, and . . . he was sanguine of success. He and Major Teel went off together and I did not see him any more...."[61]

Dawn of February 21 broke cold and cloudy as the Confederate Army of New Mexico slowly stirred to life. Details began unpacking the wagons slated for abandonment, tossing excess baggage, including "a number of saddles and old clothes" and any other equipment for which there was no space in the remaining vehicles, into heaps. One howitzer, its horses too weak to carry the burden, was left behind. The animals bawled pitifully for relief. "Men and animals were exhausted and suffering the pangs of a consuming thirst," Lt. Phil Clough of Company C, Fifth Texas remembered vividly. "The cry of the horses and mules in their agony was most pitiful."[62] To alleviate their pain, the Texans in the five companies of Pyron's Battalion saddled their mounts and headed in advance of the brigade at first light, hoping to reach and safeguard the water at the Val Verde fords within a couple of hours.[63]

In the camps, the troops pursued life as normal. "We all commenced with our usual morning duties—some digging roots, others moving their horses, and other cooking breakfast," Davidson recalled. "After . . . receiving no orders to march, we were all lounging around trying to amuse ourselves, some telling yarns, some playing cards . . . some running 'horse races' with body lice. . . ."[64]

The men of the Fourth Texas were the next to leave camp. Five companies, under Maj. Henry Raguet, followed the path of Pyron's men. Lieutenant Colonel Scurry led the balance of the regiment as well as the mountain howitzer battery as it escorted the slow-moving regimental baggage train through deep sand. The rest of the brigade remained idle, disinterested observers of the daily routine that had started anew. There was no sense of urgency. The damp, gray morning seemed unremarkable.[65]

Eventually, the men became curious about the cause for their delay; the answer came quickly. "Some of us . . . were beginning to wonder why we were not ordered to march, as usually we would have been on the march a full two hours before," Davidson wrote. Moments later, a deep booming resonated up from the Rio Grande valley. "This was a cannon shot followed by a volley of musketry," the private added. "Immediately the cry went from camp to camp and from mess to mess 'Pyron's at it!' Pyron's at it!' Every fellow sprang to his arms and for his horse. . . ." Cautious and emphatic officers ordered the men back into order. "We were pretty soon told that we had officers who would give the command when we were wanted to move."[66] Meanwhile, nervous officers gathered in close groups and speculated on what was going on just a few miles away on the banks of the Rio Grande at the wooded fords called Val Verde.

CHAPTER 8

The Battle for Empire

We turned their tactics upside down, and gave the regulars hell.
—Anonymous

Since the earliest European settlement of New Mexico, the area known as Val Verde—Green Valley—played a critical role in the region. A two-mile-wide valley dotted with cottonwoods and covered with grass, this five-mile-long park-like plain served as a favorite resting spot for travelers on the Santa Fe–to–Chihuahua road. Located at the northern entrance to the arid Jornada del Muerte, Val Verde offered the last chance at shade and water. The Rio Grande often flooded the valley, each time cutting patterns of meandering, roughly parallel channels across the sandy surface. In 1862, the river ran along the western margin of the valley, with the dry ravine of a former riverbed arching bow-like away through the trees to the east then rejoining the main channel a mile north. The flat-topped Mesa de la Contadera bounded the southern end of the valley and served as a convenient place for shepherds to inventory their flocks in earlier days. A small village at one time flourished near the river but, by 1862, its inhabitants had long since left. Recognizing its strategic importance, the U.S. Army established Fort Conrad near the village after 1846, but later abandoned the post in favor of Fort Craig a few miles south and across the river. Now, the once serene Val Verde would serve as the battlefield of empire.

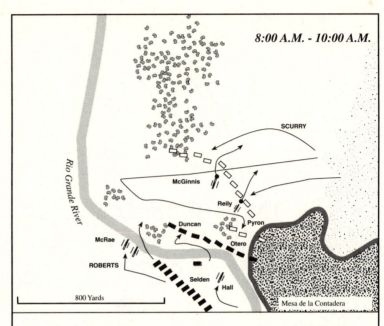

THE BATTLE OF VAL VERDE

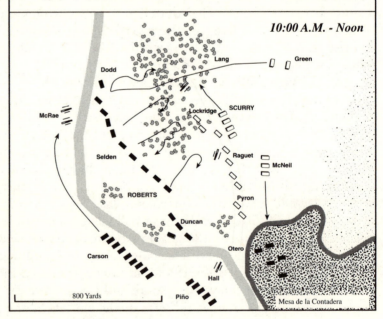

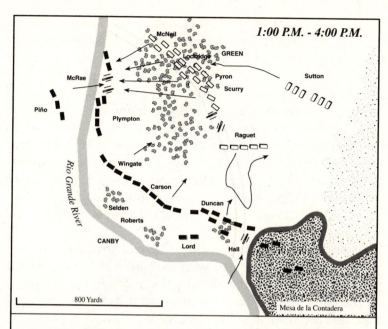

1:00 P.M. - 4:00 P.M.

McNeil

Lockridge   GREEN

McRae   Pyron   Sutton

Scurry

Piño

Plympton   Raguet

Rio Grande River

Wingate

Carson

Selden   Duncan

Roberts

CANBY   Lord   Hall

800 Yards

Mesa de la Contadera

THE BATTLE OF VAL VERDE

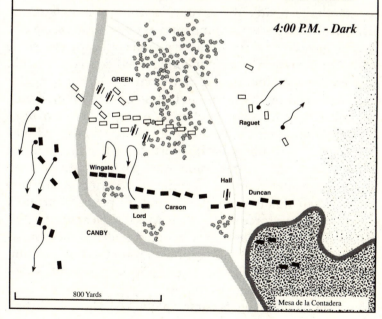

4:00 P.M. - Dark

GREEN

Raguet

Wingate

Hall

Carson   Duncan

Lord

CANBY

800 Yards

Mesa de la Contadera

Col. Edward R. S. Canby's Union army made an early start on the morning of February 21. Lt. Col. Benjamin S. Roberts and his five-hundred-man march column had already moved to seize the Val Verde fords. Maj. Thomas Duncan, leading four companies of the Third U.S. and one of the First U.S. regiments of cavalry had gone to support Capt. Miguel Otero's five mounted New Mexico militia companies who had spent the night among the cottonwoods near the Mesa de la Contadera on the Rio Grande. In all, some three hundred and fifty mounted Federals were now converging on the banks of the Rio Grande. Meanwhile, Capt. Henry R. Selden with nine companies of regular infantry and an equal number of volunteers remained poised south of the mesa, ready to strike the Rebel rear and baggage train.[1]

The vanguard of the Texan column that had broken camp early that same morning soon collided with the Union horsemen. Major Pyron led 180 soldiers of the Second Texas down a steep, dusty draw to the river, sending back word to the brigade that the road was clear and the river in sight. "As we were marching along in some glee at the prospect of getting some water," wrote Sgt. Maj. William P. Laughter of Pyron's Battalion, "we spied some tents in the timber on the east bank of the river." As the Texans entered the water, flankers detected several companies of Otero's militia cavalry to the left and gave chase through the scattered cottonwoods. These Federals fled to the river. As the pursuing Rebels crested the bank, they discovered several hundred more Unionists, Duncan's regular cavalry strengthened by the recent arrival of several hundred men from the Third New Mexico Infantry, crossing the river toward them. "It was soon apparent that we had . . . over cropped ourselves," Laughter remembered. "In short, 'bit off more than we could chew.'" The Confederates dismounted, took positions behind the bank of a dry water course, and commenced firing. Additional Union troops, four infantry companies and six pieces of artillery detached from Selden's force south of the Mesa, soon arrived. "The ping! and spud! of their bullets, the roll and thunder of their bursting bombs, and the crash of falling timber around us had no comfort in them," Laughter added.[2] As a light snow began to fall, Major Pyron dispatched a hasty note to the rear.[3]

Confederate reinforcements came up quickly. The courier first

Lt. Col. Benjamin Stone Roberts, circa 1863. Courtesy of Massachusetts Commandery, Military Order of the Loyal Legion and the U.S. Military History Institute, Carlisle Barracks, Pennsylvania.

reached Lt. Col. William Read Scurry's Fourth Texas Mounted Volunteers, already underway escorting the regimental wagons on the plateau behind and east of the Mesa de la Contadera. Scurry ordered his men to gallop immediately to Pyron's relief. "Upon receipt of this intelligence we struck a brisk trot and rode rapidly over the table land and down a long slant to the river bottom," recalled Sgt. Alfred Peticolas of Victoria. Within an hour of Pyron's request, Scurry's troops had descended the sandy slope and were rushing across the mile-wide flats to join the battle. "In high spirits and singing songs," Peticolas continued, "we crossed the valley at the same rapid pace and dismounted among the cotton woods." Maj. Henry Raguet's companies arrived first, followed within half an hour by the balance of the regiment. Once among the trees, the companies tied their horses and advanced to Pyron's right, taking a position along a slight sand bank. "As soon as we made our appearance they greeted us with a rapid discharge of small arms, but we were none of us hurt."[4]

One of the next companies in line was the "Crockett Boys" of Capt. D. A. Nunn's Company I, Fourth Texas. "Volley after volley met our advance," the captain confided in his diary. "As we came into line the balls greeted us with the viper's hiss." As the unit advanced, the second in command tumbled over, a bullet in his ankle. Nunn then hurried his men to the safety of the sand bank. "The enemy cannon balls came just over our heads, tearing the trees and cutting the limbs. . . . Their minnie muskets were whizzing by in rapid succession, clipping the trees. Now, for the first time, did I fully realize the terror of the battlefield!"[5]

Next, the Confederates hurried forward Lt. John Reily's mountain howitzer battery and companies from Green's regiment to strengthen the line. Eighteen-year-old Pvt. Frank Starr, entering combat for the first time, struggled to get his gun through the deep sand, his pulse racing as he neared the edge of the high ground before starting his descent into the valley below. "We heard the report of a cannon, then another, and another; one after the other in quick succession," he wrote. "In a few minutes we had descended into the valley urging our jaded horses on as fast as possible." Frenzied troopers from the Fourth Texas galloped past, urging the struggling gunners forward.[6]

The Union forces also poured additional troops into position at Val Verde, but seemed confused on how best to deal with the Texans. By 10:00 A.M. Major Duncan had crossed his dismounted cavalrymen across the river and had extended his skirmish line to

his left, to counter the arrival of the Fourth Texas. He had successfully denied the Rebel access to water, but had committed Union
troops to the east side of the river, an unnecessary and possibly risky
move. In addition, he had failed to capitalize on his earlier superiority in numbers and now the enemy was reinforced and in a fairly
strong position. Lieutenant Colonel Roberts, furious over his subordinate's blunder, committed additional men to the east side of the
Rio Grande, sending his infantry across while keeping his guns
safely on the west bank. There, Capt. Robert H. Hall's two twenty-
four-pounders and Capt. Alexander McRae's two twelve-pounder
howitzers and two six-pounders deployed to support the regulars.[7]

This addition of several hundred enemy rifled-muskets pinned
Scurry's troops behind the safety of the sand bank, their short-
ranged shotguns and pistols nearly useless. "We laid close to the
ground and behind the trees," Peticolas wrote. "Not a gun was fired
while we were lying there."[8] From three hundred yards away, the
Union troops fired volley after volley into the Rebel positions; the
Texans looked anxiously to the rear for additional Confederate reinforcements to save them from their plight. Though handled gal-
lantly, the lighter Texan cannons also proved ineffective. "We tried
our Howitzers upon them," Starr wrote, "but found the enemy was
too far off to do much damage."[9]

More Texans joined the battle. A section of Maj. Trevanion
Teel's old battery under Lt. Joseph H. McGinnis arrived at 10:30
A.M. and inaugurated an intense artillery duel that added to the
mayhem. The two Southern six-pounders replied valiantly but
vainly to the more powerful guns of Hall's battery. "This gallant
officer held his position and continued his firing upon the enemy,"
Scurry reported, "himself seizing the rammer and assisting to load
the pieces."[10] The duel also drew more enemy fire through the ranks
of the Fourth Texas hiding behind the sand bank. "Shell and round
shot and minie bullets came whistling in showers over our heads,"
wrote Sergeant Peticolas. "Bombs burst just behind and before, and
trees were shattered and limbs began to fall." Teel's gunners pulled
their lanyards, reset their guns, sponged the barrels, and then
rammed home fresh charges. When one crewman fell, his companions dragged him to the safety of the sand bank. Other gunners staggered and dropped. A shell burst beneath one of the gun carriages,

setting the grass on fire, but the Rebel battery kept firing.[11]

Eventually the Union fire overwhelmed the Rebel guns. After a few minutes of the uneven contest with the enemy twenty-four-pounders, only five Confederates remained to work the twin six-pounders. Some gunners were dead, others had fled. "I noticed one of Teel's sergeants of artillery squatting behind the trees and looking very much scared," Peticolas recounted, "and making a good many exclamations suggestive of alarm." One of the battery officers forced the skulker back to his post. Eventually the crews of the impotent mountain howitzers abandoned their pieces in favor of the sturdier field pieces of their beleaguered compatriots. "Reily's artillerymen were called out to man the guns," Captain Nunn remembered, "who did it with heroic daring." Even the dismounted volunteers tried to help. One enemy solid shot, bounding to a stop near the sand bank, was recovered by a soldier in Peticolas's company who, "in spite of our expostulations," wrote the sergeant, crawled out and retrieved the still warm projectile. He then offered it to the nearby Rebel gunners to fire back at the Northerners, "in hopes that it might kill some of them." The duel ended when McRae's four guns added their fire from across the river. Teel quit the uneven fight, ordering his guns to move to the left to counter an anticipated Union advance. The Union artillery now dominated the battlefield.[12]

After a morning of encouraging reports, Canby moved to exploit his gains and ordered the balance of his troops to head for Val Verde. Captain Selden, with the flower of the Union army in New Mexico, crossed the freezing Rio Grande from his position south of the Mesa de la Contadera, marched the several miles north to the battlefield, then recrossed. Col. Kit Carson and his well-drilled First New Mexico Volunteers followed. Col. Miguel Piño's Second New Mexico Volunteers, who had fled under fire the night before, escorted the Federal ammunition wagons from Fort Craig. Upon arriving, Selden's wet and weary men deployed immediately into battle, extending the line to the left. Carson moved his regiment, west of the river, to a position on the extreme Federal left to provide security on that flank. Meanwhile, Piño's troops went into reserve.[13]

Lieutenant Colonel Scurry found his position deteriorating as

Selden's regulars, crossing at a ford to the north, threatened to turn the Texan right. Leaving Major Raguet and four companies to hold the center and support Pyron, Scurry sidestepped the rest of the regiment several hundred yards to the north. The men scrambled back to their horses, untied them, and mounted. "After riding 250 yards higher up, we dismounted in a perfect hail of bullets and took our position behind the same sand bank that had protected us below; but here it was higher," wrote Sergeant Peticolas. Minié balls began to thud into men and animals. "As we were in the act of dismounting, Jones' horse was shot in the thigh, Woodapple's was crippled, and a ball tore a small peel of skin from my right thumb, which bled profusely," Peticolas confided. "Unheeding this, I tied my mule to a bending tree and went to the bank." Captain Nunn was close behind, writing "The bullets whizzed by us as thick as bees in a swarm." His forces spread desperately thin, Scurry now hoped to hold on until Col. Tom Green could bring up his troops.[14]

The Confederate command scrambled to shore up the critical situation at Val Verde. Around noon, Sibley ordered Lt. Col. John Sutton, with his five companies of the Seventh Texas and two from the Fifth Texas, to remain behind to guard the supply train on the plateau behind the mesa while Green rushed his remaining eight companies forward. Lt. Col. Henry McNeill and Maj. Sam Lockridge, with the first five companies of the Fifth Texas and two more of Teel's six-pounders, arrived at 12:30 P.M. Most of Pyron's exhausted unit, meanwhile, fell out of line and went into reserve, as the Texan artillery took positions at intervals along the line. Most of the mountain howitzers, after their marginal performance, lay abandoned as Teel distributed their crews among his six-pounders.[15]

After pummeling the Confederates with artillery and small arms fire for hours, the Federals had gained the initiative. With an advantage in men and weapons, Lieutenant Colonel Roberts, still the senior officer on the battlefield, pressed the lightly held Texan center. "I directed Captain Selden with his command," he reported, "to engage them with the bayonet."[16] The U.S. regulars—men of the Fifth, Seventh, and Tenth U.S. Infantry regiments, as well as Capt. Theodore Dodd's independent company of Colorado volunteers, began their steady advance. The brunt of the attack fell on Scurry's exhausted troops. "We could see the enemy in strength just before us about 600 yards and advancing rapidly as if to force our line in," Peticolas noted. "They were taking trees as they approached and [were] firing rapidly upon us."[17]

The jaded men of the Fourth Texas suffered anxiously as the few soldiers armed with rifles attempted to fight back while most stayed behind cover. As Texan sharpshooters left cover to take their shots, flurries of Federal bullets hit their mark. One rifleman, hit by a marksman atop the Mesa on the extreme left, fell with "heart rending groans." Another, struck in the arm, exclaimed, "O God, I'm shot;" another fell struck in both thighs. One Texan took a devastating blow to the mouth, which nearly severed his tongue. "He pulled out a part of it which was hanging ragged," Peticolas remembered, "and cut it off with his knife." Especially devastated were the regimental mounts. Rounds that whistled past the concealed Confederates wrought havoc among their animals. Heartsick men could only watch helplessly as dozens of mules and horses staggered and screamed from scores of leaden blows. "A cannon ball had shot off the right forefoot of one in 10 yards of me," Peticolas lamented. "Another had both forelegs shot off, and the last I saw of him he was trying to use and stand on the shattered stumps."[18]

On the far left, Union firepower had also devastated the Texan artillery. Captain Hall's twenty-four-pounders and hundreds of Union rifled-muskets continued to dominate the lighter Rebel guns. "One of our pieces," wrote Private Starr, now serving one of the six-pounders, "was exposed to such a heavy fire that the gun was partially disabled, the horses all killed and nearly all the men either killed or wounded." A bullet stuck the young private, sending him sprawling. "I thought at first I was shot through my thigh," Starr wrote, "but as I felt no pain, I examined and found that the ball had struck a large wide-mouthed bottle cork, which I had in my pocket, breaking it to pieces, and bruising my leg a little. Upon finding myself whole and sound, I jumped up and went to work at the cannon again."[19] Union troops, taking advantage of the suppressing fire from Hall's battery, surged forward and captured one of the disabled Rebel guns. Lockridge's men quickly counterattacked, and recovered the cannon, dragging it behind the sand bank to safety. Texan gunners also ran short of ammunition. "We fired the guns," Starr added, "until we had expended all our round shot, then we loaded it with canister and awaited the nearer approach of the enemy."[20]

As the Regulars advanced to within shotgun range, the Texans eventually achieved satisfaction. "They began to pay dearly for getting so close to us," Peticolas boasted. "Not a man shot without taking sight, for Texas boys are accustomed to the use of arms and never shoot away their ammunition for nothing. Our fire soon became extremely galling." After an intense half hour, the Federals abandoned their advance, and withdrew toward the river. Sensing victory, Rebel gunners returned to their pieces, sending blasts of canister through the cottonwoods, hurrying the Unionists out of range.[21]

By 1:00 P.M. Colonel Green arrived, escorted by the two lancer companies of his regiment, but found the Confederates situation chaotic. Sibley, still with the wagons, had retired to his ambulance and the Texans lacked any unified command. As a result, the Southerners fought piecemeal, dissipating their strength in disjointed actions. Anxious to strike back, the recently arrived Capt. Willis Lang petitioned to lead his lancer company into action. "Capt. Lang in person asked Colonel Scurry to let him charge their infantry," Lt. Phil Fulcrod noted as he served one of the cannons assigned to that end of the line. "The request was refused." The persistent Lang would not be put off, however, and Scurry eventually relented. Lang "formed . . . to the right and just in front of my battery, made them a short speech, brought them to attention, and gave the fearful order 'charge,'" Fulcrod remembered. The Texan cavalry, just over fifty strong, surged forward—walking, cantering, then galloping—across the valley toward Dodd's Coloradans on the far right, lowering their lances for the last hundred yards. As the Confederates closed the distance, many of the troopers noticed that their charge was unsupported. Some reigned in the mounts, turned, and fled. Others continued on to their doom.[22]

Though dramatic, the lancer charge was a predictable disaster. The well-disciplined Coloradans, wearing the same gray uniforms as the less steady New Mexican volunteers, firmly held their ground. "Like an avalanche, the intrepid Lang . . . charged the serried lines of the foe," Lt. Phil Clough of the Fifth Texas remembered.

"Instantly, [the Coloradans] threw themselves in position to 'resist cavalry,' the front lines on their knees with braced muskets presented a wall of bayonets." As the Texans thundered closer, the miners and frontiersmen of the second rank raised their weapons and waited for a short-range volley. "Our Captain, stepping in front, said 'Steady there my brave mountaineers'," one Union volunteer recalled. "'Waste not a single shot. Do not let your passions run off with your judgment. Steady men, guns to faces, but wait for the command to fire.'"[23] At forty yards, the Union line erupted, knocking several of the Texans from their saddles and scattering the charge.[24]

The surviving lancers flowed around the enemy infantry, but found additional Federals in position to rake them with bullets. "Reinforcing columns were at hand," Clough continued, "who quickly formed squares. On the right and left of them, and in their front, the deadly musketry played." Grapeshot carried away Captain Lang's saddle horn, wounding him severely; six other bullets also stuck the hapless officer. Twenty of his troops also fell. The milling Texans were helpless. "They appeared bewildered," a Federal recalled, "[they] did not know how or what to do." Dodd's infantry, bayonets fixed, lunged forward. A Union soldier dashed among the Texans and, according to an observer, "ran his bayonet through one and then shot the top of his head off." The few surviving Texans fled, streaming back to the safety of Confederate lines.[25] Capt. Jerome McCown's lancers, behind the Rebel lines, moved forward to aid the survivors, red pennants snapping in the breeze; Green stopped them. The charge had been a debacle and would not be reinforced. "Those men went into the very jaws of death," Fulcrod mourned. "I looked on as those lances went down to rise no more. . . . This threw a gloom over our entire line."[26]

On the Confederate left, the looming Mesa de la Contadera became hotly contested as both sides struggled to control its bolder strewn heights. During the morning, mounted Union skirmishers had climbed the slopes and had enfiladed the Texan line with a deadly fire. During the fighting, a number of Texans, as well as dozens of horses, had been felled by bullets coming from this unexpected angle. Three Confederate companies under Lt. Col. Henry McNeill responded, riding to the mesa top to confront the enemy riflemen.[27] Hall's twenty-four-pounders shelled these Texans as they rode. "In moving to this position one of our men was wounded by a grape shot," Fifty-seven-year-old Sgt. E. L. R. Patton of Parker County wrote. "I saw the shot before it struck him, it struck the ground, not three feet on my left, bounded, and hit him, striking his gun, brakeing & bending it while in his hand and forced against his knee so as to cripple him for the time. It was blue as indigo." Otero's New Mexican militia atop the mesa fled when McNeill's troopers crested the rise.[28]

The victorious Texans took control of the critical position, a fifty-man detachment from Pyron's battalion, armed with rifles, replacing McNeill's mounted troopers. "Getting behind the rocks and trees on the point of the hill," wrote Sergeant Major Laughter, "we salted and peppered them finely for awhile. I thought it was the finest fun in the world, for about five minutes. . . . We yelled and fired as rapidly as we could."[29]

The Federals responded to the snipers swiftly, clearing the mesa of the Rebel nuisance. "They turned every gun on us," Laughter wrote. "How they did hustle us out of there." The sergeant major, seeking cover behind a large boulder, felt himself safe until one of Hall's howitzers careened a solid shot off of the improvised breastwork, showering him with debris. "When I got the little pieces of rock and dust out of my eyes, I looked around and found myself alone." The prudent soldier joined his comrades in their flight down the slope. As the echoes from this exchange faded in the valley, the firing slackened along the Rio Grande, the first break since Pyron had precipitated the battle nearly five hours earlier.[30]

The respite was welcomed by Scurry's bloodied regiment. Sergeant Peticolas, exhausted from the morning's fighting, took the opportunity to add cartridges from the bottom of his box, having already used his twenty rounds of loose ammunition in the top of his tins. Next, he "ate a little piece of dried beef and suffered for water." He also took a blanket and draped it across his shoulders to combat the chill of a light snow that had begun to fall. Meanwhile, the equally tired artillery men used spades to dig a make-shift well in the bottom of the dry river bed to the water table just a few feet below.[31]

The Union army, too, was spent, but their cannons kept firing as the infantry rested. "The commands were fatigued with five hours constant action," Lieutenant Colonel Roberts reported. "The men were permitted to lunch and ordered to replenish their cartridge boxes. During this time the batteries continued to operate on the enemy."[32]

In the hour-long lull, both armies regrouped and changed leadership. General Sibley had spent the entire morning back with the wagons and finally relinquished command. By 1:00 P.M., Colonel Green, the next highest ranking Texan officer engaged, took over. Meanwhile, Union Lieutenant Colonel Roberts turned over command to his superior, Colonel Canby, who had recently arrived from Fort Craig with the last of the Federal reinforcements.[33]

Colonel Green worked to stabilize the Confederate position while assessing the course of the battle. The lack of a unified Confederate command had kept the Texans on the defensive the entire morning. What flailing attacks were made had been piecemeal and unsupported. Upon reaching the field, companies had fought under the local command of regimental officers, and knew little about the general course of the battle. The engagement had been a combat of Southern reactions to Northern actions. Green used his own, as well as Sibley's, staff to issue orders and tighten control of the army in an effort to reverse the course of the battle.[34]

Colonel Canby, after inspecting the battlefield, correctly believed his army to be in control of the situation. The Federals had denied the Confederates water all day, and had pushed the Southerners back into the safety of the old river bed, an admittedly strong and tested position. Even so, Canby reasoned that a determined push against the Texan left at the base of the mesa would enfilade this line, flushing the Confederates into the open where they could be destroyed. Union infantrymen and dismounted cavalrymen firmly held the woods along the margin of the river.[35]

Canby confidently moved to implement his plan for victory. To support his decisive push, Canby ordered the Union artillery to cross over the river and anchor the flanks, Hall on his right near the mesa and McRae on the left. Midstream, one of the fearsome twenty-four-pounders splintered an axle and had to be abandoned. Supporting Hall's remaining gun, and spearheading Canby's attack, was Major Duncan and four companies of the Third U.S. Cavalry, a company of the Seventh Infantry, and four companies of volunteer infantry. Duncan's reserve, in place to exploit the anticipated break through, was a squadron of venerable dragoons from the First U.S. under Capt. R. S. C. Lord. To support McRae's guns—augmented by the arrival of an additional six-pounder and a twelve-pounder mountain howitzer—Canby ordered two more companies of New Mexico volunteers to cross. Dodd's Coloradans and four companies of regulars from the Seventh and Tenth U.S. under Capt. P. W. L. Plympton lay behind the safety of the riverbank as an additional reserve.[36] Capt. Benjamin Wingate and four companies of the veteran Fifth U.S. Infantry and Colonel Carson's First New Mexico moved into position in the center. West of the river, Colonel Piño's Second New Mexico Volunteers stood in reserve. As they reached their various positions, the Northerners joined a steady crescendo of fire upon their Texan foes.[37]

The Union troops raked the Texan lines with bullets, grapeshot, and shell, to which the Confederates could offer only a feeble reply. Private Davidson, armed with a rifle, took his place in front of the lines to return the enemy fire. "Here I spent my last bullet," he wrote. "My rifle was no more use that day. I fell back . . . and laid in the ravine with my company." The Union artillery caused several casualties. "They were firing about six cannon shots to our one. Major Raguet . . . who was walking down our line, was struck by piece of shell," Davidson wrote. The officer staggered until helped to the ground by some comrades. "He sat down and examined his wound [and] said he was not much hurt and walked back up our line."[38]

Confederate slaves accompanied their masters into battle, sharing their fates under fire. As the men of Capt. Samuel Shropshire's Company A, Fifth Texas, took their places behind the sand bank, his servant Bob coolly kept by his side amid the incoming Federal bullets. "Bob did not seem to mind these at all," Pvt. Bill Davidson remembered, "but walked about joking with the boys." When the Union artillery began shelling that portion of the Rebel line, the bondsman quickly, and prudently, sought shelter to the rear. "The first shell went beyond us and exploded among some horses," Davidson wrote. "Bob's eyes got a foot wide. [He] put out and as far as we could see him he was making good time, the boys cheering him as he went."[39]

By late afternoon, many of the Texans were spent and severely demoralized. "I began to be weary and heartily wished the battle was over," recalled Sergeant Peticolas. The inadequacy of the Confederate weapons had been apparent all day. "We could only shoot at intervals with our small arms," Peticolas added, "as they were of an inferior kind to theirs. Now I began to feel almost disheartened."[40]

Green watched as the impressive blue lines maneuvered into position, and decided upon a battle plan of his own. A man of decisive action, he could no longer tolerate the steady attrition from Union fire and decided to attack the enemy. Green concluded that the Federals were merely feinting, and that the tactical initiative now rested with the Confederates. Even as the Union fire intensified, he sat unconcerned astride his horse. "He was asked what he thought of the fight," Sergeant Peticolas wrote. "He replied that he did not think it was intended to bring on a decisive battle."[41] Amid occasional stray bullets, Green dispatched riders with orders intending to bring the battle to decision. One of Green's aides, Lt. Tom Ochiltree, as one Texan remembered, "with his long streaming hair, gleamed like a meteor" as he hurried along the line. Troops responded, and the Confederate Army of New Mexico, although wounded, was back in motion. "Colonel Green knows nothing about military science," Davidson added, "but he knows how to fight and win battles."[42]

Green repositioned his army using the high bank of the dry stream bed to conceal its movements. He abandoned the base of the mesa as untenable in the face of Union concentrations; Union riflemen had also reoccupied the heights. Major Raguet, with three hundred men in five companies, held the Rebel left as it shifted along the sand bank. Meanwhile, the balance of Green's troops, some five hundred men, assembled on the right. At 3:30 P.M., Lieutenant Colonel Sutton arrived with the five companies of the Seventh Texas and one of the Fifth, and took his place with the concentrated Texan battalions on the right, increasing the strength to more than one thousand.[43]

Ordered to remount and extend the line to the right as part of this movement, Peticolas and the men of the Fourth Texas discovered an appalling scene. Dozens of horses and mules had been massacred in the brutal firing. "Hardly half of Co. C found horses to ride," Peticolas lamented. "Wounded and dead horses were hastily stripped, and those that were able to move were turned loose to feed around or to shiver and die." The sergeant's own mule was among the wounded. "She shivered and seemed to be suffering intense pain." The various companies reorganized themselves into mounted and foot contingents, then began their move along the sand bank. Hundreds of Texans had fled the battlefield. "I was surprised and chagrined about this time to notice how very few of our men were on our line," Peticolas wrote. "Had they left the field completely . . . that our center was protected for an extent of 250 yards by less than 100 men?"[44]

Meanwhile, the Federals executed the maneuver that would, they hoped, destroy the Texan army, eliciting a desperate reaction from Colonel Green. Canby ordered a huge wheeling movement to turn the Rebel left flank using McRae's battery as the pivot. When skirmishers from the Third U.S. Cavalry moved toward the Confederate left, Green ordered Major Raguet and his five mounted companies to drive the enemy back.[45] Dashing out in single rank onto the open ground, the troops rode hard for Hall's twenty-four-pounder. Amid bullets and canister, two hundred Texan cavalrymen galloped to within one hundred yards of the Union lines before the charge disintegrated. Gun-shy horses veered away from the enemy fire, exposing their riders to the muskets of almost the entire Union line. Panicked men and horses turned and rushed past their original positions along the sand bank and into the hills beyond. Raguet, a flesh wound in his leg, vainly tried to rally his men as they scattered.[46] The Federals took several minutes to recover from the audacity of the Confederate attack, but soon had their gun and skirmishers moving to complete the enfilade. Raguet's charge had seemingly come as a gift which allowed the Federals to clear the ravine near the mesa with minimal casualties; Canby ordered additional reinforcements brought from the center to exploit the newfound advantage. Wingate's and Carson's soldiers, obeying these orders, moved toward the weakened Rebel left, away from McRae's guns.[47]

The Confederate left predictably crumbled. "Slowly but surely, the heavy columns of infantry and the artillery were driving back our line," Peticolas recorded. "The close, heavy cannonading on the left showed us that our men could not long hold their lines against the galling fire."[48] One panicked private appealed to Captain Shropshire to do something. "Said he, 'Captain, did you see that movement on our left,' " wrote Private Davidson. "Shropshire said that he did but that he was not commanding." Before the soldier could make reply, a cannonball cut him down.[49] Peticolas prepared himself for the worst. "The enemy's artillery had nearly reached the position on our left occupied by Teel's battery in the morning. In two minutes a raking fire would slay the last man of us." McRae's gunners maintained their intensive covering barrage as their comrades continued to maneuver. "The bombs and grape were bursting and flying all around us," Peticolas added. Colonel Green recognized the danger facing his command and eagerly sought some relief, some way to check the Federal attack. The time of decision had arrived. After surveying McRae's lightly protected guns to his right, Green found his salvation. "At this critical moment, Col. Green said: 'We must charge that battery, boys!' "[50]

The order at first caused confusion. Men within hearing left the sand bank and headed for their horses. 'Back men, back,' " Green yelled, thinking the troops were fleeing. " 'Remember you are Texians!' " Lieutenant Colonel Scurry then interceded for the confused soldiers. " 'The charge must be made on foot.' " Immediately, orders went to company commanders to prepare their men for action; when the word had passed the length of the line, Green gave his signal. Scurry and Major Lockridge, rising from behind the sand bank and moving forward for all to see, yelled, "Charge, boys, charge!"[51]

On this command, the dismounted men from six companies of the Fourth, four of the Fifth, and five of the Seventh Texas Cavalry regiments hesitantly rose from their positions and ran across the grass-covered field. Captain Shropshire turned to his company and yelled " 'Come on my boys!' " as he too climbed out of the ravine.[52] McRae's surprised gunners hastily lowered their cannon sights as clumps of Texans surged forward. Sergeant Peticolas threw off his blanket and joined the rush. "I hated to get up from behind the sand bank very much indeed," he recalled. "After I had . . . gotten 10 yards from the bank on the way to the cannons, I saw a great many had not started. . . . I paused for a moment to entreat them to come on. A few more having started, I rushed on towards the battery, for I knew I could be in no greater danger than I then was." Canister and case shot knocked many men to the ground in the six hundred yards between armies, but most missiles passed overhead. "Grape shot plowed up the dust before me and whistled around me and past me as I ran, but none struck me," Peticolas added. "I chose the openest ground right in front of the enemy's battery to run on, where there were the fewest men, for I knew that the cannoneers . . . would aim at the thickest bunches of men. . . ."[53] The Texans, either from instinct or orders, fell to earth when the cannons fired, rising to resume the assault after the rounds had passed. Union small arms fire from the left raked the Rebel mob as it pressed forward. Sixteen-year-old Abe Hanna fell dazed, knocked down by a bullet passing through his hat. A blast of canister mutilated Lieutenant Colonel Sutton's leg. Forty yards away from McRae's guns, daunted by fire from front and flank, the charged wavered as Green's Texans stopped to fire at the Union gunners. "The shotguns opened," wrote Davidson, "and . . . the enemy's lines seemed to melt away."[54]

Officers and men rallied the wavering Texans, urging then on. "Lockridge, with heart of iron, led us on," Peticolas remembered. Other officers "waved their swords, shouting 'Come on my boys, don't stop here!'" Sensing the devastation among the Federal gunners, the color bearer of the Fifth Texas, waving the Stars and Bars with the motto Victory Awaits You pressed ahead, urging his comrades to "'Follow, and stick by your flag.'" Two bullets ripped through the folds of the banner as the Texans drew their pistols and the charge again rolled on. McRae's gunners, regulars all, fought stubbornly with rammers and short swords as the Confederates poured around them, but were shot down. Captain McRae ran to his supporting infantry and begged them to hurry forward before returning to die by his guns. Major Lockridge, upon reaching the cannon, exclaimed "This is mine!" Immediately, he fell to his knees as a bullet passed through his body. As he bled to death, he gasped, "Go on my boys, don't stop here."[55]

Plympton's regulars from the Seventh and Tenth U.S. joined in the melee, but the battery could not be saved. One Confederate grabbed the reins of the lead horse on a Union caisson, as its rider swung angrily with his sword. Other Texans swarmed around the vehicle, and the Yankee was carried from his saddle. In desperation, a Union artillery man detonated an ammunition chest, the explosion killing himself and several Texans amid the chaos. Some New Mexican militia, panicked by the ferocity of the Rebel charge, turned and fled, communicating their terror to the regulars that had come to save the battery.[56] "Never were double-barreled shotguns and rifles used to better effect," Colonel Green reported.[57] Dozens of the Spanish-speaking troops near McRae's guns fell amid the meleé while many more died while crossing the Rio Grande. Union Colonel Piño's supporting New Mexico infantry, for the most part, looked on, wisely refusing to cross the river under fire to join the maelstrom around the guns. As increasing numbers of Federals fled, the jubilant Confederates turned the guns around. "Lieutenant Colonel McNeill came up to where some of our company had one piece and showed them how to fire it," wrote Davidson. "From [that] time on every fellow was acting pretty much on his own hook." After eight minutes, the charge was over and the guns taken.[58]

The adrenaline-drunk Texans continued to swarm around the captured battery and scores rushed toward the Rio Grande, eager to shoot more Federals as they struggled across the icy stream. Sgt. Maj. William P. Laughter of Pyron's Battalion joined the mob, spilling down the river's sandy bank and into the water. After recovering his feet, the Texan spied an enemy horse tied nearby which he triumphantly seized, mounted, and spurred back toward the captured battery to urge more Confederates forward. There he met a cursing and excited Colonel Green—the fire of battle beaming in his eyes—who urged Laughter to find and hurry Teel's gunners forward. "I soon met Captain Teel coming with his cannon urging his horses to the top of their speed," Laughter wrote. "His face was burned with powder and streaked with sweat, until he presented a very contraband appearance."[59]

Lieutenant Fulcrod also hurried forward with his cannon, passing the skulkers of the brigade. "Having no instructions," he wrote. "I limbered up my pieces and started to follow." As his guns rumbled down the ravine, he noticed dozens of men hiding from the battle. Halfway to the captured battery, Fulcrod also encountered Colonel Green. "He asked me where I was going, and I told him I would . . . render what assistance I could." Fulcrod then reported the cowards he had passed. Green "spurred his horse . . . made him jump down . . . among them and I think he scared them worse than the enemy had."[60]

Canby reacted quickly by ordering the guns retaken. Eighty U.S. cavalrymen in reserve near the Mesa de la Contadera drew their sabres, wheeled about, and trotted toward McRae's captured battery while Union infantry began pouring volleys into the milling Rebels. "Here the firing was so rapid that it sounded like one solid crash of musketry," remembered one Texan. "The smoke was so thick that you could scarcely tell one man from another, and our faces so black with powder and dirt that we looked more like negroes than white men."[61] Private Starr arrived with the Rebel artillery which took positions to defend against the Union counterattack. "The balls were whistling around us thick as hail," he assured, "but we had by this time got used to that."[62]

The Union troops, however, balked at the idea of closing with the Texans. Captain Lord's dragoons found themselves between the volleys of friends and foe alike, and ordered his men away from the Confederates and out of danger. Meanwhile, Captain Wingate and his battalion of the Fifth U.S. Infantry ceased firing and began a determined drive toward the guns. After closing the range, he ordered his men to halt and open fire, raking the Texans with musketry. The Confederates responded with artillery and what rifles they had, stopping the Union advance. Now, Southern artillery ruled the field. Wingate fell, seriously wounded, his leg shattered. Wisely, Canby ordered his wavering veterans to halt and slowly give ground. The fight for McRae's guns was over; the U.S. regulars had been beaten. "A few volleys of small arms and the old Texas war shout completely dispersed them," Green bragged, "many of them dropping their guns to lighten their heels."[63]

The taking of McRae's battery reversed the situation on the field, and the Federals hurried to end the battle. Canby, realizing that half his men had fled, ordered those remaining withdrawn. Wingate's regulars continued to hold their line as the remaining Union troops crossed the river near the mesa. The Confederates, without an organized reserve, attempted to pursue the beaten enemy, but Green ordered his exhausted men to stop, calling back those who had already crossed the Rio Grande, thus allowing the Unionists to retire unmolested. As darkness fell, a Federal rider carrying a white flag requested a truce to bury the dead. Green agreed. As night fell, the battle of Val Verde ended.[64]

The battle had proven nothing. Its implications for the Confederacy were entirely out of proportion to its size. For the number of men involved and the modest casualty rate, considerable—even great—consequences had hung in the balance. Tactical success, though, was not enough—especially without inspired leadership on the part of the Confederates—to gain a strategic victory in New Mexico. Val Verde, while impressive in its intensity, had been a hollow conquest.

It had been, however, a battle unlike any others that had, or would, occur in the war. Many larger, and bloodier battles had already been fought across the South: Wilson's Creek the previous summer had seen the triumph of poorly equipped Rebels over Union regulars and volunteers, but not as dramatically as along the Rio Grande. Manassas, by comparison, had been a titanic clash, but lacked the savagery of Sibley's and Canby's encounter. More than anything else, the fighting in New Mexico marked the only real showdown between the frontier military tradition of Andrew Jackson, San Jacinto, and Texas Rangers and the professionalism epitomized by West Point. The "arrogant" regulars had grappled with the self-assured volunteers, and the amateurs had won.

Indeed, the Texans reveled in their victory over the well-drilled regulars. "It is not so certain that discipline is very much advantage in small armies," Sergeant Laughter boasted. His young friend, Private Hanna, was equally proud. "I have no name for this brave action," he wrote in his diary, "but I think it would be very appropriately termed a young Manassas."[65] Scurry, too, was amazed by the Rebel success. "Well I never did see such a charge as that," the veteran was reported to have said.[66] Teenaged German Joseph Faust of New Braunfels was stunned. "I entered into the fight with more courage than I thought myself capable of, cold-bloodedly walked towards the cannons and came out without a scratch."[67] In later years, one of the Texan participants, proud of triumph over the professionals, included the following lines in a poem about the battle:

> We *heeded not their great renown,*
> We *charged them with a yell,*
> We *turned their tactics upside down,*
> And *gave the regulars hell.*[68]

These broader implications seemed lost on other survivors who were just happy to have made it through the battle unharmed. "It was amusing to notice with what joy acquaintances shook hands and congratulated each other on being alive," Peticolas remembered. "They laughed and danced and shook hands with more real joy than friends must after years of absence in ordinary circumstances. Never before have I felt such perfect happiness as I did when we took the battery from our enemy."[69]

Amid the jubilation and celebration, company commanders and their noncommissioned officers attempted to reorganize their jumbled commands. "We got into line as soon as we could," Private Davidson wrote. "Captain Shropshire spoke a few words to us complimenting and congratulating us, then told us to succor our wounded and collect our dead."[70]

The men from both armies, just lately enemies, scattered across the dark battlefield to search for the wounded and the dead. A few had lanterns, others followed the groans of the fallen or hoped to chance upon their injured comrades.[71] Men carried the stricken soldiers of both North and South to various campfires, covering them with blankets and attempting to make them comfortable. Peticolas was heartbroken by the scene unfolding in the flickering light. "It was a sad sight to see these young men, so lately in all the strength and vigor of manhood, now lying pale and weak around these fires, suffering."[72]

To others fell the grim task of collecting the slain. "When we thought we had collected all our wounded, we commenced carrying our dead to the spot selected for their final resting place," Private Davidson wrote. "We hauled them in wagons, as many as we could lay side by side." This duty continued on until almost dawn.[73]

The Confederates erected a hospital tent two miles upstream

where surgeons labored over the more serious cases. Lieutenant Colonel Sutton, the proud veteran of Republic of Texas days, refused to have his shattered leg amputated; he died of blood poisoning a few days later. Captain Lang, leader of the lancer debacle, lay in torturous pain. Others also came. Lt. Benton Bell Seat of Company F, Fifth Texas, had a wound through his right arm. "Although it was not considered dangerous, . . . I had bled so profusely that I was too weak to reach the camp and had to be carried part of the way," he wrote. "By lamp light the surgeons probed the wound but found nothing and they dressed it and prepared a sling in which to carry my arm until it was healed up."[74]

The final casualty toll revealed that the battle had been bloody for both sides. The victory had cost the Rebels nearly ten percent of their force: thirty-six men killed, one hundred and fifty wounded, and one missing. Forty-three of the wounded later died. The Federals lost about sixteen percent of their force: one hundred and ten killed, two hundred and forty wounded, and thirty-five missing. Among the regulars, nearly one of every five had been hit. Captain McRae, like most of his gunners, was among the dead. His supports, mostly Spanish-speaking militia and volunteers, counted one hundred and twenty casualties in and around the battery.[75] For the Texans, perhaps the most serious loss was to their animals. Tied to trees behind the battle line, the mounts had been the only available target for many of the Yankee skirmishers. Nearly a thousand horses and mules had been killed, mostly those of the artillery and the Fourth Texas.[76]

Those not caring for the fallen scavenged the battlefield for anything of value. Shivering soldiers found dozens of discarded Union overcoats. The weary Texans claimed more than one hundred rifles along with dozens of full cartridge boxes, allowing many to retire their shotguns. Troops manhandled McRae's six guns into camp, aligning them as trophies for all the command to see.[77] Other articles—watches, accoutrements, and the like—also fell into Rebel hands. "I picked up a blanket in place of the one I had thrown off," Sergeant Peticolas recorded in his diary. Surprisingly, he discovered a stray horse to replace his dead mule. The hungry Southerners also plundered the battlefield for food. "Light bread, coffee, sugar and bacon for three days were all snugly stored away in [the Federals'] haversacks," noted Peticolas, who had dined on cold bread and dried beef, with very little water, the night before.[78]

Efficient slaves helped their Southern masters gather plunder from the field. "Lieutenant Oaks has a servant," Davidson wrote, "who . . . is a hero in his way. [He] keeps Oaks mess well supplied with horses and everything else likely to be found on a battlefield."[79]

After a cold, restless night, the men of Sibley's army awoke to finish the business of war. "The battlefield was a sad sight," wrote Pvt. William Randolph Howell. "So many poor fellows lieing cold in death and others biting the earth, horses dead and wounded. The whole seemed to be the abode of death itself."[80] A burial detail dug four long trenches, fourteen feet long, seven feet wide, and six feet deep, as others assembled the Confederate dead. Friends covered the corpses with blankets, then sewed the bodies inside. After Lieutenant Colonel McNeill performed a funeral service, the soldiers buried them. "Tearfully, tenderly, and prayerfully we laid them in their grave," Davidson wrote. "Officers and men were laid side by side."[81]

Across the river, an occasional crash of musketry echoed away from the Union stronghold. "Judging from the firing at Craig," Howell noted as he looked across the Rio Grande, "they too are burying many a poor soldier far from his relatives and the home of his youth."[82]

As the brigade buried its dead, Sibley, recovered and back in command of his army, moved to complete Green's victory. The general dispatched Lieutenant Colonel Scurry and Capt. Denman Shannon with ten men under a flag of truce to Fort Craig to demand its immediate surrender. "We were stopped within 40 or 50 yards of the fort," Private Starr wrote. "We were received by a guard of eighteen mexicans with a dutch sargeant and an Irish Corporal." The Confederate officers were granted admittance while the enlisted men waited outside. The Texans gazed suspiciously at the curious Federals looking on them from the adobe walls. "The fort was very strongly fortified, having a deep wide ditch all around, and post holes for small arms and bastions for Artillery. I noticed that the men were nearly all mexicans or foreigners."[83]

Canby, despite his army being badly demoralized, flatly refused to surrender the post. Although his companies had been shot-up, he believed they still had fight remaining. "Although defeated, my command is not dispirited," he wrote. "Large numbers of the militia and volunteers have deserted, but this adds to, rather than diminishes, our strength." He sent the Texan officers back without satisfaction. Confident he could hold Fort Craig, Canby dispatched the leavings of the New Mexico mounted militia to Socorro to block the Rebel advance up river and to destroy government property that might fall into enemy hands.[84]

Sibley faced a dilemma. His men had carried the field and beaten Canby, but the Union army had not been destroyed or even crippled, and with a month's food and supplies behind adobe walls it remained a considerable threat. Sibley's army, however, had only three-days' rations. He could not retreat to his base in Confederate Arizona—his men would starve. Canby would be foolish to offer battle in the open again. "Every opportunity was given them to try us again in a field fight," Sergeant Patton wrote his children, "but their prudence prevented."[85] Sibley would have to move north, deeper into enemy territory and away from Fort Craig, in hopes of capturing supplies at more lightly held Federal posts. The Confederate Army of New Mexico, however, was in poor condition for a march. "The command was badly torn up," remembered Lieutenant Fulcrod of the artillery. "The batteries shot to pieces and things in general in a dilapidated condition."[86] The only action that would avert disaster was to lead the army north, committing the crippled force to a much longer and more grueling campaign.[87]

On February 23, 1862, the Confederate army of empire started its trek. The shortage of horses dictated that much of the brigade equipment had to be abandoned. Soldiers piled worn-out clothing, blankets, and now-useless horse tack in great heaps, which were burned. The remaining wagons loaded up, and the army, according to Julius Giesecke, recently promoted to captain, "traveled on towards Santa Fe . . . not troubled by the enemy any more."[88]

The broken condition of Sibley's army limited its speed. Companies had been fragmented, and those still mounted pressed ahead of those afoot. Details of six men carried some of the wounded on improvised litters. Other casualties endured rough, jarring rides aboard wagons. The remaining brigade animals, already jaded from poor diet and overwork, strained at their burdens. "Our mules are about worked down and can hardly pull the . . . wagons," Davidson noted. "The consequence is the boys have to put their shoulders to the wheels and roll the wagons along. The beeves, like the mules, are so poor they can hardly walk. The truth is, the marches show as much or more heroism than the battles." At the end of the day, the brigade had traveled only six miles.[89]

That evening, a windfall buoyed the Rebel spirits. Soldiers looted the ranch and store of Col. Robert Stapleton, one of Canby's militia officers, carrying away hundreds of pounds of wheat, salt, and sugar. Some troops plundered bales of Federal uniforms while others drove work oxen and a flock of sheep to the commissary. "The wearing apparel was divided out to the different regiments and companies," Peticolas scribbled in his diary, "and we had dinner and breakfast of mutton."[90] Davidson marveled at the sudden change in attitude among his refreshed comrades, writing "they crack their jokes and sing as merrily as we did when in Texas."[91]

Meanwhile, Lt. Col. Henry McNeill, with five companies of the Fifth Texas Mounted Volunteers and two artillery pieces, trotted ahead of the brigade to capture Federal supplies at Socorro.[92] McNeill ran into opposition, forcing him to deploy for battle. Col. Nicolás Piño and two hundred of his New Mexico Militiamen had already occupied the town and appeared ready to fight. After exchanging shots, the Rebel commander deployed his cavalrymen around Socorro and demanded its surrender. When Piño refused, the Texan guns opened fire around sunset from a rise southwest of town. After a few rounds bounced off the adobe buildings of the town and ricocheted down its dusty streets, the demoralized native troops, reluctant Unionists at best, scattered. Piño, hoping in vain for reinforcements and with only a handful of his own troops staying by the colors, reluctantly surrendered the town just after midnight.[93]

The capture of Socorro secured the Texans a forward base of operations as well as much-needed supplies. Capt. Jerome McCown's Company G, Fifth Texas Mounted Volunteers, gladly exchanged their lances, which, according to that officer, were "perfectly useless in [this] peculiar kind of warfare," for an assortment of Mississippi rifles, Springfield rifles and muskets, and a few breech-loading Sharps' carbines. The commissary department seized thousands of barrels of government flour from the town. The spoils of Socorro also included three hundred Federal horses and mules.[94]

The Confederate Army of New Mexico made good use of Socorro. In the evening of February 26, Sibley's weary brigade marched into town, where the peach trees were just beginning to bloom. The troops moved into the adobe homes there and in two surrounding villages, while doctors established a brigade hospital. Nearly one hundred and fifty men, included wounded from Val Verde and those too sick to travel, were admitted, while officers assigned nurses and doctors to care for the stricken. "This was the first time we have had a house to put our sick in," mentioned Davidson, "since we left Fort Thorn more than a month ago."[95]

Tragedy, however, stalked the brigade. After settling into one of the buildings that night, Lieutenant Seat was startled by the sharp crack of a pistol nearby. Captain Lang, aided by his servant, had killed himself. "[He] was a modest nice man, well educated, and it almost made me sick to hear the sad news," Seat added. "I recalled the fact that only the week before he and I had ridden side by side for hours . . . and he was decidedly pessimistic as to the outcome of our expedition."[96]

The following day, Sibley reorganized his army. The plight of his brigade mounts was critical. "There is no forage for horses in this part of the country, either corn, hay, or grass," Peticolas wrote. In an effort to increase the efficiency of the brigade, Lieutenant Colonel Scurry asked those of his Fourth Texas who still had horses to turn them over to the quartermaster for redistribution as replacements to the better-mounted regiments. In exchange, he promised, the men would be compensated their appraised government value. "The men see a prospect of their animals starving," Peticolas mentioned pragmatically. "The idea [of surrendering their mounts] is not as repugnant to them as one would naturally supposed it would be to the cowboy of Texas."[97] The men of the Fourth Texas reluctantly agreed. "It was one of the most generous, noble, patriotic, and self sacrificing acts I have ever known men to do," wrote Fulcrod, whose artillery stood to benefit from the act. "When this was completed it placed us once more on a new footing and we were ourselves again, all gloom and despondency was banished from our camp."[98]

However, around the camp fires of the Fourth Texas, the men were grumbling. "Our horses are all turned over [and] the regiment is more depressed that it has been for months," wrote Peticolas, who turned in the horse he found at Val Verde for a $110 voucher. His friend Hanna echoed the sentiment. "To be dismounted as infantry . . . will not agree with the Texas Boys as they have never been accustomed to walking. Now, a thousand miles from home, afoot, and without a dog, . . . and in as dreary a country as this . . . and things in such a state of confusion, our prospect is but a gloomy one."[99]

With the mounts redistributed, Sibley once again faced hard choices. The troops had already eaten through much of the captured provisions. There was just enough to accomplish one of two goals: He could reverse his course and attempt to take the still formidable Fort Craig, or he could ignore that post and press deeper into New Mexico with the hopes of securing more food en route. The battle of Val Verde, although spectacular, had been far from decisive and Sibley's command, although victorious, had suffered a crippling blow to its mobility. Sibley's gamble of bypassing Canby's army to force it into the field had so far yielded few rewards. The Texans could, however, overrun the rest of the territory virtually unopposed, eventually sealing Canby's fate and securing the territory. The only obstacle to this plan lay east of the Sangre de Cristo Mountains at Fort Union, the strongest and most important position in New Mexico, but as yet only lightly garrisoned by a mixed command of several hundred volunteers and a few dozen regulars.

On the last day of February, Sibley decided to abandon communications with Confederate Arizona and ordered his troops to continue northward. "I had supposed that we would return and capture Fort Craig and Canby's army there before we attempted to proceed up the Rio Grande," Davidson remarked. "It never occurred to me that we would deliberately place ourselves between two armies, sever ourselves from the base of our operations, and cut ourselves off from all hope of assistance from home. Yet this is exactly what we did."[100]

CHAPTER 9

The Apex of Empire

An air of desolate lonesomeness reigns over the whole country.
—Sgt. Alfred B. Peticolas, Victoria, Texas

"You will probably learn from the telegraph, from rumor and from other sources that we have had a most desperate and bloody struggle with the Texans," Union Capt. Gurden Chapin, assistant adjutant general on Col. Edward R. S. Canby's staff, scrawled from his temporary office at the depot in Santa Fe. A week after the combat at Val Verde, he and the rest of the mounted regulars of the First and Third U.S. had left Fort Craig and skillfully slipped past Sibley and his army. Now these few hundred cavalrymen hurried north throughout the territory in a desperate effort to remove supplies from the path of the Texans. Federal morale remained wretched as Chapin continued his despondent and imploring dispatch to Maj. Gen. Henry W. Halleck, commanding the Department of the Missouri in Saint Louis, begging for help. "Our loss is great. The enemy is now above Colonel Canby, on the Rio Grande, and of course has cut him from all communication with his supplies. It is needless to say that this country is in a critical condition. The militia have all run away and the New Mexico Volunteers are deserting in large numbers. No dependence whatever can be placed on the natives; they are worse than worthless; they are really aids to the enemy, who catch them, take their arms, and tell them to go home." Chapin knew the stakes in this faraway campaign in the desert southwest. If only he could convince the rest of the nation. "We must look to the future. The conquest of New Mexico is a great political feature of the Rebellion. It will gain the Rebels a name and a prestige over Europe and operate against the Union cause." Chapin respected his foes, and knew their determination to extend the Confederate empire from ocean to ocean. "These Texans will not rest with the forces they have already with them, but they will have large additions to their command here, in order to extend their conquest toward old Mexico and in the direction of southern California." Only by receiving more Federal attention, especially reinforcements—at least two regiments and a battery of rifled cannon—the captain argued, could disaster be avoided. "These [reinforcing] troops cannot serve the government better than by saving this Territory. I have given you a true picture of the state of this country, and if you wish to save it, you, I hope and pray, will act immediately."[1]

Indeed, the month of March, 1862, marked the high point of the Confederate conquest of the American Southwest, and all signs seemed to indicate that the South would achieve its empire while stripping the Union of its desert territories. The Union cause in New Mexico lay prostrate. Canby's army, less its mounted arm, lay inert and still at Fort Craig, leaving New Mexico to Sibley. A few hundred Federal volunteers held Fort Union. Less than one hundred U.S. regulars guarded the tons of supplies held in Santa Fe. At the depot in Albuquerque, a sergeant's guard of twelve men were all that remained to stop the Texan juggernaut. The only immediate deliverance for the Union cause was approaching, however, in the form of nearly nine hundred Colorado volunteers that were, even then, making a forced march through the mountain snows to aid New Mexico.

Time became the key to Union salvation. As long as the Rebels remained in New Mexico, the grinding attrition on their horses, men, and supplies would continue. If Canby could somehow keep supplies from falling into Texan hands while avoiding contact with his enemies, then, he reasoned, the Confederate invasion would ultimately fail.

Fort Union was the most important position in New Mexico. Situated on a broad plain, this post straddled the Santa Fe trail as it snaked north and east to Kansas and Missouri and commanded roads leading through Raton Pass to Colorado. Thus, it was the Federal gateway to New Mexico, and the territory's lifeline to the nation. The rows of adobe and brick buildings would have to be held at all hazards. Its garrison was critically weak but its commander was a man of strength. Gabriel René Paul was a Mexican War hero and veteran of the frontier army. Formerly a major in the Eighth U.S. Infantry, he had been promoted to Colonel of Volunteers and given the task of raising the Fourth New Mexico Infantry. The fate of the territory, in large part, depended on him.

In Mesilla, meanwhile, a new regime was administering Confederate Arizona. Col. William Steele, Maj. Arthur P. Bagby, and four companies of the Seventh Texas Mounted Volunteers had arrived shortly after Sibley left Fort Thorn. What they found was an expanding territory in transition. Baylor had departed on an Apache campaign into Mexico. Capt. Sherod Hunter, Col. James Reily, and nearly one hundred men had pushed west to Tucson. The garrison at Mesilla consisted of Company A of the Second Texas Mounted Rifles, a six-pounder and a few mountain howitzers, the sick of Sibley's army, and a small detachment of dismounted troopers at Fort Thorn. After inspecting his command, Steele took over as acting governor and presided over the continuing expansion of the nation's western border.[2]

The Southern gains continued. Hundreds of miles to the southwest, the Confederate empire accomplished another important goal as Capt. Hunter secured Tucson. On February 28, his force of about seventy-five Confederates with three wagons had occupied the town after a harsh two-week march in freezing weather. "My timely arrival with my command," Hunter reported, "was hailed by a majority, I may say by the entire population, of the town of Tucson."[3] Colonel Reily presided over a ceremonial flag raising in the town square and delivered a speech. Captain Hunter then began the task of establishing Confederate control. Properties held by Union men were forfeited, and those still backing the United States were escorted out of town. Hunter then requisitioned supplies and clothing from local store owners and confiscated feed for his horses.

Maj. Gabriel Paul, circa 1863. Courtesy Civil War Library and Museum, MOLLUS, Philadelphia, Pennsylvania.

Colonel Reily left for Sonora three days later, accompanied by a twenty-man escort.[4]

The Confederate Empire had arrived at a critical time in its development. Sibley and its principal army had disappeared into the New Mexican interior—cut off from news, supplies, or reinforcements—

in a bold gamble designed to yield impressive rewards. At the same time, Governor Baylor and his band of Indian-killing veterans vented their unmitigated wrath against the Apaches. To the south, Chihuahua appeared ready to endorse the Confederacy.

Of all the Confederate military effort, the citizens of Arizona hoped most earnestly for Baylor's success in his campaign against the Apaches. In mid-February Baylor had decided to punish Apache raiders who had driven off hundreds of Sibley's animals. As the Army of New Mexico was leaving Fort Thorn to force Canby to give battle, Baylor and a force consisting of men from the Arizona Guards and other companies at Mesilla had gone west toward Pinos Altos in hopes of also forcing the Apaches into a decisive, crushing engagement.

Baylor's force, like Sibley's, soon found itself in a frustrating and fruitless march through rugged mountains in search of an elusive enemy. After arriving at Pinos Altos, Baylor made a dash to a nearby spring where Mangas Coloradas and some of his Mimbreños had been reported, but the wily old warrior was long gone. Baylor returned to the mining camps and turned his column south after other quarry, the Chiricahuas. His Mexican guide led him into the Burro Mountains, where the Confederates hunted game to sustain themselves. "Found no Indians but plenty of turkeys and black tail deer," remembered the German Hank Smith. "Laid in a good supply of both and feasted for two days." From there, the column proceeded to Stein's Peak and the Peloncia Mountains, finding signs of Apaches, but no sightings. The guide then urged Baylor to take his men south, into Mexico.[5]

Baylor agreed, and began a series of hard, circuitous marches in northern Chihuahua, where he encountered more signs of the Apaches. Near Corralitos, the Confederates discovered fresh evidence that Indians were near. While Baylor's men made camp, their guide traveled to various villages and returned with reliable information that a band of Apaches had been seen in the Tres Hermanos Mountains, fifty miles north and just inside Confederate Arizona. Because of the poor condition of their mounts, the Texans knew that a quick dash on the camp was impossible. Instead, they set out to slip around to the north of the enemy in a series of easy marches, although that would extend the journey to about one hundred miles.

After a few days ride across a barren plain with little water, Baylor and his troops were finally in position to attack. Dividing his forces, he prepared to drive the Indians down a canyon with forty men and force them into an ambush. At dawn, the Confederates started their attack.[6]

The Apaches, however, had escaped to the south; Baylor doggedly pursued them, again plunging deep into Chihuahua. Probably remembering Colonel Reily's assurances that the Mexicans tacitly approved of the principal of "hot pursuit," Baylor pushed the concept to its limits. He followed the Indians to Caretas, a remote mining village west of Casas Grandes. Here the Apaches, probably Mimbreños, took refuge in the large house of José María Zuloaga, one of the principal mine operators, and sued for peace, but Baylor ordered his men to attack. The resulting volley and pursuit by the mounted Confederates killed most of the Apache warriors and scattered the rest. Baylor and his hundred men returned to Arizona, satisfied that they had inflicted a serious defeat on the Apaches. Baylor headed for Mesilla, while Capt. Tom Helm and a detachment traveled on to Pinos Altos.[7]

Baylor's raid produced diplomatic aftershocks that rocked the region. The gore and mayhem left in the wake of Baylor's raid promised to jeopardize all Confederate diplomatic efforts in Mexico. R. L. Robertson, the United States Consul in Mazatlán, was amazed at the Rebel audacity and predicted that Mexican authorities would be furious. "The Texans are becoming daily more hateful to the Mexicans," he wrote. "The atrocities of Baylor's men . . . will not be overlooked, but . . . will serve to revive the hatred of the Chihuahuans to the Texans." The Confederates, however, seemed oblivious to the consequences of their actions.[8]

Far to the north, while Baylor had been hunting Indians and shooting up Mexican towns, Sibley had led his troops up the Rio Grande toward Albuquerque, hoping to feed his army on captured Federal supplies. "Our march was slow but sure," Lt. Phil Fulcrod of the artillery remembered. "I thought it rather unwise to leave as strong a place as Fort Craig in our rear, but I supposed it could not be avoided." On March 2, 1862, the Texan van, composed of the weary veterans of Pyron's Battalion of the Second Texas Mounted Rifles, arrived in the city just in time to see the critical provisions burning and flames erupting from government warehouses; the tiny Union garrison of the town had departed just moments before. "The greatest mistake that was made was in not sending a force on to Albuquerque as soon as Val Verde was won," Fulcrod concluded. As fire consumed the stores of tallow and pickled pork, a huge pool of melted grease flowed out of the commissary building and into the street. "There was a great quantity of . . . stores that were at that place and thereby would . . . have passed the command through the winter. It looked like a sin to destroy the necessaries of life in such a manner." Remembering the lessons of history, Fulcrod wrote, "When I saw this I thought of Napoleon and Moscow." Despite the setback, Pyron and his troops took formal possession of the city, raising a Confederate flag in the main plaza as the band played "Dixie" and "The Girl I Left Behind Me." Next the troops settled into quarters to await the rest of the army. "Major Teel assigned me to splendid quarters," Fulcrod wrote, "a fine house well furnished."[9]

The rest of the Confederate army crept up the river from Socorro, averaging a dozen miles a day. Sibley's Texans stretched out for three miles in a long snaking column. The mounted troops led. Next came the dismounted men of the Fourth Texas, "a long struggling line nearly a mile long," Pvt. Henry Wright remembered. After these troops came a small rear guard followed by the wagons and finally the artillery. Stragglers lined the roadside. "The boys often stopped to rest and then dragged on," Wright added. "I would often stop by the side of the road to read or write, or mend my clothes."[10]

As the troops consumed the last of their rations, hunger and disease again swept the ranks; the Texans became despondent. "We buried four men," Bill Davidson of the Fifth Texas wrote. "Pneumonia, measles, small-pox, itch, and body lice are getting in their work on us."[11] Pvt. William Henry Smith of the same regiment reported "great dissatisfaction among the soldiers." The bleak winter hills of New Mexico aggravated homesickness among the Texans. "The country is worthless, fit for nothing," he added. "Think this country never was intended for white folks. The first man that ever came . . . ought to have been killed by the Indians."[12]

Nowhere was the grumbling as severe as in the Fourth Texas. The men had not made the transition to infantry gracefully. "It being the first traveling we had done on foot," wrote teenager Abe Hanna, "there was considerable growling among the Boys."[13] Upon stopping for the day, the weary soldiers collapsed where they stood. "Many a foot was blistered," Sgt. Alfred Peticolas wrote. "I have a blister on my heel about as large as a quarter . . . from which the skin is peeled, but I washed my feet thoroughly in cold water, and they feel tolerably comfortable now." As the march progressed, the wind blew colder and firewood became a luxury. The troops quickly burned anything that would light.[14] "Our only chance for a fire," Hanna wrote, "was to gather old dry cow chips." Blowing sand and fierce winds made the task even more daunting. "Cooking tonight was a more desperate undertaking than it has yet been," Peticolas complained. "I was tempted to give it up two or three times."[15]

Desperate for sustenance, the army foraged among the natives, wreaking economic ruin on the tiny villages of Belén, Pajarito, Valencia, Peralta, La Joya, Sabinal, Lemitar, Bosque, Polvadera, Los Lunas, Los Chávez, Las Nutrias, and Los Lentes. Soldiers confiscated livestock, household goods, saddles and tack, cooking utensils, and even roof poles and house frames. "We had to force the alcalde to furnish wood," Smith wrote. "There is no grass or wood in this country." Foraging parties scoured the land, with some success. Pvt. William Randolph Howell found adequate food for both him and his horse in the hamlets of La Joya and Sabinal. "Get plenty [of] corn and tops for my horse and two or three tortilla dinners for myself," he wrote in his diary. Days later, as his scrounging efforts continued, he scribbled "After confiscating some goods, we set out."[16]

When foraging, the "foot-pads" of the Fourth Texas had only the leavings of their better-mounted compatriots to choose from, leading to even greater discontent. Sergeant Peticolas lamented, "We are now beginning to experience about the greatest of the manifold hardships of war. Upon the battlefield there was the fierce din of conflict and the danger to face, but we had our courage and convictions of the importance of winning the day to sustain us. . . . But to trudge along day after day with nothing to eat save beans . . . to go from early breakfast till late supper and feel the weakness and gnawing of hunger . . . is a feature of soldiering without any redeeming trait."[17] On March 3, Hanna recorded his desperation in his diary. "We are now entirely out of everything in the way of provisions and yet thirty miles to Albuquerke, our promised paradise."[18]

On March 4, Sibley's column crossed the Rio Grande to the east side. While most suffered on short rations and had to walk, several officers rode, with sacks of flour and slabs of bacon strapped to their saddles. While crossing the icy Rio Grande, some of the leaders inspired the men while others earned their contempt. "Some of the captains waded; the others crossed on horseback, being too delicate to wade," recorded Peticolas sarcastically.[19]

As the troops straggled on, the situation for the Texan rank and file looked bleak, and many began to lose heart. In some instances, this morale breakdown bordered on mutiny. "A council . . . was held to ascertain the feelings of the officers whether they were willing to travel or not," wrote Pvt. William Henry Smith. "A majority of them is opposed to going on. Starvation seems to stare us in the face." A day later, the soldier's acid pen added that "the field officers [are] drunk all the time, unfit for duty—incompetent to attend to their duty." Lieutenant Colonel Scurry of the Fourth Texas Mounted Volunteers tried unsuccessfully to resign his commission. Sibley's campaign, like his soldiers' resolve, appeared to be falling apart.[20]

Federal patrols shadowed the Texans. New Mexican militia and detachments of the First and Third U.S. Cavalry regiments triggered daily rumors and alarms among the Confederates, but no contact was made. Occasionally these roaming Northerners caused real trouble for Sibley's men. Rebel couriers, pursued by enemy troopers, destroyed a load of mail destined for the Texans to keep it from capture. The regulars also canvassed the countryside ordering the locals to hide their possessions. "The enemy have . . . persuaded the Mexicans to hide their corn and wheat," Davidson reported, "and drive their cattle and sheep beyond our reach."[21]

To ease the suffering of the troops, Col. Tom Green organized a foraging corps from among his mounted troops. Private Davidson was among those appointed. Daily, riders brought in several bushels of wheat and corn confiscated from stores and homes. Scouts occasionally discovered large caches of supplies, calling for wagons to be sent from the column to haul away the plunder. Mules, too, fell prey to the Texans. "Just below Peralto I saw an ambulance streaking up the river, and I streaked it up that way, too," Davidson wrote. He soon overtook the wagon and its two mules, abandoned, near an adobe hovel. "Both have the 'U.S.' brand upon them. I took the mules and left the ambulance; I could not find the driver although I searched every nook and corner for two miles around." These raiding expeditions sometimes resulted in running gun battles. "I got another fine mule," Davidson boasted, "but it took a ten mile race to get it, and the fellow shot at me eight times." The Yankee eventually dismounted and fled to a nearby mountain on foot. "He was nothing but a private and I did not care much about getting him."[22]

As the Confederates moved north into more populated regions, the natives received the Texans as liberators. Peticolas and a few companions happened on one Hispanic homestead while searching for food and received what appeared to be a hearty welcome. "While the boy was cooking us something to eat, the man of the house was recounting his trials with the Federals when they tried to force him into service," he wrote. "He showed us a bayonet wound where they stabbed him trying to force him along." The Fourth Texas veterans feasted on broiled beef, mush, and eggs. The family "seemed to give with a free will," Peticolas reported. "I gave him my tobacco. We told him we had no money, but he said he wanted no pay and could hardly be persuaded to take . . . tobacco."[23]

By March 7, the bulk of Sibley's army began arriving in camps near Albuquerque. "I go up to town and see several things that look a little similar to a civilized country," Private Howell reported, "dry goods stores, church, frame work about houses, and several American citizens. The Confederate Flag is waving on the splendid pole, instead of the old Stars and Stripes."[24] Half of the Fifth Texas bivouacked near town, and Sibley established his headquarters on the plaza. The rest of the army camped a few miles south on the large estate of Spruce M. Baird, the former Texan commissioner.

An ardent secessionist, Baird flew a Confederate flag from his house and welcomed the arrival of Sibley's army. He showered the men with food and firewood and entertained the brigade officers in his home. Baird also encouraged the soldiers about their prospects for success. "He says the inhabitants of the towns above are all for us and are willing to sell us anything they have on credit of our government," Peticolas wrote. "He says that in Albuquerque it would take a very strong force to get us out, and that in Santa Fe, forty thousand men would hardly do it."[25]

As the bulk of the army filed into their camps for a few days rest, restless foragers and Southern sympathizers lucked onto a bonanza of government goods. Southern partisans at the village of Cubero, sixty miles west of Albuquerque, confiscated a Federal depot that had been established before the war for an anticipated campaign against the Navajos. Capt. Sturgis Thurmond and his company from the Seventh Texas Mounted Volunteers rode to secure this capture. Meanwhile, in the mountains to the east of Albuquerque, a Union supply train headed for Fort Craig fell prey to Confederate horsemen. Altogether, these two events provided another fifty wagon loads of provisions for the starving Rebels, enough to last forty days. Commissary agents located additional food among the homes of Albuquerque—the local citizens had looted the Federal warehouses as soon as the garrison had left, and had saved nearly half the depot from the flames. Their plunder now fell into Confederate hands.[26]

While Sibley's men consolidated their gains, Sibley was secretly being assailed by his own subordinates in the Mesilla Valley. Baylor was impatient and bitter over his treatment by the general; he sincerely hated Sibley. Baylor had been superseded in command, then left behind in Mesilla in an administrative position. He quietly resumed his machinations, with Steele's encouragement, to restore his own control over the region. Knowing that the twelve-month enlistments of the Second Texas Mounted Rifles would soon expire, he encouraged those men remaining in Mesilla to return to Texas, where he would supervise their reorganization. The Indian fighter, already anxious to get back to Texas, submitted his resignation and abandoned his post without waiting for reply. As a safeguard, though, he recruited local Hispanics to draft a message in Spanish that endorsed his policies, and forwarded it to Pres. Jefferson Davis.[27]

In mid-March, Baylor's Indian raid apparently bore fruit as news arrived from Pinos Altos that Mangas Coloradas had requested a peace parley with Captain Helm. Baylor was ecstatic at the prospect of eliminating this nemesis. "You will . . . use all means to persuade the Apaches or any tribe to come in for the purpose of making peace," he wrote Helm, "and when you get them together kill all the grown Indians and take the children prisoners and sell them to defray the expense. . . ." He encouraged the captain to ply the natives with whiskey, the costs of which would be reimbursed. Secrecy was vital. "Say nothing of your orders until the time arrives," he admonished. "Leave nothing undone to insure success, and have a sufficient number of men around to allow no Indian to escape." Baylor even offered to send troops from the stay-behinds of the Second Texas to aid in the massacre. "To your judgment I entrust this important matter and look to you for success against these cursed pests. . . ." He prefaced the note, however, with a statement which would later prove to be his downfall, asserting that "the Congress of the Confederate States has passed a law declaring extermination to all hostile Indians." In fact, the Rebel government was dedicated to the old U.S. policy of pacification, and had never passed any such law. The scheming Baylor blatantly misrepresented his government's policy. To him, however, the end would justify the means.[28]

Baylor then quit the territory, meeting Sgt. Morgan Wolfe Merrick, still serving as a hospital orderly in the Mesilla Valley, a few days before his departure. "He told me I had better go to San Antonio and wait for the reorganization," Merrick wrote. "It was not exactly an order but could be so construed." The orderly, who had served as a Knight of the Golden Circle in a state company, had never formally enlisted in the Confederate army. "I was still in the service, but a sort of free lance—no one to command and no one to command me," he added. "I told him I would follow his instructions. He then told me he would see me again before he left Mesilla, and would hand me a letter that would be favorable to me in the reorganization." Merrick and two companions soon left their posts in the hospital at Fort Fillmore and began their journey back to Texas. By the end of March, Baylor boarded a stagecoach and returned to Texas to pursue his plan for empire.[29]

Baylor's ally, Colonel Steele forwarded an urgent letter to the nation's capital at the same time to facilitate his friend's rise to power. Steele deliberately sabotaged Sibley. He sent an urgent note to Richmond describing the deplorable conditions in Arizona, bitterly criticizing his superior's actions. He reported that the Federals had successfully kept all supplies out of Sibley's hands and that the Confederate Army of New Mexico might be marching to disaster. "Our army will find itself in the midst of a population . . . possessing no very friendly spirit towards us—a country nearly or quite exhausted as regards forage and other army supplies." He lambasted Sibley for willingly placing himself between two strong enemy forces. "Either of which," Steele wrote, "is too strong to assail with the means at our command." The Colonel hinted that the army might mutiny. "There is a spirit of insubordination and prejudice against General Sibley which appears to have been aggravated by the fact that [he] was sick during the battle near Fort Craig." As a final blow, Steele noted that some of the soldiers accused Sibley of "a deliberate plan to deliver his command into the hands of the enemy."[30]

Sibley had no idea of the conspiracy unfolding in Mesilla; he faced other concerns. With circumstances for his army improving, Sibley reorganized his command for continuing the campaign. The commissary department established a depot in Albuquerque, carefully shepherding all of the confiscated goods into warehouses. The pro-Southern Otero brothers—Miguel, who had represented New Mexico in Congress just prior to the war, and Rafael—turned over their fortunes and the contents of their stores to the Texans. Brigade officers detailed two units, Capt. Gotch Hardeman's Company A, Fourth Texas, and Bethel Coopwood's San Elizario Spy Company, as the Albuquerque garrison. The Confederates also created a hospital in town, which soon filled with dozens of pneumonia cases. Sibley, a keen organizer, had returned his army to a military footing. This attention to detail had an immediate and positive affect on his troops. Rations—molasses, flour, mutton, and beef—revived the soldiers and their spirits. With his army back in shape, the general renewed his call for all New Mexicans to abandon the Union cause, promising complete amnesty for those who had fought the Confederacy.[31]

One detachment of the Confederate Army of New Mexico,

however, faced difficult times and found themselves between the lines. Sibley had unencumbered his combat troops by leaving hundreds of their sick and wounded comrades at Socorro. Now these hapless troops found themselves facing starvation. Federal patrols from Fort Craig made frequent visits to the town, but offered no relief unless the stricken Texans surrendered. "If we do not," wrote Dr. Hal Hunter of the Seventh Texas, "we get nothing." Eventually, a Union detachment occupied Socorro. "They are unfeeling wretches . . . surely they would not annoy our wounded with their presence." Fit Rebels, those who had recovered from wounds or served as hospital stewards, grew increasingly annoyed at their enemy neighbors. "[The Yankees] are drunk and talking rather too glib. I fear our boys will tip some of them off their pins."[32] In response to the hospital's plight, three wagons of flour and bacon arrived in Socorro from the Confederate depot at Albuquerque. The Union troops graciously allowed the train to pass through.

Sibley charted the conquest of the rest of the territory. On March 8, shortly after arriving in Albuquerque, he ordered the bulk of the command—nine companies of the Fourth Texas and the five-company battalion of the Seventh Texas—east into the Sandia and Manzano Mountains, intending to quarter them in the sheltered canyons and valley villages. There, with an abundance of grass and wood, the men could rest, creeping north in easy marches toward the town of Galisteo, as they regained their strength. These troops would also block the main road from Fort Craig to Fort Union. Meanwhile, a mounted column composed of Maj. Charles Pyron's ad hoc battalion of Texans and Arizonans would strike north and capture Santa Fe and the Union depot only forty miles away. Four companies of the Fifth Texas Mounted Volunteers led by the recently promoted Maj. John Samuel Shropshire would stay near Albuquerque to rest their horses, then follow Pyron north. Col. Tom Green, who also faced crippling mobility problems, was to rebuild the strength of his mounts and possibly cross the Sandia Mountains. Then he was to ride toward Fort Union, blocking the eastern approach to Glorieta Pass and interdicting any Federal traffic from Santa Fe or Fort Craig. By this move, Green's troopers would turn any Northern defensive position in the Sangre de Cristos. Sibley planned for his three converging columns to fall on the last enemy stronghold by the end of the month.[33]

Preparatory to renewing the advance, Major Teel reconditioned the Rebel artillery. "He had a great deal of work to do in getting up horses, blacksmiths, and wood work on the caissons," Lt. Phil Fulcrod recalled. "Everything was put in good condition. General Sibley inspected the artillery as soon as it was reported in good condition and we commenced drilling."[34] Two guns accompanied Pyron to Santa Fe.

As the Confederates dispersed, an unexpected change in weather exposed the Texans to some of the most severe climatic conditions that occur in springtime New Mexico. As the infantry column turned east toward the Sandia Mountains, a severe sandstorm blew in from the west, sending clouds of sand and gravel stinging the Texans' backs. The hills and valleys eventually sheltered the command from the biting west wind, but the altitude brought snow. Captain Giesecke noted that "frequent showers of snow claim our exclusive attention, for we shiver around the best fire we can make, all wrapped up in our overcoats." Across the camp, Peticolas observed, that "it was amusing to see the men as they woke and looked around with bewildered expressions, raking the snow out of their hats and shoes." On the plains near Albuquerque, Private Smith and his companions shivered in the open, the camp equipment long ago abandoned due to the shortage of draft animals. "The whole face of the earth was covered with snow. It is severe upon our soldiers without any tents or anything to shelter from the snow." For the next week, the changeable weather brought beautiful days but several inches of snow at night. Privates, who tried vainly to keep their hands warm around a smoky fire made from green pine and cedar, saw little benefit to their situation. Thawing snow turned the camps into bogs. "Everything was wet and sloppy. All the soldiers were today engaged [in] drying blankets."[35]

As the soldiers made the best of the situation and settled into their camps, however, they enjoyed enough leisure time to rest, eat, and recuperate in preparation for continuing the campaign. Peticolas wrote, "the boys [are] getting rested and recruited a little, [and] are now more lively than usual." Every other night music drifted across the mountain darkness as fandangos enlivened the small adobe houses of the mountain villages. Reading materials also abounded, providing additional diversions. "I had a magazine to read, and did not suffer any inconvenience from being on guard," Peticolas added. Short novels with chivalrous Victorian titles such as *The Monk Knight of St. John* and *The King and the Cobbler* circulated through the camps. And when the troops did not dance or read, they played cards.[36]

The Texans also used their respite from campaigning to make up deficiencies in equipment. Many of the soldiers wore Federal uniforms confiscated from prisoners or pillaged from U.S. government stocks; the destitute men received some items of replacement clothing while in the mountains. The Rebels also prized tools of war, and traded among themselves. Peticolas swapped his Bowie knife for a sturdy blade, "a tremendous weapon, about 2 feet long and made of first rate metal. It is . . . more formidable in the hands of a man able to wield it than a sword." The troops also moved into the relative warmth of the Mexican houses and mountain caves—most of the brigade tents had been abandoned because of the lack of draft animals and wagons—forcing the locals to serve as unwilling hosts.[37]

In spite of the rest and refitting benefits, the stay in the mountains destroyed the health of many of the men. Private Howell, assigned as a hospital attendant in Albuquerque, lamented that a "great many more come in from the mountains and report snow all over everything, blankets and all. That foolish move out in those mountains will cause the death of many a poor fellow." Maladies from heartburn to pneumonia plagued the command. The soldiers, well stocked with medicines of questionable quality, treated diseases with the harsh cures of that time. Many began to show signs of the respiratory problems that would eventually kill them. Peticolas noted, while on outpost duty, that "the men are all lying around on the floor, some asleep and some talking in a low tone. But the coughing is distressing."[38]

As the men waited around their fires, Sibley's conquest lost its momentum. Soldiers who had anticipated a quick conclusion to the campaign after Val Verde seemed bewildered by a lack of decisive action on the part of their leaders. Four company commanders resigned.[39] Sibley, his aides, and presumably the regimental staffs also came under criticism, mostly for drinking too much. Young Private

Hanna wrote: "head quarters is generally . . . a figure head, and has never been any other way lately and never having any notion of what is ahead."[40]

The Texans' progress remained slow, and opportunity flitted away as the Federals continued to keep their supplies out of Rebel hands. In advance of the main portion of the army, Major Pyron pushed his worn mounts to make up lost time, his veterans thundering into Santa Fe on March 10, eight days after taking Albuquerque. Given that much advance notice, the Federals had easily evacuated the valuable government stores. Some 120 fully laden wagons, escorted by only 150 regulars and volunteers, had already rumbled through Glorieta Pass to the safety of Fort Union a week before. The territorial government fled northeast to the village of Las Vegas. "I am glad to say," Union Maj. J. L. Donaldson reported, "that the enemy has gained nothing along the line"[41]

The newly arriving Confederates found Santa Fe in a state of chaos, but moved quickly to set it to rights. The Federal evacuation had sparked a wave of looting as the local population plundered government property. Pyron's troops returned order. The wives and families of several U.S. officers, including Louisa Canby, had remained behind, and welcomed the Texans as a stabilizing force, thankful to have the riots ended. The pro-Union *Santa Fe Gazette,* abandoned by its owners, resumed operation as a Confederate press, Sibley's amnesty offer being among the first documents printed and distributed. In the town square, Northern troops had chopped down the flagpole; Southerners replaced the mast and had the Stars and Bars flying within days. Confederate troops now occupied the capital of New Mexico, but total victory eluded them.[42]

On March 20, Major Shropshire left Albuquerque to reinforce Pyron. Evidence abounded of continued Union vigilance in the area as Texan foragers and Federal patrols clashed. Private Davidson and three companions happened upon several companies of enemy cavalry in the hills south of Santa Fe. "As we rose [atop] one mountain . . . they appeared on the top of another, two miles distant. We kept counting until we reached a hundred, when they charged us." The Texans turned and fled. "We made those . . . 'Yanks' run ten miles faster than they ever did before in their lives." After a suspenseful chase, the shaken Confederates rejoined Shropshire's column and the Federals gave up the pursuit. By March 22, the two hundred additional Rebels joined Pyron in the capital.[43]

Elsewhere, the haphazard Confederate advance also returned to life, although fitfully. On March 21, Lt. Colonel Scurry started his column north toward the mining town of Galisteo, strategically located almost equidistant from Santa Fe and Albuquerque. Pyron and Shropshire, meanwhile, remained ensconced in Santa Fe, patrolling occasionally. Green and his men, however, idled at Albuquerque, unable or unwilling to begin their turning movement to the northeast.[44]

Scurry's men, the principal Confederate column, kept to a leisurely four-day pace as they marched to the new bivouac. Even though the troops complained about the rough country through which the hilly road traveled, many marveled at the spectacular panoramas. Peticolas wrote, "The mountain scenery in places is picturesque and interesting, but an air of desolate lonesomeness reigns over the whole country." Many of the men got their first view of a gold mining operation as they marched past the open pits and steam-operated ore crushers at the village of Real de Dolores. Soldiers, enjoying the diversions of the march, used prairie dogs along the route for target practice, while mounted foragers took sheep and goats taken from ranches along the way to feed the column. Some Texans brought in pregnant ewes. "When many of them were opened," Sharp Whitley of the Seventh Texas reported, "the lambs that came out of them were able to get up and walk." Unknown to these distracted troops, enemy patrols were only twenty miles away.[45]

The lumbering progress of Sibley's army had aided the Federals immensely, furnishing them with ample time to recover, react and save the territory for the United States. Colonel Canby remained at Fort Craig with 1,800 regulars and New Mexico volunteers, but he had rallied his beaten army, rebuilding the confidence lost at Val Verde. Meanwhile, the few regulars at Fort Union, northeast of Santa Fe, erected a star-shaped earthwork complete with bombproofs, making the post virtually impregnable to Rebel attack. The Texans' slow progress had also allowed Union reinforcements, 900 miners of Col. John P. Slough's First Colorado Volunteers, to arrive on March 10, after a grueling march that covered four hundred miles in thirteen days. Their arrival raised the number of Federal troops in the Fort Union garrison to more than 1,342. While Sibley's combined force outnumbered either element of the opposing army, Canby's or Slough's, it would be hard-pressed to continue garrisoning both Albuquerque and Santa Fe, while defeating the enemy in detail. If the Northern armies united, the Confederate invaders faced disaster.[46]

Colonel Paul had already made plans to unite with Canby. He had marshaled a strike force composed mostly of his regulars and the newly arrived Coloradans and had planned on rendezvousing with the other Union army in New Mexico, somewhere east of Albuquerque. Canby instead urged caution. "Fort Union must be held and our communications with the East kept open. All other points are of no importance." Canby, although ordering Paul stay put, did urge active patrolling as long as the security of Fort Union was not in jeopardy. "Harass the enemy by partisan operations; obstruct his movements and remove any supplies that might fall into his hands." He clarified his intentions by repeating "Do not move from Fort Union to meet me until I advise you of the route and point of junction."[47]

By the time Canby's orders reached Fort Union, however, Colonel Paul was no longer in command. Colonel Slough of the First Colorado, a short-tempered martinet who at one time had been suspected as a Southern sympathizer, held his rank for a few weeks longer than Paul and claimed seniority. Informed that the hotheaded Colorado colonel now commanded the Fort Union garrison, Canby dispatched another note north. "Keep your command prepared to make a junction with this force," he wrote. "I will indicate time and route." Canby knew that the Rebels faced a difficult strategic situation. Fort Craig could hold out for another three months, and Sibley was trapped between two strong and well-provisioned forts. He wrote confidently that "the question is not of saving [Fort Craig], but of saving New Mexico and defeating the Confederates in such a way that an invasion of this Territory will never again be attempted." He again directed the Fort Union garrison to annoy the Texans. "Use the mounted volunteers for these purposes and keep the regular cavalry in reserve. Feed their horses well." Fearing that Slough might indeed try and engage the Rebels single-handed, Canby added "If you . . . act independently against the enemy, advise me of your plans and movements, that I may cooperate. In this you must be governed by your own judgment but nothing must be left to chance."[48]

Despite the talk of command unity and strategic coordination, the leaders of the Union forces, hundreds of miles apart and separated by a powerful enemy army, both moved independently to seize the strategic initiative. On March 22, Canby cautiously started patrols up the Rio Grande past Socorro—he planned a bold march on Albuquerque within a fortnight. He remained uninformed, however, as to the movements of his counterpart at Fort Union. That same day, the impetuous Slough, stretching his order to "harass the enemy" as far as possible, launched an offensive from that post with a 1,300-man force divided into two columns. The 418-man advance element was under Maj. John Chivington of the First Colorado—a Methodist minister turned soldier—and consisted of three infantry and one mounted company from his regiment and 150 troopers from the First and Third U.S. Cavalry regiments. The main force, commanded by Colonel Slough, was composed of six companies of the First Colorado, Capt. Hiram Ford's independent company of Colorado Volunteers, a handful of New Mexico volunteers, and various unassigned and detached troops from the First and Third U.S. Cavalries. In addition, a few companies of the Fifth U.S. Infantry served and supported two artillery batteries—one of four field guns under Capt. John F. Ritter, and one of four mountain howitzers under the command of Lt. Ira Claflin. While unwary Rebel troops tramped up mountain by-ways and roamed the streets of Albuquerque and Santa Fe, bold and formidable blue columns snaked up the Rio Grande and down the Santa Fe Trail.[49]

Colonel Paul, wounded over being superseded in command and concerned over the safety of his troops and his fort, fired off an angry note to officials in Washington. "I wrote [Colonel Slough] urging him to leave me a part of the troops for the defense of this post. To this letter he paid no attention whatever and left with his column. I am thus left with a feeble garrison and no suitable artillery for the defense of the principal and most important post in the Territory. My object in this communications is to throw the responsibility of any disaster which may occur on the right shoulders."[50]

News of these Federal movements arrived quickly at Sibley's headquarters in Albuquerque. Shocked out of lethargy, the general ordered his two mounted columns to probe for the now-mobile enemy. Colonel Green led his six companies out of their camps and down the road toward Fort Craig to fix Canby's position in a quick reconnaissance before resuming the march through the mountains toward Fort Union.[51] At the same time, Rebel Majors Charles Pyron and Sam Shropshire led some 380 of the Santa Fe garrison east along the Santa Fe Trail to ascertain Slough's intentions. On March 25, this command camped at the entrance to Apache Canyon, the western side of Glorieta Pass, in the southern Sangre de Cristo mountains. Pyron led his force into the defile the next day, his weary men fatigued from hard riding and a frosty, sleepless night. Meanwhile, he ordered forward a number of pickets through the canyon and over the pass to watch for the Federals.[52]

That same week, hundreds of miles to the southwest, Confederate Capt. Sherod Hunter had moved against the other Union army exerting pressure on the Confederate Empire, James H. Carleton's California Volunteers. From Tucson, the Rebels had pressed even further west, establishing contacts with the friendly Pima, Papago, and Maricopa Indians on the Gila River while breaking up Union operations. At the "Pima Villages," Hunter arrested Unionist Ami White, destroyed his flour mill, and confiscated several hundred sacks of wheat intended for the California Column. "This I distributed among the Indians," Hunter reported, "as I had no means of transportation, and deemed this a better policy of disposing of it than to destroy or leave it for the benefit of the enemy." Also at the Pima villages, Hunter and his troops enjoyed another important triumph. Capt. William McCleve and nine men of the First California Cavalry rode unaware to White's Mill, expecting to find dispatches from Colonel Canby. Instead, they were promptly surrounded and captured.[53]

Hunter, now encumbered by eleven prisoners, divided his command. The captain and most of his unit returned to Tucson, where his men took quarters in private buildings and stabled their horses at the old Overland Mail lot. Meanwhile, a small detachment continued west on the stage road, destroying caches of hay at abandoned mail stations to deny its use to the Federals. These daring

Confederates ventured to within eighty miles of Fort Yuma and the California border. At Stanwix Station, a series of windmills on the south bank of the Gila River, two Union pickets refused to surrender when confronted by the Rebel raiders on March 23. The Southerners fired, striking one of the Californians in the shoulder as he rode away. After receiving news of the affair, a detachment from Company D, First California Cavalry, pursued the Confederates for several miles, but turned back at dusk. Tucson and western Arizona had fallen to the empire, but the California Column—over a thousand men strong—was coming to take it back.[54]

In the last week of March, the Confederate Empire was at its greatest expanse. In the north, Confederate troops occupied Santa Fe, strengthening the Southern claim to New Mexico, and Majors Pyron and Shropshire maintained their post in Apache Canyon, guarding against a Union move through Glorieta Pass against the territorial capital. The territory's other major town, Albuquerque, served as Sibley's headquarters as well as the Rebel supply depot, and housed 150 veterans. To the south, Colonel Green and his four hundred horsemen protected the Rebel depot from Canby's advance. Halfway between these two towns, Lieutenant Colonel Scurry led the largest Confederate element, one thousand men, in an easy march toward the north. Sibley's plan was in motion and his forces—the Army of New Mexico—were scattered, no longer able to converge quickly on Fort Union. Distance and momentum prevented any sudden changes. Instead, outside of the original mission, the Confederates were limited to reacting to Federal initiatives.

Even farther south, Colonel Steele and six hundred men held the Mesilla Valley and Confederate Arizona. At Pinos Altos, a few dozen men stood guard while the miners carved out their meager livings. Governor Baylor of Arizona, his resignation resting in Steele's Mesilla office, was already back in Texas, advancing his own version of empire. Far to the west, Captain Hunter and his command waited to serve—either as the vanguard for the empire's drive to the Pacific, or as its first line of resistance. From Tucson to Santa Fe, the Texans had unwittingly—and prematurely—assumed the defensive.

CHAPTER 10

Empire Repelled

There is a sort of gloom resting on the company.
—5th Sgt. Alfred B. Peticolas, Victoria, Texas

"The weather was so cold, and our covering so light, that we could not sleep much at night," wrote Pvt. Bill Davidson. On March 26, Majors Charles Pyron and John Shropshire had led their troops into Apache Canyon to block the road to Santa Fe and to shelter their men from the cold wind. None of the 380 Confederates had managed to get much rest the previous night, so the officers let the troops nap during the warmth of the following day. The various companies scattered across the canyon, selecting soft ground on which to spread their blankets. Pockets of snow still clung to patches of shade along the granite walls. As a precaution, Pyron sent fifty men forward to the summit of Glorieta Pass and beyond to warn of any enemy approach. By the time the New Mexico sun had burned away the chill of the previous night, the Texans and Arizonans had peacefully drifted to sleep.[1]

"We were rudely awaked by a volley of gunfire fired into camp," Davidson continued. "In a moment, every fellow was on his feet, gun in hand." That morning, Maj. John Chivington and his command—the vanguard of Col. John Slough's command from Fort Union—had unexpectedly forged ahead on the Santa Fe trail and captured the Rebel pickets as they played cards at Pigeon's Ranch, a few miles east of Glorieta Pass. The Federals had then surprised another twenty Rebels without a shot at the summit of the pass. Encouraged by his early success, Chivington had continued over the pass and into Apache Canyon to where Pyron and his three hundred men snoozed unsuspecting.[2]

Although caught by surprise, Pyron's and Shropshire's veterans scrambled into battle. Unfurling a red flag bearing a single white star, the two Confederate six-pounders started firing on the advancing enemy as the rest of Pyron's troops tried to reorganize. Two bursts of canister from the guns stopped the Federal advance for a moment, allowing the Texans to withdraw their pieces. Chivington, after rallying his men, directed them to scale the canyon walls to envelop the Southerners and to pursue the retreating cannon. "Pyron and Shropshire [moved] back and forth calm, cool, and deliberately restoring order and forming us in line to meet the foe." The Texan effort, however, failed, and almost immediately the fight became a confusing melee as the two forces intermingled. As Union soldiers fired down at the milling Texans, Pyron ordered his men to form a line further back down the canyon in a narrower, more defensible position. Company C "got into a kind of pocket so that the enemy was on three sides," Davidson wrote. "Here [they] lost a good many . . . men. But by dint of hard fighting and good running, [they] finally got [out] to us." As his troops fell back, Pyron dispatched a courier with orders to locate Lt. Col. William Read Scurry and hurry his command forward.[3]

The Federals continued advancing on the Texans, enveloping both of the Rebel flanks while keeping the mounted Coloradans and some regulars in reserve. The fighting soon became a series of individual gun battles, the Confederate artillery proving ineffective against the open enemy formations. The Unionists' greater numbers began to tell as they overlapped the Texan lines, gaining the rear. Pyron again ordered his men to retreat, this time forming them across the mouth of a valley that ran perpendicular into Apache Canyon. Gunners again hastily limbered their pieces and hauled them to safety but triggered a moment of uncertainty in the Southern ranks. The Texan line dissolved in panic, and Pyron's force scattered into separate clusters of men trying to fight their way out of the trap. Taking advantage of this confusion, Chivington ordered his horsemen forward. Scores of Texan muskets, shotguns, and pistols fired on the advancing cavalry, dropping the lead captain's horse and hitting the officer in the thigh and foot, but the Unionists kept coming. Jumping an arroyo and riding directly into the Rebel ranks, the one hundred–man column scattered dozens of their disoriented enemies, capturing many. The Confederates had been surprised, and now routed.[4]

In the swirling skirmish, Davidson's company was cut off from the rest of Pyron's troops and faced disaster. Major Shropshire, who had originally commanded the unit, galloped through Union fire to rescue his friends and neighbors. "Like an avalanche he came to us . . . in his eyes . . . there gleamed the fierce light of battle. The storm cloud of war rested dark upon his brow." Reining in his mount, Shropshire ordered the beleaguered troops to draw their Bowie knives and follow him to the new line. The Federals yelled "shoot . . . the man on the white horse," Davidson recalled. "This may account for why they were overshooting us." The men of Company A eventually reached the third, and final, Confederate line. Over twenty, though, were missing. "Shropshire was a noble man, but on that particular day and at that particular time he was grand, mighty and magnificent."[5]

Chivington decided to pursue the Rebels no further. Counting the pickets he captured earlier, the Colorado major had taken seventy-five prisoners. With the enemy in flight and the conditions farther down the canyon unknown, Chivington recalled his troops and retired toward Pigeon's Ranch. Unknown to him at the time, he had just inflicted the most crushing defeat to the Texans thus far.[6]

Both the Federals and Confederates retreated after the fight to count their casualties and gather reinforcements for continuing the struggle. Major Pyron's force had been mauled: besides the dozens of prisoners, the Texan lost four killed and twenty wounded. With nearly a third of his command lost, Pyron fell back to the mouth of Apache Canyon to dig in and wait for Scurry. Chivington and his men, meanwhile, fell back past Pigeon's Ranch to where Colonel Slough and the main column waited. In the Union advance column, the Battle of Apache Canyon had claimed five killed and fourteen wounded. Slough had intended to harass the enemy, and so far the results had been amazing.[7]

Lt. Col. John M. Chivington, 1st Colorado Infantry, circa 1862.
Courtesy Colorado Historical Society, Denver.

Meanwhile, Scurry received Pyron's frantic dispatch late in the afternoon of March 26, while his men loitered at the mining town of Galisteo. He ordered his footsore troops to march immediately to Johnson's Ranch, fifteen miles distant over the mountains. The Texans gathered their equipment and fell into ranks on the road;

then, with the sun setting, they began the trek northward. Sgt. Alfred Peticolas wrote, "We started off at a brisk gait and made the first six miles of our journey in a very little time, but footsore and weary we did not travel from that point so fast as we had been doing, but there was no murmuring at our suffering. . . . Every man marched bravely along and did not complain at the length of the road, the coldness of the weather or the necessity that compelled the march." At 3:30 A.M., the column reached Johnson's Ranch.[8]

"I was glad to see them," Davidson wrote upon Scurry's arrival. "I thought they were the finest looking men I ever saw in my life." The reunited Texans then spent the night discussing the day's events. Pyron and Scurry reviewed their few options: The victorious Federals, they believed, would be back in force at daybreak. The Texans opted for defense.[9]

The next day, Confederate officers and men prepared to receive what they considered an inevitable Federal attack. Soldiers dug rifle pits atop a small, steep-sided hill covering the entrance to Apache Canyon. This knoll would provide the Texans with a clear field of fire at an approaching enemy, who would be clustered together along the road in the narrow defile. Artillerymen emplaced Pyron's two guns, along with the two brought up with Scurry, in strong positions behind the infantry line. Sharpshooters deployed along the rocky slopes of the canyon to flank any Yankee attack. The various companies of the Second, Fourth, Fifth, and Seventh Texas then rested and waited, the men cooking supper while teamsters and quartermasters parked the supply trains alongside a creek, beyond the anticipated line of fire.[10]

Scurry understood Sibley's intentions. He, Pyron, and Shropshire would block Glorieta Pass. There, the army would wait for Green to pass over the Sandia Mountains to the south with his three hundred horsemen and arrive behind Slough, cutting off his retreat. Then, the northern division of the Union army in New Mexico could be surrounded and destroyed in the field. Scurry, however, like his Union antagonist, was not a patient man.[11]

After spending March 27 burying the dead and fruitlessly waiting in ambush, Scurry decided to find the Federals the following morning. He anticipated locating the enemy retreating somewhere beyond Glorieta Pass toward Fort Union and he planned to attack

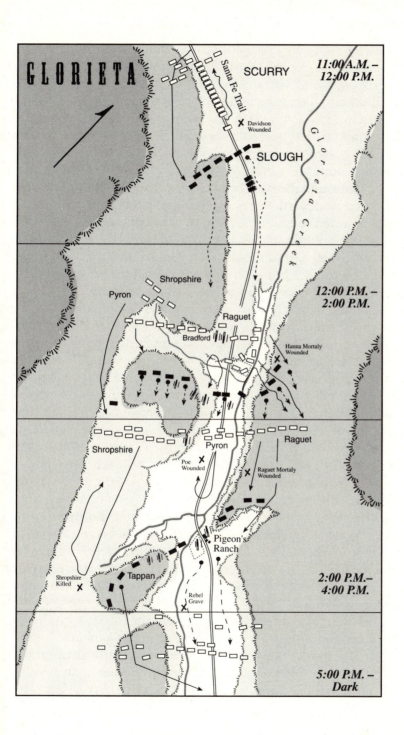

GLORIETA

11:00 A.M. –
12:00 P.M.

Santa Fe Trail

SCURRY

Glorieta Creek

X Davidson
Wounded

SLOUGH

12:00 P.M. –
2:00 P.M.

Shropshire

Pyron

Raguet

Bradford

Hanna Mortaly
Wounded

Shropshire

Pyron

Raguet

Poe
Wounded

Raguet Mortaly
Wounded

Pigeon's
Ranch

2:00 P.M.–
4:00 P.M.

Shropshire
Killed
X

Tappan

Rebel
Grave
X

5:00 P.M. –
Dark

them and maintain contact until Green could come up. Leaving a six-pounder field piece atop the hill at Johnson's Ranch at the mouth of the canyon, along with small details to guard the wagons, more than a thousand Texans marched along the Santa Fe Trail, heading generally eastward toward the enemy. Late that morning, the Rebel column, with mounted troops under Shropshire and Jordan in advance, passed the summit of Glorieta Pass, William Kirk and the now infamous "Brigands" in the lead. At 11:00 A.M., the "sharp report of a gun, and the sharper whistle of a minnie ball," Peticolas reported, revealed Northern troops in line of battle, 250 yards down the road. Private Davidson, riding at the head of the Texan column, fell in the first volley with a bullet through his thigh. A cocky Coloradan called out "Get out of our way you damned sons of bitches, we are going to take our dinner in Santa Fe!" The irascible Kirk responded "You'll take dinner in hell!" as the Brigands and the rest of the mounted Rebels quickly withdrew and dismounted, and the infantry and artillery came forward.[12]

Union commander Colonel Slough, unwittingly mimicking his Texan counterpart, had waited a day for the enemy advance as his own forces concentrated, and then also returned to the offensive on March 28. He expected Pyron to have been reinforced—maybe with an additional four hundred men—but assumed that the supposed outnumbered Rebels would maintain their position in Apache Canyon. He was surprised to encounter the Rebels in the pass, for he had planned to trap them near Johnson's Ranch between his forces and those of Chivington, which had departed on a flank march early that morning. The combined Union columns would then envelop and overwhelm the outnumbered Texans from front and rear. Slough's calculations, like his enemy's, were all wrong. Scurry, east of the summit of the pass, now enjoyed a numerical superiority; Chivington and his four hundred troopers were too far away to help the Federals now. The hard-pressed Coloradans and regulars gave ground.[13]

Colonel Slough deployed two heavy flanking forces, while keeping his guns and a heavy reserve in the center. Company I, First Colorado, composed mostly of Germans, moved forward on the Union right, while Company D went left. Three other infantry companies supported the Union guns while the some seventy regulars

Col. John P. Slough, 1st Colorado Infantry, circa 1862. Courtesy Colorado Historical Society, Denver.

from the First, Second, and Third U.S. Cavalries remained as a mounted reserve.[14]

The Texans recovered from the surprise encounter and maneuvered to gain a positional advantage over the enemy. Scurry deployed his troops across the little valley where the pines, rocks, and gullies reduced visibility, causing confusion as the soldiers advanced.

Major Pyron commanded the right, aided by Major Shropshire, and pushed the Federals from the brow of a small hill, across a boggy draw, and onto a second ridge line one hundred yards away. In the center, the Texans placed three guns atop the captured rise as Scurry pointed to gunners and told them where to shoot. The rugged terrain was already causing companies to become intermingled, and few soldiers had a clear view of the enemy. "We could not see anything in the world to shoot at," Peticolas wrote, "but Scurry must have seen them." The Confederate leader decided on a ruse to provide his troops with better targets. He turned to the company directly supporting the artillery and issued some perplexing orders. "We were instructed to run like we were scared to death when our cannon fired," reported Corporal Sharp Whitley of the Seventh Texas. The troops, following his unusual wishes, feigned a route. The opposing Coloradans could not believe their fortune and rushed from behind cover to capture the Rebels guns before they reloaded. "They came within twenty steps . . . when a lot of men that Scurry had concealed . . . rose up and began peppering them, and they began getting away as fast as their legs could take them. . . . This is the only time in a annals of history that anybody ever tricked a Yankee."[15]

The fighting became a contest of skirmishers. "The character of the country," Slough reported, "was such as to make the engagement of the bushwhacking kind." Soldiers drew their pistols as they sought targets amid the cedars. On the left, a gully bordered by a fenced field cut across the level ground in the bottom of the pass, causing the companies there under Maj. Henry Raguet to bunch up and stop short of the high ground beyond. The Texan advance stalled. Even as increasing numbers of Southerners added their muskets to the fight, the Federals consolidated their position atop the second rise and stubbornly resisted.[16]

The Texan advance faltered in the face of the increased Union fire; two Federal batteries on the opposite ridge began throwing case shot and shell into the Rebel lines. Bullets whistled among the Confederate artillerymen, one gunner falling across the barrel of his piece, shot through the heart. Dying horses writhed in their harnesses, as additional soldiers fell. Soon, Federal bullets were striking the Rebel positions from both the front and the left. Section commander Lt. James Bradford, himself wounded, ordered the guns withdrawn behind the hill. The supporting infantry of the Fourth Texas took cover behind the pine posts of a nearby field. "To this fence a good many of us repaired when the firing grew hot," Peticolas wrote. Scurry furiously ordered two of his guns back into action, then tried to organize and rally his scattered command. The Brigands, answering his call, gamely rolled the cannons forward under fire.[17]

As the Texans fought the stubborn Federals, Confederate reinforcements, Scurry's now-dismounted troops, hurried up the road to rejoin the battle, passing the casualties of the earlier fighting. "We found Davidson on the side of the road, his pipe in his mouth, cursing the world and the Yankees," one soldier observed. The wounded private had removed his uniform coat and pants to dress his wound. "He . . . was tearing up his shirt and tying it around his leg." When asked how he was doing, the stricken soldier could only reply that the "Yankees had ruined his breeches—tore two big holes in them."[18]

As the fighting intensified, the Federals faced a daunting problem. The high slopes of the valley would enable the numerically superior Texans to overlap either flank. Riding with his mounted reserve, Slough scaled the eastern hillside to survey his line. The fighting was then raging near the junction of two ravines. However, far to the left, the ground rolled gently toward Glorieta Mesa, giving the Confederates an easy path to the rear of the Union line. Lt. Col. Samuel Tappan of the First Colorado brought Slough's attention to two hills, one behind the other in the valley floor, that would serve as a natural position to oppose such an enemy move. These knolls, coupled with Pigeon's Ranch in the center and a rocky precipice to the right, would serve nicely as a fall-back position. Slough dispatched Tappan with just twenty-five men to cover the huge interval between the Union left and the hills.[19]

As Slough feared, the Southerners' superior numbers began to tell as the opposing forces attempted to outflank each other. Confederates on the right fired from behind trees, reloaded, then advanced a few paces to fire again, pinning the Yankees behind cover. "The firing . . . began to be very rapid and hot," Peticolas remembered. Soon the Texans had worked around the Union position, sending bullets ricocheting amongst the rocks; almost surrounded, the Coloradans here withdrew. "We heard a cheer from Pyron's and Shropshire's men announcing that the enemy was retiring there." On the Texan left, the Germans of Company I, First Colorado, had penetrated the Rebel line, advancing under cover of the ravine. The Yankees, who had been firing rapidly into the Texans, emerged from the ditch intending to capture Scurry's guns as they withdrew; instead, they found themselves overrun by scores of Raguet's troops, who "dashed down upon them with a yell and, plunging into the gully, came to a hand-to-hand conflict with them." The Texan shotguns were especially devastating at close quarters. "We reakon they thought an earthquake had struck them. . . . [The] old *swie*-barrel gun did the business." In the melee, several Northerners were killed or wounded by Texan knives and pistols. Five of the Germans surrendered, and the rest scattered up the northern slope of the valley. Discouraged that his companies were being overwhelmed piecemeal, Colonel Slough ordered his troops and guns to withdraw across the half-mile of open fields in front of Pigeon's Ranch into the third series of hills. To cover the retreat, the frontier veterans of Company E, Third U.S. Cavalry dismounted and scaled the eastern slope of the valley.[20]

The entire Confederate line surged forward to press their advantage but company cohesion disintegrated as individuals continued fighting their own private battles. Peticolas and a companion followed Pyron and Shropshire to the right; the rest of his company moved on to the extreme left to engage some U.S. regulars threatening the Texan flank. Major Pyron, seeing the Federal cavalrymen taking cover, recklessly galloped into the open to warn Scurry. A well-aimed Union cannon ball tore his horse's head off, tumbling the officer and his mutilated mount into a heap. Shaken but unhurt, Pyron removed his pistols from their saddle holsters and finished his errand. In response, dozens of men, among them the Victoria County men of Company C, Fourth Texas, pressed uphill as the Northerners fired rapidly upon them. As the opposing soldiers closed to within thirty yards, sixteen-year-old Abe Hanna fell, a bullet breaking his spine in the lower back before severing a major vein in his pelvis. One Texan knelt to aid the grievously wounded teenager; he quickly fell dead after a minié ball entered his shoulder and ranged through the length of his body. The Federals on the hillside, having dropped several of their enemies, withdrew under pressure of the Rebel attack, surrendering the field to Raguet and his men.[21]

The battle had scrambled the Confederate command as soldiers relied on sounds of battle to maintain the advance. "We could see no distance along our line and only knew that we were advancing from the fact that the firing was going back all the time," Corp. Whitley of the Seventh Texas remembered. The officers of the brigade would "pass along by us once in a while and encourage us, and tell us how it was going at other points. There was and could be no regular order in that place and where the firing became most rapid we would work our way to help our side."[22]

The firing died down by early afternoon, as the Confederates stopped short of the open fields and deployed along the second line of hills; Scurry surveyed the strong Union position across the valley. On his left, atop the high, steep ridge composing the north slope of the pass, blue-uniformed troops could barely be seen taking cover behind the huge boulders that studded its side. To his right, two hills running one behind the other down the middle of the valley, anchored that end of the Federal line. In the gap between the eastern slope and hills, the adobe ranch buildings and stockaded corral wall of Pigeon's Ranch, bordered by the Santa Fe Trail and a small creek, afforded the enemy a strong fortification. A granite precipice jutted out from the valley's eastern slope and afforded the Yankees a clear view of the entire area. Everywhere, save the ranch itself, Slough's Coloradans and regulars held the high ground, with plenty of trees and rocks to provide cover. It would be a difficult position to carry.[23]

Scurry could not see the enemy clearly but believed that one more solid push would drive them from the field. To complete his victory, Scurry organized his jumbled command into three columns. "Major Shropshire was ordered sent to the right, with orders to move up among the pines until he should find the enemy. . . . Major Raguet, with similar orders, was dispatched to the left." Scurry would lead the men in the center, himself, in an assault of the adobe corral wall in front of Pigeon's Ranch. First, however, he would use his artillery to draw the Union fire.[24]

Across the valley, Union Colonel Slough was worried; he had not really recovered from the shock of finding the Confederates so far forward. The terrain added to his apprehension because the enemy, too, was hard to see. "The fighting was done in thick covers of cedars, and having met the enemy where he was not expected the action was defensive from its beginning to its end," he explained. He knew his small army held a strong position, but he worried that it could not last long against the superior numbers of the Texans. His only hope, he believed, was for Major Chivington to ride to the sound of the guns, descending from the mountain to the west to strike Scurry's rear. Slough sent a lieutenant of his staff to find the major and his horsemen and to lead them into the battle.[25]

Lieutenant Colonel Tappan meanwhile hurried to organize his defense of the Federal left. Knowing that two dozen men were inadequate to hold the critical hills, he sought any other unassigned troops to bolster his defense. Behind Pigeon's Ranch, seventy-five soldiers serving as the wagon guard stood idly alongside the road. Tappan ordered these troops to follow him up the hillside, where he deployed them as skirmishers in a great arc, three-quarters of a mile long. "This position commanded the valley in part," he wrote. "The irregularities of the surface afforded excellent protection for the men from the fire of the enemy."[26]

The battle resumed with an uneven artillery duel. While the Rebel infantrymen took their positions, the two six-pounders rumbled down the road, crewed by trained gunners and eager volunteers. From the safety of cover, Peticolas watched as the "artillery was ordered up to tear the corrals to pieces," probing for the Union guns. The gunners quickly placed their pieces then began shelling the ranch. The four Federal field guns—two twelve-pound howitzers and two six-pounders—cooperated by returning the Confederates' fire, supported by four mountain howitzers and Union marksmen. The Federal fire was effective, and almost immediately a round shot struck one of the Texan guns on the muzzle, dismounting the barrel and smashing the carriage. Next a limber box exploded. Pvt. William Kirk, urging the desperadoes of the Brigands on, fell heavily with a gunshot wound in the leg. The Southern artillery was doomed. With the crews falling, and their equipment destroyed, the Confederate battery commander ordered the pieces withdrawn, leaving the Union gunners in control of the field. Scurry had found the enemy guns.[27]

Around 3:00 P.M. Major Shropshire launched his attack, leading whatever soldiers he could find on a right oblique, aiming for the hill where he assumed the enemy to be. "Up we went," Peticolas wrote, "taking advantage of every bush and tree to shelter us." As the troops struggled over the broken ground and scrub brush, many of the Texans took cover and straggled off. "There was then not over ten men each in [the] companies," Whitley reported. Some soldiers of the Seventh Texas, dressed in captured Union overcoats and uniforms, made contact first. "A party approached my line, dressed in the uniform of the Colorado Volunteers," Lt. Colonel Tappan wrote. He hoped that they were Chivington's men arriving from their raid. "They were allowed to come within a few paces of us when . . . recognizing them as Texans, my men were ordered to fire." The stunned Confederates fell back through the trees.[28]

Major Shropshire, with about fifty men, pressed on as Texans stumbled to the rear. He tried to rally the men, telling them to "come on and take that position, or stay back and look at men who would." A few turned and rejoined the advance, as Shropshire dismounted and led his squad blindly through the trees. After advancing a few dozen yards, a volley cut through the brush and into the Confederates. Shropshire, now aware of the ambush and seeing several Union troops just thirty feet away in the woods, raised his hand and motioned to his troops. "By the time his hand was even with his head, the fatal bullet went crashing through his scull," fifteen-year-old Private J. H. Richardson of the Seventh Texas remembered. "I was looking at him when the minie ball cut his hat band." Capt. Charles Buckholts of Milam County and three others also fell. The Texans fled, leaving their dead. Capt. Denman Shannon, stunned by the sudden burst of gunfire, surrendered. "Finally we rallied some, about 50 yards from where the ambush was, and shielded ourselves behind trees," Richardson added. Soldiers of the First Colorado sprang from their cover to pursue the enemy and loot the bodies. "I took two shots at four Yanks who came down to Shropshire to take his pair of ivory handled six-shooters and his watch. I shot with my double barrel shot gun with buck and ball— you ought to have seen them git when I opened on them." The assault then degenerated into a confused gun battle, with men sniping at each other from behind cover.[29]

Peticolas, dressed in a captured uniform, had become separated from the main body of Confederates and passed through the heavy foliage undetected. To the left of Shropshire's advance, Peticolas had heard the volley that killed the major, and had inadvertently moved through the Union lines figuring incorrectly that it was his comrades that were driving the Federals back. He remained ignorant of his mistake as he found himself alone on the edge of the hill, overlooking the enemy artillery in the valley below. "I began to take part in the battle again by . . . firing at every opportunity down at the enemy." While reloading after his sixth shot, Peticolas turned to his right to find a blood-chilling sight. "I . . . to my astonishment, saw that I was in two feet of a line of 100 men, all strangers to me." He had stumbled onto some of the Colorado volunteers, positioned in the woods to support the artillery. "I thought, well, I'm a prisoner after all." The Federals, however, mistook the Texan for one of their own. "The major of the enemy . . . said, looking straight into my face, 'you had better watch out . . . or those fellows will shoot you.'" The Northerner was motioning to some approaching Confederates. "Who will?," Peticolas nervously asked. "Why those fellows over yonder, there are two or three of them shooting at us." Peticolas saw his chance to escape. "'Is there,' said I. 'Then I'll go over that way and take a shot at them.' I started off with my gun at charge bayonets . . . as if advancing on a real foe. . . . In a dozen steps further I was out of sight and over in our own lines once more . . . thanking an overriding Providence for my escape."[30]

Scurry, his face bleeding from a grazing wound, observed the repulse on the right and sent his troops in the center forward to try to retrieve the situation. The Federals kept up a steady fire on the advancing Texans, forcing them to take cover. Pvt. Henry C. Wright, before he advanced, made a pact with his hometown friend and bunkmate, John Poe: If one was wounded, the other would see to their safety. As the Rebels left their cover and started across the open toward the Union center, Poe jerked backwards and rolled along the ground, a gunshot wound in the chest. One of Poe's uniform buttons had been driven into the wound. Wright recovered his friend and dragged him behind a tree, promising to return after the charge.

"I pressed on, caring for nothing but to avenge my friend." His determination was futile. Behind the corral wall, Ritter's Battery, the target of the Texan assault, threw canister among the Rebels, killing several more and dispersing the rest, including Wright. The fleeing Southerners, once they had found protection behind an out-building, tree, or wall, returned the fire.[31]

The Confederate advance stalled, and the battle turned into a blazing firefight, rifle duels adding to the list of casualties. All along the front the Texans, disorganized and now fighting in squads, kept up a steady fire on the Union positions. Yankee gunners, exposed as they reloaded their pieces, fell as bullets ricocheted off the dried mud wall. Between the lines lay the casualties—men mangled by canister, others bleeding to death from painful body wounds.[32]

On the Texans' left, Majors Raguet and Pyron at last started their advance, ordering their men to scale the north slope of the valley and drive the Federals from the ridge. The men crossed a small creek and arroyo and then began their attack. Colorado troops fired down at the Texans, but without effect. Atop the rocky precipice, dis-mounted cavalrymen fired their carbines, enfilading the Rebel line, again without stopping the assault; Raguet's men rapidly closed the distance between the lines, the firing becoming point-blank. "The intrepid Raguet and the cool, calm, courageous Pyron had pushed forward among the rocks, until the muzzles of the guns of the op-posing forces passed each other," Scurry reported. "Inch by inch was the ground disputed." Outnumbered and overrun, the Union-ists retreated, covered by Ritter's Battery firing from the ranch.[33]

The Federal right had been turned, and the situation of the Union center soon became desperate. The Confederates pursued along the top of the ridge while Scurry's troops, who had taken cover in the fields below, renewed their advance toward Pigeon's Ranch. Yankee cavalrymen, veterans of years on the frontier, desperately pushed cartridges into their breech-loading carbines and fired at the oncom-ing Texans, but eventually abandoned their position. As he urged his men forward, a second bullet grazed Scurry's face. Major Raguet, seeing a party of Federals fortified behind some boulders, led a squad to root them out. Bullets cut the officer's sleeve as he urged his men on, waving his sword overhead—eventually he dropped with a mortal bullet wound in the abdomen. His men, witnessing the fall of their leader, rushed the rocks and drove the enemy from the ridge.[34]

With his gunners falling around him and Texans occupying the heights above, Federal Captain Ritter ordered his men to limber the guns. The Union artillerymen cut dead horses from their traces and whipped the teams through the noise and confusion down the road to safety. Scurry was jubilant. "So precipitate was their flight that they cut loose their teams and set fire to two of their wagons." By 4:30 P.M., the Southerners controlled Pigeon's Ranch and the ridge to the north, but the Unionists had managed to get their guns away. Slough, and the bulk of his army, retreated down the Santa Fe trail.[35]

Lieutenant Colonel Tappan, with his defenders on the Union left, now faced encirclement as the Texans looked for more targets. "Considering it extremely hazardous to remain longer . . . I ordered my men to fall back and close in the rear of the retiring column." Confederates, sensing victory, followed closely, at times mingling with the retreating Federals. Private Whitley recalled one Rebel officer who found himself in personal combat with a heroic Coloradan. "In crawling through the brush, Lieutenant Phil Clough and a Pike's Peaker came suddenly upon each other, and both fired and Clough missed him." The Southerner, however, had been grazed. "Here was done some of the fastest loading that was done that day, but Clough got loaded first and the Pike's Peaker threw in the sponge. He had to." Eventually Tappan and his men, although cut off from the rest of Slough's army, evaded their pursuers in good order and reached the safety of the Union lines two miles down the road.[36]

Near sunset, Slough organized one last stand, nearly a mile south of Pigeon's Ranch, where the valley walls narrowed on the road. The Union artillery commanded the center while the rest of the Union forces took cover in a ravine to the rear. Scurry's men made one more charge before dark, but the combined fire of eight Union guns drove the Texans back as night fell. After dark, as scattered survivors of the command wandered in, Slough ordered his demoralized and exhausted men back to Kozlowski's ranch, ten miles away. Chivington, the Union's best hope of winning the battle, had never arrived.[37]

Night brought an end to the fighting as the Texans failed to pursue the withdrawing Unionists. Southerners scoured the battlefield and gathered their dead and wounded. Scores of Rebels lay cold and stiff in death—one soldier's face had been mangled by canister. Soldiers had to force one dead trooper's feet together with a piece of harness leather so that he would fit into a grave—his legs had stiffened in death at odd, gruesome angles. The serene-looking body of Major Shropshire lay where his friends had arranged him.[38]

Elsewhere, messmates rendered what aid they could to stricken friends. Abe Hanna, barely seventeen years old, lay pale and calm, a bullet in his spine making his legs useless, as a severed vein drained him of life.[39] His companion, Peticolas, mourned for the young soldier. "Abe Hanna died about an hour into the night very easily. He said he felt no pain save that his limbs were numb and dead from his hips down."[40]

Scurry forwarded a flag of truce to the Federals, inviting them to recover their wounded and bury their dead. Eventually, several dozen did return, bringing shovels and medical supplies which they shared with their enemies. Forty-six Rebels were dead, or soon would be; another sixty lay wounded. The Federals suffered sixty-four wounded, while forty-six dead were placed in graves near Pigeon's Ranch.[41]

Snow fell that night. "Several of our wounded froze to death," Private Davidson wrote. "We took off our coats and piled them upon them; we built the best fires we could build for them; we rubbed their limbs and bodies but all to no avail. They died in spite of all we could do."[42]

Although victorious, most of the Texans felt a general foreboding on the night of March 28. No one issued rations. Officers and their commands were scattered. Twenty-five Rebels remained missing. The troops, tired and shivering, spent a cold night huddled around fires, wishing for their blankets back with the wagons. Mild panic had also spread through the ranks as rumors placed the Federals in control of the Confederate line of retreat to Santa Fe. Food was scarce. Some dried buffalo meat and a small flock of sheep confiscated from a nearby ranch provided the only rations some of the exhausted soldiers had eaten in thirty-six hours.[43]

The uneasiness of the Rebel rank and file was well founded. For the Confederates, the biggest loss had come not in the fields around

Pigeon's Ranch but back at Johnson's Ranch. Union Major Chivington, with his four hundred–man detachment, had crossed the mountains guided by Lt. Col. Manuel Chávez of the Second New Mexico. Originally intended as a flank movement in conjunction with Slough's push up the valley, Chivington's troops were apprehensive as the day wore on, and Slough never appeared in the pass. Pvt. Charles Gardiner of the First Colorado suspected that something had gone wrong. "His plans were unsuccessful as [the Texans] 'wouldn't drive worth a cent.'" As Chivington's command waited, some Federal pickets stumbled upon an unexpected discovery. "While we were waiting for the [Texans] to be drove to us, our scouts bro't in information that their entire train with a two-gun battery and three hundred men, were two miles below us in the mouth of the pass." Chivington took advantage of the intelligence and ordered his command into action. Gardiner wrote that the Unionists "crowded through the mountains in almost perfect silence" until taking position on a slope overlooking the Texan wagons. The Rebels had seemed oblivious to the danger. "We sat and rested near an hour, watching the unconscious Texans, jumping [and] running foot races."[44]

After observing the unsuspecting enemy, Chivington ordered his men to descend the nearly perpendicular slope. "We were ordered in rather an unmilitary style, 'go fur em,' at which we all raised the 'Injun' yell and commenced pitching down the hill, some on their heads, some on their feet," Gardiner wrote. The Texans, now fully aware of the enemy presence, scrambled to their weapons. A Colorado officer, in an act of bravado, yelled from the mountain "who are you down there?" which brought a response of "Texans, god damn you." The officer continued with "We want you!" The Southerners obliged. "Come and get us, god damn you, if you can!" The surprised Rebel wagon guard fired only two rounds from their six-pounders, which burst harmlessly along the slope. Panic gripped the Texans as they watched hundreds of Federals scramble down what had been considered an impossible slope.[45]

Outnumbered, most of the Texans fled despite their previous bravado, as the Colorado volunteers and U.S. regulars, having re-formed their ranks, systematically destroyed the supply base. Soldiers overturned and destroyed the eighty Confederate vehicles.

"The boys were allowed to ransack and keep whatever valuables they could find," Gardiner recalled. "There was a great deal of fine officer's clothing, fine Mexican blankets and all kinds of military stores, wines, Brandies, pickles, cand fruit, oysters, Navy Revolvers, [and] double barrel shot-guns. . . . But to reclimb that hill with much of a load was next to impossible. So they were all committed to the burning element." Three hundred small arms were broken. The Federals spiked the Rebel cannons and rolled them off into a ravine, smashing wheels and carriage. Soldiers drove off or killed five hundred mules and horses. A number of Union prisoners, taken early in the fighting at Glorieta, were freed. These men delivered the first news Chivington had received of the fighting at Pigeon's Ranch. "You had better get away from here quick," one Northerner reportedly said, "the damn Texians are whipping our men in the canyon like hell." As ammunition exploded and a column of smoke spiraled skyward, Chivington ordered his troops back up the mountain, where they met a courier, hours overdue, urging them to march to Pigeon's Ranch. The Federals remounted and instead trudged through the night, planning to rejoin Slough's command at Kozlowski's. Chivington's absence from the battle had cost the Union a victory, but his success against the Texan wagons would eventually yield much greater rewards. As a final insult, locals plundered the burning wagons as soon as the soldiers were gone, carrying off anything of value that had not been totally consumed by fire.[46]

March 29 dawned as a miserable day for Scurry's Texans camped around Pigeon's Ranch, now serving as a Confederate hospital. A burial detail had laid the dead in a common trench, three layers deep—the dead men's arms folded across their chests, personal items like a "Jews harp" or clay pipe clutched in their lifeless hands. Soldiers dug a separate grave for Major Shropshire a few feet away.[47] Elsewhere, men wandered looking for food. Private Wright discovered his friend Poe and a dozen other wounded men in a well-stocked cabin over a mile away. "I, thinking of my friend's welfare, secreted a sack of flour and a bale of dried buffalo meat. In a dug-out I found a hen setting on 11 eggs. The eggs were still fresh and the hen very fat. I confiscated her for the good of the service, and she made soup enough . . . for two days."

Scurry faced a crisis. He moved a portion of his army back toward Johnson's ranch. Here the dispirited soldiers gazed on the smoldering ruins of their supply train. "The Mexicans were busy stealing everything they could lay their hands on," Peticolas reported. "I didn't mind losing anything save my watch and my journal." The Confederate army was now strung out over nearly a dozen miles. Low on ammunition and with no provisions, Scurry realized his situation was untenable, so he ordered a retreat. A few volunteers stayed with the wounded, who would be collected as soon as wagons could be procured. That night, the battle-weary Texans began the long, cold march to Santa Fe. The troops straggled badly, many building fires along the way to rest and wait for daylight. Amidst ringing of church bells, the veterans of Apache Canyon and Glorieta filed into town the next morning, taking quarters mainly in half-burned, abandoned government buildings.[48]

That same day, March 30, Brigadier General Sibley's brass band assembled in the plaza at Albuquerque, as a Confederate major unfolded an official-looking paper. Glancing at the collection of soldiers that had gathered around him, the officer began to read the contents—Lieutenant Colonel Scurry's report of the victory at Glorieta. As he finished, the men raised a rousing cheer while the band struck up the lively strains of "Dixie."[49]

The effect of such news was electric to the men, who promptly distorted the contents of the report to put an even more positive light on the event. "We this morning received glorious news," Pvt. William Henry Smith confided to his diary. "Colonel Scurry . . . whipped five regiments of Kansas soldiers, whipped the Kansas fellows greatly." Of course, the enemy troops were Coloradans, but to the Albuquerque garrison such distinctions were of secondary importance. "Our loss was thirty killed. The enemy lost three hundred. It seems that we are unlucky in the way of majors; we have had two killed."[50]

The Texan high command, though, reacted cautiously to Scurry's optimistic news of the battle. "General Sibley was very much surprised at the intelligence," Lt. Phil Fulcrod observed. "He was afraid Colonel Scurry had suffered himself to be surprised."[51] At 3:00 A.M. Col. Tom Green ordered his six companies of the Fifth Texas Mounted Volunteers, along with a section of two mountain howitzers, to mount up and move for Santa Fe. The remaining one hundred–man garrison, composed of a company each from the Fourth Texas and the Seventh Texas, an artillery battery of three twelve-pounder mountain howitzers and a six-pounder field piece, prepared to defend the town against attack and to protect the valuable Confederate supply depot. "Major Teel ordered me to have the horses shod, lumber chests filled and cannon and caisson's wheels greased and to be ready to move at a moment's notice," Fulcrod wrote. Meanwhile, the artillerymen buried the eight mountain howitzers from the light batteries of the Fourth and Fifth Regiments—now without ammunition to fire or horses to carry them—in a garden, where they could eventually be recovered. The next day, Capt. Bethel Coopwood and twenty-five members of his San Elizario Spy Company arrived from Mesilla, having avoided the Federals moving out of Fort Craig by taking a rough trail through the San Mateo and Magdalena Mountains west of that post.[52]

With brigade strength and supplies dwindling, the Confederates had reached a crisis in the campaign. The general first dispatched his aide, Tom Ochiltree, with a letter to Richmond, telling of the recent events of the campaign and closing with, "I must have re-enforcements. . . . Send me re-enforcements." In a letter to Texas Gov. Francis R. Lubbock, he again requested more troops and supplies. While waiting for this hoped-for aid, Sibley and his officers followed Green's command north to Santa Fe.[53]

While Sibley weakened the garrison at Albuquerque, Union Col. Edward R. S. Canby pressed north. On April 2, the Federals arrived in Socorro and formed up in front of the Rebel hospital. "Some of the boys became frightened and burned up my letters that were in care of an express man," lamented Dr. Hal Hunter, surgeon of the Seventh Texas and commander of the post. The next day, Canby passed through the town in an ambulance. "I had the honor of seeing Canby who is a very ordinary looking man. We expect a fight at Albuquerque as our men are there." Unknown to Hunter, the majority of the Texas troops had already gone from that town, leaving the depot dangerously exposed.[54]

Sibley was concentrating against the wrong foe. Ironically, Slough, the man Sibley feared most and had concentrated his army against, considering himself beaten. He had intended to lead a reconnaissance in force toward Santa Fe—a simple raid. In fact, Slough had unwittingly launched a spoiling attack that blunted the Confederate offensive. His impetuous move, while yielding impressive strategic results, had also put his small Union army in grave jeopardy. If not for Chivington's luck in finding the Texan wagons, the Federals might have been in dangerous straits. As it turned out, the Confederates would soon be desperate for supplies. Meanwhile, fifty miles from Santa Fe at his camp at Kozlowski's Ranch, the Colorado colonel was shaken by the battle. He decided that it was time to follow Canby's orders more closely.

Slough led his army back to Fort Union, carrying his wounded and some one hundred prisoners with him. Private Gardiner of the First Colorado was amazed by the Texan captives. "They are the most ignorant set of white people I ever came across in my life. If I was asked once, I was twenty times, in good earnest, if it was a fact that Abe Lincoln was a Mulatto. They are mostly boys from 15 to 20, though there are some very intelligent Germans among them. They say they were compelled to enlist or loose their farms." Once back at Fort Union, Slough resigned and left soon after for Colorado.[55]

CHAPTER 11

Empire Retreating

Sibley is gone to Texas—we are sold.
—Dr. Hal Hunter, Palestine, Texas

As he settled into new quarters in Santa Fe, Scurry faced a morale crises as the magnitude of the disaster at Johnson's Ranch and the aftermath of Glorieta became readily apparent. Capt. Julius Giesecke noted that his exhausted troops' "greatest concern was to rest and eat." Hungry soldiers bartered whatever possessions they had for food. The industrious German captain traded some extremely roasted coffee salvaged from the wreckage of their supply train to a local merchant for whiskey and bread. Having to find clothing and blankets for nearly one thousand men taxed the quartermaster and commissary departments. Meat, especially pork, was rare; corn meal, prepared in various creative ways, provided the main sustenance of the Rebel garrison.[1]

The Confederates established a military hospital in Santa Fe that was soon filled with sick and wounded soldiers. The casualties from Glorieta, in wagons with canvas slings to cushion the soldiers from road shock, arrived after their rough four-day journey. New arrivals trundled in daily. Several hundred men convalesced in the facility, which was fully staffed with attendants and physicians, but lacking food and drugs. The chief surgeon was Maj. Powhatan Jordan, commander of the battalion of the Seventh Texas Mounted

Volunteers and a physician before the war.[2] According to Pvt. Henry C. Wright, the medical staff had to rely on "nature's remedies," including "cold water applications, under which treatment the wounded and fever stricken rapidly recovered."[3]

The suffering of the destitute Texans eventually led Louisa Canby to intervene. "Mrs. Canby was an angel," remembered Bill Davidson, suffering from his flesh wound in the thigh. "I was at the hospital at Santa Fe. . . . Mrs. Canby came there and a girl with her [carrying] two baskets of delicacies for the wounded." Col. William Scurry noticed her arrival and "met her at the door and told her about the burning of our train, clothing, and bedding, the suffering of the boys and freezing of some of our wounded." Mrs. Canby wept, and she said "Colonel, these men must not suffer any more." The compassionate lady then revealed large caches of government supplies hidden by Union troops as they evacuated Santa Fe. After two days' effort, thirty thousand dollars' worth of equipment turned up. By April 1, the equipping had succeeded to the point that every three men had two blankets, a welcome relief from the cold New Mexico nights. Clothing and shoes, too, had been gathered and distributed, replacing the worn-out Federal uniforms worn by many. Cooking utensils, though, remained in short supply.[4]

As the Texans became aware of the gravity of their precarious situation, morale began to plummet. Casualties had thinned the ranks. Sergeant Peticolas wrote, "there is a sort of gloom resting on the company. We have lost three companions who were very dear to all of us, and though a soldier's life is calculated to render a man properly callous, it will be long before we forget [them]." He noted that the men "seldom sing . . . save when liquor abounds. . . . The sound of a violin makes me sad."[5]

Whatever the cause of their discontent, most of the Rebels in Santa Fe agreed on their hatred of New Mexico. "This country is verry disagreeable. I do not see [what] the inhabitants have ever done to live here so long. If the Lord will spare me to get out of this country I will never come [back]," Pvt. William Henry Smith vowed. The alien culture in which the soldiers found themselves also annoyed the men, Peticolas recording that the capital, "like all Catholic towns . . . abounds in bells, and it is not very harmonious to hear them all chiming for matins or vespers morning and

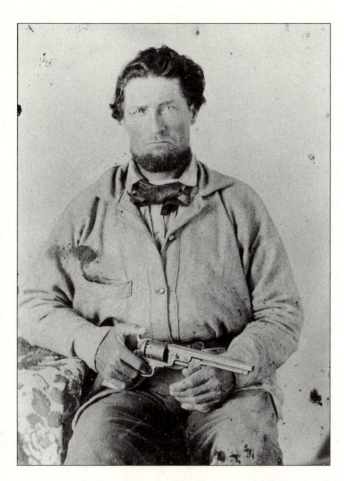

Capt. Isaac Adair, Company H, 7th Texas Mounted Volunteers, 1861. The thirty-five-year-old captain probably posed for this tintype after his Houston and Leon County command arrived in San Antonio in October. Captain Adair received a mortal wound at Glorieta on March 28, 1862, and died on April 9 in the hospital at Santa Fe. The photograph was handed down through four generations of Adair descendants. Courtesy of the James H. Healey family.

evening, for they do not chord by any means . . . the noise is rather disagreeable." Pvt. William Randolph Howell agreed, writing, "I am completely disgusted with church bells and Mexicans generally." Despite the Confederacy's imperial ambitions, the troops were eager to turn south and leave the despised territory behind.[6]

The soldiers analyzed the cause of their misfortunes, and heaped praise or disgust on those they deemed responsible. Regimental officers, notably Scurry, Raguet, Shropshire, and Pyron, received accolades. Artilleryman Frank Starr observed that, "Our regimental officers one and all have, in battle, shown themselves gallant, brave men—always in the front where the balls flew thickest." The men also took pride in their achievements, calling Glorieta the toughest fight of the campaign. Lieutenant Colonel Scurry, in his "General Order No. 4," praised his troops for their prowess, stating that the soldiers could proudly take a place in history with the heroes of San Jacinto; Peticolas responded to the honor in his diary by writing, "From all I hear of San Jacinto, that battle was not near such a hotly contested fight as the battle of Glorietta or Val Verde either." The initiative of the men, their disdain for the drill and tactical movements they had been taught, and confidence in their native ability to fight led one trooper to note, "Our drill has been useless—it would ruin us to charge the enemy in a column . . . our officers say 'come on boys!' and away they go, every man for himself." The current reverses, the troops reasoned, were the fault of the overall leadership in the campaign. "I can say this," Capt. Lee Alexander wrote, "The *men* did *their* duty."[7]

Spirits lifted a bit when reinforcements began arriving, dispelling some of the gloom. On April 3, Colonel Green, his six mounted companies and two cannons arrived in Santa Fe to aid Scurry, bringing the news-hungry veterans word from farther south. "They report everything quiet below," reported Sgt. Alfred Peticolas. Other rumors had Canby evacuating Fort Craig and fleeing to the mountains. Gen. Henry Sibley, who had not been on hand to witness the misery and suffering of Scurry's command, remembered his arrival in Santa Fe the next day in glowing terms. "Upon my arrival, I found the whole exultant army assembled. The sick and wounded had been comfortably quartered and attended; the loss of clothing and transportation had been made up from enemy's store and confiscations, and, indeed, everything done which should have been done." The confident general set up a territorial government. Sibley, however, was ill. The same painful disease that had dogged him at Val Verde, aggravated by drinking, was crippling that officer.

Much of the time, unknown to the rank and file, Sibley was drunk.[8]

Soon the restless and recovering men began to look for ways to pass their time while the officers planned the army's next move. The brigade band provided concerts in the main plaza; the troops, however, sought other entertainment. There were fandangos and the Milam County boys in Company E, Fourth Texas Mounted Volunteers hosted a two-day party starting April 6, 1862. The elaborate funeral—complete with muffled drums—provided for Major Raguet, mortally wounded at Glorieta, relieved some of the boredom. The newcomers in Green's regiment took time to tour the town. "I . . . find it to be a pretty sharp Mexican city," remarked Private Howell, still suffering signs of illness that had hospitalized him once. Even so, curiosity led him out of bed. "I was surprised to see a Catholic nunnery close by my quarters." And if such activities were not enough to occupy the men's attention, they practiced with their pistols—one careless soldier shot himself in the head.[9]

Women, whether as a source of revery or companionship, also helped soldiers pass the time. "I have seen very few American ladies as yet," noted Peticolas, who was tired of gawking at the native Hispanic girls. Other Texans scaled the wall of the nearby convent to catch a glimpse of the Anglo nuns. Private Smith discreetly avoided blatant voyeurism and instead pined for his sweetheart at home, romantically scrawling, "Sweet girl, I often think of you in these wild woods of New Mexico, where . . . no kind female friend is near to watch over us so tenderly as our girls did at home." This same warrior seemed to have forgotten his sentimentality as he admired the "two beautiful daughters" of a local merchant. "I have got to loving one of them—she is so pretty," he wrote. "I believe I will marry her and take her home with me and show her to the homefolks."[10]

While his army recovered, Sibley and his officers faced serious problems. Reinforcements and supplies were badly needed. At the same time, two Union armies—Canby's to the south and Slough's to the north—stood poised to unite, trapping the Texans in Santa Fe. The Confederates decided to leave the capital in favor of a more strategic position. "After the occupancy of the capital of the Territory for nearly a month from the time of our first advance upon it," Sibley wrote, and "the forage and supplies obtainable there having become exhausted, it was determined to occupy, with the whole army, the village of Manzano, intermediate between Fort Union, Albuquerque, and Fort Craig." By moving his troops to this point, Sibley argued, the Union troops could be kept from uniting. At Manzano, with clear lines of communications to Texas via the Pecos River valley, the Confederate Army of New Mexico would await reinforcements and supplies.[11]

Sibley also put plans in motion that would facilitate the second phase of his imperial ambitions—the conquest of Colorado. Believing the rumors of pro-secession sentiment among the Rocky Mountain miners, Sibley sent George Madison and a handful of followers from the "Brigands" north to help organize Confederate sympathizers. The Rebels had been stopped by Union patrols in the Sangre de Cristos, but were quickly released. The marauders eventually entered southern Colorado. Once there, Madison and his guerrilla band would continue their war against the Union by interdicting the Federal mail and communications with New Mexico and the East.[12]

Having rested and recovered in Santa Fe, the Confederate Army of New Mexico received orders to change its base. Before Sibley's plans could be acted upon, however, the Federals seized the strategic initiative. Daily couriers brought news that Canby was moving on Albuquerque. As the tension rose among the Rebel high command, the soldiers gathered their few belongings. On April 6, riders on lathered horses informed Sibley and Green that the Federals would indeed attack Albuquerque within a few days. Green ordered his men of the Fifth Texas mounted and ready to move. "Immediately upon receiving the news we were ordered to march," Davidson, still in the hospital, remembered. Those wounded able to travel left their beds and joined the column, "preferring that to staying in Santa Fe and being captured." Howell, again under doctor's care, decided to leave. Sergeant Davidson, back in the commissary, took command of the regimental wagons. "Colonel Green . . . seeing that he could make no time in getting to the relief of [Albuquerque] encumbered with the train, came to me and told me the situation." Davidson—aided by the sick, wounded, and two guns—promised to "take that train to Albuquerque or bust hell out of its socket."[13]

Pvt. Wady T. Williams, Company C, 5th Texas Mounted Volunteers.
From a quarter-plate tintype, circa 1861. Courtesy Lawrence T. Jones III collection, Austin, Texas.

Meanwhile, on April 8, 1862, Union Colonel Canby, with 860 regulars and 350 New Mexico volunteers from his Fort Craig garrison, had indeed arrived outside Albuquerque and began probing the defenses. A few cannon shots and maneuvering by cavalry marked the skirmish as the 120-man Texan garrison fired at long range, hitting a major but no one else. "By rapid changes of position, [we] were able to present such a front to the enemy [that] they retired," wrote Rebel Capt. Jerome B. McCown. Even so, the

Confederates spent an uneasy night, preparing to defend the town against assault. Around 10:00 P.M., Green arrived amid the cheering of the received garrison. In the morning, the Federals were gone. Canby, his road to Fort Union now open, hurried into the mountains. He could not be sure of the strength of the Texans holding the town, but had hoped that his feint would pull the Confederates away from Santa Fe in order to defend their depot. In this he was correct.[14]

Meanwhile, at Fort Union, the troops there had reorganized. The zealous Colonel Slough was gone and the more prudent Col. Gabriel Paul was again in command of the garrison, while reliable Lt. Col. Samuel Tappan took command of the First Colorado. Paul, in keeping with Canby's original orders, dispatched militia and volunteer cavalry to harass Santa Fe. A courier arrived soon afterward bearing news of Canby's movements with orders to march to a rendezvous east of Albuquerque. The garrison, already veterans of hundreds of miles of marching, readied itself for more of the same.

To the south, Canby's bluff had worked. The Federal attack forced the Rebels to react. The rest of Sibley's army followed the mounted Fifth Texas to Albuquerque on foot, divided into small groups in order to conceal their intentions from Union spies. Sibley ordered his Texans to maintain a grueling, thirty-mile-a-day pace as they hurried to save their supply base. The straggling Confederate foot soldiers began arriving on April 10, Sibley reported, "too late to encounter the enemy but time enough to secure [the] limited supplies from the contingency of capture."[15]

While the forced march punished the mounted troops, it tortured the foot soldiers. "In spite of new shoes and long rest, we marched rapidly, but towards night the wagon guard got very strong," noted Peticolas as his men straggled to the rear. "Numbers we would pass on the road lying flat on the ground, entirely given out. Many clung to the wagons and sat on the tongues to get a little rest." Some of the thirsty troops broke open a cask of "first rate wine" plundered along the way; a number drank heavily while others swallowed just enough to "strengthen and refresh" themselves. On the morning of April 11, the last of the Texans shuffled into Albuquerque.[16]

That same day, mounted Union troops clattered through Santa Fe in pursuit of the retreating Rebels. Nearly two hundred invalid

Texans and their attendants had remained behind in the capital and now faced an uncertain fate. At first the Rebels were largely ignored as Federals kept clear of the hospital. The defenseless Texans remained somewhat defiant of their enemies until rations got short. Private Wright, who had remained behind to nurse his wounded friend, noted that "our provisions were exhausted and our officers were obliged to appeal to [the enemy] for assistance." In exchange for food, the Texans agreed to become prisoners of war. "Then liberal supplies of everything we needed were issued to us. Food such as we had not enjoyed for many months was in abundance. Coffee, sugar, and other luxuries that we had long been deprived of made me think that life was again worth living." Medicines, too, were issued. "Sad to say, when fresh medical supplies were furnished and the old system of strong medicines revived, . . . the fatalities increased in an astonishing way and two or three funerals a day was common."[17]

Likewise, the beleaguered Rebel hospital in Socorro faced starvation. While Sibley led his men to relieve Albuquerque, his forgotten casualties from Val Verde had to beg from Col. Kit Carson at Fort Craig. "Our food for the last three weeks has been the poorest of beef which we could only get half the time," complained Dr. Hal Hunter. "A little coffee, some sugar and tea. Our rations of flour for today has been ground wheat without sifting or bolting. This is life in New Mexico." Eventually the Rebels agreed to capture and parole in exchange for supplies. This agreement, wrote Dr. Hal Hunter, "can be broken on our part at any time if we let the [Federals] know." Some 116 men took the oath, promising to avoid any "connection in any way with our army or do anything against the U.S. so long as we are in the hospital." As promised, Carson forwarded ten days' rations of sugar, coffee, tea, salt, bacon, molasses, vinegar, and flour. Thirty-three men, led by Pvt. Herman Lowenstein of Teel's Battery, refused to submit to this indignity and left town heading north hoping to find Sibley.[18]

By now, the Confederate prospects for renewing the campaign had become increasingly gloomy. Union forces from Forts Craig and Union would finally link up in a few days in the mountains east of Albuquerque, giving the Federals a numerical superiority. A mere ten days' rations existed for the Texans in the Albuquerque depot, and there was not enough ammunition for a prolonged fight. Attrition had taken its toll on the army: more than two hundred Confederate sick and wounded, along with their attendants, had been left in Santa Fe, and half that many remained at Socorro; 150 Rebels had died in combat or from wounds. Others died daily from pneumonia or other diseases. "I don't see how as many of us escaped as have," wrote Private Howell, "taking into consideration the hardships and exposures we have had in this cold climate the past winter." Meanwhile over a hundred Texans remained unparoled prisoners. Sibley's Army of New Mexico had lost more than 600 men while the Unionists had lost less than half that number, mostly battlefield casualties. With a powerful enemy close by, and the prospects of starvation growing daily, Sibley decided that a retreat to Mesilla was his only recourse. There, shielded by Col. William Steele's battalion of fresh garrison troops, he would await the arrival of reinforcements and supplies from Texas.[19]

Informed that the army would be evacuating Albuquerque immediately and heading south, regimental officers moved to put their commands in shape for the march. Foraging details scoured the countryside to seize whatever food could be found. Late in the day, Commissary Sgt. Davidson of the Fifth Texas took several wagons and a strong guard to confiscate a large cache of corn at a ranch twenty-five miles north of town. At sundown, the Rebel column spotted two companies of Union cavalry, probably New Mexico militia, in the distance. "Thinking this an attempt to cut me off I sent a courier . . . back to Colonel Green, but [the courier] was mortally wounded and never got back." The Texans pressed on through the darkness and eventually reached the ranch where they filled fourteen wagons with corn before promptly turning south. "I knew that the Mexicans would take [this] news back to the Federal army," Davidson recounted, "and that my safety depended on the rapidity with which we traveled." Daybreak found the foragers twelve miles north of Albuquerque on a ridge. "I could see . . . a heavy dust arising far to our rear which told me they were in pursuit. I directed the men to hurry up the mules, which they did, and the mules were doing some pretty tall traveling, when pretty soon I saw a heavy dust in our front."[20]

Seemingly trapped, the detachment of the Fifth Texas Mounted

Volunteers braced for a fight. "I told them to hurry along and get as near Albuquerque as possible when we would park the wagons," Davidson wrote. "Perhaps Colonel Green would hear the firing and come to our relief." After traveling two miles further, the Texans circled the wagons and awaited the enemy. As the riders from the south came closer into view, Davidson and his men felt a wave of relief and sent up a spontaneous cheer. "They proved to be Lieutenant Darby, of Company I of the 5th, with 100 men." The combined forces then turned to face the other pursuers. As the Federals crested a ridge to the north, they could see that Davidson had been rescued. "Their desire to come further south was entirely appeased." The foragers continued on to Albuquerque without incident.[21]

On April 12, the Confederates began evacuating Albuquerque, destroying those items that could not be carried and leaving part of its scant rations to subsist the hospital. Many of the sick, including Private Howell, refused to be left and mustered their strength to rejoin their units. The three remaining six-pounders of Teel's Battery and the guns captured at Val Verde proudly rolled out of town. Scurry's men, along with the troops of the Seventh Texas, forded the Rio Grande to the west side, while Green's and Pyron's soldiers headed down the east bank, looking for a better crossing. Pro-Southern citizens accompanied the army, adding a refugee element to the retreating column. Judge Baird, the veteran politician whose ranch had hosted the Confederates just a few weeks earlier, watched as his fellow Texans retreated past his home. Reluctantly he prepared his family to join the column.[22]

The apparent Rebel defeat emboldened local partisans who had kept a tentative peace up to that point. Having suffered under Rebel occupation, locals turned resentment into violence. On April 14, Captain McCown sent ten soldiers from his company to Las Padillas to escort "a gentleman and his family who were going to Texas intending to accompany us as far as El Paso." While camped and cooking supper, this detachment found itself faced by a company of Spanish-speaking militia cavalry. "They were surrounded," McCown wrote. One of the Confederates dropped his belt and holstered pistols to surrender. "The leader of the Mexicans immediately placed a pistol to his breast and shot him dead." The rest of the Texans scrambled to a nearby wall and began firing. In the ensuing fight, another Southerner died and a third was wounded. In response to this "bushwhacking," a company of Texans, under former Ranger Capt. Alfred Sturgis Thurmond, returned to Las Padillas to bury the dead. The Texan slain, however, had already been interred. "Before they left the place they sent a few greasers to their father, the devil, in payment for their treachery."[23]

Although somewhat harassed by partisans and Union militia cavalry, the Rebel retreat was far from hurried. "The enemy," according to Sergeant Peticolas of the Fourth Texas, "will go to [Fort] Union. We are expecting, however, to have a fight down at Craig." Heavy sand on bad roads and the poor condition of the Texan animals dictated a slow pace. Unconcerned about Canby and his Union army, which had disappeared into the eastern mountains, the Texans divided their forces on either side of the Rio Grande and observed poor march and camp discipline. The Texan column straggled over miles of road. Few guards remained with the wagons and stubborn teamsters constantly disobeyed orders, causing the trains to fall even further behind the army. Colonel Green and his regiment halted their march on April 14, at the village of Peralta. That night of April 14, the officers of Green's Fifth Texas, confident in their position, enjoyed a raucous fandango in the pillaged residence of Henry Connelly, the U.S. Territorial Governor of New Mexico.[24]

Sergeant Davidson, tasked with bringing in the wagons, spent that same day and night overcoming a series of frustrations, as he attempted to accomplish his orders. Teamsters, tired of fighting the deep sand and bad roads, finally abandoned the effort at various points on the route and unhitched their teams to graze. Many of the heavier wagons stood hub deep in sand, miles away from the army, with their precious cargoes in danger from roving partisans. Davidson, furious over the situation, organized a relay of smaller vehicles to transfer the loads and carried them into camp. The work was exhausting. The backbreaking effort was still underway at 2:00 A.M., when the wounded sergeant gave up and went to sleep in camp.[25]

Again, the Confederates underestimated their adversary. Colonel Canby had finally united the Federal forces of New Mexico the day before at Tijeras Canyon. The garrison of Fort Union, after a hard march, had arrived, and Canby immediately ordered a pursuit of the Confederates. Troops left behind heavy baggage and other

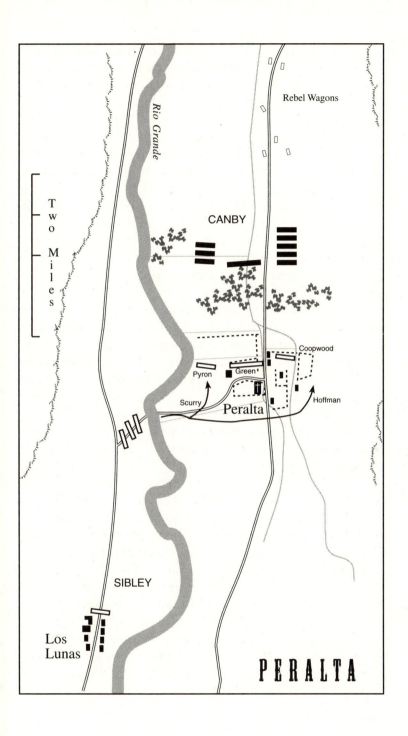

Rio Grande

Two Miles

CANBY

Rebel Wagons

Coopwood

Pyron   Green

Scurry

Peralta

Hoffman

SIBLEY

Los
Lunas

PERALTA

encumbrances and started on yet another trek. The footsore regulars, Coloradans, and New Mexicans, turned to the southwest and marched toward Albuquerque, keeping a grueling pace. Roving mounted New Mexican militia effectively prevented any Rebel scouts or stragglers from noting the movement, blinding the enemy. After a final thirty-five-mile forced march, the Federal forces finally caught up with the retreating Confederates in the darkness at Peralta—the hard-marching miners and regulars were outpacing the mounted Texans. Fiddle music was drifting from Governor Connelly's house and hundreds of dying campfires twinkled in the distance as the Union troops arrived. This was the crucial moment that Canby had been seeking. While the main force of Canby's army took positions near the town, planning to surprise the Rebels at daybreak, other detachments scouted the enemy forces, discovering the stranded wagons. For the Federals, the news was all good. The Rebel army was divided by the Rio Grande and, better yet, was totally unaware of his presence. At first light, Colonel Paul and some of his Federal horsemen swooped upon the outlying Rebel wagons and killed, scattered, or captured their surprised guards after a brave defense. Meanwhile, Union gunners fired twenty-four-pounder shells into the Southern camps, and infantry massed for an assault.[26]

Lt. Benton Bell Seat had just started breakfast when the firing started. "I was sitting down at our fire with a frying pan in my hand frying bacon when the enemy . . . opened fire. One ball struck the center of the pan I held and knocked the pan and its contents into the fire."[27] The Confederates, although surprised, quickly recovered and made a defense. "We were aroused from our peaceful slumbers by a volley fired right into our sleeping camp," Davidson recounted. "This . . . was very rude and ungentlemanly yet a very effectual way of waking a fellow up." Daylight also revealed something Canby had not counted on—the flat terrain around the town was sectioned off into fields, bordered by adobe fences and irrigation ditches, which served as ready-made breastworks for the Rebels. Their position was, he said, "the strongest (except Fort Union) in New Mexico." Canby's men were tired and hungry—many had not eaten in a day and a half. Unwilling to send his weary men against such strong defenses, Canby began probing for a weak point.[28]

Both armies, amid the steady boom of artillery fire, maneuvered troops and attempted to gain an advantage on the enemy. Paul's Coloradans moved into a strip of woods west and north of town, which masked the bulk of the Union army from sight. Rebel skirmishers, mostly Coopwood's Arizonans, fought from behind fences and walls in the center and right as the Federals continued to deploy around the Confederate position. Maj. Charles Pyron's men faced north and held the crucial ground between Peralta and the river. Green's Fifth Texas held the right. In a matter of moments, it seemed, the Federals would realize their numerical advantage and would rush the Texan line.

Green, anxious to discover the enemy's intentions, placed lookouts in the tower of the Peralta church on the left-center of his line. "Col. Green gave me a field glass and sent me up in a cupola to observe and report to him the movement of the enemy," Sergeant Davidson remembered. "I went up and had a fine view of the surrounding country and the enemy which I thought to be about three thousand strong." Green commanded under a thousand. The lookout then reported a new development. "They finally massed their forces, placed a battery at the head of the column, and started on our left in between the river and the town."[29]

Green, realizing his danger, ordered artillery to support Pyron at this threatened point. Lt. Phil Fulcrod led four six-pounders around the church and, after his gunners pulled down an adobe wall to clear the path, trotted the pieces to the left. The Texan guns took position as Federal guns began to find their range; a long-distance duel of solid shot erupted. From his perch in the bell tower, Davidson saw "cannon balls rolling along like a parcel of marbles . . . without the least respect for persons." The Unionists, checked in their advance on Pyron and the Rebel left, doubled back behind the woods to threaten Coopwood's men on the right. The Texan lookout in the tower called out their movements, and Green shifted his forces to meet the new danger.[30]

Federal artillerists decided to destroy the church tower and thus end the Rebel reconnaissance. "The enemy ran a cannon upon a little mound directly in front of our center," Davidson recalled, "a puff of smoke and then a ball passed directly over the house and about twenty feet in rear of the cupola. They sent another ball still closer than the first." The third shot crashed into the tower. The Texan lookouts, shaken but alive, quit the position after recovering from the shock.[31]

The Federals continued to maneuver in the face of Rebel resistance. Green ordered the men on his left to sally forth and take a wall two hundred yards south of the tree line. The Texans leapt over adobe walls and rushed to the position, opening on the Union defenders in the trees as they arrived. The Northerners withdrew. On the Texan right, however, Lt. Col. Benjamin Roberts had massed his regulars—the veterans of Val Verde—for a grand assault against Coopwood's position. Green sent an urgent note to Fulcrod to bring his guns back around. The Federals, however, did not attack.[32]

As the firing echoed across the valley, General Sibley at his headquarters with the rest of the Confederate army at Los Lunas, quickly ordered the foot soldiers of the Fourth and the mounted troops of the Seventh Texas Mounted Volunteers to cross at Peralta Ford and reinforce Green's position. The Texans, after leaving a force behind to guard the regimental wagons, waded across the river. By 11:00 A.M., the Confederate reinforcements gathered on the east bank. Scurry, leading the column, immediately headed for Coopwood's position on the threatened right. "The enemy were marching and maneuvering around us and making demonstrations . . . and we were beginning to think that the time had come to pass in our checks," Davidson wrote, "when a yell from the right announced that something had occurred." Green had been saved. "Hats went into the air, and [a] yell went from our throats, for there coming up the road, was brave Scurry with the 4th and 7th at his heels." The reinforcements took positions to strengthen the line—Scurry and his regiment on the left near the river, and Maj. Gustav Hoffman leading the Seventh to the right.[33]

Sibley, accompanied by his chief of artillery Maj. Trevanion Teel and a few other staff officers, attempted to cross the river and join the action. Union pickets, however, blocked their way. The general and his entourage, under fire, returned to Las Lunas.[34]

The battle of Peralta continued with unabated fury at ranges of several hundred yards. The artillery of both sides, almost equal in the number and weight of guns, carried the action. Infantrymen on both sides took cover to stay out of the line of fire. Davidson remembered a close call. "While we were laying behind the wall . . . the enemy were dropping shells among us. . . . One shell fell right behind our company. The fuse was burning 'chew, chew.' Of course I was spread out as thin as I could, but it still seemed to me that I was nineteen feet thick and forty-eight feet long, and when the thing exploded it was bound to hit me." A courageous comrade picked up the sputtering missile and heaved it over the wall into a ditch of water. "Said it was better for it to kill him than the whole company."[35]

Union shells caused mischief all along the Rebel line. One shell burst amid the Texan hospital. Another spooked the beef herd, causing them to stampede toward the Federal lines. Major Hoffman, of the Seventh Texas, immediately ordered some of his men to mount up and pursue the stricken beeves. With a dash and a yell, the Confederates galloped across the flat toward the animals. "The enemy," Davidson wrote, "supposing it was another charge on their battery, limbered up and started off the field." With the cattle recovered, Hoffman led his men back to cover as the cannonading resumed.[36]

Across the river, the Rebel troops in Los Lunas were having troubles of their own. Soldiers standing on top of the flat-roofed houses spied a party of cavalry on the west side of the river rapidly approaching the town. The Southerners hauled cannon into the streets and began building makeshift barricades, determined to resist. The Rebels then dispatched a mounted scouting party to ascertain the intentions of the coming cavalry. Tension mounted as men watched the fighting across the river and waited for the coming enemy. The tension ended, however, as the Confederate horsemen returned to report that the threatening troops in the distance were, thankfully, Texans.[37]

Canby had not attacked all day. He had, as he intended, discovered the strengths and weaknesses of the Rebel position. He also allowed his men, who were near collapse, the better part of a day to rest. He would attack in the morning. The Battle of Peralta ended when a howling sandstorm descended on the opposing armies, putting an end to the artillery duel.

That night, Sibley evacuated his troops to the west side of the river. By 4:00 A.M. on the morning of April 16, the Confederates reached Los Lunas, "wet and sleepy." The Rebels had lost seven wagons and twenty-two men captured, along with four killed and eight wounded—a slight loss considering that the Federals had missed the opportunity to destroy a third of the Texan army. After a few hours rest and reorganization, the Rebel column resumed its march. Even so, Davidson remembered, the engagement had taught the Southerners a valuable lesson. "The events of Peralto have disclosed the fact to our leaders, which they ought to have known at first, that we have a wise and vigilant foe, who is keeping a close watch on our every move."[38]

All the next day, amid clouds of blowing sand, the Union army kept pace with its retreating foes. Federal horsemen harassed the Rebel column throughout the day. Sergeant Peticolas remarked that "two or three companies of Cavalry have been dogging us down the river all day, trying to pick up stragglers but cautious to keep out of range." The Confederate column, sensing urgency in their situation, began to abandon extra baggage. "We burnt and destroyed everything we had . . . save blankets, cooking utensils, a suit of clothes, and overcoats. This was to lighten our teams so that we could travel more rapidly." The next morning, April 17, the blue shadow remained. "We discovered that confounded cavalry of the enemy right opposite us on the other side of the river this morning." As the day progressed, all of Canby's army came into view, and the opposing armies marched within a mile of each other, with only the Rio Grande between. Pickets sniped at each other, but neither side seemed interested in bringing on a general engagement. "We looked for an attack all day," Peticolas wrote, "but did not have our expectations realized."[39]

The Union tactic puzzled the Confederates. "Marching together, halting together, one imitating every move of the other, neither seeming anxious to bring on a battle, yet neither trying to avoid it," mused Davidson. A friend, mounted on a mule, dashed toward the pursuing Federals, with bravado in mind. Reining in within earshot of his enemies, the soldiers asked the blue coats what they intended to do. The Union pickets replied with lead. "I don't think they tried to hit him, but merely intended to admonish him to stay with his own crowd." By early afternoon, the Texans camped on the banks of the Rio Puerco. "The enemy, who had now become like our very shadow, stuck with us like a love-sick swain following the footsteps of his sweetheart, went into camp too."[40]

The unexpected turn of events over the last few days left the Texan high command in trouble. Within a day's march, lay a narrowing of the Rio Grande valley at the village of Polvadero. Canby could, by beating Sibley's slow-moving column to this chokepoint, gain the heights that commanded the road and destroy the Texan army. Davidson, like many of the troops, realized their predicament. "The alternative was now presented to us of continuing down the river to the 'narrows,' make battle at Pulvadeer with the enemy's cannon sweeping every inch of ground, exhaust our ammunition in a futile attempt to go through their lines, make an honorable surrender, and pine away in a Northern prison." Even if the Confederates escaped this trap, they would remain hemmed between Canby's army of twenty-five hundred men and Kit Carson's eight-hundred-man garrison inside the strong defenses at Fort Craig. The eighteen-hundred-man Texan command found itself in desperate straits. As his troops filed into their camps along the Rio Puerco, Sibley called his officers together to discuss their position.[41]

The men of the Confederate Army of New Mexico had already drawn their own conclusions. In the ranks of the Second Texas Mounted Rifles—the vanguard up the Rio Grande and the rearguard down—men were strapping food and ammunition to their saddles. "I asked the cause," Davidson wrote. "They replied that there was talk of going down to Pulvadeer, making a fight, and then surrendering; they would go down, fight as long as Sibley said fight, but the moment he said surrender, they were going . . . into the mountains and make their way to Texas."[42]

Tempers flared as the debate raged; Sibley, who at one point threatened to arrest one of his captains, finally agreed that the river road had to be abandoned. The Confederate Army of New Mexico was doomed, it seemed, unless an alternative route could be used to bypass the Union road blocks. Capt. Bethel Coopwood, the veteran campaigner and frontiersman, suggested using the same mountain trail he had used days earlier to make his way from Mesilla to Albuquerque. Sibley's council debated the question. Colonel Green at first favored Coopwood's plan, but as the debate wore on, he became sullen and detached realizing, according to one observer, that one plan meant "death in a northern prison, the other death in the mountains." One of Sibley's staff argued that if the route proved successful, Sibley would get the credit. If not, the failure would be known as Coopwood's folly. With his reputation thus safeguarded, this officer argued, the general should take the risk. "The discussion waxed hot," remembered Davidson, "and Coopwood got mad and left the council. The [others] lounged about seemingly indifferent as to the course the leaders concluded to adopt." Eventually the meeting concluded that Coopwood's gamble—an arduous march through the hills without roads suitable for wagons—was the army's only hope. The rude trail around the north end of the rugged Magdalena Mountains in front of the San Mateo range, some twenty miles west of Fort Craig, seemed the only possible salvation for the army. The officers adjourned and went to prepare their commands. Maj. Alexander M. Jackson, Sibley's adjutant, took sixteen men and rode hard for Mesilla with news of the retreat for Col. William Steele.[43]

On the night of April 17, with a full moon illuminating the way, Sibley's Army of New Mexico began its move behind the Magdalena Mountains. Clothing that could not be taken was burned. The Rebels crammed their pockets and cartridge boxes with ammunition and destroyed the rest. Troops packed the small supply train, strapping ten days' rations, blankets, and cooking utensils to the backs of worn-out mules. Artillerymen, determined to save the brigade's only trophies, hitched the "Val Verde" battery to available limbers. Company by company, the Confederate Army of New Mexico shuffled off into the darkness and to an uncertain fate. "Now commenced," recorded Sergeant Peticolas of the Fourth Texas, "one of the most remarkable retreats ever read of."[44]

Behind lay more than thirty wagons and the sick of the brigade. Comrades passed slowly by to bid these unfortunates farewell. "They had come on this far to save being made prisoners, and now they had to be made prisoners at last," Davidson recalled. Huddled around a fire with the yellow flag waving over them from the corner of a wagon, the wounded and infirm shook hands with their friends, fearful that they may never meet again. Peticolas, moved by the pathos, watched sadly. "It was affecting to see the brave companions in arms of these sick men grasping them . . . and bidding them an affectionate farewell." Slowly, pathetically, the abandoned Texans watched as their comrades moved quietly away in the moonlight.[45]

The next morning, Union scouts brought Colonel Canby news of the Rebel retreat. The Federal commander, somewhat surprised, remained master of the situation. "After making arrangements for securing the property abandoned by the enemy the march continued to Polvadera." He was unsure, however, as to the final destination of the retreating Rebels. One route would take the Texans, by way of the Mimbres River, to Cook's Canyon, and then by the Tucson road to Mesilla. The other trail emerged near the battle-scarred village of Alamosa. "If they have taken the route by the Mimbres it will be impossible to overtake them. If they have taken that by Cañada Alamosa I am not without hopes of intercepting them, although my scouts report that they have abandoned everything that would encumber them in their flight." The weary Union army continued its march at a reduced pace down the Rio Grande toward Fort Craig.[46]

The small colony of Texans in Socorro followed rumors of Sibley's advance carefully, hoping for rescue. When the Confederates failed to arrive, men began to worry. "We hear nothing of old [Sibley]," Dr. Hunter wrote. "The cry is still they come." A few days later, Major Jackson's party clattered through the dusty streets with bad news. "Is this to be the glory of our brave men," lamented Hunter. "Must they suffer reproach for their General? This is more than human nature can bear. We soon will be taken prisoners. Sibley stampeded last night and went to the mountains leaving his sick and wounded with a part of his train in the road unprotected with no medicine, no physician and but few attendants. Sibley is gone to Texas—we are sold."[47]

The Confederate Army of New Mexico was now moving into an unforgiving wilderness, beginning a week-long struggle "through scenery the grandest and most picturesque imaginable," that would test the endurance of the entire command. Water was scarce, for brackish waterholes or creeks were often a day's march apart. The one-hundred-mile trail led over high ridges and across steep-sided canyons. The higher altitude also brought cold, uncomfortable nights. And, as an added menace, Indians prowled the area;

stragglers and those too sick to continue the march faced an uncertain fate.[48]

In the beginning, spirits remained buoyant and hopeful. The first night, traveling over firm roads by moonlight, the troops covered fourteen miles but made a dry camp. The few remaining wagons even made the journey without trouble. Coopwood's shortcut had proven successful.

The next day, however, conditions worsened. Wagons bogged down in deep sand. Frustrated soldiers abandoned the vehicles, turning the sick and wounded still with the column out to walk. The troops suffered terribly from poor water and inadequate rations. Upon reaching the first spring along the route, Capt. Julius Giesecke wrote, "It was so salty that we could hardly use it for coffee." Sgt. Alfred Peticolas added that since the daily staples were "nothing but coffee and bread, we had pretty hard fare."[49]

The next day, April 19, was a disaster. Thirst soon drove many soldiers to relish even the saltiest water. "The strong," observed Peticolas, "pressed feverishly and frantically on . . . the cry [becoming] more intense and universal for water." An unfortunate bear and several unlucky antelope happened by the brigade line of march; hundreds of weapons fired, dropping the game which was then carved, cooked, and devoured by members of the column.[50] Fatigue added to the misery, and discipline quickly evaporated. "No order was observed, no company staid together, the wearied sank down upon the grass, regardless of the cold, to rest and sleep," Peticolas observed. "A great many of the infantry, tired of marching through the heavy sand, have picked up mules, little poor scrawny things, upon which they tie a fold of blankets for a saddle, and with a rope for a bridle strike out, every man for himself." As darkness fell and camps formed, echoes rang along the slopes as soldiers straggled in and searched for their units where food and blankets could be found. "For hours, as the scattered men came in, a confusion of voices hallooing for different companies, individuals, and regiments rendered the place a perfect babel." Fatigue soon overshadowed the lack of food and water, Pvt. William Randolph Howell, still with the army despite a raging illness, wrote "this is my first day on foot and me very feeble, I don't get into camp until 10 P.M. as all have gone to bed, I can't find my company and have to lay by the fire all night without my blanket."[51]

Abandoned equipment littered the trail the Texans traveled, but they were committed to bringing the Val Verde guns through. With little sleep, empty canteens, and bad rations, the soldiers struggled with the pieces, oftentimes dragging them up and down canyons with teams of men working ropes. By April 20, the ragged Texans began talking of leaving the guns. "Some talk of spiking the artillery and leaving it," Peticolas wrote. "Green [has] gotten tired . . . of helping their battery along." Lt. Col. William Read Scurry, obsessed with saving the battery, took charge of getting the guns through and himself aided the men as they manhandled the weapons over the formidable terrain. Teams of soldiers lowered the guns by ropes down the steep sides of canyons then dragged them up the other side. The backbreaking effort sapped strength, but Scurry refused to let his men give up. Eventually the officers assigned responsibility for a cannon to each of several companies; troops then destroyed all of the remaining caissons, limbers, and ammunition.[52]

Refugees added to the chaos of the column. Several New Mexican families, who had aided the Rebels during the conquest, were now part of the army struggling through the wilderness. "We have quite a number of women along, the wives and daughters of Mexican citizens who have thought it most prudent for them to leave because of their southern principles," noted Peticolas. "These people have light wagons and ambulances along, to take their provisions and property." The sight of these civilians, as well as Sibley and his staff, riding in relative comfort worked hard on some men's morale. Private Howell was outraged. "My health is very bad yet. I am compelled to walk while mean Mexican women ride."[53]

Former Texas Ranger Capt. Alfred Sturgis Thurmond was less subtle in his outrage. While leading his men through a narrow defile during the retreat, the column halted while Sibley and his entourage passed through. Riding ahead to ascertain the cause of the holdup, the Texan bellowed, "What the hell are those damned wagons waiting for?" Sibley, occupying one of the offending vehicles, shouted out, "Who the hell is that talking so loud?" Thurmond, by now totally enraged, shot back "I'm Captain Thurman of the Rangers, by God, who the devil are you?" Sibley, who had already had trouble with this officer, ordered the captain's arrest.

Maj. James Magoffin, charged with the task, hesitated. "Yes, let him come here," Thurmond yelled as he turned his horse, "and I'll damn sure 'Goffin' him!"[54]

On April 21, the leading elements of the Confederate Army of New Mexico passed along the eastern slope of the San Mateo Mountains and could see the Rio Grande away to the east. Sergeant Peticolas noted the irony. "On this day, marking the 2nd month since our Val Verde battle, we . . . passed in sight of Ft. Craig. Every man knew the table mountain and could distinguish the glistening waters of the river away down in the valley 10 miles from where we were crawling along the side of the mountain. We traveled along in full view of this rather (to us) noted place for two hours."[55]

The last Union obstacle had been passed, but after five days and nearly eighty miles of the mountain ordeal, the Confederate Army of New Mexico had been eliminated as an effective military force. Little discipline was observed, and unit organizations faded as the misery of the march became acute. Stragglers and refugees stretched in a column nearly fifty miles long. What little ammunition had been carried into the mountains now littered the trail. Civilian carriages, military ambulances, and artillery limbers lay abandoned in the sand. Wounded and sick soldiers, too stubborn to be left behind at Santa Fe, Albuquerque, Peralta, or the Rio Puerco, now lamented their decision. William Kirk, the onetime wagon master, spy, and soldier, endured the amputation of his leg from a wound received at Glorieta. Surprisingly, he survived, and after a little rest, continued the journey with help from his friends. Union scouts under Capt. James "Paddy" Graydon shadowed the Rebels—on occasion, even mingled with them by their firesides—and reported back to Colonel Canby all that they had seen. A final battle for New Mexico, these spies reported, would not be necessary.

On April 24, relief for the tattered Texans arrived. As Sibley's column crossed the last of the foothills and descended into the long canyons that led to the Rio Grande, scouts from Col. William Steele's battalion of the Seventh Texas Mounted Volunteers stationed at Mesilla greeted the footsore brigade with letters and news from home. Sibley's soldiers, sensing that their ordeal was nearly over, marveled at their own achievement: "Surely such a march over such a country and made by men mostly on foot, not accustomed to walking, was never surpassed," wrote Howell. "It reminds one of . . . Bonaparte's celebrated march over the Alps."[56]

That night, excited soldiers gathered around the campfires, reading their first news from home in over two months and greeting friends left behind at the beginning of the campaign. "Messes sat up late reading letters and discussing their contents and talking with the *green* men who had come in, and there was a great and general stir in camp that did not calm down till 10 o'clock that night," wrote Peticolas. The newcomers also brought word that Steele's command was no more than six miles away.[57]

Col. James Reily, Sibley's diplomat, resumed command of the Fourth Texas. Lt. Col. William Scurry, the hero of Glorieta and the savior of the Val Verde guns, received a promotion to colonel, with orders to return immediately to Texas to raise a regiment of his own. Although eager to be on his way, Scurry did tarry long enough to bid his troops farewell and to let them finish letters home that he would carry with him. "Scurry . . . made an effecting speech to the men . . . in which he referred to our victories, our trials, and our privations," Peticolas wrote. He "said that it was like taking leave of wife and children to take leave of us who had fought with him so bravely and been with him so long. He shed tears as he bade the men farewell. Thus we lost the best officer, most polished gentleman, most sociable gentleman, and most popular Colonel in the whole outfit."[58]

Leaving the mountains behind, Sibley's hungry veterans started early the next morning, looking for Steele and a promised provision train. The two forces finally united that evening on the banks of the Rio Grande, but the supply train was still a day's march away. On the morning April 27, after eating "a rib or two of an old brokedown work ox," the soldiers started south, finally meeting the wagons seven miles above Fort Thorn. Here the famished Texans feasted, according to Howell, on "a little pickle pork . . . [with] bread baked in a frying pan."[59]

News from Mesilla was not good either, as conditions in the Mesilla Valley had also been difficult. While Sibley had been pushing into the interior, the Mescaleros had posed the most serious threat to Confederate Arizona as they raided skillfully and often. While Texans fought at Glorieta and Peralta, eighteen-year-old Felix

Robert Collard of Polk County had spent the spring chasing these Indians. On several occasions small parties of Apache raiders, camouflaged by oiling their bodies and rolling in the dirt, had stolen dozens of horses and mules from well-guarded enclosures. "This was generally done when the moon was on the wane," Collard wrote, "just before moon-rise. Then, quiet as a cat, [they] would step over the sleeping men, and be among the horses . . . cutting all halters and ropes." Next, the raiders would stampede the herd through the camp, spreading havoc among the sentries. "The Indian on the inside would mount a horse, one hand under his neck and [with] a good hold of the mane, his foot over the horses loin, yelling and jabbing him with the knife," Collard remembered. "The other horses . . . frightened, would run over anyone trying to stop them."[60]

On these occasions the alarmed camp would pursue the marauders with varying success. To aid in the chase, the Confederates often employed local scouts and Indian hunters. "We had trailers . . . half-breed indians and half-breed mexicans, or some trapper who had spent his life in the wilds," Collard wrote. The Apaches scattered the herd, keeping on the hardest ground where tracking was most difficult, regrouping only at water holes. A lone Indian scout remained behind to warn of the approach of pursuers. On the rare occasions that soldiers overtook the raiders, the Apaches simply abandoned their prize and scattered into the surrounding hills to ride another day. "Then where are you?" Collard asked. "A hundred and fifty miles from anywhere, with a lot of run down horses— those that the indians have stolen and those that have been following."[61]

Occasionally, camp guards and sentinels foiled the Apache attempts to steal horses. Collard recalled one sergeant who encountered the raiders sneaking into the Rebel camp. "He discovered a strange looking object near the line," he wrote. "He covered this object with his six-shooter and called 'halt!' At the word . . . an arrow whizzed past his head. At the same instant he pulled the trigger. . . ." The target, two Apaches, ran into the darkness as the Texan fired another shot. The camp, now alerted by the firing, gathered around the sergeant, and a small party of armed men cautiously pursued the Apaches. "Four or five men, six-shooters in hand, . . . found a dead indian and a little farther along a drag which they started to follow. . . ." The Texans, wary of straying too far from camp, postponed the chase until sunup. In the morning, after following the trail for nearly a mile, they discovered the second warrior, who "raised up to a sitting position and let fly an arrow," Collard wrote. "We had to back off and shoot him with a rifle. They neither give nor ask quarter."[62]

Besides chronic problems with Apaches, Colonel Steele had to counter the steadily eroding discipline and morale. At Robledo, on April 16, recently promoted Lt. Col. Arthur P. Bagby of the Seventh Texas Mounted Volunteers, serving as officer of the day, was drunk. Capt. Hiram Mack Burrows, one of his company commanders and a Methodist preacher, confronted him over this dereliction of duty. Bagby responded by going for his pistol, but was too inebriated to draw it from its holster. The incident passed without injury, but Burrows immediately pressed charges and Bagby submitted his resignation. He caught the next stage for Texas, leaving Steele with no second in command.[63]

A glimmer of good news. though, came from Tucson. In early April, Colonel Reily and his escort had returned from Sonora, and Capt. Sherod Hunter used the opportunity to send dispatches and prisoners to the Mesilla Valley. The nine enlisted Federals captured at the Pima Villages received paroles, but the captain and the mill owner accompanied the Confederate diplomatic mission east as prisoners. As the detachment rested amid the ruins of Fort McLane, a belated dispatch arrived informing Reily of the battle of Val Verde. "A glowing account . . . was read to the rebel [company] stating that they easily whipped the Union troops for which three cheers were given with joyful acclamations," recalled the Californian prisoner, Capt. William McCleve. Reily and his party continued their journey, arriving at the capital of Arizona after a hard week's journey. Steele greeted the returning Confederates with enthusiasm, and congratulated them on their victory, while sending the prisoners to jail. He then began fortifying Mesilla against an inevitable attack by the approaching Californians.[64]

While trying to minimize the implications, Reily had to admit that his diplomatic mission had achieved little. The Colonel had asked Sonora Gov. Don Ignacio Pesqueira for an agreement concerning pursuit of Apaches and for news regarding Federal intentions. But most importantly to the Southern empire, Reily had sought Confederate rights of transit from the port of Guaymas to Tucson. He had achieved mixed results. Reily apparently visited the port to appraise its facilities, but found Pesqueira reluctant to concede anything, although professing support for the Confederate cause. Reily returned to Arizona optimistic but without any firm commitments from Mexico.[65]

Some important—and hopeful—news that had yet to be delivered, however, was that Hunter had bested the Californians again in western Arizona. On April 15, soon after Reily and his party arrived in Mesilla, and while Sibley was fighting Canby at Peralta, a squad of Captain Hunter's Confederates laid an ambush three hundred miles to the west. The place was a narrow defile northwest of Tucson where the stage road rambled near a towering rock column called Picacho Peak. As the Rebels waited, an advance party of ten soldiers from the First California Cavalry entered the pass about 2:00 P.M., while another detachment secretly circled around to flank the dangerous position. The Confederates unleashed a volley at the main body of the enemy, wounding two Federals and scattering the rest. As those Californians regrouped, their other column surprised three Southerners who surrendered. The Union lieutenant, emboldened by this success, ordered his troops toward the Rebel ambush point. The Federals immediately came under fire, forcing them back. After regrouping, the Unionists continued firing for another hour before retreating. Three Federals lay dead and three others wounded.[66]

Captain Hunter reacted to the skirmish at Picacho Pass with guarded optimism. It had been an obvious psychological blow for the California column. The Union vanguard, around two hundred men, hastily retreated one hundred miles back into the Gila Desert, after greatly exaggerating Rebel strength at Tucson. This misinformation would delay the advance of the Federal column for several weeks. Hunter knew, however, that even with his valiant handful and the time they had purchased at Picacho, he could not resist the thousand-man Union army for long, without help. "Our position is rather critical," he wrote in a report of the fight, "though with a reinforcement of 250 men we can hold in check all the forces that can be sent from Calafornia [sic]."[67]

CHAPTER 12

Empire in Ruin

The Territory of New Mexico is not worth a quarter of the blood and treasure expended in its conquest.
—Brig. Gen. Henry H. Sibley

The Union officers in New Mexico knew they had ended the Texan menace. Colonel Canby allowed his troops to rest after they had arrived at Fort Craig on April 22. Canby had accomplished his goal—the Texans were retreating out of New Mexico. After taking inventory of his own dwindling supplies and the jaded condition of his men and horses, he ended the pursuit. The colonel decided to reorganize his own command and to await the arrival of the Californians and other reinforcements from Kansas before delivering the coup de grace. Col. Benjamin Roberts commanded the northern subdistrict of New Mexico, with headquarters at Santa Fe, while Col. Gabriel Paul commanded in the south from Fort Craig. After reviewing the accomplishments of the past two weeks, all these Union commanders were confident. The Texans had left, besides hundreds of casualties, a wake of abandoned equipment, including sixty wagons and two guns. Paul, closest to the enemy, knew that the Confederates were finished. "The enemy is in a disorganized state . . . and is making his way out of the Territory." Roberts, writing to headquarters in Washington, echoed this belief. "According to the most reliable information, General Sibley has

[only] 1,200 men of the army of 3,000 that appeared before Fort Craig on February 13, and his retreat is the complete annihilation of his remaining forces."[1]

Sibley and his troops were indeed beaten. Not just physically, but spiritually as well. The will to fight had been crushed, replaced by the overwhelming desire to go home. There were no longer any delusions of empire. Just memories of lost friends, futile marches, and missed opportunities. During the last week of April, refreshed by adequate rations, Sibley's Brigade straggled south past Fort Thorn to where the various regiments would camp. Green's Fifth Texas stayed at Mesilla; Reily's Fourth Texas and the five "veteran" companies of the Seventh Texas continued on to Fort Fillmore, Franklin, and Fort Bliss. Col. William Steele and his untried battalion maintained the rear guard at Fort Thorn. Once in camp, the units were to rest and refit, while Sibley, Steele, and their officers determined what to do next. The empire was crumbling.[2]

Sibley's command remained disorganized, dispirited, and scattered as it retreated toward Mesilla. Discipline had eroded. The shortage of mounts aggravated the troops' low morale. Pvt. William Randolph Howell lamented, "I have never before known the value of a horse. A man . . . afoot can only know." One resourceful group, tired of marching and carrying its own gear, built a raft to float their equipment down the Rio Grande, which was flooding from the spring thaw. They did not, however, take into account the cataracts and snags along the way; the river eventually claimed the unfortunate soldiers' blankets and provisions.[3]

Even so, the Confederate Army of New Mexico remained intact. The brigade officers kept the men moving at an easy pace, and by May 5, a week after the ragged command came out of the mountains, order and morale began improving. "Every now and then," observed Alfred Peticolas, "some member of Company C can be heard humming a tune, some familiar air or favorite love song, but often the tune is stopped when memory brings back some remembrance of our hardships . . . but a better trend of feeling and more cheerfulness begins [to] characterize the company and faces look less care worn and elongated." Company by company, regiment by regiment, in squads and sometimes alone, the soldiers filed into their camps along the Rio Grande to rest and make sense of the ordeal through which they had passed.[4]

One feeling was universal to these weary veterans: no one trusted Sibley. "The feeling and expression of the whole brigade is never to come up here again unless mounted and under a different General," Peticolas wrote. "Among the soldiers I hear ridicule and curses heaped upon the head of our genl," added young Frank Starr. "They call him a coward, which appears very plausible too, for he has never been in an engagement or where there was any appearance of there going to be one." Starr, in a letter home, revived the specter of drunkenness among the field officers, stating that those men would "stay in comfortable quarters in towns soaking themselves with rum and whiskey while others are doing the work." Private Davidson echoed the sentiment. "This old brigade never saw the day that they would not have swapped Sibley for Canby."[5]

Sibley unwittingly added to the dissatisfaction among the troops by returning a number of officers to the ranks. At the start of the campaign, he had commissioned several men to command the howitzer batteries assigned to the Fourth and Fifth regiments—since these artillery organizations no longer existed, many of these artillery officers were ordered back to their companies. "After those officers have gone through this entire campaign, they are plainly told that they can report themselves to their original captain for duty as privates—infact a disgrace to them, although they themselves were innocent," wrote the irate Starr. "I would not be surprised if [they] resigned and went home to seek service again under some leader more capable than the one we have here."[6]

As his troops refitted, Sibley ordered the creation of the "Val Verde Battery" armed with the two twelve-pounder field howitzers and three six-pounder guns taken during the brigade's first fight; he unwittingly added to his unpopularity. Enlisted men from the Fifth Regiment received commissions and filled four of the five officer positions. The unit commander, Capt. Joseph Draper Sayers, had been promoted from the staff of Colonel Green. While most of the members of the new battery had seen action with the Fifth Regiment's howitzer battery, the officers were all recent appointments, an additional snub to those men stripped of their rank. Sibley had intended to create the battery to boost morale. Instead, it worsened.[7]

These disaffected soldiers, politicians, and civilians penned scores of letters, looking to lay blame and brewing a political tempest at home. "It is hoped that there will be some courts-martial and Courts of Inquiry," wrote irate Capt. Lee Alexander of Nacogdoches. "I could a tale unfold that would make Texas too damned hot to hold some men, that up here have been carrying high heads." Green and Sibley enjoyed a close relationship, as the artillery appointments might indicate, and when angry officers wrote home, they often mentioned the colonel's name in an unfavorable light.[8]

The leadership crisis came to a head when Colonel Steele of the Seventh Texas, at the request of Capt. Sturgis Thurmond of Company A, issued formal charges against Sibley and forwarded them to Richmond. The captain accused the general of drunkenness on duty, of inhumane treatment of the sick and wounded by abandoning them along the line of retreat, of cowardice, and of misappropriation of confiscated goods. Sibley was shown the charges, and he knew that he would soon have to defend himself in Confederate military courts.[9]

Not only were the troops spiritually wounded, but their health suffered too. Fatigue, malnutrition, and disease plagued the Confederate Army of New Mexico. "All the men are more or less unwell, and it is distressing to notice how general is the debility in camp," Private Howell recorded. Measles, smallpox, and pneumonia ravaged the commands, filling both the hospital and cemetery at Franklin. Peticolas noted that many of the soldiers, although not sick enough to occupy a bed, "have disease planted in their systems, which will hereafter reveal itself, caused by the exposure and hardships they have undergone in this disastrous campaign." Some troops suffered from bleeding gums and toothaches—symptoms of scurvy and vitamin deficiency.[10]

Medical staffs struggled to deal with the sick. Doctors and attendants gave stricken soldiers goat's milk to rebuild their strength. Many recovering patients received medical discharges and headed for home. A number of them never recovered, their deaths hastened by the crude medical remedies of the times. Starr, observing the medical staff, wrote home that "those who have succeeded in getting through the campaign without letting the doctors get their hands on [them], can go through anything."[11]

As the month of May passed, the salubrious, late spring weather in the Franklin area slowly revitalized the recovering soldiers as they rested from the campaign. "I now for the first time, so far as concerns my body, feel [the most] comfortable and rested since this brigade left San Antonio last October," recounted Starr in mid-month, adding "we are having beautiful weather. . . . Very opportune too, for the health of our broken down soldiers."[12]

By May 12, the arrival of the payroll officer boosted spirits while giving hustlers and entrepreneurs an opportunity to relieve the men of their hard-earned currency. "Gambling is extensively practiced by the troops that have been paid off, and large sums in Confederate notes change hands here daily over the gambling tables," recorded Peticolas. Captain Giesecke, taking advantage of his spare time and the proximity of the Rio Grande, purchased fishing tackle from a local merchant. One Rebel started a bakery, selling pies to his hungry comrades. A German named Goldman, from Victoria, Texas, started a business, buying such items as wine, chocolate, and water kegs in the Mexican city of El Paso and selling the marked-up merchandise to his fellow soldiers in Franklin for cash.[13]

The soldiers of the brigade were well armed but almost destitute of clothing or blankets. Many still wore the clothes they had drawn in Santa Fe. The arrival of packages from home, containing clothing and other items, was cause for celebration. Some boxes came addressed to companies, others to individuals. Peticolas, the suitor of several girls in Victoria, received one roll of bandages, a large bed quilt, and seven pairs of socks, but relied on company stocks for practical items such as shirts and pants.[14]

With health and morale improving, the newly restored soldiers began fighting boredom. Regimental commanders ordered companies with officer vacancies to elect replacements, and the attendant campaigning kept many busy. Peticolas took advantage of his new-found leisure to read an eighteen-hundred-page *History of the French Revolution*. The novel *Reveries of a Bachelor* also circulated among the troops. By far, the favorite source of reading material was the mail; Starr read an account of the fall of New Orleans, remarking prophetically that, "those gunboats seem to be terrible things."[15]

While in their camps, company commanders drew up muster rolls and made an accounting of their commands which revealed how badly the army had been damaged. Captain Alexander reported, "I have scarcely 10 men in my co. fit for duty and seven of my best men are dead, 16 are prisoners of war in New Mexico. . . . We have many sick, none dangerously, . . . there are many complaining and some just getting over measles, being quite weak." Capt. Jerome B. McCown in the "mounted" Fifth Texas reported, "The most, in fact nearly all, of the horses of my company have either been killed in battle or died of starvation; we have supplied their places in a measure with mules, but still nearly half of my company is on foot."[16]

The Texan army that had so eagerly invaded New Mexico a few months earlier now lay in shambles. Less than 1,800 men remained of the 2,515 that had moved up the Rio Grande in February. Combat casualties accounted for at least 170 soldiers while more than 67 men had died of disease. Hundreds that had not succumbed to infirmities had become prisoners, as they lay helpless in hospitals. Federals had also captured dozens more in battle. Scores of these prisoners found themselves heading across the plains to Fort Riley, Kansas, and from there to internment at Camp Douglas, Illinois. The Unionists paroled or exchanged the balance—primarily those too sick to travel—and returned them to Texas as soon as they had sufficiently recovered. Daily, small groups of Confederates straggled in from the north as parolees. Many of the returning men had been taken at Socorro, others wandered in from faraway Santa Fe. All had horror stories of their separate, but equally terrible, ordeal.[17]

The arrival of these survivors buoyed the hopes of friends and relatives, who anxiously awaited news of comrades left behind in hospitals. Until they arrived, however, officers reported them as "missing." Peticolas wrote, "of all the accounts of the way in which soldiers go, set down upon the face of the muster roll, this is the saddest, suggests the greatest variety of ideas, and is the most painful." One party of soldiers, which had left the hospital in Socorro in an effort to rejoin the brigade—a violation of their paroles—had mistakenly gone north toward Albuquerque, where they supposed the Texans to be. There, Yankees from the First New Mexico informed them of their error and escorted them to Fort Union as prisoners.[18]

Piece by piece, Sibley's New Mexico campaign had fallen apart. Chronic logistics problems had plagued the Confederates throughout the ordeal, and rations, although stockpiled, could not be adequately distributed to the troops in the field. When the Texans failed to win a decisive victory at Val Verde, they unwittingly jeopardized their chances of success. Sibley's decision, born of necessity, to leave Canby in his rear at Fort Craig had committed the Army of New Mexico to an extended mission in a hostile environment. But the Federals had successfully denied the Southerners most of the food stockpiles in the territory, as might have been expected. The loss of the wagon train during the Battle of Glorieta was a staggering blow, but the Rebels had managed to recover, and they doggedly pursued their goals, until forced to retreat under pressure from the combined Union army in New Mexico. They eventually reached the relative security and caches of food in the Mesilla Valley, but Sibley's army, though still intact, was badly battered. Victorious in battle, it had never managed to crush its enemies. The result was a decline in morale among the troops. The empire simply was no longer worth dying for; the men of Sibley's Brigade were defeated.

The soldiers, of course, knew or had opinions on what had caused their calamity. The days before and after the battle of Val Verde were perhaps the most critical of the campaign. As Sergeant Peticolas observed, "bad management has been the cause of our ruin—when we advanced upon Fort Craig we had rations for no longer than two weeks! And with that we passed around Fort Craig and left it in our rear. . . . It was a desperate piece of Generalship and proved . . . to be so." Private Howell agreed: "General Sibley's idea of cutting off the enemy's supplies was [a] bright one indeed. We had about three days rations and the enemy I suspect had at least six months rations in the Fort." Most critical was the failure to secure the Union depot at Albuquerque. "A quick movement . . . would have put us in possession of it all," Howell wrote. "That alone would have saved us from this disgraceful retreat." Throughout the campaign, Sibley's broken-down animals never allowed him the speed and mobility required to overrun the territory as he had envisioned. These Texans were not the centaurs of the saddle, as their state's military reputation had promised.[19]

Sibley's Texans turned bitter. Captain McCown, of the Fifth

Texas, remarked that the command should be glad to return home, instead of "throwing our lives away in . . . a country which is not worth the life of one good man, of the many who have breathed their last on its arid sands." Starr agreed, stating, "it is the opinion of everyone that this country is not worth the loss of lives and money necessary for its conquest. I do not think it is worth the life of a single Texian."[20]

The veterans of the New Mexico fighting also felt cheated. "Well sir, we gave the Yankees the devil in every fight up the country, but in the long run they got the better of us by a long ways," Captain Alexander wrote. Starr listed the gains made during the fighting as only "the name of our victories, the fine battery of six guns taken from the enemy at Valverde, and 800 or 1000 stand of small arms taken in several engagements."[21]

Discontent among the troops of the Confederate Army of New Mexico spread until it soon approached mutiny. On May 12, while most of the troops were distracted by the sutlers, a self-appointed council of officers from the Fifth Texas, including most of its company commanders, met at Ward's Hotel in Las Cruces. They debated two options: to resume the campaign, or to abandon the territory. Before deciding, however, the men passed several resolutions outlining their mission. The first two called for officials in the commissary, quartermaster, and medical departments to report on the state of the regiment, the quality of its rations, and its future prospects. The council next called for the compilation of an official report of the campaign to be compiled. For humanitarian reasons, the officers also requested Col. Tom Green to make arrangements for the evacuation of the wounded and sick to San Antonio. The last directive required "that the General commanding this brigade be requested to move this regiment to some other scene of action, where their services could be more useful to their country." The council then adjourned, to meet again in three days.[22]

By May 15, all of the reports from the regimental departments had arrived, painting a grim profile of the unit. Capt. J. H. Beck, the Fifth Texas Assistant Commissary, reported a large quantity of flour on hand, but little else. "Amount of breadstuffs on hand," he wrote, "ninety-three days rations for 600 men. This comprises the whole amount . . . in the Territory of Arizona." Little livestock remained to subsist the regiment. "The beef in possession is only about fifteen days' rations, is very poor, and almost unfit for use. Under ordinary circumstances it would be condemned as unwholesome food for troops. There is neither pork nor bacon . . . and none can be procured at any price. . . ." Lard and tallow were also unavailable, and what few beans could be gathered would have to be taken from the locals. Also, there was no sugar, coffee, or rice. Soap and candles were available only in limited quantities. There was, however, an abundance of vinegar and salt, both of which fetched highly inflated prices on the local market.[23]

Regimental quartermaster Capt. Thomas G. Wright could offer little encouragement. With some effort, he gathered fifteen wagons, drawn by 170 mules that were in "a bad condition." Feed for these animals was scarce, consisting of a small supply of corn supplemented by "hay of an inferior quality." For the troops, reduced to wearing tattered uniforms, new clothing could not be had.[24]

The report of Assistant Surgeon John M. Bronaugh was even more discouraging. "I have no hesitation in stating that the rations now issued are of an unwholesome nature," he asserted. "You will readily understand from so unwholesome a diet, that indigestion, diarrhea, dysentery, & c., must necessarily prevail in the regiment." He also addressed the army's lack of clothing. "Many of the men are now almost in a state of nudity . . . at no time has it been properly clad for even a summer campaign. Much of the mortality of the past winter was attributable to these causes."[25]

To the assembled officers of the Fifth Texas Mounted Volunteers, the course they should follow was clear. They collated a report and supporting documents, sending a set to the secretary of war in Richmond, another to the governor of Texas, and a third to the Houston *Tri-Weekly Telegraph*. "We have endeavored to discharge our duty as good soldiers, fighting for Southern independence and laboring together with our compatriots in arms, to establish a government that will receive the respect and admiration of the world," the document stated. "We respectfully ask that this report receive your favorable consideration, and that we be transferred to some other field of operation, where . . . our efforts in the great struggle for independence may result more profitably to the cause. . . ." The document ended with a resounding condemnation of the territory encompassed in the would-be empire. "In this remote region . . . there is nothing to stimulate the heart of the patriot or to nerve the arm of the soldier."[26]

Their general needed little persuading. Sibley, the grand strategist of the Confederate Empire, had second thoughts. "The Territory of New Mexico," he wrote his superiors, "is not worth a quarter of the blood and treasure expended in its conquest."[27] His New Mexico campaign was intended as the first step on the way to California; now that dream seemed unobtainable. Like his men, Sibley was beaten.

Sibley recognized the mood of his troops and sincerely sympathized with his suffering men. "I cannot speak encouragingly for the future, my troops having manifested a dogged, irreconcilable detestation of the country and the people," he wrote to his superiors in Richmond. "They have endured much, suffered much, and cheerfully; but the prevailing discontent, backed up by the distinguished valor displayed on every field, entitles them to marked consideration and indulgence."[28]

Unknown to the Confederates, the New Mexico campaign had been hard on the Federals as well. Canby also rested and rebuilt his small army, while awaiting reinforcements for his final drive against the Texans. The Yankees had been roughly handled in two battles, and their veterans respected the prowess of their adversaries. Canby made no attempt to pursue the Texans into the mountains— the best moment for trapping the entire Confederate command— because he had no rations to feed prisoners and his men were exhausted. Many Northern officers believed that the retreat to Mesilla was as good as annihilation for the Texans. Brig. Gen. James H. Carleton's California Column, containing elements of several fresh volunteer regiments, would add fourteen hundred new troops to the area. By early May, the Californians were once again moving against Tucson, and would soon be scouting the way to the Rio Grande.[29] Four regiments were also expected from Kansas. At Fort Craig, officers maintained their commands, drilling their troops while detachments guarded the cavalry mounts grazing across the river at Paraje.[30]

At Mesilla, the one undefeated Confederate leader—Col. William Steele—seized an opportunity to strike the Federals, while Sibley and his battered veterans rested. According to eighteen-year-old Pvt. Felix Robert Collard of Polk County, the colonel ordered his officers to "go thru the six hundred horses" of his untested battalion and "pick one hundred that could march . . . without food or water." His target was the Union remuda at Paraje, hundreds of horses under a small guard, cut off from Fort Craig by the flooded Rio Grande. Thomas O. Moody of Tarrant County commanded the one hundred–man party, with instructions to "arrive . . . just at daybreak while the horses were corralled . . . run in on [the enemy] camp, and capture not only horses but also the men guarding them." At 1:00 P.M. on May 18, the Texan raiding party left Doña Ana, crossed the river, and headed into the dusty plains of the waterless Jornada del Muerte—Spanish for "dead man's journey."[31]

The expedition proved to be more difficult than expected. While the Rio Grande made a large, western bend, the sixty-mile Jornada formed a shortcut, running due north from the meandering river road and rejoining it at Val Verde. The arid waste, however, was devoid of drinkable water. As the Rebels rode northward toward the town of Paraje, they happened upon a pond. Although their horses refused to drink, many thirsty soldiers, glad for the relief, dismounted and drank heavily. The pond was, however, heavily alkaline, or "poison," and scores of the men, including Moody, became incapacitated with severe stomach cramps, vomiting, and "purging." The command then fell to Lt. Isaac Bowman, also of Tarrant County. After riding all night, the remaining Texans found themselves within a few hundred yards of the Union position. Instead of charging at first light, as were his orders, Bowman dispatched a courier with a demand for the surrender of the town. Two Texans rode toward the town and found the enemy totally unprepared. A lone sentinel paced atop the flat roof of a building near the corral. As the Rebels came into view, this guard fired a shot and disappeared.[32]

Bowman's delay cost the Texans the victory. The Federals, forty-five regulars from the Third U.S. Cavalry, although surprised, quickly hustled out of bed, loaded their weapons, and took up positions among the adobe houses. The Union commander, Capt. Joseph G. Tilford, replied to the Confederate lieutenant that "a compliance to his demand depended altogether on his ability to enforce it." With the element of surprise lost, the Texans exchanged a few long-ranged shots with the enemy, then retreated. Bowman decided the battle was useless, and gave orders to return to Doña Ana. "To know that the Confederacy had such a commissioned officer," Collard wrote, "makes me blush."[33]

Fifteen of the raiders determined to continue the attack. "We dismounted under cover of a hill, and crept around, shielded from view by a ledge of rocks," Collard continued. When within a little more than one hundred yards of the town, the Texans took positions and opened fire. The Federal garrison responded with two mountain howitzers. "The first thing I knew a load of canister . . . struck in our midst with a crash, tearing up the rocks. This was the first time we had ever been under fire." These Texans joined their comrades in retreating back down the Jornada del Muerte.[34]

As the Confederates started back down the Jornada, Collard's mount gave out. "My horse all of the sudden stopped. I spurred him, he staggered, straddled out his legs, and reeled." The teenager from East Texas now faced a dangerous ordeal, afoot, and miles from friendly territory or drinkable water. His comrades nobly offered to stay with him. Instead he asked them to go on ahead to the river and return with full canteens. They agreed and trotted off into the distance. "I felt kinder lonesome when the last man rode out of sight. My father owned slaves, and I was a soft 'feather-bed' kind of boy, unused to hardship." he remembered. "Now I was catching it in the neck." Collard stripped his exhausted mount— his father's gray thoroughbred—then attempted to prod the animal along. After worrying with the stricken beast for the rest of the day, the Texan abandoned him to his fate. "He would whinny after me. It was like going off and leaving a child." That night he slept on the trail—alone.[35]

After a sleepless night, Collard continued down the Jornada on May 22, desperate for water but vigilant. "I walked on, looking back for the enemy, looking forward, looking to the right, looking to the left expecting Indians." After a day of this terrifying routine, the soldier began seeing signs of hope—more dead or exhausted horses. His friends must be near. He found a concealed position, then slept, dreaming that night of "Blue Branch, near my father's home," he wrote. "[I] Dreamed of laying down in that limpid stream, in a blue pool, and drinking like a fish."[36]

On the third day of his ordeal, the boy felt that death was near. "I chewed bullets, trying by these means to excite the salivary glands," he remembered, "the very air was dry, my lips and throat parched." Around midday, however, he found something else to add to his fears. More dead horses, but these had been stripped of blankets and saddles. Surrounding the carcasses were moccasin tracks. "Indians, like sleuth hounds, had followed the trail in the dark." His decision to conceal himself the night before had saved his life. "My bloody scalp was not dangling from an Apache's belt, but the demons were on the trail ahead of me." Collard made a deal with God. "I promised . . . along about that time, if He would bring me through that peril, that I would try and live a better boy."[37]

Collard never saw the Indians and reached water and his comrades that evening. His friends had filled buckets from a spring and returned to the Jornada to find the stragglers. Upon finding fresh Indian signs, however, they gave up hope. When the half-dead teenager stumbled into camp, the Confederates were amazed. "Twenty men were on their feet in an instant," Collard wrote. The Texans made the boy drink slowly. "I never got enough, but like the boy who attempted to eat a barrel of sugar, I reached a point where it didn't taste good." Reunited with the rest of the ill-fated raiders, Collard shared a mount for the final fifteen-mile ride to Doña Ana, reaching the town on May 24. This embarrassing horse-stealing expedition, and a picket skirmish near Fort Craig on May 23, marked the end of fighting between Union and Confederate troops in Arizona.[38]

At the same time, the western bastion of Confederate Arizona was crumbling. Capt. Sherod Hunter, aware of the conditions of the main Confederate Army, had decided to abandon Tucson to the Californians and retreat to the Rio Grande. After they passed through Apache Pass, a war party of Chiricahuas attacked the Confederates at Dragoon Springs, killed four, and drove off a number of horses. In desperation, Hunter armed his few prisoners to help ward off additional Indian attacks. The Rebels cautiously continued their march, arriving at the Rio Grande on May 27.[39]

As Hunter's veterans arrived in Confederate Arizona, Sibley received word that he was to be reinforced in accordance with his earlier requests. Col. Xavier Debray's Twenty-sixth Texas Cavalry had already left the Gulf Coast, en route to Fort Bliss. Gen. Robert E. Lee, military adviser to Pres. Jefferson Davis, authorized the diversion of an additional regiment from Arkansas to ride to Arizona. Davis, after meeting with Capt. Thomas P. Ochiltree, who had left New Mexico in early April, included a personal note to Sibley in an attempt to put a good light on the plight of the Confederate cause in the Far West. "With the assistance of the two regiments sent to you from Texas," the president wrote, "I trust you will be able to meet the more immediate and pressing exigencies that may arise. . . ." He added that Sibley's military ability and the valor of his troops should make up for the shortage of supplies and ammunition in Arizona.[40]

Although two regiments sounds trifle, compared to fighting in Virginia or Tennessee, their arrival would have made a huge difference. In a place like New Mexico, this equated to being reinforced by a corps in the larger theaters of the war. The fact that Lee and Davis would release troops from the hard-pressed front in Arkansas is significant. The Confederate high command was beginning to show an active interest in Sibley's success. Like many other ideas that sprang forth during the brief life of the Confederacy, however, Davis's interest was characteristically too late to be of any use.

Despite the president's optimism, Sibley remained gloomy and pessimistic. "The mail of last week brought unofficial reports from various sources of the intention of the Government to reinforce this army with one or more regiments," he wrote to the commander of the department of Texas. "And finally, . . . that New Mexico and Arizona are to be held at all hazards. My purpose in addressing their communication to you is to inform you distinctly of the resources of this country and New Mexico. Any forces sent to operate in this quarter should not depend upon the productions of the country." The result of his letter, Sibley believed, would be a halt of any additional reinforcements. Even if Lee and Davis did send troops, Sibley did not want them unless they were packing their own chow. The dream of empire, at least with him, was dead.[41]

As summer approached, Sibley's army dwindled. The enlistments for the Second Texas had already expired, and Maj. Charles Pyron led his veterans, along with the Val Verde Battery, back to San

Antonio late in May. These men—veterans of the early days of secession, the capture of the Federals at San Agustín Springs, and the first up the Rio Grande and the last down—were quitting the adventure. The men who came to Arizona with John Robert Baylor had been the finest warriors, and Sibley's Texans, Davidson among them, hated to see them leave. "No purer patriot, no braver soldier, no truer man, and no better officer wore the gray than C. L. Pyron. . . . There never breathed braver soldiers, or purer patriots, than the little band of brothers who followed him."[42]

Many of the troops that had been recruited locally took the same opportunity to separate themselves from the Confederate service. Many of the locally recruited companies dissolved. "Having served out our twelve months enlistment," wrote Cuban Enrique D'Hamel of the San Elizario Spy Company, "we were paid off and told . . . we would be called on again to enlist for 3 years or during the war. I, with many others and a caravan of Mexican families were leaving, fearing the Federals, and Indian invasion." A large caravan of Southern sympathizers prepared to depart for Chihuahua City. "They allowed us to join . . . on condition that we were to stand guard and help take care of the stock." D'Hamel and his companions gladly accepted, and left Arizona for good, eventually returning to Texas by way of Laredo.[43]

At the same time, thousands of miles to the east, John Robert Baylor, continued to press his ambitious imperial schemes. Commissioned colonel in Richmond on May 29, Baylor received formal authorization to raise his Arizona Brigade. Traveling by rail through Alabama and Georgia, he called on influential merchants to discuss his plan for supplying the western armies through a Pacific port. Texas cotton, exchanged for munitions and supplies coming through Sonora, would supply his troops. In Marietta, Georgia, Baylor boasted, "I am now in relation with the parties . . . representing the foreign buyers, and am satisfied that the occasion now offers for importing arms, medicines, munitions, & c. into Texas and Arizona by the way of Guaymas, in Mexico, on the Gulf of California. The port . . . is not suspected by the enemy, and a large supply of winter clothing, powder, & c. can thus be imported. There is cotton enough in Texas thus utilized to arm and equip an army." He was too far away to know that the empire was already dead.[44]

Closer to the scene of disaster, Sibley grew despondent, lashing out at his superiors. "I have made report after report to the Government, but up to this date have received not a single line of acknowledgment or encouragement," he lamented. Because of the mood of his soldiers, his own poor health, and his chronic lack of supplies, Sibley's confidence collapsed. His heart was no longer in the mission, and he readily abandoned his dream of empire. The disheartened general ordered the bulk of his command to abandon Arizona. Meanwhile Col. William Steele and his four hundred troopers would hold the territory as long as possible until help arrived. This final, brutal act—in effect the collapse of Confederate Arizona—would be the crowning agony of Sibley's Brigade.[45]

A lack of adequate transportation crippled the evacuation, and men lightened their loads, as officers sought creative ways of moving their gear toward San Antonio. The Fourth Texas Mounted Volunteers built a flatboat to carry regimental provisions down the swollen Rio Grande to Fort Quitman, as an advance depot for the retreating column. Sergeant Peticolas reported for duty as one of the crew, and on June 1, the expedition was ready to depart. "We were with the flatboat all day and got it loaded with 200 sacks of flour. When we got it loaded the boat sprung a leak." The soldiers frantically unloaded the boat and threw its precious cargo on the river bank. "This was severe work, and before we could get it all out about 60 sacks got wet. . . . Thus our flatboat expedition was brought to a close."[46]

Five days later, the Fourth Texas Mounted Volunteers, led by the recently promoted Lt. Col. William Hardeman, started out of Franklin on a seven-week odyssey on foot that would return them to San Antonio. Peticolas's cosmopolitan company from Victoria was happy to be going home. "All the sounds in camp intimate a fast recovering cheerfulness. Linn is laughing and joking his friends, Fenner congratulating himself on the cheerfulness of the camp; Roeder rousing himself from his usual profound apathy and indolence and summing up energy enough to cut his hay for his own horse, and broil a piece of beef." A blend of old and new-world music drifted from the camp. "Powell is singing old-time baptist hymns, and the rich strains of some of the most celebrated German airs rise from the lower end of the company where the Germans are camped; tenor, soprano, bass, and all complete." Despite this early optimism, the same trail that had caused so much misery the previous fall would again punish the Texans—this time at the height of summer.[47]

Pvt. William Lott Davidson, with the rest of the Fifth Texas and the five veteran companies of the Seventh Texas, departed a week later. "Be it known that we did not march in line, but every man for himself and the wagons take the hindmost." The midsummer heat immediately scorched the footsore troops, forcing them to travel only the dark hours between dusk and dawn. After leaving the Rio Grande at Fort Quitman, water along the route was short. Mescalero Apaches filled many of the springs and wells along the route with dirt and rotting animal carcasses. The suffering was intense. "Hot, hot, and no shade, vine or cloud to hide the sun or break it parching rays from us. Many . . . threw themselves down . . . to die. Many kept on forward with their tongues so swollen that they could not articulate a word, more crazed than rational."[48]

Sibley and his escort, including the diarist William Randolph Howell, left June 19, bringing up the rear of the column. "Prepare to go home," he wrote. "Glorious thought!" The general and his companions trotted along the line of march, passing the army along the route. Sibley passed Green's veterans just outside Franklin and started away from the Rio Grande and into the interior on June 23. "Leave it for ever, I hope." Poor grass, deep sand, and insects plagued the command. "Gnats thick as grains of sand," Howell noted. "Almost in possession of the territory." General Sibley, his staff, and escort had frequent brushes with Indians, probably Mescaleros and maybe Comanches. At Eagle Springs, marauders raided the party's mounts. "Indians pay us a visit tonight, stealing one horse and shooting two mules with arrows." Two days later, at Dead Man's Hole, three of Sibley's mules disappeared. Hardship and Indians, it seems, did not recognize rank.[49]

Despite the harsh conditions along the march, a rare summer thunderstorm would provide occasional relief to the stumbling troops as they trudged along through the night. "A dark cloud rapidly covers the heavens, one by one shutting from our view the glimmering little stars," Davidson wrote. "Heavy and long the thunder rolled." The ensuing rain would drench the grateful travelers. In the heat of the day, "men, tired weary men, bared their heads to let it fall upon and cool their burning brows; men, brave dauntless men fell down upon their backs and opened their mouths to let it run down and cool their parched and burning thirsts; men . . . fell down upon their faces and drank it as it lay on the ground."[50]

The battered Confederate Army of New Mexico retraced its path of the previous fall, passing familiar landmarks. The Fourth Texas, in the lead, crossed the Pecos River on July 2, and camped at Fort Lancaster. Three days later, the troops slept at Beaver Lake on the Devil's River. On July 10, Sibley and his entourage caught up with the head of the column near San Felipe Springs. The general and his men traveled on, eager to be back. On the afternoon of July 15, the men of Sibley's escort rode into view of that city. "Get in sight of San Antonio . . . and rejoice at the sight!" Howell wrote. "Once at San Antonio, we know it is not difficult to get home."[51]

The folks at home, too, came to the aid of their returning soldiers. At Prairie Lea, in Caldwell County, a committee of twenty-two leading citizens gathered $401 in contributions, which went to purchase clothing and sundries. In addition, various farmers brought in half a ton of bacon, six wagons, and the necessary mules to pull them. The heavily laden column headed west to succor their soldiers, sons, and neighbors.[52]

The arrival of these wagons of relief supplies restored Sibley's army. The first vehicles reached the troops along the Devil's River. Additional arrivals came daily, driven by older men from the various counties. The men responded with "joy and happiness on meeting what their fathers, mothers, and friends had sent them," Private Davidson wrote. "Clothing, soap, and other cleansing articles such as combs were . . . received, to say nothing of the good fresh corn meal, sugar, salt, bacon, coffee . . . with some tobacco, the first seen by many in several days." Additional wagons met the army near D'Hanis. "The boys were in no way . . . selfish or tight fisted with what they received, but divided freely and to the last."[53]

Dreams of empire had turned into a nightmare from which Sibley's army was slowly waking. Late in July, the battered, but proud, Confederate Army of New Mexico trickled into San Antonio. The Fourth Texas Mounted Volunteers began arriving July 18, 1862. Officers directed the men to their old camp grounds along

Salado Creek. Troops continued to wander in for the next few weeks. After resting in camps for a few days, company officers mustered their men. Then they sent them home on an extended furlough. For the bulk of Sibley's army, the ordeal was over.

The camps along the creek bustled with activity. Parents arrived with wagons to look for their boys. Survivors answered their inquiries as best they could. Others packed for home. Private Howell and a friend started on the road for Plantersville. Alfred Peticolas and the "Victoria Invicibles" broke camp and started southeast toward the coast. Captain Giesecke and some of his neighbors from Austin County reversed the journey that had begun nearly a year before—simple things were now precious; the battle-hardened officer stopped in Gonzales for "several bottles of gingerpop." Behind them, along the road to El Paso and on the lonely fields of New Mexico, lay scores of their friends and neighbors—the price of empire.[54]

In the summer of 1862, the Confederacy's situation was much different from what it had been the previous year, when Sibley had first presented his ambitious plan. While the Texans had been in New Mexico, stirring events elsewhere in the South had overshadowed their desperate struggle. Before Val Verde had been fought, the Tennessee strongholds of Forts Henry and Donelson had fallen. While Confederates shivered in the mountains east of Albuquerque, the battle of Pea Ridge was fought on March 7 and 8; a month later, Glorieta was over, and the crucial battle of Shiloh had been fought. George Wythe Baylor, the governor of Arizona's brother, had watched as his fallen chief, Gen. Albert Sidney Johnston, was buried. The largest city in the South, New Orleans, had fallen on April 29, an event that drastically altered the fate of Sibley's veterans and the nation. While the Texans rested in the Mesilla Valley in May and June, Thomas J. "Stonewall" Jackson won fame in the Shenandoah Valley, and Joseph E. Johnston fell wounded at Seven Pines. As Sibley's army retreated from Franklin, Robert E. Lee fought to save Richmond during the Seven Days Battles. The news from those fronts depressed New Mexico veteran Frank Starr, who wanted his sufferings—which seemed in vain—to have meant something. "We all think that our operations out here will all be lost in history when such great struggles are going on nearer home."[55]

CHAPTER 13

Echoes of Empire

Instead of fighting Yankees since Sibley left,
we have to fight the Mexicans.
—Pvt. John A Kirgan, Company E, Seventh T.M.V.

Col. William Steele and his rear guard, in Arizona alone and un-supported, faced perilous times as they attempted to keep the ter-ritory—for the sake of the nation and Governor Baylor—in the Confederacy. Only three hundred men of the Seventh Texas Mounted Volunteers and three of Maj. Trevanion Teel's six-pound-ers remained to hold the territory against the combined forces of a growing Union Army. Steele consolidated what was left of the locally raised cavalry companies into the nominal First Arizona Bat-talion Mounted Rifles under Lt. Col. Philemon Herbert. It was only a shadow organization; its members, quite aware of what was hap-pening around them and never fully committed to the secessionist cause, deserted in large numbers. German Hank Smith—miner, Indian fighter, and veteran of Baylor's campaigns—was among them. He was later reported as missing, along with "one minie musket." California Capt. William McCleve, released from the Mesilla jail by his deserting guards, accompanied four former Con-federates north along the Rio Grande. On their way, the party cut ferry ropes and attempted to do their part in disrupting Rebel operations.[1]

Colonel Herbert, the longtime champion of all things Southern—from Willard's Hotel to California—also felt disillusioned. Desiring a truly independent command, he had been instead given a mockery of a unit. The former member of Congress instead chafed under the command of Colonel Steele, whom he described as a "perfect martinet." One observer noted that "as Herbert is compelled to come under discipline and to toe the mark, it is rather against the grain."[2]

Colonel Steele, meanwhile, felt Arizona slipping away. The miners near Pinos Altos requested protection; he had none to offer. Others suggested buying peace from the Apaches by giving them food. "I regret that it is out of my power to comply with your wishes," he wrote, "there being a scarcity of provisions in the country. At the present time there is not even a sufficiency for the troops destined to remain in the territory. I can not, therefore, make peace with the Indians on the basis of furnishing them with rations. Neither am I in a condition to chastise them." Steele hoped to maintain his position until the corn crop could be gathered in the coming weeks; his chances grew increasingly unlikely. He doubted if he could hold on that long.[3]

The soldiers of the Seventh Texas Mounted Volunteers also sensed that their tenure in Arizona would be short and most made frantic preparations for the eminent evacuation. Men on foot needed mounts. Occasionally, troops on patrol would receive a windfall as they recovered loose horses and mules. One lucky squad found an abandoned U.S. mule, a highly prized mount in that rugged country, during a foray against Apaches. A lucky sergeant gained sole possession of the animal in a friendly game of poker, leaving him with two mounts—the mule and "Pete," a mustang and thoroughbred mix.[4]

One private in his company, eighteen-year-old Felix Collard, had lost his mount in the ridiculous raid down the Jornada del Muerte and was facing the prospects of making the thousand-mile-trip home afoot. He negotiated with the sergeant. "I knew it was of no use to talk . . . about buying the mule, but bantered him for Pete. After dickering for a few minutes, we traded." The young soldier made a down payment for the animal out of emergency funds that his father had sent with him, and signed a note for the balance.[5]

Collard adored his new friend. To a cavalryman, and especially a Texan, the personality of your mount was very important; soldiers a long way from home developed understandably close bonds with their animals. Pete was typical of the range ponies many of the troops rode. "He had a very large stomach," Collard wrote admiringly. "He was shaped like a bale of cotton, with a leg on each corner, . . . had a Roman nose and a course mustache as long as the wing-feathers of a frying sized chicken." Pete, full of personality, also had a voracious appetite and was not particular about what items were on the menu. "Meat skins, jerked mutton, bread and biscuit were a delicacy," Collard remembered. "He would turn over the cooking vessels, spilling their contents on the ground. He was ever ready to dodge chunks of fire. After turning over the bread (when we had any) he would return . . . and pick up the pieces."[6]

The mule-borne sergeant, however, had cause to regret selling the mischievous horse. His sturdy mount was promptly confiscated for use with the regimental wagons. The disgruntled soldier returned to Collard and demanded to buy back Pete. "I told [the sergeant] that I thought a great deal of him," Collard responded, "but not enough to walk."[7]

As Steele's Texans prepared to evacuate, they found themselves facing an increasingly belligerent citizenry. The Hispanic residents of the Mesilla Valley, in addition to Mexican citizens from Chihuahua, now openly resisted Confederate foraging details. Pvt. John A Kirgan wrote: "Instead of fighting Yankees since Sibley left, we have to fight the Mexicans. . . . They refused to let us have transportation, and we went to press them into service, thereby creating a civil war with them." In mid-June, as Sibley's army headed home, soldiers from Company E, Seventh Texas had clashed with the residents of Socorro, Texas. After exchanging small arms fire, the ruthless Confederates brought two of Maj. Trevanion Teel's six-pounders to bear on the village. "We killed 20 and wounded a great many," Kirgan wrote, "besides destroying their church and otherwise damaging the town." The Rebels had only two horses wounded. Two weeks later, fifteen soldiers returned to the stricken hamlet "for the purpose of pressing articles we needed into service," wrote Kirgan. Fifty enraged civilians charged the detachment, killing one, seizing five others, and scattering the rest.[8]

In early July, Company D of the Seventh Texas ran into similar trouble near Mesilla. A large force of Spanish-speaking citizens attacked Capt. William H. Cleaver's Angelina County command as it, too, foraged for food, sending the Confederates scurrying for cover. In the following melee, the fighting became close and deadly. One Confederate lieutenant reportedly killed three attackers with his Bowie knife. Elsewhere, rifles and pistols dropped the attacking civilians as they rode into the fight. After an afternoon of heavy fighting, Captain Cleaver and seven other East Texans were dead, and over forty of the Hispanic partisans had been wounded. A local civic leader, Plácido Romero, sent a letter to Union forces at Fort Craig. "The Southern soldiers here . . . have destroyed everything, even to the growing crops," he wrote. "The people here are with their eyes open toward the North, in the hope of being relieved from the devastation of these locusts."[9]

Collard, his lieutenant, and five companions participated in one late-afternoon raid, targeted at a few beeves in the villages of Isleta and San Elizario. "We found the cattle and drove them into a corral. We had nothing to pay for them, [so] we tuck 'em." The alcalde of the town threatened to order an attack on the Texans if the cattle were not returned. The Confederates took positions behind the adobe-walled pen and prepared for battle. The men spotted one civilian rider galloping out of town, evidently to get help. One soldier, "laid his gun up on the wall, and when it fired, the horse ran off riderless." The locals did not attack, and after dark the Texans prepared to make their escape. "We cut out the cows, the calves, and the poor," wrote Collard. The lieutenant then ordered his men to "make them pant." The Texans emerged from the corral at a gallop driving the healthier beeves before them, returning to their camps safely.[10]

Amid the growing racial tensions and the increasingly perilous job of keeping Confederate Arizona from spontaneously collapsing, a few more veterans of Sibley's shattered army wandered in from the wilderness. Pvt. Henry C. Wright of the Fourth Texas Mounted Volunteers emerged near Las Cruces and could not believe his good fortune.

His June trip down the Rio Grande to freedom was epic. He had stayed behind in Santa Fe to nurse his bunkmate wounded at

Glorieta. He had been captured, paroled, then thrown in jail on trumped-up charges. Union authorities eventually released the soldier after an inquiry and allowed him to return to Texas, but the proceedings had taken so much time that many of his fellow comrades and parolees had long since left the capital. Wright managed to ride with a Federal party as far as Fort Craig. From that point south, the road was perilous. He joined a six-man Union patrol scouting the road, observing, among other things, a party of Indians in the distance, with a huge flock of stolen sheep. The patrol stopped thirty-five miles north of Mesilla near Fort Thorn. "Here we expected to find our picket post." There were no Confederates for Wright to join. "The commander of our little party announced that this was as far as he had orders to go." The Texan faced a dilemma. "To return [with the patrol] meant separation from home and friends for an indefinite time—perhaps the duration of the war. To go on was to face unknown dangers—Indians, Mexicans, wild beasts. . . . The call of home and mother was too strong, and I determined to go forward at all risks." His Union escort had provided the Rebel with a rifle, twenty rounds of ammunition, and all the provisions he could carry. Armed but afoot, Wright had continued his journey alone.[11]

Wright kept east of the flooded Rio Grande to avoid the Indians he had seen before and struggled over the ridges and foothills until reaching Las Cruces. "Here the people ran out to meet me. My Yankee clothes were all that saved me. Had they known I was one of the hated Texans they would have torn me to pieces." The Rebel convinced the mob that he was scouting for the Union army, and the citizens gladly told him of the whereabouts of the closest Confederates. "I hurried on . . . glad to escape with my life." After going another five miles without finding a friend, Wright quit for the night. "I saw a wolf trotting up from the river . . . and knew that no person could be near." The next morning, Wright woke up with a start. A solitary Hispanic man was walking by and told the soldier that Texans were a half-mile further on, preparing to cross the river. "Oh, joyous sight. . . .They welcomed me heartily [and] gave me something to eat. . . . It seemed to me then, as it does now, that it was a providential happening in my favor."[12]

By July, Steele knew that prolonging his efforts was futile. Captured Union correspondence indicated that Tucson had fallen to the California column in mid-June. On July 5, an advance party from that army occupied Sibley's old headquarters at Fort Thorn. Canby, already reinforced from Colorado and Kansas, would soon join the Californians. Steele, now facing an army of some three thousand men only a few days march to the north, recognized that his position was hopeless. Baylor and his chimerical Arizona Brigade would never arrive in time, and Sibley had turned back reinforcements from Texas. On July 8, Steele abandoned Confederate Arizona, withdrawing his troops to Fort Bliss. "At this place," Wright noted, "we found a disorderly lot of men, formed of sick and wounded from the hospital. Also many attendants who had waited on them, and a good many stragglers of one kind and another . . . all anxious to get away." On July 12, after securing what transportation and supplies he could, Steele and his command followed Sibley's army to San Antonio.[13]

His men improvised for their lack of adequate equipment on the march. Collard, noticing that his warhorse Pete was walking tenderly with sore unshod feet, made him some moccasins from green cow hides. "These lasted for several days." Passing through Franklin, he found an itinerant blacksmith who shoed the horse properly. "He had a kind of pouch around his neck that contained a set of horse shoes, nails, a horse-shoe hammer, and a rasp. He used a wet gunny sack for tongs, a wagon tire for anvil and [an] iron pin . . . for a hammer. I paid him a dollar and a quarter a shoe, and had the shoes pulled off three hundred miles east of San Antonio."

Before he could resume his travels, however, Collard almost lost his trusty steed. While the young soldier attended to other business, Pete wandered alongside a two-wheeled oxcart, loaded with sacks of corn. A hole in one of the bags had leaked kernels through the boards of the wagon bed, forming a cone. The famished horse wanted this tidbit badly, but could reach the morsels from neither the front nor the back of the vehicle. The intelligent animal instead knelt beside the cart and, threading his head between the spokes of the large wheels, munched happily on his prize. "Something frightened him," Collard wrote. "He jumped up and fastened his head near the hub." The horse went into a panic. "He was pulling back, all four feet braced, and twisting his neck from side to side."

His owner arrived just in time, and hurried to Pete's relief. "I ran and fell across his neck and pushed it down to the ground. He, in his struggles, had rubbed the hair off behind his ears." Once freed, the angry horse made several circles around the cart, snorting. After calming the animal, Collard rejoined his unit on the road to San Antonio.[14]

Steele's retreat, like that of the rest of the brigade, was a rambling, undisciplined affair. The command was unevenly mounted and what animals were available were in wretched shape. Troops drove a small herd of sheep behind the column. This odd menagerie of men on half-starved horses, soldiers afoot, government wagons, and civilian carts managed only about ten miles a day. The balance of the Confederates in Franklin, mostly parolees forbidden by their oaths to associate with the army, or bedridden wounded, made their way east as best they could.

Collard and six other mounted Texans asked and received permission to ride ahead of the column. After purchasing a burro to carry their gear, the squad pushed ahead of the army. Another soldier, simply called "Jack of Clubs," asked to go along, although unmounted. "He took a survey of our horses and said, 'I can keep up that layout, afoot.'" The crew presented a motley appearance: one soldier rode with a shirt wrapped as a turban over his head; two were barefoot. A shotgun swinging from his saddle, Collard sported a "flap wool hat that had the crown gone—a drawstring in the brim to keep it from flapping in my eyes; a lindsey shirt, dirty and worn; a pair of tanned leather breeches; no underwear; and a pair of boots with the toes sticking out. Fine thing that it was summertime."[15]

Indians raided this small, vulnerable detachment on Limpia Creek, near Fort Davis. The soldiers had camped in a bend of the creek, letting their horses graze near the margin of the water. "Some [were] dragging ropes, some foot loose, Pete among them," Collard recalled. That night, Indians took advantage of a full moon to approach the herd. "Neither an Apache or Comanche could steal Pete. Whenever either came around . . . his heart would thump, thump, thump as if he were nearly scared to death." On this occasion, the horse began pacing nervously. At the same instant, a cacophony echoed down from the surrounding hills. "It sounded like half-a-dozen gongs, or, two skillet lids rubbed together, or tin pans beaten. The noise, echoing and reverberating around in the rocks and cliffs [was] like pandemonium turned loose." Under cover of the racket, Indians darted from rock to rock, lassos in hand. "The horses were running around . . . the men were up and yelling at them, driving them back." Pete snorted and stamped his hooves. The Texans fired at one silhouette. Then, silence. The nervous men kept a careful watch, but the Indians were gone.[16]

After this close call, the squad renewed their efforts to get home. At Leon Holes, however, another peril waited. Rattlesnakes infested the rocks near the water. "These were striking at our horses, which smelled the water and wanted to get at it," Collard remembered. "We just had to stop. Part of us were holding the horses, part killing snakes." Smaller serpents died beneath hurled stones; larger ones fell to buckshot. "Finally we cut a lane through the snakes and got the horses to the water."[17]

The soldiers did what they could to ease the suffering of their malnourished mounts. Saddle and equipment had rubbed a large sore on Pete's skinny back. "I could not get that sore healed," Collard lamented. Pete, after being rubbed down, wallowed in the cool mud.

"He jumped up suddenly with a little ground rattlesnake sticking to his head just behind the ear." The wounded animal shook the viper off, then resumed his roll in the shallows. "His head swelled up as big as a flour barrel before night." The horse's eyes were swollen shut. Collard had to lead his temporarily blinded horse. As the group continued their journey, Collard gathered mesquite beans for his poor pony. "I . . . held them to the horse's nose. After smelling, he ate and whinnied for more." The Texans gathered as many pods as they could, tied them in a blanket and loaded it on their burro for future use. At Dead Man's Hole, the squad found the still-smoldering campfires of a recently passed caravan. Pete, just barely able to see again, stepped in the embers. "Pete ran off, keeping the road in the right direction. He would keep just out of reach. He made me walk four or five miles before he got over his mad fit."[18]

As the eight companions traveled east, food became more abundant for the men. Turkeys and antelope fell to bullets and buckshot. On the Devil's River, large catfish, chummed in with goat entrails, kept the soldiers fed. "We had no grease to fry them with, so we had fish stew." Near San Felipe Springs, the Confederates encountered a pioneer family. These settlers provided the grateful troops with buttermilk, and their mounts with a little shelled corn. "Every day," Collard remembered, "we were getting nearer and nearer civilization."[19]

The horses, however, were failing. As the men neared San Antonio in early August, the animals made just a few miles a day. Maggots had "blowed" the sore on Pete's back. "He looked like the map of Mexico after a big battle," Collard remembered. "His ribs had rubbed raw, his hip bone was bleeding, his sore back bleeding, and his tale and mane were full of mud. "Still afoot, Jack of Clubs left the others and their crippled animals behind, pressing on at a quicker pace. According to Collard, "he beat us into San Antonio by four days."[20]

That quick-stepping soldier alerted the town that another cluster of Sibley's expedition was on its way. Upon reaching San Antonio, a brass band met Collard and his companions and escorted them into the city. "There were ladies on the front porches and at up stairs windows, and on verandahs, waving handkerchiefs." The tired, dirty, and bedraggled Rebels passed through the streets, taking their horses to a livery stable, while at the same time seeking out the closest saloons.

Both men and mounts emerged refreshed. Collard purchased "new clothes, new shoes, under-wear and all." The soldiers then collected flour, bacon, coffee, and sugar. Pete, meanwhile, got a bath in the San Antonio River. "Two Mexicans . . . took him out into the water where it was only knee deep and scoured him." After rinsing the suds, the two grooms put a clean blanket on his back and fed him a peck of shelled oats. That night the squad camped a few miles north of town, near brigade headquarters at San Pedro Springs.[21]

For Collard and Pete, the ordeal was nearly ended. Like the rest of Sibley's Brigade, these soldiers received furloughs to return home and re-equip. The teenager, instead of heading out immediately, let his mount rest, grazing him in an abandoned cornfield nearby. After a few days, Collard's father arrived. "I can't describe the feeling when I heard the voice of our old negro carriage driver as he turned out of the road and approached our camp, and then my father's voice as he made inquiry." Reunited, the men spent that night in camp.

The next morning, the Collards and driver prepared to go home. "My father took a survey of Pete, and said 'turn him loose and let him go. Get in the hack or on the mule and let's go home.'" The boy could not bear to abandon his boon companion of so many hard miles. His father replied sharply, "He is too stove up and worn out. I wouldn't give two bits for him." Young Collard still refused. "I replied that I was attached to Pete and that if it had not been for him, that I would yet be a long ways back among the Comanches and that I did not want to leave him to starve." His father finally relented, and the party headed for home. "Pete lived and made a good farm horse till after the surrender at Appomatox. Peace to his ashes."[22]

Back in Arizona, Private Wright, like many captured Confederates, actually honored his parole and refused to travel with the army; he now found himself virtually alone. "Judge Hart, who had a mill on the river . . . was preparing to flee from the approaching enemy with a train of well-equipped wagons. The Judge was aware, should they capture him, his life would pay the forfeit." Wright agreed to escort the refugees as they abandoned far West Texas. "He said he would give me twenty dollars a month," Wright noted. "I told him I wanted no wages, only my passage, but he refused to take me except on his terms." Simeon Hart, one of the key players in the scheme of Confederate Empire, left his palatial home in late July and traveled toward an uncertain future, choosing the less-traveled upper road toward the Concho River. "Many were the envious looks and remarks of the men I was leaving behind," Wright remembered, and "at what they called my good luck at getting off." The only Rebels left behind were the brigade chief surgeon and twenty-five men convalescing at the hospital in Franklin. By August 16, the arriving Californians added these men to the list of prisoners. The Confederate tenure in Arizona, and the yearlong attempt to create an empire, had ended.[23]

The ordeal for many of Sibley's soldiers, however, was far from over. Many of the healthier soldiers captured at the Santa Fe hospital found themselves unexchanged and without parole. Instead of returning to Texas, they marched north along the Santa Fe Trail as prisoners of war. Robert Thomas Williams had stayed behind to care for his ailing younger brother. Instead, he found himself headed for Kansas. On April 23, Federal troops had collected, counted, and prodded this collection of three dozen prisoners northeast to Fort Union. Five days later, the misguided prisoners that had refused to surrender at Socorro joined the band. On April 30, these Texans had left New Mexico for good, marching on to Kansas.[24]

Amazing sights awaited these hundred men as they entered the Great Plains. Herds of antelope dotted the prairie. Regiments of Kansas and Wisconsin troops, responding to the emergency in New Mexico, passed them on the road. Snow-capped peaks dominated the western horizon. The prisoners and guards kept a thirty-mile-a-day pace, finally reaching Bent's Fort on May 12. Following the Arkansas River, the Confederates saw Cheyenne and Kiowa Indians, and supposedly even a few Kaw and Sioux.[25] On May 30, these captured Confederates participated in a grand "buffalo chase." By June 5, the prisoners waited in camps at Fort Riley, Kansas. Here the Rebels whiled away the month, waiting to be exchanged.[26]

On July 1, the Texans again took the trail heading east, through the heart of abolitionist Kansas. After crossing a floating bridge on the Big Blue River, the Confederates neared Topeka on Independence Day. The citizens fired cannons to celebrate the passage of the enemy prisoners, adding to the festivities of the day. Two days later, the prisoner column reached Fort Leavenworth and camped. Some two hundred Arkansas prisoners joined the train here, and later several dozen Confederate Cherokees entered the compound. For their first time in their service, the Texans mingled with units from other Rebel armies from other theaters of the war. This combined collection of soldiers remained in eastern Kansas until mid-August.[27]

The odyssey continued for these veterans. On August 22, the Texans began a three-hundred-mile trip by steamboat and rail that would eventually land them in Camp Douglas, Illinois, two days later. For the rest of the month, the well-traveled Texans renewed acquaintances with old friends from other regiments who were also serving time in the Chicago prison.[28]

On the afternoon of September 3, Union authorities declared the

New Mexico prisoners and hundreds of other Confederates officially exchanged, loaded them aboard trains for Cairo, Illinois, and shipped them south. Two days later, the men loaded onto steamers for the long trip to Vicksburg, which they reached two weeks later. Private Williams immediately gorged himself. "Eat to much" his diary reads, followed by "Sick." The Texans waited in camps, until finally heading for home early in October. One month later, Williams reached his parents house. "All well," he scribbled, "Meeting with old friends."

At the same time, one of the last Confederates out of New Mexico was Lt. Edward Robb. He was wounded at Glorieta. After the evacuation of Santa Fe, he, like the rest of the bed patients there, had been abandoned to his fate. When the Federals reoccupied the town, Robb surrendered and was paroled. On August 25, he, and more than ninety other recovered Texans who had missed the trip to Chicago, instead headed out of Santa Fe for the long walk to Texas.

These soldiers retraced the route of the campaign, passing by sites made famous by the battles of the spring. The journey through Union-controlled New Mexico seemed pleasant, and the Texans often reveled alongside former enemies at local fandangos in towns along the way. Upon reaching Fort Craig, however, the travelers received reminders of the failed push for empire. "Passed the old battleground . . . where so many of our brave boys fell," Robb scribbled in his diary. "The river has been up and covered the whole field, nothing remains of it except the lanes ploughed through the woods by the artillery." The expedition took the Jornada del Muerte back to the Mesilla Valley, hearing rumors of Mescalero depredations from passing California troops en route. The journey passed without incident, and Robb and his companions went into quarters at Fort Fillmore on September 12.[29]

The Confederate parolees, however, soon received reminders that they were still under Union control and in dangerous territory. When several bolted across the Rio Grande, the remainder found themselves under close arrest. "A strong guard was placed around us and we were not even allowed to speak," Robb wrote. That night, Indians raided the Union herd and rode away with several horses. Escaping prisoners and rampaging

Apaches were just business as usual in New Mexico.[30]

Union troops escorted their charges as far as Fort Quitman. From there to San Antonio, though, the Texans were on their own. As the well-armed and well-equipped Federals rode off to the west, Robb noted that the fort was "very much dilapidated." The surrounding countryside, essentially abandoned to the Apaches, he described as "deserted and going to wreak." The Confederates continued east, passing reminders of their failed campaign. At Eagle Springs, rotting horses and several graves greeted the men. "This is one of the worst places on the road," Robb wrote. The ruined stage stands along the way added to the sense of desolation. "It is astonishing how men, for a pittance of 30 or 40 dol[lars] per month will risk their lives in these dreary places. . . . Not a stand we pass but what some men have been killed by Indians. Dead oxen and horses, remains of wagons are scattered all along the road—not a stick of timber to be seen anywhere. Everything betokens a God forsaken country."

Fort Davis, one of the promising strongholds of the Confederate empire, also lay deserted and destroyed. "Found the fort in ashes, don't know how it was burnt," Robb recorded. The reminders of human tragedy were abundant. "In the hospital of the fort found some of the hair of a man who had been left, probably to die. The worms were thick where his body had lain."

The column moved on. On October 4, Robb noted that he "killed a large tarantula this morning, of which there are a great many . . . also centipedes." That same day, in a reflective moment, he added "one year ago today I was mustered into the C.S. Service at the Sallado 8 miles north of San Antonio." A few days later, the caravan reentered Confederate held territory. Their first sign of civilization was the lightly garrisoned Fort Stockton. Here, the men received corn and watermelon rations. After crossing the Pecos River the Texans pushed on to Fort Lancaster, where "We had the good luck to find another Beef here—a fine one with a large sore on his back about the size of a man's hand," Robb wrote. "As fresh meat is not to be had in this country, a few sores on the beefes are not noticed." These latecomers finally wandered into San Antonio by the end of the month, about the same time as the parolees from Camp Douglas. The role of Texas soldiers in Sibley's drive for empire had ended.[31]

Their efforts, it seemed, were in vain. In the final analysis, though, a variety of factors had contributed to the disaster. The general himself had provided, at best, mediocre leadership; he certainly had unrealistic expectations for supplying his men and horses. The Confederacy itself, far away and out of touch with the rapidly changing events in the Far West had been of little help. None of the Southern leaders had anticipated the chaos caused by the Apaches.

The Texas soldiers, though, bear much of the blame. They were amateurs at war, and played the part. Although mounted, few kept proper care of their animals, and brigade mobility suffered. This collection of "mounted volunteers" failed miserably in traditional roles of cavalry: screening, interdiction, and reconnaissance. Union garrisons never suffered for supplies, rarely had their mail intercepted, and always knew Confederate movements. Sibley's Texans, however, let supplies burn within galloping distance and let slow-moving wagons trundle away to safety. These same soldiers allowed themselves to be surprised twice—once by exhausted infantry! Many of their field officers, like their brigadier, were professional soldiers. Drill and training had at first been energetic. This discipline, however, did not survive contact with long marches and hard fighting. These troops, like their Mexican War and Texas Revolution predecessors, had proven to be fine warriors, but poor soldiers, ironically in keeping with the frontier military tradition they so well represented.

A belated rising of Colorado secessionists underscored the lost opportunities for the Confederacy in the Far West. Starting that spring, a regiment had been forming at Mace's Hole, near Pueblo. By midsummer some six hundred men had wandered in to join the unit. "Really there was never this number in the hole at once," Southern sympathizer Daniel Ellis Conner wrote, "but this was the headquarters." He, too joined. "Everybody was presumed to have a decided choice. There was no escaping, whether there was an individual expression or an overt act committed or not. Amid this confusion . . . the public mind became unsettled and impatient."[32]

The Secessionists kept their mustering point secret. "No new recruit was ever allowed to come directly to Mace's Hole," Conner continued. "They were recruited and sent to a small camp above Pike's Peak, more than fifty miles from Mace's Hole." From there, once Rebels had verified their intentions and loyalty, the new men would follow guides to the main encampment. "By this means a traitor could not jeopardize the safety of any but the little recruiting squad."[33]

Meanwhile, Confederate partisans operated against Union targets in the territory. Capt. George Madison, on commission by Sibley, had been raiding Federal mail lines in the area. In August, his band of thirty-five men robbed the Fort Garland mail. Authorities offered a reward for Madison's capture, but to no avail. With increased Rebel activity in the territory, and the Texan threat removed from New Mexico, attention turned toward Colorado.[34]

The Rebels, it seemed, were ready to strike. Fort Garland, near the New Mexico border, was the target. Agents among the Union garrison would allow the secessionists access to the fort. The Confederate commanders then assigned men to various tasks, including seizing the post artillery, securing the livestock, and capturing the fort commander. Others were to capture small arms and ammunition, then blow up the magazine. "The calculation was that a sufficient number of men were to be near at hand to overpower the fort within its walls," Conner wrote, " and to have the matter ended before it was known what had happened. All these preparations were complete and the regiment was only waiting to call in its little recruiting camps and for the appointed day to arrive."[35]

The opportunity for this Rebel coup, however, passed. The men at Mace's Hole, chaffing under the light military discipline imposed on the camp, became dissatisfied and began deserting wholesale. Some of these would-be soldiers informed Union commanders of the scheme, and soon Federal troops arrived at Mace's Hole. The place was deserted. Those secessionists that could made their way to Texas or Arizona. Colorado remained loyal.[36]

Despite the collapse of Confederate Arizona, Southern imperial aspirations continued throughout the rest of the war. Two men, Lansford Hastings and John Robert Baylor, each presented various schemes in the later stages of the war that were designed to bring the Southwest into the Confederacy. William M. Gwin, Mississippi native and former California senator, proposed to Emperor Louis Napoleon of France an expedition to seize Sonora. Even as the prospects of Southern independence waned, a few national leaders still sought ways of pushing on to the Pacific.[37]

The factors that inspired these imperial delusions were the same as in 1861. Exaggerated reports of renewed secessionists' activities in California and Colorado continued to filter east. The natural reaction among Southerners was another attempt to succor these territorial compatriots, but the time for such action had passed. The small fires of disunion burning on the Pacific slope and in the Rocky Mountains had been systematically snuffed out.[38]

Of all the imperial schemers, John Robert Baylor remained the most persistent, and he surrounded himself with men who shared his dream. After Sibley evacuated Arizona, the mercurial Texan found himself a governor without a territory, but he continued with his plans for raising an Arizona Brigade. Five small battalions, each claiming six companies, formed near Hempstead, Texas, officered by men prominent in the original conquest of the West. Brother George Wythe Baylor, who had accompanied Albert Sidney Johnston from Mesilla, commanded one. Peter Hardeman, one of the original captains of the Second Texas Mounted Rifles, led another. Former Texas official Spruce M. Baird, lawyer Philemon Herbert, and other ex-residents of the desert southwest served as officers. The veterans of the Arizona companies Baylor had raised formed the nucleus of the brigade, and some evidence suggests that he intended to include Col. Charles Pyron's recently reorganized Second Texas Cavalry in his plans.[39]

During the summer of 1862, as Sibley's troops wandered home, Baylor's plans for the reconquest of his jurisdiction proceeded apace. According to Union reports, Confederate agents had been spotted in Monterrey, Mexico, purchasing supplies for the expedition. Determined not to repeat Sibley's mistakes, Baylor planned a new invasion route. This time his army would strike through northwest Texas to the Santa Fe Trail, in southwestern Kansas or southeastern Colorado. His army would then control the Union line of supplies and communications in the territory. The Federals would have to fight or starve. James H. Carleton, who had replaced Edward R. S. Canby as head of the Department of New Mexico upon the latter's promotion and transfer to the East, took the new Texan threat seriously and stockpiled food and ammunition to counter the anticipated invasion.[40]

Texas in 1862, however, was vastly different than it had been the year before. No longer did hundreds of eager recruits flock to join the army; of Baylor's anticipated force of three thousand men, only five hundred had enlisted by the end of the year. The brigade horses, too, became a nuisance as they voraciously consumed all of the available forage in the vicinity of Hempstead; the men also consumed supplies desperately needed for other units guarding the coast. Many Texans were fighting in Arkansas, Tennessee, and Virginia, while others, including Col. Edwin Waller's battalion, served in Louisiana. The resources of Texas could no longer support armies raised for quixotic adventures in the west.[41]

Baylor refused to believe that recruits could not be found and he actively sought additional men. His only success was a company he dubbed the "Ladies Rangers," because it was equipped with donations by the women of Houston, Galveston, and San Antonio. His sister stitched its flag, and Baylor tied it to a Comanche lance he had captured years before. This one unit, though, was hardly sufficient.[42]

Even as his task grew increasingly difficult, Baylor's plan for reconquest received a deadly blow from an unexpected quarter. Official documents from the Confederate tenure in Arizona had trickled east. Couriers, like Sibley's aide Tom Ochiltree, carried some; others accompanied the army as it withdrew to San Antonio. One notorious piece of government business, however, had been penned by Governor Baylor in March, when he ordered Capt. Tom Helm to lure the Apaches into a peace parley and then murder them. This letter, upon its arrival in Richmond, was dubbed the "Extermination Order."[43]

Confederate Pres. Jefferson Davis reacted angrily to the infamous correspondence. Baylor had misrepresented the government by stating that Congress had passed a law to exterminate the Apaches. Quite the contrary was true, for Richmond espoused conciliation, pacification, and other policies inherited from the United States. By October, Davis fired Baylor, removed him from command of his brigade, revoked his commission, and ordered the expedition abandoned. For the second time in his short association with the Confederacy, Baylor's plans had been sabotaged.[44]

The other prophet of the Confederate Empire, Henry Hopkins

Sibley, fared little better. On September 9, he had moved the head-quarters of his brigade to Marshall, Texas, settling his family in a large home in that city. He then spent the fall defending himself against charges arising from his mismanagement of the New Mexico campaign. Numerous delays plagued the process, and the necessary paperwork had difficulty finding its way through the proper government channels. Eventually, President Davis intervened on Sibley's behalf and dismissed the charges. In December, he ordered Sibley to rejoin his brigade, with his commission intact, but his reputation in shambles. He left immediately, planning to meet his men in the field.[45]

Other minor players in the imperial scheme continued a shadow government, which they claimed represented the interests of Confederate Arizona. Establishing their capital-in-exile at San Antonio, these men remained true believers. Californian Dan Showalter, an early proponent of West Coast secession, entered the state via Chihuahua and made time to meet Colonel Baylor's mother. Others, including "Grant" Oury, territorial delegate to the Confederate Congress, James Magoffin, Alexander M. Jackson, and Maj. Bethel Coopwood stayed in hotels downtown near the Alamo. The Confederate government, in tacit approval of at least the idea of regaining Arizona, sent Mississippian Robert Josselyn to act as governor. This close friend of Jefferson Davis drew a salary, as did three other "territorial officials." For the rest of the war, secessionists schemes continued to simmer, and disaffected citizens continued wandering in with stirring tales of conditions in the West, but with no result.[46]

The Confederacy, too, had changed dramatically; as the fall of 1862 brought fresh horrors to the nation, calls for reinforcements came from every front. Hood's Texas Brigade, crippled at Antietam, sought aid from home, and Sibley was instructed to move his command immediately to Virginia. Before that dispatch had traveled halfway to Austin, a second document ordered the veterans to Vicksburg, where Gen. John C. Pemberton prepared his citadel on the Mississippi River. An even more plaintive call, however, came from Louisiana. Gen. Richard Taylor, newly arrived in Alexandria, called for troops to help him hold his native state against overwhelming odds. After the fall of New Orleans, Union troops under Nathaniel Banks had ravaged the area; Taylor needed more men to provide an adequate defense. Levies from the Pelican state went to Virginia or Mississippi, but few remained to protect their homes. Its salvation would have to come from Texas. When Sibley's troops received orders to report back to the brigade, they discovered that their destination was the exotic region around New Iberia, on the black and winding Bayou Teche. Baylor's so-called Arizona Brigade would eventually also find itself east of the Sabine River. The requirements of Southern defenses had claimed the last of the Army of New Mexico.

For Sibley, the war was as good as over. While serving under Gen. Richard Taylor in Louisiana, the spectre of alcohol again intruded. During the battles of Bisland and Irish Bend in April, 1863, Sibley mismanaged his duties and abandoned his troops in the middle of a chaotic retreat. Later that year, he faced a second court martial which, amazingly, cleared him of misconduct. He was not, however, restored to command. He spent the next few months attempting to find a command worthy of his rank. Eventually, he traveled back to Richmond where government bureaucrats shuttled the officer from one office to the next, seeking a suitable assignment. Sibley, the man who had started the war with dreams of carving a Confederate Empire, finally got his chance to serve in Mexico, although not in the capacity he imagined. Late in the war, he received orders to return to the Trans-Mississippi to wait for an assignment, but by that time travel to the West was difficult. He ultimately opted to take a steamer from Mobile, via Havana, to Matamoros, Mexico. From here, the road-weary general had to travel up the south bank of the Rio Grande to Laredo to gain entrance back into Texas. Sibley, however, spent the last days of the war haunting Shreveport with no official duties. He had arrived at Gen. Edmund Kirby Smith's headquarters looking for an assignment, to no avail. Undaunted, he remained in the city, but sent his family through Union lines to live with his in-laws in Brooklyn, New York. He was still in Shreveport in June, when Kirby Smith surrendered the Department of the Trans-Mississippi.[47]

A final irony awaited, though, for Sibley, the man whose name has become so intimately linked to the Confederate dream of empire. A few weeks after the surrender, while the general waited to rejoin his family, occupying Union troops had perpetrated an indignity against that weary old warrior, symbolically reminiscent of the campaign in New Mexico years earlier. Sibley promptly scribbled a formal protest, addressing his letter to, oddly enough, Union Maj. Gen. Edward R. S. Canby, the acting occupation commander in Louisiana. Some Federal soldier, Sibley complained, had stolen his horse.[48]

John Robert Baylor, meanwhile, emerged from the disaster of the Confederate Empire as its greatest champion. The lion-hearted warrior served amid the flying iron at the Battle of Galveston on January 1, 1863, in his shirtsleeves, as a volunteer artilleryman. Afterward, Baylor successfully ran for Congress. Once in Richmond, he continued his lobbying for a reconquest of Arizona. He eventually met with Jefferson Davis on the matter, taking the opportunity to improve his reputation with the president. As late as December 21, 1864, Baylor continued agitating for a Confederate return to the Southwest in a letter to Secretary of War James Seddon. Even as Union cannon thundered in the distance, and the very survival of the nation seemed in jeopardy, a converted Davis reviewed the letter and gave his blessing to a reconquest of Arizona and New Mexico. On March 25, after a tedious cycle of bureaucratic wrangling, Baylor was reinstated as a colonel in the army and assigned to raise a command to restore the Confederate empire. This authorization, however, was one of the last acts of the Rebel government. Fifteen days later, Robert E. Lee surrendered at Appomattox.[49]

Epilogue

The conflict in New Mexico should be regarded
as one of the decisive campaigns in the war.
—Latham Anderson

By mid-1862, Union planners in the West relaxed, but they realized that the threat to the nation posed by Sibley and his army had been extremely dangerous. In later years, one Northern observer, Brig. Gen. Latham Anderson, wrote: "The remote and unimportant territory of New Mexico was not the real objective of this invasion. The Confederate leaders were striking at much higher game—no less than the conquest of California, Sonora, Chihuahua, New Mexico, Arizona, and Utah—and above all, the possession of all the gold supply on the Pacific coast." The consequences if the South had been successful, Anderson feared, would have been devastating. "The conquest alone of this vast domain, in all probability, would have insured the recognition of the Confederacy by the European powers. The conflict in New Mexico should be regarded as one of the decisive campaigns in the war."[1]

Indeed, if the concept of a Southern nation was to succeed, then the Confederacy needed more territory. Territorial expansion for the sake of extending slavery had started after the Missouri Compromise and became a driving force behind Southern politics. Secession, the ultimate expression of Southern nationalism, had been in part fueled by Southern frustrations over perceived limits to slavery in the territories. The Confederacy had to expand—the right to own slaves in the territories was part of the Southern catechism.

Northwestern Mexico was lagniappe, some might argue *leben-sraum,* a little extra real estate as insurance for the future. Slavery, and by extension the Confederacy, required an empire. The legitimacy of the nation had been at stake.

Even if successful, the question of the Confederacy's ability to hold the western territories remains. Troops seemed to be available, and if prewar figures are to be trusted, many more awaited the arrival of Southern troops. Evidence of secessionists from Nevada to Montana exists, and these men would have, in theory, materially aided the Confederacy. The Union's control in the region was tenuous early in the war, held together by Republican politicians and Federal bayonets. Once this cement was removed, recapturing the West for the Union would have been tough.

California, however, presents a unique case when considering the implications of a Confederate Empire. Two ports, Los Angeles and San Francisco, would have provided safe haven for Rebel shipping, while proving difficult to blockade. Union vessels would have had to have been diverted from Asia and the Atlantic to deal with the problem, and friendly ports would have been scarce. Eventually, either facilities in Oregon would have been developed, or the United States might themselves have seized Guaymas or Acapulco, as was often suggested at the beginning of the war. If the U.S. Navy was unsuccessful in its two-coast blockade, then California gold might have flowed freely to European creditors willing to arm the South. Instead of paying for commerce raiders with promises of cotton, the South might have been able to pay cash. Monuments in the gold fields of Nevada and California allude to the fact that western minerals saved the Union. In this scenario, they might have just as easily sustained the Confederacy.

With the stakes so high, the question arises over the wisdom of entrusting the chore to General Sibley. The fault seems to lie with Jefferson Davis. Sibley was everything the president looked for in the leadership of his army: a fellow West Point graduate, Mexican War veteran, and man of influence. Davis saw Sibley as an expression of his belief in the professionalization of war. Something as big as empire could not be trusted to amateurs. In Davis's defense, however, Sibley was the only man to formally propose conquering the West. He arrived at a critical time in the life of the Confederacy, offered a plan that promised to be self-sustaining, and a distracted Davis bought it.

Ultimately, the Federals had the most to do with Confederate failure in New Mexico. Canby made few mistakes, although some would argue that he lost Val Verde after Roberts already had the battle won. Even so, he denied Sibley any meaningful victories. He shepherded his meager resources, and used them to their best advantage. His men were brave and long-suffering, his subordinates capable and creative. They saved the West for the Union.

Even if Canby and his troops had failed, Abraham Lincoln would not have allowed a western Confederate Empire to remain unchallenged. Besides the Californians, a fresh brigade from Kansas was on its way to New Mexico, even as Sibley's army evacuated the region. Even had Fort Union fallen, the Texans would have faced many hard battles between Las Vegas and Denver City. Had fortunes still favored the South, even more regiments from Kansas and Wisconsin would have headed west, probably augmented by units from Iowa, Minnesota, Missouri, and even Nebraska, Indian Territory, and Oregon. This apocryphal "Army of the Plains" or "Army of the Missouri" would have been supplied from Saint Louis via Kansas City and the Santa Fe Trail, employed some ten thousand otherwise unoccupied troops, and would have been an impressive force as it marched across the prairie. The American Civil War would have become even more of a continental conflict.

The true winners in such a scenario would probably have been the Native American inhabitants of the plains and the mountains of the West. The Union troops who would have faced a "Confederate Army of the Rockies" would not have been available to hunt Apaches in Arizona or massacre the Southern Cheyenne at Sand Creek. Historian Alvin Josephy argues that the American Civil War was a time of unparalleled cruelty for the indigenous peoples of North America. If the whites had been killing each other by the thousands on the Great Plains and in the Rockies, they would not have been killing Indians.

Sibley's failed adventure might have provided one of the few prospects for Southern independence. The creation of a Confederate Empire would have secured western wealth and European recognition. The hopes for the campaign had indeed been high—much greater than what history has remembered—but the dream came to a tragic end. The empire, like the Confederacy, was not to be, despite the investment of so much blood and treasure.

Notes

CHAPTER 1. TEXANS, SOUTHERNERS, AND DREAMS OF EMPIRE

1. Trevanion T. Teel, "Sibley's New Mexico Campaign: Its Objects and the Causes of Its Failures," in Robert U. Johnson and Clarence C. Buel, eds. *Battles and Leaders of the Civil War,* new ed., 4 vols., 2:700; see also William Need to Simon Cameron, Sept. 27, 1861, *The War of the Rebellion: A Compilation of the Official Records of the Union and Confederate Armies,* 128 vols., 1st ser., 50, 1:635–41, (hereafter cited as *OR; all references are to series 1, unless otherwise indicated).

2. Robert E. May, *The Southern Dream of a Caribbean Empire, 1854–1861,* pp. 235–44; Robert E. May, "Young American Males and Filibustering in the Age of Manifest Destiny: The United States Army as a Cultural Mirror," *Journal of American History* 78 (Dec., 1991): 859, 865.

3. Important works on American expansionism include Richard Van Alstyne, *The Rising American Empire,* a study of the growth of the American nation-state. A. K. Weinberg, *Manifest Destiny: A Study of Nationalist Expansionism in American History,* argues that the moral justification of the imperialistic impulse was sincere. Fredrick Merk and Lois Bannister Merk, *Manifest Destiny and Mission in American History: A Reinterpretation,* argue that the sense of mission in American expansionism was sincere and noble, but that Manifest Destiny corrupted this ideal by force of arms. William Goetzmann, *When the Eagle Screamed: The Romantic Horizon in American Diplomacy 1800–1860,* suggests that American imperialism in the early nineteenth century was inspired by romantic notions carried over from Europe, including beliefs in national grandeur and destiny. For source documents, see Norman Graebner, ed., *Manifest Destiny,* an anthology of primary materials relating to the subject. Valuable articles on the subject include Richard Van Alstyne, "The Significance of the Mississippi Valley in American Diplomatic History, 1686–1890," *Mississippi Valley Historical Review* 36 (Spring, 1949): 215–38; and Charles Vevier, "American Continentalism: An Idea of Expansion," *American Historical Review* 65 (Summer, 1960): 323–25.

4. D. W. Meining, *Imperial Texas: An Interpretive Essay in Cultural Geography,* pp. 38–39. This work deals extensively with the concept of Texas imperialism.

5. William C. Binkley, *The Expansionist Movement in Texas, 1836–1850,* p. 29.

6. Columbia *Telegraph and Texas Register,* Sept. 16, 1837. See also Binkley, *Expansionist Movement in Texas,* pp. 16–42.

7. Herbert Pickens Gambrell, *Mirabeau Buonaparte Lamar: Troubadour and Crusader,* p. 245. See also Asa K. Christian, *Mirabeau Buonaparte Lamar;* and Mirabeau B. Lamar, *Papers,* 6 vols., ed. C. A. Gulick; see also John Edward Weems and Jane Weems, *Dream of Empire: A Human History of the Republic of Texas, 1836–1846.*

8. Quoted in Meining, *Imperial Texas,* p. 42.

9. Janet Lecompte, *Rebellion in Rio Arriba, 1837,* pp. 61–62.

10. The three expeditions included Gen. Hugh McCleod's attempt in 1841, Col. Charles Warfield's 1843 raid on the village of Mora, and Col. James Snively's "Battalion of Invincibles" expedition the same year.

11. A discussion of Manifest Destiny serving as a cure to national instability can be found in Thomas R. Hietala, *Manifest Design: Anxious Aggrandizement in Late Jacksonian America.*

12. Binkley, *Expansionist Movement in Texas,* pp. 170–73.

13. Texas Legislature, *Senate Journal,* Third Legislature, pp. 285–87; Edmund T. Miller, *Financial History of Texas,* p. 118.

14. Meining, *Imperial Texas,* pp. 39, 63; Loomis Morton Ganaway, *New Mexico and the Sectional Controversy, 1846–1861,* p. 22.

15. Binkley, *Expansionist Movement in Texas,* pp. 177–79.

16. Kenneth Franklin Neighbours, *Robert Simpson Neighbors and the Texas Frontier 1836–1859,* pp. 87–94; W. H. Timmons, "American El Paso: The Formative Years, 1848–1850," *Southwestern Historical Quarterly* 87 (July, 1983): 16–19.

17. Quoted in Mark E. Nackman, *Nation within a Nation: The Rise of Texas Nationalism,* p. 120.

18. Benjamin Rush Wallace to Thomas J. Rusk, Jan. 16, 1850, Thomas J. Rusk Papers, Eugene C. Barker Texas History Center, University of Texas, Austin (hereafter, cited as BTHC).

19. U. B. Phillips, ed., *The Correspondence of Robert Toombs, Alexander H. Stevens, and Howell Cobb,* pp. 192–93.

20. Nackman, *Nation within a Nation,* pp. 122–23; See also Kenneth F. Neighbours, "The Taylor-Neighbors Struggle Over the Upper Rio Grande Region of Texas in 1850," *Southwestern Historical Quarterly* 61 (Apr., 1958): 431–63.

21. *Clarksville Northern Standard,* Sept. 7, 1850.

22. Binkley, *Expansionist Movement in Texas,* pp. 216–17; Nackman, *Nation within a Nation,* pp. 123–25.

23. Randolph Campbell, "Texas and the Nashville Convention of 1850," *Southwestern Historical Quarterly* 76 (July, 1972): 10–14; for a discussion of Texas and its reasons for seceding, see Walter L. Buenger, "Texas and the Riddle of Secession," *Southwestern Historical Quarterly* 87 (Oct., 1983): 151–82.

24. See Campbell, "Texas and the Nashville Convention," pp. 1–14.

25. J. Fred Rippy, "The Negotiation of the Gadsden Treaty," *Southwestern Historical Quarterly* 27 (July, 1923): 6–8.

26. For the standard, though very dated, work on the Gadsden Treaty, see Paul N. Garber, *The Gadsden Treaty.* For a discussion of conflicts over control of the Indians, taken mainly from published sources, see Joseph F. Park, "The Apaches in Mexican-American Relations, 1843–1861: A Footnote to the Gadsden Treaty," *Arizona and the West* 3 (Summer,

1961): 129–46.

27. Ganaway, *New Mexico*, pp. 106–107. See also W. H. Goetzmann, "The United States–Mexican Boundary Survey, 1848–1853," *Southwestern Historical Quarterly* 60 (Oct., 1958); Joseph Richard Werne, "Partisan Politics and the Mexican Boundary Survey, 1848–1853," *Southwestern Historical Quarterly* 90 (Apr., 1987): 329–46. Park, "Mexican-American Relations," pp. 129–46.

28. Clement Eaton, "Frontier Life in Southern Arizona," *Southwestern Historical Quarterly* 36 (Jan., 1933): 177–78.

29. Ibid., p. 174; Mills, "Personal Narrative," p. 1.

30. May, *Southern Dream*, pp. 147–48.

31. As quoted in May, *Southern Dream*, pp. 145–46. A study of the problem of slaves fleeing to Mexico can be found in Rosalie Schwartz, *Across the River to Freedom: U.S. Negroes in Mexico*.

32. As quoted in May, "Young American Males and Filibustering," *The Journal of American History*, p. 885.

33. May, *Southern Dream*, pp. 235–36; David M. Potter, *The Impending Crisis: 1848–1861*, p. 198.

34. May, *Southern Dream*, pp. 148–49.

35. [George Bickley], *Rules, Regulations and Principles of the K.G.C., issued by Order of the Congress of the K.C.S. and the General President*, pp. 6–7.

36. Roy Sylvan Dunn, "The KGC in Texas, 1860–1861," *Southwestern Historical Quarterly* 70 (Apr., 1967): 543.

37. *Dallas Herald*, Feb. 29, 1860, p. 1.

38. Dunn, "The KGC in Texas," pp. 555–57.

39. Jimmie Hicks, ed., "Some Letters Concerning the Knights of the Golden Circle in Texas, 1860–1861," *Southwestern Historical Quarterly* 65 (July, 1961): 80–86.

40. Ibid., p. 84.

41. Alvin M. Josephy, Jr., *The Civil War in the American West*, p. 19.

42. Elijah R. Kennedy, *The Contest for California in 1861: How Colonel E. D. Baker Saved the Pacific States to the Union*, pp. 72–73; Latham Anderson, "Canby's Services in the New Mexican Campaign," in Johnson and Buel, *Battles and Leaders of Civil War*, 2:697–99.

43. Kennedy, *The Contest for California*, pp. 73, 219.

44. Winfield Scott Hancock to William W. Mackall, May 7, 1861, *OR*, 50:479–80.

45. *Charleston [South Carolina] Mercury*, Nov. 7, 1860.

46. Kennedy, *The Contest for California*, pp. 72–73.

47. Buenger, "Texas and the Riddle of Secession," pp. 181–82; Francis R. Lubbock, *Six Decades in Texas: The Memoirs of Francis R. Lubbock, Confederate Governor of Texas*, ed. C. W. Raines, pp. 305–308.

48. *Charleston Mercury*, Dec. 7, 1860, n.p.; *Macon [Georgia] Daily Telegraph*, Feb. 28, 1861, n.p.

49. May, *Southern Dream*, p. 232.

50. Ana Irene Sandbo, "The First Session of the Secession Convention of Texas," *Southwestern Historical Quarterly* 18 (Oct., 1914): 166.

51. R. H. Williams, *With the Border Ruffians: Memories of the Far West, 1852–1868*,

p. 159. See also Charles Anderson, *Texas, Before, and on the Eve of the Rebellion.*

52. Williams, *With the Border Ruffians*, pp. 159–60. In his memoirs, Williams claims to have joined a San Antonio castle. However, he later served under Capt. James Paul of the Castroville Castle, KGC.

53. Ibid., pp. 188–91.

54. Ibid., pp. 243, 246.

55. Ernest W. Winkler, ed., *Journal of the Secession Convention of Texas*, pp. 45, 67.

56. As quoted in Bernard Mandel, *Labor, Free and Slave*, p. 151.

57. Frederick Law Olmstead, *The Papers of Frederick Law Olmstead*, ed. Charles Capen McLaughlin, 2:381–84.

58. Bernard Mandel, *Labor, Free and Slave*, p. 151.

59. Ganaway, *New Mexico*, pp. 105–107; Anne Merriman Peck, *The March of Arizona History*, pp. 153–54; Eaton, "Frontier Life in Southern Arizona," p. 151.

60. Ganaway, *New Mexico*, pp. 60–76.

61. J. J. Bowden, *The Exodus of Federal Forces From Texas*, pp. 42–44.

62. James Reily to John H. Reagan, Jan. 26, 1862, *OR*, 50:825–26.

63. May, *Southern Dream*, p. 243.

CHAPTER 2. BEGINNINGS OF EMPIRE

1. Dunn, "KGC in Texas," p. 568; David E. Twiggs to L. Thomas, "Report of Bvt. Maj. Gen. D. E. Twiggs, U.S. Army, of the seizure of U.S. Arsenal and Barracks at San Antonio, and surrender of military posts, & c., in the Department of Texas," *OR*, 1:503–504; Thomas J. Devine, Sam Maverick, and P. N. Luckett to J. C. Robertson, n.d., cited in J. T. Sprague, *The Treachery in Texas: The Secession of Texas and the Arrest of the United States Officers and Soldiers Serving in Texas*, pp. 116–17.

2. Jerry Thompson, *Colonel John Robert Baylor: Texas Indian Fighter and Confederate Soldier*, pp. 24–34; Martin Hardwick Hall, *The Confederate Army of New Mexico*, pp. 295–97; George W. Baylor, *John Robert Baylor: Confederate Governor of Arizona*, ed. Odie B. Faulk, pp. 4–5.

3. Thompson, *Baylor*, pp. 3–4; Baylor, *Baylor*, pp. 20–21.

4. Thompson, *Baylor*, p. 4; Hall, *Confederate Army of New Mexico*, p. 295; Baylor, *Baylor*, p. 24.

5. Thompson, *Baylor*, p. 5; Hall, *Confederate Army of New Mexico*, p. 296; Baylor, *Baylor*, p. 25.

6. Thompson, *Baylor*, pp. 5–6; Baylor, *Baylor*, p. 25.

7. John Robert Baylor to "Emy" [Emily Hanna Baylor], Nov. 9, 1853, Baylor Family Papers, BTHC; Neighbours, *Neighbors*, p. 159; Thompson, *Baylor*, pp. 6–9.

8. Baylor, *Baylor*, pp. 33, 35.

9. Neighbours, *Neighbors*, pp. 177, 180; Baylor to "Fan," Mar. 30, 1856, Baylor Papers, BTHC; Thompson, *Baylor*, pp. 8–11.

10. Neighbours, *Neighbors*, pp. 166, 181; Thompson, *Baylor*, p. 11; Baylor to "Fan," Apr. 5, 1857.

11. Thompson, *Baylor*, pp. 1–22; Baylor, *Baylor*, pp. 1–4. An oil painting of Baylor on display at the Alamo depicts him in a curious uniform of a dark blue frock, gray trousers,

and a circular golden pin. The pin is of a design described in J. W. Pomfrey, *A True Disclosure and Exposition of the Knights of the Golden Circle, including the Secret Signs, Grips, and Charges, of the Three Degrees, as Practiced by the Order*, pp. 29, 46. Baylor apparently was a member of the second, or financial, degree. Baylor's uniform is described in detail in [Bickley], *Rules, Regulations and Principles*, p. 13.

12. Williams, *With The Border Ruffians*, p. 163; Caroline Baldwin Darrow, "Recollections of the Twiggs Surrender," Johnson and Buel, *Battles and Leaders of Civil War*, 1:34–35; Josephy, *Civil War*, p. 24.

13. Jerry Thompson, ed., *From Desert to Bayou: The Civil War Journal and Sketches of Morgan Wolfe Merrick*, pp. ii–iv; Ronnie C. Tyler, *Santiago Vidaurri and the Southern Confederacy*, pp. 23, 32–33.

14. Thompson, *From Desert to Bayou*, p. 6.

15. Ibid.; Larkin Smith to [C. A. Waite], Feb. 23, 1861, "Report of Bvt. Maj. Larkin Smith, Eighth U.S. Infantry, of the seizure of U.S. Property at San Antonio, Tex.," *OR,* 1:519–20.

16. Thompson, *From Desert to Bayou*, pp. 6–8.

17. Twiggs to Thomas, pp. 503–504; Devine, Maverick, and Luckett to Robertson, p. 117; Thompson, *From Desert to Bayou*, p. 8.

18. Ben McCulloch to J. C. Robertson, n.d., cited in Sprague, *Treachery in Texas*, p. 118.

19. Williams, *With The Border Ruffians*, p. 164; Thompson, *From Desert to Bayou*, pp. 6–8.

20. Johnson and Buel, *Battles and Leaders of the Civil War*, 1:38–39; Twiggs, "General Order No. 5," Feb. 18, 1861, cited in Sprague, *Treachery in Texas*, p. 118; see also Devine, Maverick, and Luckett to Robertson, Mar. 9, 1861, pp. 119–21; C. A. Waite to L. Thomas, Feb. 26, 1861, *OR,* 1:521–22.

21. Ralph A. Wooster, *The Secession Conventions of the South*, pp. 132–35; Lubbock, *Six Decades in Texas:*, p. 310; Ben Procter, *Not Without Honor: The Life of John H. Reagan*, pp. 125–27.

22. L. P. Walker to Ben McCulloch, Mar. 4, 1861, *OR,* 1:609–10; L. P. Walker to John Hemphill, Apr. 11, 1861, ibid., pp. 621–22; Stephen B. Oates, "Recruiting Cavalry in Texas," *Southwestern Historical Quarterly* 64 (Apr., 1961): 465.

23. For a lengthy, and innovative, discussion of this frontier military ideal, see Tom W. Cutrer, *Ben McCulloch and the Frontier Military Tradition*.

24. For an excellent essay on the riddle of Southern individualism, see John Shelton Reed, "The Same Old Stand?" in Fifteen Southerners, *Why the South Will Survive*, pp. 13–34; see also "Two Types of American Individualism" and "Two Orators" in Richard M. Weaver, *The Southern Essays of Richard M. Weaver*, ed. George M. Curtis, III, and James J. Thompson, Jr., pp. 77–133.

25. W. J. Joyce, *The Life of W. J. Joyce, Written by Himself: The History of a Long, Laborious, and Happy Life of Fifty-Seven Years in the Ministry in Texas—From the Sabine to the Rio Grande*, p. 1.

26. Ganaway, *New Mexico*, pp. 113, 119; Duane A. Smith, *The Birth of Colorado: A Civil War Perspective*, pp. 12, 18, 20, 27, 108–109; Oscar Lewis, *The War in the Far West: 1861–1865*, pp. 20–24; Joseph Allen Stout, Jr., *The Liberators: Filibustering Expeditions into Mexico, 1848–1862, and the Last Thrust of Manifest Destiny*, pp. 159, 163.

27. Peck, *March of Arizona History*, pp. 153–54; Ganaway, *New Mexico*, pp. 111–19.

28. W. Hubert Curry, *Sun Rising in the West: The Saga of Henry Clay and Elizabeth Smith*, pp. 9–16.

29. Ibid., pp. 13–39.

30. Ibid., p. 70.

31. Daniel Ellis Conner, *A Confederate in the Colorado Gold Fields*, p. 120; Smith, *Birth of Colorado*, pp. 12–20.

32. Conner, *Colorado Gold Fields*, pp. 98–109.

33. Ibid., pp. 122–23.

34. Martin Hardwick Hall, *Sibley's New Mexico Campaign*, pp. 16–17; Ganaway, *New Mexico*, pp. 112–13; Norman K. Johnson, "Satanic-looking Colonel John R. Baylor fought Yankee, Indians and one unfortunate newspaper editor," *America's Civil War* 3 (Jan., 1991): 10; L. Boyd Finch, "Sherod Hunter and the Confederates in Arizona," *Journal of Arizona History* 10 (Autumn, 1969), p. 145.

35. W. W. Loring to L. Thomas, Mar. 23, 1861, *OR*, 1:599–600; Isaac Lynde to "Assistant Adjutant General, Headquarters Department of New Mexico, Santa Fé," Mar. 11, 1861, ibid., p. 600; see also Edward R. S. Canby to "His Excellency Governor of Chihuahua," June 23, 1861, ibid., 4:43.

36. Hall, *Sibley's New Mexico Campaign*, pp. 10–13; see also Martin Hardwick Hall, "The Mesilla Times: A Journal of Confederate Arizona," *Arizona and the West* 5 (Winter, 1963).

37. Ganaway, *New Mexico*, pp. 85–90; Hall, *Sibley's New Mexico Campaign*, pp. 7–8; Calvin Horn, *New Mexico's Troubled Years: The Story of the Early Territorial Governors*, pp. 85–86.

38. Anonymous editorial, *Houston Tri-Weekly Telegraph*, May 12, 1862, p. 1.

39. Teel, "Sibley's New Mexican Campaign," 2:700.

40. Anderson, "Canby's Services," 2:697–99.

41. Williams, *With The Border Ruffians*, pp. 165–66; Dunn, "KGC in Texas," p. 569; Thompson, *From Desert to Bayou*, pp. 8–9.

42. Bowden, *Exodus of Federal Forces*, pp. 97–109; Samuel Cooper to Earl Van Dorn, Apr. 11, 1861, *OR*, 1:623; Henry McCulloch to Leroy P. Walker, Apr. 17, 1861, ibid., p. 627.

43. W. W. Heartsill, *Fourteen Hundred and 91 Days in the Confederate Army: A Journal Kept by W. W. Heartsill for Four Years, One Month, and One Day or Camp Life; Day by Day, of the W. P. Lane Rangers from April 19, 1861 to May 20, 1865*, ed. Bell Irvin Wiley, p. 2.

44. Ibid., pp. 3–4.

45. Ibid., p. 5.

46. Bowden, *Exodus of Federal Forces*, pp. 101–11; Earl Van Dorn to [Samuel Cooper], May 10, 1861, "Reports of Col. Earl Van Dorn, C.S. Army, of the surrender of the U.S. troops in Texas, and of his subsequent operations," *OR*, 1:572–73. Among the U.S. vessels captured at Saluria was the celebrated *Star of the West*.

47. Williams, *With The Border Ruffians*, pp. 172–73; Isaac V. D. Reeve to Lorenzo Thomas, May 12, 1861, *OR*, 1:568.

48. Heartsill, *Fourteen Hundred and 91 Days*, p. 11.

49. Bowden, *Exodus of Federal Forces*, p. 111; Reeve to Thomas, p. 570.

50. Bowden, *Exodus of Federal Forces*, pp. 99, 107, 111; Williams, *With The Border*

Ruffians, p. 174; Sprague, *Treachery in Texas,* p. 139; Reeve to Thomas, p. 570.

51. Edward Clark to Jefferson Davis, Apr. 4, 1861, *OR,* 1:621; Lubbock, *Six Decades in Texas,* pp. 387, 355–56.

52. Leroy Walker to Edward Clark, Apr. 11, 1861, *OR,* 1:623; Van Dorn, "General Orders No. 8," May 24, 1861, ibid., pp. 574–75.

53. Martin Hardwick Hall, "Native Mexican Relations in Confederate Arizona, 1861–1862," *Journal of Arizona History* 8 (Autumn, 1967): 171; Martin Hardwick Hall, "Negroes with Confederate Troops in West Texas and New Mexico," *Password* 13 (Spring, 1968): 11; Edgar A. Treadwell, Fort Bliss, Texas, to Dr. E. W. Treadwell, [Palestine, Texas], Aug. 11, 1861, typescript in possession of Jerry Thompson, Laredo, Texas; Martin Hardwick Hall, ed., "The Taylor Letters: Correspondence from Fort Bliss, 1861," *Military History of Texas and the Southwest* 15 (Fall, 1980): 54. County residence information was gathered from Hall, *Confederate Army of New Mexico,* and cross-referenced with the Eighth Census of the United States, 1860: Harrison, Upshur, Austin, Lavaca, Harris, Cherokee, Nacogdoches, Anderson, and Bexar counties, Texas, population schedules; agricultural information for the counties of origin for the Second Texas Mounted Rifles came from Census Office, *Agriculture of the United States in 1860; Compiled from the Original Returns of the Eighth Census, Under the Direction of the Secretary of the Interior* (Washington, D.C.: Government Printing Office, 1864).

54. Josephy, *Civil War,* pp. 34–35; Hall, *Sibley's New Mexico Campaign,* pp. 23–24.

55. Earl Van Dorn to John S. "Rip" Ford, May 27, 1861, *OR,* 1:577; Hall, *Sibley's New Mexico Campaign,* p. 26; Josephy, *Civil War,* pp. 29–30.

56. Joyce, *Life of W. J. Joyce,* p. 10.

57. S. W. Merchant, "Fighting With Sibley in New Mexico," *Hunter's Magazine* 1 (Nov., 1910): 12; Hall, *Confederate Army of New Mexico,* pp. 345–46.

58. E. B. D'Hamel, *The Adventures of a Tenderfoot: History of 2nd Regt. Mounted Rifles and Co. G, 33 Regt. and Capt Coopwood's Spy Co. and 2nd Texas in Texas and New Mexico,* pp. 8–9. The drill instructor was probably 1st Sgt. James H. Coulter (Hall, *Confederate Army of New Mexico,* p. 347).

59. A. L. Anderson to Isaac Lynde, June 30, 1861, *OR,* 4:50–51; D'Hamel, *Adventures of a Tenderfoot,* p. 8; W. W. Mills, "A Personal Narrative of W. W. Mills of El Paso. Union Side of the Story," *Galveston News,* Nov. 24, 1883, p. 1.

60. Heartsill, *Fourteen Hundred and 91 Days,* p. 14.

61. Thompson, *Baylor,* pp. 24–25; Baylor, *Baylor,* pp. 4–5.

62. Dunn, "KGC in Texas," pp. 569–70; Hall, *Confederate Army of New Mexico,* pp. 336–37.

63. Meining, *Imperial Texas,* p. 42; J. R. Baylor to Earl Van Dorn, Aug. 14, 1861, *OR,* 4:22–23.

64. Thompson, *From Desert to Bayou,* p. 18; Hall, *Confederate Army of New Mexico,* pp. 337–38.

65. Van Dorn to Ford, p. 577; Edward R. S. Canby to "Assistant Adjutant General," June 11, 1861, ibid., p. 606; Hall, *Sibley's New Mexico Campaign,* p. 20; Josephy, *Civil War,* pp. 35–36, 40–42.

66. Jerry Thompson, *Henry Hopkins Sibley: Confederate General of the West,* pp. 1–87; Hall, *Confederate Army of New Mexico,* pp. 43–44.

67. Ibid.

68. Thompson, *Sibley*, pp. 209–10; Isaac Lynde to Edward R. S. Canby, July 7, 1861, *OR*, 4:58.

69. As quoted in Josephy, *Civil War*, p. 37.

70. H. H. Sibley to W. W. Loring, June 12, 1861, *OR*, 4:55–56; Hall, *Sibley's New Mexico Campaign*, p. 21.

71. Hall, *Sibley's New Mexico Campaign*, p. 21; Thompson, *Sibley*, p. 212.

72. Thompson, *Baylor*, pp. 25–26; Thompson, *Sibley*, p. 212.

CHAPTER 3. THE FIRST BLOW

1. Hall, *Sibley's New Mexico Campaign*, pp. 21, 25–26; Sibley to Loring, pp. 55–56.

2. Samuel Cooper to H. H. Sibley, July 8, 1861, *OR*, 4:93; Walker to Clark, July 8, 1861; Samuel Cooper to Earl Van Dorn, July 9, 1861, ibid.; Lubbock, *Six Decades in Texas*, p. 398.

3. Merchant, "Fighting With Sibley in New Mexico," p. 12; *Mesilla Times*, July 11, 1861, p. 1; Hall, *Confederate Army of New Mexico*, pp. 297, 300, 345–46; Hall, "Native Mexican Relations, p. 172.

4. Hall, "Taylor Letters," p. 54–55.

5. Shell jackets are waist-length uniform coats with seven or nine brass buttons; kersey is a coarsely woven woolen, dyed sky blue, used in Federal uniform pants; kepis are the billed hats patterned after French headgear and worn on campaign.

6. Hall, "Taylor Letters," p. 55.

7. Ibid., pp. 56–57.

8. Ibid., p. 56.

9. Ibid., p. 57.

10. Joyce, *Life of W. J. Joyce*, p. 4.

11. Ibid., p. 5.

12. Treadwell to Treadwell.

13. Hall, "Taylor Letters," p. 57.

14. Ibid.

15. Joyce, *Life of W. J. Joyce*, p. 3.

16. Hall, *Confederate Army of New Mexico*, pp. 297, 320, 354, 374; Thompson, *From Desert to Bayou*, pp. 23–24.

17. Josephy, *Civil War*, pp. 23–24; Thompson, *Baylor*, pp. 25–26, 243; Finch, "Sherod Hunter", pp. 146–47.

18. Edwin R. Sweeney, *Cochise: Chiricahua Apache Chief*, pp. 183–84; for an excellent survey of all the Apache tribes, see Donald E. Worcester, *The Apaches: Eagles of the Southwest*.

19. James B. O'Neil, *They Die But Once: The Story of a Tejano*, pp. 40–41.

20. Hattie M. Anderson, ed., "With The Confederates in New Mexico During the Civil War: Memoirs of Hank Smith," *Panhandle Plains Historical Review* 2 (1929), pp. 66–69; Curry, *Sun Rising on the West*, p. 65.

21. Anderson, "Memoirs of Hank Smith," pp. 66–69; Curry, *Sun Rising on the West*, pp. 66–68.

22. Martin Hardwick Hall, "The Skirmish at Mesilla," *Arizona and the West* 1 (Winter, 1958): 346; J. R. Baylor to Capt. T. A. Washington, Sept. 21, 1861, *OR*, 4:17–20; Baylor, *Confederate Governor of Arizona*, p. 11.

23. Anderson, "Memoirs of Hank Smith," pp. 71–72; Curry, *Sun Rising on the West*, p. 72.

24. C. L. Sonnichsen, *Roy Bean: Law West of the Pecos*, p. 43. Wagon master Roy Bean helped organize the "Free Rovers."

25. Hall, "Skirmish at Mesilla," p. 347; Lynde to "Acting Adjutant General," July 26, 1861, *OR*, 4:4–5.

26. Hall, "Taylor Letters," p. 58; Hall, "Skirmish at Mesilla," p. 348; C. H. McNally, "Statement of Capt. C. H. McNally, Third U.S. Cavalry," n.d., *OR*, 4:14; Baylor to Washington, pp. 17–20; Curry, *Sun Rising on the West*, pp. 73–74; Anderson, "Memoirs of Hank Smith," p. 73; D'Hamel, *Adventures of a Tenderfoot*, p. 10.

27. Anderson, "Memoirs of Hank Smith," p. 73; Curry, *Sun Rising on the West*, p. 75.

28. Anderson, "Memoirs of Hank Smith," pp. 74–75; Curry, *Sun Rising on the West*, pp. 75–77.

29. Anderson, "Memoirs of Hank Smith," p. 77; Curry, *Sun Rising on the West*, p. 77.

30. Hall, "Skirmish at Mesilla," p. 349; Baylor, *Confederate Governor of Arizona*, p. 11.

31. Hall, "Taylor Letters," p. 58; Treadwell to Treadwell.

32. Baylor to Washington, pp. 17–20; Hall, "Taylor Letters," p. 58; Baylor, *Confederate Governor of Arizona*, pp. 6–7; D'Hamel, *Adventures of a Tenderfoot*, p. 11.

33. Timothy J. Reese, *Syke's Regular Infantry Division, 1861–1864: A History of Regular United States Infantry Operations in the Civil War's Eastern Theater*, pp. 161–62; D'Hamel, *Adventures of a Tenderfoot*, pp. 11–12.

34. Thompson, *From Desert to Bayou*, p. 25.

35. Charles P. Roland, *Albert Sidney Johnston: Soldier of Three Republics*, p. 255; Martin Hardwick Hall, "Albert Sidney Johnston's First Confederate Command," *McNeese Review* 13 (1962): 7; Thompson, *Baylor*, pp. 44–77.

36. Baylor to Van Dorn, pp. 22–23; Baylor, "Proclamation: To the People of the Territory of Arizona," Aug. 1, 1861, *OR*, 4:20–21; Baylor, *Baylor*, pp. 9–10.

37. Cornelius C. Smith, Jr., *William Sanders Oury: History-Maker of the Southwest*, p. 113.

38. Thompson, *Baylor*, p. 66; Mills, "Personal Narrative," p. 1.

39. Anderson, "Memoirs of Hank Smith," pp. 82–83; Curry, *Sun Rising on the West*, pp. 84–85.

40. Hall, "Johnston's First Confederate Command," pp. 9–11; Curry, *Sun Rising on the West*, pp. 86–89; Roland, *Soldier of Three Republics*, pp. 255–56.

41. Roland, *Soldier of Three Republics*, pp. 244–49; Thompson, *Sibley*, p. 18.

42. E. V. Sumner to E. D. Townsend, Apr. 28, 1861, *OR*, 50, 1:472.

43. Elijah R. Kennedy, *The Contest for California in 1861: How Colonel E. D. Baker Saved the Pacific States to the Union*, pp. 210–15, 217–18; Aurora Hunt, *The Army of the Pacific: Its Operations in California, Texas, Arizona, New Mexico, Utah, Nevada, Oregon, Washington, Plains Region, Mexico, etc. 1860–1866*, pp. 19–21.

44. Townsend to Sumner, June 5, 1861, *OR*, 50, 1:498–99.

45. C. L. Sonnichsen, *The Mescalero Apaches*, pp. 93–94; Barry Scobee, *Old Fort Davis*, p. 47; Hall, *Confederate Army of New Mexico*, p. 320; Baylor to Van Dorn, Aug. 25, 1861,

OR, 4:25–26.

46. John R. Pulliam to J. R. Baylor, Aug. 25, 1861, OR, 4:24–25; Thompson, *From Desert to Bayou,* p. 105, n. 32; Hall, *Confederate Army of New Mexico,* p. 320; Sonnichsen, *Mescalero Apaches,* pp. 90–91.

47. O'Neil, *They Die But Once,* pp. 41–42.

48. Ibid., pp. 43–44.

49. Sweeney, *Cochise,* pp. 183–84; O'Neil, *They Die But Once,* pp. 41–42.

50. O'Neil, *They Die But Once,* pp. 45–46.

51. Wayne R. Austerman, *Sharp's Rifles and Spanish Mules: The San Antonio–El Paso Mail, 1851–1881,* p. 181.

52. *San Antonio Herald,* July 5, 1862, p. 1.

53. Austerman, *Sharp's Rifles and Spanish Mules,* pp. 183–84.

54. The man Mills is referring to is probably acting sheriff Albrecht Kuhn (Thompson, *Baylor,* p. 66); Mills, "Personal Narrative," p. 1; Mills also mentions a James McGarvey as being one of his captors, see Hall, *Confederate Army of New Mexico,* p. 331.

55. Mills, "Personal Narrative," p. 1; Thompson, *Baylor,* pp. 66–67.

56. Donald C. Stith to A. L. Anderson, July 20, 1861, OR, 4:59–60; Thompson, *Baylor,* pp. 66–67. The stolen train was undoubtedly the work of William Kirk; see Lynde to Assistant Adjutant General, p. 600.

57. Mills, "A Personal Narrative," Nov. 24, 1883, p. 1; Stith to Anderson, pp. 59–60; William Byrd to Henry McCulloch, Sept. 9, 1861, OR, 4:103–104.

58. Curry, *Sun Rising on the West,* pp. 84–85, 88; Anderson, "Memoirs of Hank Smith," p. 82.

59. William C. Adams to Henry McCulloch, Oct. 21, 1861, OR, ser. 2, 2:1526–27; J. R. Baylor to W. C. Adams, Oct. 3, 1861, ibid., p. 1527; Emory Gibbons to "President of Presidio del Norte," Oct. 16, 1861, ibid.; Benigno Contreras to Gibbons, Oct. 16, 1861, ibid., pp. 1527–28; A. F. Wulff to W. C. Adams, Oct. 16, 1861; ibid., pp. 1528–30.

60. J. R. Baylor to H. H. Sibley, Oct. 25, 1861, OR, 4:133; Hall, *Confederate Army of New Mexico,* pp. 222, 373–74; War Department, Adjutant General's Office, "General Orders No. 174," Oct. 30, 1862, OR, ser. 2, 4:669.

61. D'Hamel, *Adventures of a Tenderfoot,* p. 12; Baylor to Van Dorn, p. 24.

62. Baylor to Van Dorn, p. 26.

63. Canby to Assistant Adjutant General, Aug. 16, 1861, OR, 4:64; Josephy, *Civil War in the American West,* p. 35.

64. Canby to Assistant Adjutant General, June 20, 1861, OR, 4:41–42.

65. Baylor to Van Dorn, pp. 22–23; Baylor, "Proclamation," pp. 20–21; Baylor, *Baylor,* pp. 9–10.

CHAPTER 4. THE IMPERIAL BRIGADE

1. Lubbock, *Six Decades in Texas,* pp. 324–26, 344–51; T. R. Fehrenbach, *Lone Star: A History of Texas and Texans,* p. 352–54.

2. Baylor to Van Dorn, pp. 22–23.

3. Ibid., p. 23.

4. Thompson, *Sibley,* pp. 218–19; Josephy, *Civil War,* pp. 52–53.

5. Hall, *Confederate Army of New Mexico*, p. 44; Thompson, *Sibley*, pp. 33–219ff; Teel, "Sibley's New Mexico Campaign," p. 700; Don Alberts, ed., *Rebels on the Rio Grande: The Civil War Journal of A. B. Peticolas*, p. 16; Hall, *Sibley's New Mexico Campaign*, pp. 31–32.

6. Teel, "Sibley's New Mexico Campaign," 2:700; Josephy, *Civil War in the American West*, pp. 52–53.

7. H. H. Sibley to Samuel Cooper, Nov. 16, 1861, *OR*, 4:141–43; Lubbock, *Six Decades in Texas*, p. 396; Thompson, *Sibley*, pp. 224–25.

8. Sibley to Cooper, pp. 141–43.

9. Hall, *Confederate Army of New Mexico*, pp. 45–47.

10. Edward R. S. Canby to Adjutant General of the Army, Jan. 25, 1862, *OR*, 4:89; Sibley to Cooper, Nov. 8, 1862, ibid., p. 132; Simeon Hart to H. H. Sibley, Oct. 27, 1862, ibid., 50, 1:683.

11. Hart to Sibley, p. 134.

12. Hall, *Confederate Army of New Mexico*, pp. 52–53.

13. Ibid., pp. 53–54; John Salmon Ford, *Rip Ford's Texas*, ed. Stephen B. Oates, p. 21.

14. Hall, *Confederate Army of New Mexico*, pp. 133–34.

15. Richard Taylor, *Destruction and Reconstruction: Personal Experiences of the Late War*, p. 178.

16. Francis B. Heitman, *Historical Register and Dictionary of the United States Army, from its Organization September 29, 1789 to March 2, 1903*, 3 vols., 1:679; Post returns, Fort Stanton, New Mexico Territory, Apr.–May, 1861, Martin Hall Collection, Texas State Library and Archives, Austin.

17. William Walker, *The War in Nicaragua*, p. 355; Laurence Green, *The Filibuster: The Career of William Walker*, p. 292.

18. Charles H. Brown, *Agents of Manifest Destiny: The Life and Times of the Filibusters*, p. 403.

19. William O. Scroggs, *Filibusters and Financiers: The Story of William Walker and His Associates*, pp. 237, 261, 278–83, 370; Brown, *Agents of Manifest Destiny*, p. 447; Tyler, *Santiago Vidaurri*, p. 32.

20. Col. William Steele to Ben W. Hall, Oct. 11, 1861, Hall Family Papers, BTHC. The competition for recruits and the unwillingness of some to serve under appointed officers conspired against success. On Oct. 10, 1861, Ben W. Hall received his letter from Colonel Steele authorizing him to raise a company for service in the brigade. Six months later, well after the last of Sibley's Army had departed for New Mexico, Hall still did not have his own command and he began to despair. Eventually, he struck a deal, joining his few converts with those of another recruiter and forming a company in Col. George Flournoy's Sixteenth Texas Infantry, serving as an infantry lieutenant, instead of a cavalry captain.

21. *Bellville Countryman*, Aug. 28, 1861, p. 1.

22. Steele to Hall, Oct. 11, 1861, Hall Family Papers.

23. Williams, *With The Border Ruffians*, pp. 177–79; Hall, *Confederate Army of New Mexico*, pp. 167–68.

24. Hall, *Confederate Army of New Mexico*, p. 143; John Samuel Shropshire to "Carrie" [Caroline Tait Shropshire], Sept. 28, 1861, John Samuel Shropshire Letters, Shropshire-Upton Confederate Museum, Columbus, Texas.

25. J. W. Carson to Mrs. E. L. Gordon, May 31, 1930, John Samuel Shropshire Letters.

26. Theophilus Noel, *A Campaign From Santa Fe to the Mississippi: Being a History of the Old Sibley Brigade From Its First Organization to the Present Time; Its Campaigns in New Mexico, Arizona, Texas, Louisiana and Arkansas in the Years 1861–2–3–4,* ed. Martin Hardwick Hall and Edwin Adams Davis, pp. 10–12.

27. Demographic information was gathered from Hall, *Confederate Army of New Mexico,* and cross-referenced with the Eighth Census of the United States, 1860: . . . Agriculture.

28. Ibid.

29. William H. Cleaver, "Last Will and Testiment," Probate Records, Angelina County, Lufkin, Texas.

30. H. C. Wright, "Reminiscences of H. C. Wright of Austin, "Wright Memoir, BTHC, p. 1; [William Lott Davidson], "Reminiscences of the Old Brigade on the March—In the Front of the Field—as Witnessed by the Writers during the Rebellion," *Overton Sharp-Shooter,* Oct. 13, 1887.

31. Jerry Thompson, ed., *Westward the Texans: The Civil War Journal of Private William Randolph Howell,* p. 50; Hall, *Confederate Army of New Mexico,* pp. 159–60.

32. Wright, "Reminiscences," p. 1; Hall, *Confederate Army of New Mexico,* pp. 93–94.

33. Don E. Alberts, *Rebels on the Rio Grande,* pp. 135–36.

34. Ibid.

35. Alberts, *Rebels on the Rio Grande,* pp. 1–10; John Nathan Cravens, *James Harper Starr: Financier of the Republic of Texas,* pp. 126–27; biographical information was gathered from the Eighth Census of the United States, 1860: Victoria, Polk, Nacogdoches, and Comal counties, Texas, population schedules.

36. Noel, *Santa Fe to the Mississippi,* pp. xxi–xxii.

37. George W. Walling to Thomas Burrowes, Feb. 5, 1866, Burrowes Family Papers, BTHC; [Davidson], "Reminiscences of the Old Brigade," p. 1.

38. Wright, "Reminiscences," p. 3.

39. Walter A. Faulkner, ed., "With Sibley in New Mexico; The Journal of William Henry Smith," West Texas Historical Association *Year Book,* 27 (Oct., 1981): 114.

40. William Randolph Howell to "Home Folks," Aug. 28, 1861, Howell Papers, BTHC.

41. Ibid.

42. S. L. R. Patton to Warren Patton, Oct. 14, 1861, in possession of Sandra Browning, Burleson, Texas.

43. Shropshire to "Carrie," Aug. 22, 1862.

44. Howell to "Home Folks," Sept. 1, 1861.

45. [Davidson], "Reminiscences of the Old Brigade," p. 1; ibid., Oct. 27, 1887, p. 1.

46. Shropshire to "Carrie," Nov. 14, 1861.

47. Hall, "Negroes with Confederate Troops" pp. 11–12; [Davidson], "Reminiscences of the Old Brigade," Dec. 15, 1887.

48. Howell to "Home Folks," Sept. 1, 1861; Noel, *Santa Fe to the Mississippi,* p. 12.

49. United States Army, *Revised United States Army Regulations of 1861, with an Appendix: Containing the Changes and Laws Affecting Army Regulations and Articles of War to June 25, 1863,* pp. 76–79; Noel, *Santa Fe to the Mississippi,* p. 12.

50. The major primary sources for the Fourth Texas Mounted Volunteers include Noel, *Santa Fe to the Mississippi;* Wright, "Reminiscences,"; David B. Gracy, II, ed., "The New

Mexico Campaign Letters of Frank Starr, 1861–1862," *Texas Military History* 4 (Fall, 1964): 171; Martin Hardwick Hall, ed., "The Journal of Ebenezer Hanna," *Password* 3 (Jan., 1958): 28–34; Alberts, *Rebels on the Rio Grande;* Martin Hardwick Hall, ed., "An Appraisal of the 1862 New Mexico Campaign: A Confederate Officer's Letter to Nacogdoches," *New Mexico Historical Review* 51 (Oct., 1976): 45–50; Robert Thomas Williams Diary, Fourth Texas Cavalry File, Harold B. Simpson Confederate Research Center, Hill College, Hillsboro, Texas; Ruth Waldrop Hord, ed., "The Diary of Lieutenant E. J. Robb, C.S.A., from Santa Fe to Fort Lancaster, 1862," *Permian Historical Annual* 18 (Dec., 1978): 19–45; Oscar Haas, trans., "The Diary of Julius Gieseke, 1861–1862," *Military History of Texas and the Southwest* 18 (Oct., 1988): 53–70; John E. Hart Diary, Texas Confederate Museum, Waco.

51. Primary sources for the Fifth Texas Mounted Volunteers include [Davidson], "Reminiscences of the Old Brigade," a series of articles in the *Overton [Texas] Sharp-Shooter* from Oct., 1887 to Mar., 1889; Shropshire Letters Collection; Benton Bell Seat Memoir, Special Collections, University of Arkansas Library, Fayetteville; Faulkner, "With Sibley in New Mexico"; Thompson, *Westward the Texans;* and the correspondence of Joseph Faust, in the Oscar Haas Papers, BTHC.

52. Gracy, "New Mexico Campaign Letters of Frank Starr," p. 171; Joseph Faust to Hermann Seele, Nov. 1, 1861, Haas Family Papers, BTHC; Faulkner, "With Sibley in New Mexico," pp. 114–16; Noel, *Santa Fe to the Mississippi,* pp. 12–14.

53. Noel, *Santa Fe to the Mississippi,* pp. 12–13.

54. Thompson, *Westward the Texans,* pp. 67–68.

55. Confederate States Ordnance Bureau, *The Field Manual for the Use of the Officers on Ordnance Duty,* pp. 91, 107, 116.

56. Confederate States Ordnance Bureau, *Field Manual,* pp. 91, 107, 116; Hall, *Confederate Army of New Mexico,* pp. 127–30, 211–13; Gracy, "Campaign Letters of Frank Starr," p. 169.

57. Howell to "Home Folks," Sept. 1, 1861.

58. Sibley to Cooper, pp. 142–43.

59. [Davidson], "Reminiscences of the Old Brigade," p. 1; ibid., Oct. 27, 1887, p. 1.

60. Noel, *Santa Fe to the Mississippi,* pp. 13–15; Faulkner, "With Sibley in New Mexico," p. 114.

61. Hall, *Confederate Army of New Mexico,* pp. 217–35. Sibley had at least two "spare" companies on hand at the end of September, prompting him to extend his recruiting.; Faust to Seele, Nov. 1, 1861, Joseph Faust Letters. For a reference to lances, see Haas, "Diary of Julius Gieseke," p. 53; Thompson, *Westward the Texans,* p. 71; Gracy, "Campaign Letters of Frank Starr," p. 171. The three lancer companies were G, Fourth Texas Cavalry, and B and G, Fifth Texas Cavalry.

62. Hall, *Confederate Army of New Mexico,* pp. 217–18.

63. Ibid., pp. 218–19; J. W. Wilbarger, *Indian Depredations in Texas: Reliable Accounts of Battle, Wars, Adventures, Forays, Murders, Massacres, etc., etc., Together with Biographical Sketches of Many of the Most Noted Indian Fighters and Frontiersmen of Texas,* pp. 63–64.

64. Martin Hardwick Hall, "The Court-Martial of Arthur Pendleton Bagby, C.S.A.," *East Texas Historical Journal* 19 (1981): 61.

65. Demographic information was gathered from Hall, *Confederate Army of New Mexico,* and cross-referenced with the Eighth Census of the United States, 1860: . . . schedules.

66. Primary sources for the Seventh Texas Mounted Volunteers include the Dr. Harold J. Hunter Diary, Ben Johnson Papers, Smith County Archives, Tyler, Texas; Felix Robert Collard, "Reminiscences of a Private, Company 'G', Seventh Texas Cavalry, Sibley Brigade, C.S.A.," typescript in possession of Dr. Don Alberts, Albuquerque, New Mexico.

67. [Davidson], "Reminiscences of the Old Brigade," Oct. 27, 1887, p. 1; ibid., Nov. 3, 1887, p. 1.

68. Faulkner, "With Sibley in New Mexico," p. 114.

CHAPTER 5. EMPIRE IMPERILED

1. L. Boyd Finch, "Arizona's Governors without Portfolio: A Wonderfully Diverse Lot," *Journal of Arizona History* 26 (Spring, 1985): 83–84.

2. G. W. Randolph to J. R. Baylor, Apr. 14, 1862, *OR*, 9:706; Randolph to Baylor, May 29, 1862, ibid., 50, 1:1108.

3. J. R. Baylor to Henry McCulloch, Nov. 10, 1861, *OR*, 50, 1:716–17; Thomas Robinson to [G. Wright], n.d., ibid., 9:628; J. M. McNulty to W. A. Hammond, Oct., 1863, ibid., 9:594–603.

4. Baylor to McCulloch, pp. 716–17; Edwin A. Rigg to James H. Carleton, Jan. 29, 1862, ibid, p. 825; Ammi White to Edwin A. Rigg, Feb. 9, 1862, ibid., pp. 867–68; Edwin A. Rigg to B. C. Cutler, Mar. 1, 1862, ibid., pp. 898–99; Robinson to [Wright], p. 628; McNulty to Hammond, pp. 594–603.

5. J. R. Baylor to Maj. S. B. Davis, Nov. 2, 1861, *OR*, 4:149.

6. Henry H. Goldman, "Southern Sympathy in Southern California, 1860–1865," *Journal of the West* 4 (Oct., 1965): 582; William Gilpin to Edward R. S. Canby, Oct. 23, 1861, *OR*, 4:73; *Mesilla Times,* Dec. 12, 1861, p. 1.

7. Baylor to Van Dorn, Oct. 1, 1861, *OR*, 4:30–31; Canby to Assistant Adjutant General, pp. 63–65.

8. Edward D. Tittman, "Confederate Courts in New Mexico," *New Mexico Historical Review* 3 (Oct., 1928): 347–56. This article contains discussion of the Confederate legal records of the Doña Ana County probate court.

9. Hall, "Native Mexican Relations," pp. 171–72; *Mesilla Times,* Oct. 10, 1861, p. 1; the post returns for Fort Davis also mention a company of "Mexican cavalry," see Post Returns of Fort Davis, Texas, Nov. 1861, Martin Hardwick Hall Papers, Texas State Archives, Austin; *Mesilla Times,* Dec. 12, 1861, p. 1.

10. Hall, "Taylor Letters," pp. 58–59; Hall, *Confederate Army of New Mexico*, pp. 303–309; Joyce, *Life of W. J. Joyce*, p. 9.

11. Thompson, *From Desert to Bayou*, pp. 30–31.

12. D'Hamel, *Adventures of a Tenderfoot*, pp. 12–13.

13. Joyce, *Life of W. J. Joyce*, p. 15.

14. Bethel Coopwood to J. R. Baylor, Sept. 29, 1861, *OR*, 4:31; Sibley to Cooper, p. 132.

15. John Minks to Edward R. S. Canby, Sept. 29, 1861, ibid., 4:27–29.

16. Ibid.

17. Coopwood to Baylor, p. 31.

18. Ibid., p. 32. In August, the mounted regiments of the old army received new designations according to seniority as the United States expanded its forces. The First and

Second Dragoons became the First and Second Cavalry, the Regiment of Mounted Rifles became the Third Cavalry, the First Cavalry changed to the Fourth Cavalry, and the Second Cavalry became the Fifth Cavalry, and the newly authorized Third Cavalry was instead designated the Sixth Cavalry (Gregory J. W. Urwin, *The United States Cavalry: An Illustrated History* [New York: Blandford Press, 1985], p. 112).

19. D'Hamel, *Adventures of a Tenderfoot,* p. 15; Coopwood to Baylor, p. 32.

20. D'Hamel, *Adventures of a Tenderfoot,* p. 16; Coopwood to Baylor, p. 32.

21. Joyce, *Life of W. J. Joyce,* p. 15.

22. Robert M. Morris to H. R. Selden, Sept. 29, 1861, *OR,* 4:29–30; Coopwood to Baylor, pp. 31–32.

23. Sweeny, *Cochise,* pp. 187–88; Curry, *Sun Rising on the West,* p. 53.

24. Curry, *Sun Rising on the West,* p. 52.

25. Sweeny, *Cochise,* pp. 187–88; Curry, *Sun Rising on the West,* p. 52.

26. Curry, *Sun Rising on the West,* pp. 52–53.

27. Sweeny, *Cochise,* pp. 187–88; Curry, *Sun Rising on the West,* pp. 53–54.

28. William Markt to the Commander in Chief of the Confederate Troops in Arizona Territory, Oct. 8, 1861, *OR,* 4:120–21; Baylor to McCulloch, Oct. 14, 1861, ibid., 4:120.

29. Peter Hardeman to J. R. Baylor, Oct. 8, 1861, *OR,* 4:33.

30. George L. MacManus to W. C. Adams, Nov. 6, 1861, ibid., 4:147.

31. J. R. Baylor to "The Commanding Officer C.S. Troops, October 24, 1861," ibid., 4:127–28; *Memphis Daily Appeal,* Dec. 7, 1861, p. 3; *Weekly [Austin] Texas State Gazette,* Dec. 7, 1861, p. 2.

32. J. R. Baylor to Simeon Hart, Oct. 24, 1861, *OR,* 4:128–29; Hall, "Mesilla Times," pp. 348–50; *Weekly [Austin] State Gazette,* Dec. 7, 1861, p. 2.

33. J. F. Crosby to H. H. Sibley, Oct. 27, 1861, *OR,* 4:133.

34. Simeon Hart to H. H. Sibley, Oct. 27, 1861, ibid., 4:134.

35. Baylor to Hart, pp. 128–29.

36. J. R. Baylor to "Commander Department of Texas," Oct. 25, 1861, ibid., 4:129.

37. Baylor to Sibley, p. 133.

38. Heartsill, *Fourteen Hundred and 91 Days,* p. 47.

39. *Mesilla Times,* Dec. 12, 1861.

40. Hall, "Mesilla Times," p. 349.

41. Anderson, "Confederates in New Mexico, pp. 90–91; Curry, *Sun Rising on the West,* p. 92.

42. Curry, *Sun Rising on the West,* pp. 93–94; Anderson, "With The Confederates in New Mexico," p. 91.

43. Johnson, "Satanic-Looking Colonel John R. Baylor," pp. 20, 72; *Weekly [Austin] Texas State Gazette,* Jan. 4, 1862, p. 2.

44. Curry, *Sun Rising on the West,* p. 93; Anderson, "Confederates in New Mexico," p. 91.

45. Smith, *William Sanders Oury,* pp. 113–17.

46. Granville Oury to Members of the Provisional Congress from the State of Texas, Feb. 1, 1862, in Smith, *William Sanders Oury,* pp. 116–17.

47. Johnson, "Colonel John R. Baylor," pp. 18, 20; *[Tucson] Arizonian,* Aug. 10, 1861, p. 1; Smith, *William Sanders Oury,* pp. 116–17.

CHAPTER 6. EMPIRE RESCUED

1. [Davidson], "Reminiscences of the Old Brigade," Nov. 3, 1887.
2. Noel, *Santa Fe to the Mississippi*, pp. 15–16.
3. Williams, *With the Border Ruffians*, p. 201; Noel, *Santa Fe to the Mississippi*, pp. 15–16.
4. Haas, "Diary of Julius Gieseke," p. 50; Hall, *Sibley's New Mexico Campaign*, pp. 41–42; Noel, *Santa Fe to the Mississippi*, p. 16; Raguet led Companies A and F; Scurry led Companies B, D, G, and H; Reily led Companies C, E, I, and K.
5. Sibley to Cooper, p. 132.
6. Faulkner, "With Sibley in New Mexico," p. 115; William Randolph Howell Diary, Nov. 7, 1861, Howell Papers; Noel, *Santa Fe to the Mississippi*, pp. 15, 17; Hall, *Sibley's New Mexico Campaign*, pp. 41, 43.
7. Seat, "Memoirs," p. 89.
8. Noel, *Santa Fe to the Mississippi*, p. 17; [Davidson], "Reminiscences of the Old Brigade," Nov. 3, 1887, p. 1.
9. Shropshire to "Carrie," Nov. 14, 1861.
10. Faulkner, "With Sibley in New Mexico," pp. 115–16; Thompson, *Sibley*, p. 237; Hall, *Sibley's New Mexico Campaign*, p. 44.
11. Hall, *Sibley's New Mexico Campaign*, 41–45; Noel, *Santa Fe to the Mississippi*, 16–18; Thompson, *Sibley*, p. 237; Hall, *Confederate Army of New Mexico*, p. 21–23; Hunter Diary, Nov. 28, 1861, Smith County Archives, Tyler, Texas; Lt. Col. John Schuyler Sutton, who had first made the trip to New Mexico as a captain in the Texan Santa Fe Expedition of 1841, led Companies A, B, F, H, and I westward. Companies C, D, E, and G departed Dec. 15.
12. Howell Diary, Nov. 15, 25, 27, Dec. 3, 1861; Faulkner, "With Sibley in New Mexico," p. 115; Haas, "Diary of Julius Gieseke," p. 50.
13. Faulkner, "With Sibley in New Mexico," p. 123; Hall, *Sibley's New Mexico Campaign*, pp. 49–50; Austerman, *Sharps Rifles and Spanish Mules*, pp. 7–8.
14. Wright, "Reminiscences," p. 5.
15. Hall, *Army of New Mexico*, p. 183; Howell Diary, Dec. 11–12, 1861.
16. Hart Diary, Nov. 28, 1861.
17. Faulkner, "With Sibley in New Mexico," p. 114; Howell Diary, Nov. 25, 1861; Heartsill, *Fourteen Hundred and 91 Days*, pp. 49, 51; Haas, "Diary of Julius Gieseke," p. 50; Howell Diary, Nov. 20, 1861; Faulkner, "With Sibley in New Mexico," pp. 117, 123.
18. Haas, "Diary of Julius Gieseke," p. 52; Howell Diary, Dec. 15, 1861.
19. Williams Diary, Feb. 1, 2, 4, 1862.
20. Howell Diary, Nov. 12, 1861.
21. Haas, "Diary of Julius Gieseke," p. 50.
22. Ibid., p. 51.
23. Faulkner, "With Sibley in New Mexico," p. 112.
24. Howell Diary, Dec. 3, 8, 11–12, 1861.
25. Wright Memoirs, p. 5.
26. Shropshire to "Carrie," Dec. 6, 1861.
27. Hart Diary, Nov. 14, 1861; Howell Diary, Nov. 18, 1861; Faulkner, "With Sibley in

New Mexico," p. 122.

28. Faulkner, "With Sibley in New Mexico," p. 117; Noel, *Santa Fe to the Mississippi,* p. 17; Williams Diary, Jan. 17, 1862.

29. Hart Diary, Dec. 12, 1861.

30. Faulkner, "With Sibley in New Mexico," pp. 120–24; Heartsill, *Fouteen Hundred and 91 Days,* pp. 48, 51; Noel, *Santa Fe to the Mississippi,* p. 18; Howell Diary, Dec. 30, 1861, Jan, 7, 9, 11, 1862; Hall, *Confederate Army of New Mexico,* p. 182; Williams Diary, Jan. 6, 1862.

31. Faulkner, "With Sibley in New Mexico," pp. 115, 117, 123; Howell Diary, Nov. 25–26, 1861; Haas, "Diary of Julius Gieseke," p. 53.

32. [Davidson], "Reminiscences of the Old Brigade," Nov. 10, 1887.

33. Shropshire to "Carrie," Nov. 14, 1861.

34. Shropshire to "Carrie," Dec. 6, 1861.

35. Shropshire to "Carrie," Dec. 7, 1861.

36. Shropshire to "Carrie," Dec. 26, 1861.

37. Shropshire to "Carrie," Dec. 12, 1861.

38. Shropshire to "Carrie," Dec. 6, 1861.

39. Thompson, *Sibley,* p. 237; Heartsill, *Fourteen Hundred and 91 Days,* p. 50.

40. Alexander M. Jackson, "General Orders No. 10," Dec. 14, 1861, *OR,* 4:157–58; J. R. Baylor to Judah P. Benjamin, Dec. 14, 1861, *OR,* 4:157.

41. Hall, *Confederate Army of New Mexico,* pp. 295–301.

42. Faulkner, "With Sibley in New Mexico," p. 124; Hall, *Confederate Army of New Mexico,* p. 23; Alberts, *Rebels on the Rio Grande,* p. 29.

43. Henry Sibley, "Proclamation of Brig. Gen. H. H. Sibley, Army of the Confederate States, to the people of New Mexico," Dec. 20, 1861, *OR,* 4:89.

44. Ibid., p. 90.

45. Ibid.

46. Shropshire to "Carrie," Dec. 26, 1861.

47. Faulkner, "With Sibley in New Mexico," pp. 122, 127–29.

48. Shropshire to "Carrie," Dec. 26, 1861.

49. [Davidson], "Reminiscences of the Old Brigade," Nov. 10, 1887.

50. Shropshire to "Carrie," Dec. 26, 1861.

51. Thompson, *Westward the Texans,* p. 76.

52. Faulkner, "With Sibley in New Mexico," p. 122.

53. Hunter Diary, Dec. 25, 1861; Heartsill, *Fourteen Hundred and 91 Days,* p. 49.

54. [Davidson], "Reminiscences of the Old Brigade," Nov. 17, 1887; Hall, *Confederate Army of New Mexico,* p. 183; Seat Memoir, p. 90.

55. [Davidson], "Reminiscences of the Old Brigade," Nov. 17, 1887.

56. Ibid.

57. Hart Diary, Dec. 14, 1861.

58. Wright Memoirs, pp. 7–8.

59. [Davidson], "Reminiscences of the Old Brigade," Nov. 10, 1887.

60. R. L. Robertson to G. Wright, Apr. 18, 1862, *OR,* 50, 1:1012–13.

61. Thompson, *From Desert to Bayou,* pp. 23–24.

62. Finch, "Sherod Hunter," pp. 141–63; Hall, *Confederate Army of New Mexico,*

pp. 361–65.

63. Finch, "Arizona's Governors," p. 87.

64. Hart Dairy, Dec. 24, 1861.

65. Howell Diary, Jan. 16, 1862; Collard, "Reminiscences,"; Haas, "Diary of Julius Gieseke," p. 54; Noel, *Santa Fe to the Mississippi,* p. 20; Faulkner, "With Sibley in New Mexico," p. 126; Williams Diary, Jan. 11–12, 1862.

66. Howell Diary, Jan. 16, 1862; Collard, "Reminiscences"; Haas, "Diary of Julius Gieseke," p. 54; Noel, *Santa Fe to the Mississippi,* p. 20; Faulkner, "With Sibley in New Mexico," p. 126; Williams Diary, Jan. 11–12, 1862.

67. Edward R. S. Canby to J. L. Donaldson, Jan. 3, 1862, *OR,* 4:82–83; Williams Diary, Jan. 4, 1862; Noel, *Santa Fe to the Mississippi,* p. 20. Companies F and H, Fourth Texas Cavalry, and Companies B, D, and E of the Second Texas Mounted Rifles rode to Alamosa.

68. Sibley to Cooper, Jan. 3, 1862, *OR,* 4:167.

69. Noel, *Santa Fe to the Mississippi,* p. 20.

70. Hall, *Sibley's New Mexico Campaign,* p. 51.

71. Hall, *Army of New Mexico,* pp. 188–89; Faulkner, "With Sibley in New Mexico," p. 124.

72. Thompson, *Westward the Texans,* p. 80.

73. Faulkner, "With Sibley in New Mexico," p. 124.

CHAPTER 7. THE ADVANCE OF EMPIRE

1. Williams Diary, Jan. 8, 1862.

2. Hart Diary, Jan. 4, 1862.

3. Wright, "Reminiscences," p. 8.

4. Hart Diary, Jan. 8, 1862.

5. Wright, "Reminiscences," p. 8.

6. Faulkner, "With Sibley in New Mexico," p. 125; Haas, "Diary of Julius Gieseke," p. 55; Howell Diary, Feb. 15, 1862; Ebenezer Hanna Diary, Feb. 19, 1862, Holbrook Collection, Texas State Library and Archives, Austin; Noel, *From Santa Fe to the Mississippi,* pp. 23–24.

7. [Davidson], "Reminiscences of the Old Brigade," Nov. 17, 1887.

8. Noel, *Santa Fe to the Mississippi,* p. 18; Hall, *Confederate Army of New Mexico,* p. 23; Faulkner, "With Sibley in New Mexico," p. 125; Alberts, *Rebels on the Rio Grande,* p. 31. The five local companies would eventually receive the designation of First Battalion, Arizona Brigade.

9. Faulkner, "With Sibley in New Mexico," pp. 124–25.

10. Thompson, *Sibley,* pp. 239–40; Hall, *Confederate Army of New Mexico,* p. 23; Alberts, *Rebels on the Rio Grande,* pp. 31–32, 42; Noel, *Santa Fe to the Mississippi,* pp. 20–21; Howell Diary, Feb. 7, 1862; Faulkner, "With Sibley in New Mexico," p. 125.

11. Hall, *Confederate Army of New Mexico,* pp. 335–37; [Davidson], "Reminiscences of the Old Brigade," Feb. 16, 1888.

12. Haas, "Diary of Julius Gieseke," pp. 55–56; Faulkner, "With Sibley in New Mexico," p. 123; Noel, *Santa Fe to the Mississippi,* p. 24; Hanna Diary, Feb. 13, 1862; Williams Diary, Jan. 26, 1862.

13. Noel, *Santa Fe to the Mississippi*, p. 23; Haas, "Diary of Julius Gieseke," p. 55; Thompson, *Sibley*, pp. 252, 311; Williams Diary, Feb. 9, 1862.

14. Haas, "Diary of Julius Gieseke," pp. 54–55.

15. Faulkner, "With Sibley in New Mexico," p. 126.

16. Haas, "Diary of Julius Gieseke," pp. 54–55.

17. Wright Memoir, p. 9.

18. Faulkner, "With Sibley in New Mexico," pp. 127–28; Noel, *Santa Fe to the Mississippi*, pp. 21, 24; Williams Diary, Dec. 26, 1961, Jan. 6, 9, 16, Feb. 19, 1862.

19. [Davidson], "Reminiscences of the Old Brigade," Nov. 17, 1887; Wright Memoir, p. 8.

20. Faulkner, "With Sibley in New Mexico," pp. 127–29.

21. [Davidson], "Reminiscences of the Old Brigade," Nov. 24, 1887.

22. Ibid., Nov. 17, 1887.

23. Ibid., Nov. 24, 1887.

24. Curry, *Sun Rising on the West*, pp. 165–67; Faulkner, "With Sibley in New Mexico," p. 126.

25. Curry, *Sun Rising on the West*, p. 92; Finch, "Sherod Hunter," pp. 165–67; Faulkner, "With Sibley in New Mexico," p. 126.

26. Hunter Diary, Feb. 9, 1862; Faulkner, "With Sibley in New Mexico," p. 127.

27. [Davidson], "Reminiscences of the Old Brigade," Nov. 17, 1887.

28. Shropshire to "Carrie," Jan. 26, 1862.

29. Alberts, *Rebels on the Rio Grande*, pp. 34–35, 45; Hall, *Sibley's New Mexico Campaign*, pp. 73–74; Thompson, *Sibley*, p. 248; William M. Nicodemus, "Circular," Feb. 14, 1862, *OR*, 9:630–31; William Clark Whitford, *Colorado Volunteers in the Civil War: The New Mexico Campaign in 1862*, p. 44.

30. Hunter Diary, Jan. 25–Feb. 3, 1862.

31. Hunter Diary, Feb. 4, 1862; Thompson, *Sibley*, pp. 239–40; Hall, *Confederate Army of New Mexico*, p. 23; Noel, *Santa Fe to the Mississippi*, pp. 20–21.

32. Hunter Diary, Feb. 5, 7, 1862.

33. Haas, "The Diary of Julius Gieseke," p. 55; James Reily to H. H. Sibley, Jan. 20, 1862, *OR*, 4:171–72.

34. Haas, "Diary of Julius Gieseke," p. 55; Finch, "Sherod Hunter," pp. 165–67.

35. Robertson to Wright, p. 1013; Finch, "Sherod Hunter," pp. 165–67.

36. Thompson, *Sibley*, pp. 239–40; Hall, *Confederate Army of New Mexico*, p. 23; Noel, *Santa Fe to the Mississippi*, pp. 20–21.

37. Shropshire to "Carrie," Jan. 26, 1862.

38. Hart Diary, Jan. 10, 1862.

39. Hall, *Confederate Army of New Mexico*, pp. 373–76.

40. [Davidson], "Reminiscences of the Old Brigade," Nov. 24, 1887.

41. Ibid.

42. Ibid.

43. Ibid.

44. Ibid., Dec. 22, 1887; Hanna Diary, Feb. 20, 1862; Howell Diary, Feb. 11–14, 1862.

45. Thompson, *Westward the Texans*, p. 85.

46. [Davidson], "Reminiscences of the Old Brigade," Jan. 5, 1888; Thompson, *Westward*

the Texans, p. 86; Faulkner, "With Sibley in New Mexico," pp. 131–34.

47. Hanna Diary, Feb. 20, 1862; Howell Diary, Feb. 11–14, 1862.

48. Hunter Diary, Feb. 14, 1862.

49. Howell Diary, Feb. 16, 1862; Alwyn Barr, ed., *Charles Porter's Account of the Confederate Attempt to Seize Arizona and New Mexico,* p. 14; Alberts, *Rebels on the Rio Grande,* pp. 35–37; Hall, *Sibley's New Mexico Campaign,* pp. 77–78.

50. Faulkner, "With Sibley in New Mexico," p. 154.

51. Howell Diary, Feb. 16, 1862; Barr, *Charles Porter's Account,* p. 14; Alberts, *Rebels on the Rio Grande,* pp. 35–37; Hall, *Sibley's New Mexico Campaign,* pp. 77–78.

52. [Davidson], "Reminiscences of the Old Brigade," Nov. 24, 1887.

53. Hunter Diary, Feb. 16, 1862.

54. Howell Diary, Feb. 16, 1862; Barr, *Charles Porter's Account,* p. 14; Alberts, *Rebels on the Rio Grande,* pp. 35–37; Hall, *Sibley's New Mexico Campaign,* pp. 77–78.

55. [Davidson], "Reminiscences of the Old Brigade," Jan. 5, 1888; Thompson, *Westward the Texans,* p. 88; Faulkner, "With Sibley in New Mexico," p. 135.

56. Wright Memoir, p. 10.

57. Howell Diary, Feb. 19, 1862; Alberts, *Rebels on the Rio Grande,* pp. 37–39; Hall, *Sibley's New Mexico Campaign,* pp. 79–80.

58. Hunter Diary, Feb. 20, 1862; [Davidson], "Reminiscences of the Old Brigade," Jan. 5, 1888.

59. [Davidson], "Reminiscences of the Old Brigade," Jan. 5, 1888; Gracy, "Campaign Letters of Frank Starr," p. 172; Howell Diary, Feb. 20, 1862; Alberts, *Rebels on the Rio Grande,* p. 39.

60. Haas, "Diary of Julius Gieseke," p. 54; Gracy, "Campaign Letters of Frank Starr," p. 173; Alberts, *Rebels on the Rio Grande,* pp. 41–42.

61. [Davidson], "Reminiscences of the Old Brigade," Jan. 5, 1888.

62. Ibid., Dec. 22, 1887.

63. Haas, "Diary of Julius Gieseke," p. 54; Gracy, "Campaign Letters of Frank Starr," p. 173; Alberts, *Rebels on the Rio Grande,* pp. 41–42.

64. [Davidson], "Reminiscences of the Old Brigade," Dec. 1, 1887.

65. Alberts, *Rebels on the Rio Grande,* pp. 41–42.

66. [Davidson], "Reminiscences of the Old Brigade," Dec. 1, 1887.

CHAPTER 8. THE BATTLE FOR EMPIRE

1. Charles Fitzpatrick and Conrad Crane, *The Prudent Soldier, The Rash Old Fighter, and the Walking Whiskey Keg: The Battle of Val Verde, New Mexico, 13–21 February 1862* (Fort Bliss, Texas: Air Defense Artillery School, 1984), pp. 68, 78; Conrad Crane, "A Careful Examination of the Field of Battle: Military Lessons from the Battle of Val Verde," p. 7, paper presented at the Fort Craig Conference, Socorro, New Mexico, 1989.

2. [Davidson], "Reminiscences of the Old Brigade," Jan. 19, 1888.

3. Charles L. Pyron to Alexander M. Jackson, Feb. 27, 1862, *OR,* 9:512; Thomas Duncan to Charles Meinhold, Feb. 23, 1862, ibid., 9:497–98; Alberts, *Rebels on the Rio Grande,* p. 51.

4. Alberts, *Rebels on the Rio Grande,* p. 42.

5. *Crockett Courier,* July 12, 1928.

6. Gracy, "Campaign Letters of Frank Starr," p. 173.

7. Henry Raguet to Alexander M. Jackson, Feb. 23, 1862, *OR,* 9:517; Duncan to Meinhold, p. 497; William R. Scurry to Alexander M. Jackson, Feb. 22, 1862, *OR,* 9:514; Fitzpatrick and Crane, *Prudent Soldier,* pp. 84–88.

8. Alberts, *Rebels on the Rio Grande,* p. 42.

9. Scurry to Jackson, pp. 513–14; Alberts, *Rebels on the Rio Grande,* p. 42; Raguet to Jackson, p. 516.

10. Scurry to Jackson, p. 514.

11. Gracy, "Campaign Letters of Frank Starr," p. 171; Alberts, *Rebels on the Rio Grande,* p. 43; Scurry to Jackson, p. 514.

12. Gracy, "Campaign Letters of Frank Starr," p. 171; Alberts, *Rebels on the Rio Grande,* p. 43, 63; Scurry to Jackson, p. 514; *Crockett Courier.*

13. Fitzpatrick and Crane, *Prudent Soldier,* pp. 92–94; Crane, "Careful Examination," p. 10.

14. Scurry to Jackson, pp. 514–15; Trevanion Teel to Alexander M. Jackson, Feb. 27, 1862, *ibid.,* 9:524–25; Alberts, *Rebels on the Rio Grande,* p. 43.

15. Companies A and D of the Fifth Texas filled the gap in the Rebel line between Pyron and Raguet, while E, I, and K remainined mounted as a ready reserve. Powhatan Jordan to Alexander M. Jackson, Feb. 27, 1862, *OR,* 9:523; Thomas Green to Alexander M. Jackson, Feb. 22, 1862, ibid., 9:519; Scurry to Jackson, p. 514. The wagon train was originally guarded by Companies C and H of the Fifth, and A, B, F, H, and I of the Seventh Texas Mounted volunteers. All but Company H of the Fifth Regiment were later committed to the fight. *Crockett Courier,* July 12, 1928.

16. Benjamin S. Roberts to William J. L. Nicodemus, Feb. 23, 1862, *OR,* 9:495.

17. Alberts, *Rebels on the Rio Grande,* p. 43.

18. Ibid., pp. 43–44, 64.

19. Gracy, "Campaign Letters of Frank Starr," p. 175.

20. Ibid., p. 173; [Davidson], "Reminiscences of the Old Brigade," Jan. 5, 1888.

21. Alberts, *Rebels on the Rio Grande,* pp. 44–45.

22. [Davidson], "Reminiscences of the Old Brigade," Jan. 12, 1888; Alberts, *Rebels on the Rio Grande,* p. 46.

23. Fitzpatrick and Crane, *Prudent Soldier,* p. 102.

24. [Davidson], "Reminiscences of the Old Brigade," Jan. 5, 1888.

25. Frank Calvert Oltorf, *The Marlin Compound,* p. 84; Whitford, *Colorado Volunteers,* pp. 66–67; Green to Jackson, p. 519. Canby's map of the battle of Val Verde appears to show Dodd's company to be in a square during the lancer attack.

26. [Davidson], "Reminiscences of the Old Brigade," Jan. 26, 1888.

27. Companies E, I, and K of the Fifth Texas.

28. [Davidson], "Reminiscences of the Old Brigade," Jan. 26, 1888; W. L. R. Patton to "Dear Children," Mar. 17, 1862, in possession of Sandra Browning, Burleson, Texas.

29. [Davidson], "Reminiscences of the Old Brigade," Jan. 26, 1888.

30. Ibid.

31. Alberts, *Rebels on the Rio Grande,* pp. 51, 66; Gracy, "Campaign Letters of Frank Starr," p. 174.

32. Roberts to Nicodemus, p. 496.

33. Roberts to Nicodemus, p. 496; Sibley to Cooper, Feb. 28, 1862, *OR*, 9:506.

34. Green to Jackson, pp. 518–21.

35. Canby to Adjutant General, Mar. 1, 1862, *OR*, 9:487–93.

36. Companies A and H, Tenth U.S.; C and F, Seventh U.S.

37. Crane, "Careful Examination," pp. 12–14.

38. [Davidson], "Reminiscences of the Old Brigade," Dec. 8, 1887.

39. Ibid., Dec. 15, 1887.

40. Alberts, *Rebels on the Rio Grande*, p. 46.

41. Ibid.

42. [Davidson], "Reminiscences of the Old Brigade," Dec. 8, 1887.

43. Crane, "A Careful Examination," p. 10.

44. Alberts, *Rebels on the Rio Grande*, pp. 44–45.

45. Barr, *Porter's Account*, pp. 15–16; Canby to Adjutant General, p. 490.

46. Alberts, *Rebels on the Rio Grande*, pp. 46–48; Raguet to Jackson, p. 517. Raguet lead Companies B, E, G, and H of the Fourth and D of the Fifth in this assault.

47. Barr, *Porter's Account*, pp. 15–16.

48. Alberts, *Rebels on the Rio Grande*, pp. 46–48.

49. [Davidson], "Reminiscences of the Old Brigade," Dec. 8, 1887.

50. Alberts, *Rebels on the Rio Grande*, p. 46.

51. Ibid., p. 48.

52. [Davidson], "Reminiscences of the Old Brigade," Dec. 15, 1887.

53. Alberts, *Rebels on the Rio Grande*, p. 65.

54. [Davidson], "Reminiscences of the Old Brigade," Dec. 15, 1887.

55. Ibid; Alberts, *Rebels on the Rio Grande*, pp. 48–49; Scurry to Jackson, pp. 512–13; Canby to Adjutant General, pp. 490–91. Companies A, C, D, F, I, and K of the Fourth, Companies A, E, H, and I of the Fifth, and A, B, F, H, and I of the Seventh participated in the charge.

56. Crane, "Careful Examination," pp. 14–16; [Davidson], "Reminiscences of the Old Brigade," Dec. 8, 1887; Alberts, *Rebels on the Rio Grande*, pp. 48–49; Scurry to Jackson, pp. 512–13; Canby to Adjutant General, pp. 490–91.

57. Green to Jackson, p. 521.

58. [Davidson], "Reminiscences of the Old Brigade," Dec. 15, 1887.

59. Ibid., Jan. 26, 1888.

60. Ibid., Jan. 12, 1888.

61. Ibid., Jan. 26, 1888.

62. Gracy, "Campaign Letters of Frank Starr," p. 174.

63. Fitzpatrick and Crane, *Prudent Soldier*, p. 125; Green to Jackson, p. 520.

64. Green to Jackson, p. 521; Hall, *Sibley's New Mexico Campaign*, p. 105; Gracy, "Campaign Letters of Frank Starr," p. 172; Alberts, *Rebels on the Rio Grande*, p. 49.

65. Hall, "Journal of Ebenezer Hanna," pp. 28–34.

66. Alberts, *Rebels on the Rio Grande*, p. 66.

67. Alberts, *Rebels on the Rio Grande*, pp. 46, 51; Hall, *Confederate Army of New Mexico*, pp. 77, 49; Faust to Seele, May 2, 1862, Haas Papers, BTHC.

68. [Davidson], "Reminiscences of the Old Brigade," Jan. 26, 1888.

69. Alberts, *Rebels on the Rio Grande*, pp. 49, 65.

70. [Davidson], "Reminiscences of the Old Brigade," Dec. 15, 1887.

71. Ibid., Feb. 9, 1888.

72. Alberts, *Rebels on the Rio Grande*, p. 67.

73. [Davidson], "Reminiscences of the Old Brigade," Feb. 9, 1888.

74. Seat, "Memoirs," p. 95.

75. Major Pyron reported four killed, seventeen wounded, and one missing from the Second Texas. Lieutenant Colonel Scurry of the Fourth Texas counted eight men killed and thirty-six wounded. Green's Fifth Texas Cavalry suffered twenty killed, sixty-seven wounded. The Seventh Texas lost two men killed and twenty-six wounded. Major Teel's old battery lost two gunners killed, and four wounded—a third of its men. Dodd's Colorado company lost over fifty percent of its men. Howell Diary, Feb. 22, 1862; Canby to Adjutant General, p. 493; Green to Jackson, p. 520–21.

76. [Davidson], "Reminiscences of the Old Brigade," Feb. 16, 1888; Alberts, *Rebels on the Rio Grande*, p. 44; Noel, *Santa Fe to the Mississippi*, p. 24.

77. Alberts, *Rebels on the Rio Grande*, pp. 49–51; Haas, "Diary of Julius Giesecke," p. 56; Howell Diary, Feb. 21, 1862.

78. Alberts, *Rebels on the Rio Grande*, pp. 49–50; Howell Diary, Feb. 21, 1862; Sibley to Cooper, May 4, 1862, *OR*, 9:508.

79. [Davidson], "Reminiscences of the Old Brigade," Dec. 15, 1887.

80. Howell to "Home Folks," Mar. 2, 1862, Howell Papers.

81. [Davidson], "Reminiscences of the Old Brigade," Feb. 16, 1888.

82. Howell Diary, Feb. 22, 1862; Canby to Adjutant General, p. 493; Green to Jackson, pp. 520–21.

83. Gracy, "Campaign Letters of Frank Starr," p. 173.

84. Canby to Adjutant General, p. 487.

85. Patton to "Dear Children."

86. [Davidson], "Reminiscences of the Old Brigade," Feb. 9, 1888.

87. Haas, "Diary of Julius Gieseke," p. 56; Thompson, *Sibley*, p. 270; Hall, *Sibley's New Mexico Campaign*, pp. 105–106.

88. Haas, "Diary of Julius Gieseke" p. 56.

89. Hunter Diary, Feb. 22, 1862; [Davidson], "Reminiscences of the Old Brigade," Feb. 16, 1888.

90. Alberts, *Rebels on the Rio Grande*, p. 52.

91. [Davidson], "Reminiscences of the Old Brigade," Feb. 9, 1888.

92. Sibley to Cooper, May 2, 1862, *OR*, 9:509, 511–12.

93. Hall, *Confederate Army of New Mexico*, p. 29; Alberts, *Rebels on the Rio Grande*, p. 53; Thompson, *Sibley*, p. 271; Colton, *The Civil War in the Western Territories: Arizona, Colorado, New Mexico, and Utah*, p. 37; Thompson, ed., "Major Charles Emil Wesche," pp. 43–45.

94. James B. McCown to Editor, *Bellville Countryman*, June 7, 1862; Alberts, *Rebels on the Rio Grande*, p. 53; Howell Diary, Feb. 28, 1862.

95. Hunter Diary, Feb. 26–27, 1862; Alberts, *Rebels on the Rio Grande*, p. 54; [Davidson], "Reminiscences of the Old Brigade," Feb. 16, 1888.

96. Seat Memoir, p. 96.

97. Alberts, *Rebels on the Rio Grande*, p. 55.

98. [Davidson], "Reminiscences of the Old Brigade," Feb. 16, 1888.

99. Hall, "Diary of Ebeneezer Hanna," p. 32.

100. [Davidson], "Reminiscences of the Old Brigade," Feb. 16, 1888.

CHAPTER 9. THE APEX OF EMPIRE

1. Gurden Chapin to Henry W. Halleck, Feb. 28, 1862, *OR*, 9:634–35.

2. Hall, *Confederate Army of New Mexico*, p. 29; Thompson, *Sibley*, p. 241.

3. Sherod Hunter to J. R. Baylor, Apr. 5, 1862, *OR*, 9:707–708.

4. James Carleton to George Wright, Mar. 22, 1862, *OR*, 50, 1:944; Finch, "Sherod Hunter," pp. 171–73.

5. Curry, *Sun Rising on the West*, pp. 94–95. Mangas Coloradas was estimated to be sixty-seven years old at this time.

6. Ibid., pp. 96–97.

7. Thompson, *Baylor*, pp. 76–77.

8. Robertson to Wright, p. 1013.

9. [Davidson], "Reminiscences of the Old Brigade," Feb. 16, 1888. In Napoleon's 1811–12 Russian campaign, the Russians employed "scorched earth" tactics to deny the French any supplies. When Napoleon arrived in Moscow, deep in the throws of a very severe winter, he found the city in ashes and the land stripped of subsistence, causing him to retreat.

10. Wright, "Reminiscences," p. 15.

11. [Davidson], "Reminiscences of the Old Brigade," Feb. 16, 1888.

12. Faulkner, "With Sibley in New Mexico," pp. 136–37.

13. Hall, "Journal of Ebenezer Hanna," p. 28.

14. Alberts, *Rebels on the Rio Grande*, pp. 57–58.

15. Ibid., pp. 56–57.

16. Thompson, *Sibley*, p. 273; Hall, *Confederate Army of New Mexico*, p. 29; Herbert M. Enos to James L. Donaldson, Mar. 11, 1862, *OR*, 9:527–28; Howell Diary, Feb. 28–Mar. 1, 1862; Faulkner, "With Sibley in New Mexico," p. 137.

17. Alberts, *Rebels on the Rio Grande*, pp. 57–58.

18. Hall, "Journal of Ebenezer Hanna," p. 32.

19. The diarist, Sgt. Alfred B. Peticolas, listed Captains Lesuer, Hardeman, Crosson, Alexander, and Giesecke as the officers he saw wading the river (Alberts, *Rebels on the Rio Grande*, p. 70).

20. Faulkner, "With Sibley in New Mexico," p. 137.

21. [Davidson], "Reminiscences of the Old Brigade," Feb. 16, 1888; Gracy, "Campaign Letters of Frank Starr," p. 176.

22. [Davidson], "Reminiscences of the Old Brigade," Feb. 16, 1888.

23. Alberts, *Rebels on the Rio Grande*, p. 58.

24. Thompson, *Westward the Texans*, p. 93.

25. Alberts, *Rebels on the Rio Grande*, p. 59.

26. Hall, *Confederate Army of New Mexico*, p. 29; Thompson, *Sibley*, p. 275; Howell Diary, Mar. 8, 1862; Alberts, *Rebels on the Rio Grande*, p. 63; Haas, "Diary of Julius Gieseke," p. 57; Williams Diary, Mar. 7–8, 1862; Alfred Sturgis Thurmond to Officer

Commanding C.S. Forces, Mar. 20, 1862, *OR,* 9:528–30.

27. Thompson, *Baylor,* pp. 78–79.

28. Thompson, *From Desert to Bayou,* p. 31. J. R. Baylor to Thomas Helm, Mar. 20, 1862, *OR,* 50, 1:942.

29. Thompson, *From Desert to Bayou,* p. 31.

30. William Steele to Samuel Cooper, Mar. 7, 1862, William Steele, "Letters Sent," Record Group 109, United States Archives, Washington, D.C.

31. Thompson, *Westward the Texans,* p. 93; Thompson, *Sibley,* pp. 275–76.

32. Hunter Diary, Mar. 12, 1862.

33. [Davidson], "Reminiscences of the Old Brigade," Feb. 28, May 17, 1888; Sibley to Cooper, p. 509.

34. [Davidson], "Reminiscences of the Old Brigade," May 17, 1888.

35. Haas, "Diary of Julius Gieseke, 1861–1862," p. 57; Hanna Diary, Mar. 8, 1862; Alberts, *Rebels on the Rio Grande,* pp. 67–69; Faulkner, "With Sibley in New Mexico," p. 138.

36. Williams Diary, Mar. 12, 14, 16, 21, 1862; Alberts, *Rebels on the Rio Grande,* pp. 67–69, 72–73.

37. Howell Diary, Feb. 24, 1862; Faulkner, "With Sibley in New Mexico," p. 138; Haas, "Diary of Julius Gieseke," p. 57; Alberts, *Rebels on the Rio Grande,* p. 52; Hanna Diary, Mar. 13, 1862.

38. Howell Diary, Mar. 13, 1862; Haas, "Diary of Julius Gieseke," p. 57; Alberts, *Rebels on the Rio Grande,* pp. 69–70, 72.

39. Capt. David A. Nunn, Company I, Fourth Texas Cavalry, and Capt. George W. Campbell, Company F, Fifth Texas, resigned during this phase of the campaign; the other two cannot be identified (Hall, *Confederate Army of New Mexico,* pp. 114, 180).

40. Alberts, *Rebels on the Rio Grande,* pp. 55–56, 58; Hanna Diary, Mar. 10, 1862; Faulkner, "With Sibley in New Mexico," p. 137.

41. J. L. Donaldson to Gabriel R. Paul, Mar. 10, 1862, *OR,* 9:527.

42. Thompson, *Sibley,* p. 277.

43. "Shrop" Shropshire was captain of Company A, Fifth Texas Cavalry and was promoted to replace Maj. Samuel Lockridge, killed at Val Verde (Hall, *Confederate Army of New Mexico,* pp. 29, 62); Faulkner, "With Sibley in New Mexico," pp. 138–39; Howell Diary, Mar. 18, 1862; [Davidson], "Reminiscences of the Old Brigade," Feb. 23, 1888.

44. Powhatan Jordan was captain of Company "A", Seventh Texas Cavalry and was promoted to major after the death of Lt. Col. John Schuyler Sutton from wounds sustained at Val Verde. The new lieutenant colonel of the Seventh Texas was Arthur Pendleton Bagby, commanding troops in Mesilla (Hall, *Confederate Army of New Mexico,* pp. 221–22).

45. Alberts, *Rebels on the Rio Grande,* pp. 73, 75; Haas, "Diary of Julius Giesecke," p. 58; Williams Diary, Mar. 26, 1862; [Davidson], "Reminiscences of the Old Brigade," Feb. 23, 1888.

46. Hall, *Confederate Army of New Mexico,* p. 31; Thompson, *Sibley,* p. 279; Colton, *Civil War in the Western Territories,* p. 48; Whitford, *Colorado Volunteers,* pp. 79–81.

47. Edward R. S. Canby to Gabriel Paul, Mar. 16, 1862, *OR,* 9:653.

48. Edward R. S. Canby to J. P. Slough, Mar. 18, 1862, *OR,* 9:649.

49. Alberts, *Rebels on The Rio Grande,* p. 75; Colton, *Civil War in the Western*

Territories, p. 48; Whitford, *Colorado Volunteers,* pp. 81–82; Thompson, *Sibley,* p. 279; Hall, *Confederate Army of New Mexico,* p. 31; John M. Chivington to Edward R. S. Canby, Mar. 26, 1862, *OR,* 9:530–31.

50. Gabriel Paul to Adjutant General, Mar. 24, 1862, *OR,* 9:652.

51. Hall, *Confederate Army of New Mexico,* pp. 29, 62; Faulkner, "With Sibley in New Mexico," pp. 138–39; Howell Diary, Mar. 18, 1862; Williams Diary, Mar. 21, 1862.

52. Hall, *Confederate Army of New Mexico,* pp. 31, 143, 151, 160, 168, 312, 328, 346, 354, 374; Thompson, *Sibley,* pp. 278–79; Colton, *Civil War in the Western Territories,* pp. 48–49; Alberts, *Rebels on the Rio Grande,* p. 75.

53. Hunter to Baylor, p. 708; Finch, "Sherod Hunter," pp. 176–77.

54. Finch, "Sherod Hunter," p. 178; Hunt, *Army of the Pacific,* p. 87.

CHAPTER 10. EMPIRE REPELLED

1. [Davidson], "Reminiscences of the Old Brigade," Feb. 23, 1888.

2. Whitford, *Colorado Volunteers,* pp. 85–87; Colton, *Civil War in the Western Territories,* pp. 50–51; Thompson, *Sibley,* pp. 279–80; Chivington to Canby, pp. 530–31; [Davidson], "Reminiscences of the Old Brigade," Feb. 23, 1888.

3. Whitford, *Colorado Volunteers,* pp. 88–89; Colton, *Civil War in the Western Territories,* pp. 51–52; Chivington to Canby, pp. 530–31; [Davidson], "Reminiscences of the Old Brigade," Feb. 23, 1888.

4. [Davidson], "Reminiscences of the Old Brigade," Feb. 23, 1888.

5. Ibid.

6. Whitford, *Colorado Volunteers,* pp. 90–93; Thompson, *Sibley,* pp. 281–82; Hall, *Confederate Army of New Mexico,* p. 31; Colton, *Civil War in the Western Territories,* pp. 52–55; Alberts, *Rebels on the Rio Grande,* p. 75; Chivington to Canby, pp. 530–31.

7. Alberts, *Rebels on the Rio Grande,* p. 75; Whitford, *Colorado Volunteers,* p. 96; Colton, *Civil War in the Western Territories,* pp. 55–57; Williams Diary, Mar. 27, 1862.

8. Williams Diary, Mar. 26, 1862; Alberts, *Rebels on the Rio Grande,* p. 76; Hanna Diary; Mar. 26–27, 1862; Haas, "Diary of Julius Giesecke," p. 57.

9. [Davidson], "Reminiscences of the Old Brigade," Feb. 23, 1888.

10. Alberts, *Rebels on the Rio Grande,* p. 77; Williams Diary, Mar. 27, 1862; Hanna Diary, Mar. 27, 1862; Haas, "Diary of Julius Giesecke," p. 58.

11. [Davidson], "Reminiscences of the Old Brigade," May 17, 1888.

12. Alberts, *Rebels on the Rio Grande,* p. 77; Hall,*Confederate Army of New Mexico,* p. 32; Thompson, *Sibley,* pp. 283–84; Scurry to Jackson, Mar. 31, 1862, *OR,* 9:543; [Davidson], "Reminiscences of the Old Brigade," Mar. 1, 1888.

13. Alberts, *Rebels on the Rio Grande,* pp. 78–79; Colton, *Civil War in the Western Territories,* pp. 60–61; John F. Ritter to Gurden Chapin, May 16, 1862, *OR,* 9:540; Samuel F. Tappan to Gurden Chapin, May 21, 1862, ibid., 9:536; John P. Slough to Adjutant General, U.S. Army, Mar. 30, 1862, ibid., 9:534–35.

14. Slough to Adjutant General, p. 538.

15. [Davidson], "Reminiscences of the Old Brigade," Mar. 1, 1888.

16. Whitford, *Colorado Volunteers,* pp. 106–107; Colton, *Civil War in the Western Territories,* p. 61; Ritter to Chapin, p. 540; Scurry to Jackson, p. 543; Tappan to Chapin, p. 536;

Slough to Adjutant General, p. 533.

17. Alberts, *Rebels on the Rio Grande,* p. 79; Walling to Burrowes, Sept. 27, 1863; Whitford, *Colorado Volunteers,* p. 107; Colton, *Civil War in the Western Territories,* p. 61; Scurry to Jackson, p. 543.

18. [Davidson], "Reminiscences of the Old Brigade," Mar. 1, 1888.

19. Tappan to Chapin, p. 536.

20. Alberts, *Rebels on the Rio Grande,* p. 81; Colton, *Civil War in the Western Territories,* pp. 61–62; Whitford, *Colorado Volunteers,* pp. 108; Tappan to Chapin, p. 536; [Davidson], "Reminiscences of the Old Brigade," Mar. 1, 1888.

21. Alberts, *Rebels on the Rio Grande,* p. 86; [Davidson], "Reminiscences of the Old Brigade," Mar. 1, 1888.

22. [Davidson], "Reminiscences of the Old Brigade," Mar. 8, 1888.

23. Alberts, *Rebels on the Rio Grande,* pp. 79–81; Scurry to Jackson, pp. 543–44; Tappan to Chapin, p. 537; Whitford, *Colorado Volunteers,* p. 109.

24. Alberts, *Rebels on the Rio Grande,* p. 82; Scurry to Jackson, p. 544; Thompson, *Sibley,* p. 286.

25. Chivington to Canby, May 21, 1862, *OR,* 9:537, 539.

26. Tappan to Chapin, pp. 536–37.

27. Alberts, *Rebels on the Rio Grande,* p. 81; Thompson, *Sibley,* pp. 284–86; Scurry to Jackson, p. 544; Ritter to Chapin, p. 540.

28. [Davidson], "Reminiscences of the Old Brigade," Mar. 8, 1888.

29. Alberts, *Rebels on the Rio Grande,* p. 82; Tappan to Chapin, p. 537; Whitford, *Colorado Volunteers,* p. 110; [Davidson], "Reminiscences of the Old Brigade," Mar. 8, 1888.

30. Alberts, *Rebels on the Rio Grande,* pp. 82–83.

31. Whitford, *Colorado Volunteers,* p. 110; Scurry to Jackson, p. 544; Scurry to Jackson, p. 544; Colton, *Civil War in the Western Territories,* pp. 64–65.

32. Charles J. Walker to N. M. MacRae, May 20, 1862, *OR,* 9:532; Slough to Canby, Mar. 29, 1862, ibid., p. 533; the description of the wounds comes from forensic examinations of the skeletal remains of Confederate casualties unearthed at the battlefield in 1987; see also Inventory of Effects of Pvt. Burton R. Stone, Late of Co. D 4th Regt. Texas Cavalry, Inventory of Effects of Private William Staughen, Late of Co. D 4th Regt. Texas Cavalry, and Inventory of Effects of Private E. R. Slaughter, Late of Co. D 4th Regt. Texas Cavalry, Moritz Maedgen Papers, Texas Collection, Baylor University, Waco, Texas.

33. Scurry to Jackson, p. 544; Colton, *Civil War in the Western Territories,* p. 67; Whitford, *Colorado Volunteers,* p. 114.

34. Gracy, "Campaign Letters of Frank Starr," p. 179; Scurry to Jackson, p. 544; Sibley to Cooper, Mar. 31, 1862, p. 541.

35. Scurry to Jackson, p. 544; Sibley to Cooper, p. 541; Ritter to Chapin, p. 540.

36. Tappan to Chapin, pp. 536–39; [Davidson], "Reminiscences of the Old Brigade," Mar. 8, 1888.

37. Slough to Adjutant General, p. 535; Tappan to Chapin, p. 537; Alberts, *Rebels on the Rio Grande,* p. 85.

38. Casualty descriptions taken from archeological and forensic studies performed on skeletons of Confederate soldiers discovered at the Glorieta Battlefield in 1987; Scurry to Jackson, pp. 544–45.

39. Don Alberts, interview by author, Mar. 24, 1989, Santa Fe, New Mexico; Confederate skeletal remains from the battlefield reveal a number of individuals with gunshot wounds to the head, including fired pistol balls removed from inside the cranium, possibly showing a mercy killing by friends of the suffering, mortally wounded soldiers.

40. Alberts, *Rebels on the Rio Grande,* p. 86.

41. Scurry to Jackson, pp. 544–45; Alberts, *Rebels on the Rio Grande,* p. 85.

42. [Davidson], "Reminiscences of the Old Brigade," Mar. 1, 1888.

43. Haas, "Diary of Julius Gieseke," p. 58; Alberts, *Rebels on the Rio Grande,* pp. 86–87; Williams Diary, Mar. 29, 1862; Wright, "Reminiscences," p. 21.

44. Donald Gaither, ed., "The 'Pet Lambs' at Glorieta Pass: Charles Gardiner called the battle 'the severest stroke the Texans ever received at our hands, in this country,'" *Civil War Times Illustrated* 15 (Nov., 1976): 33.

45. Chivington to [Canby], Mar. 28, 1862, *OR,* 9:538–39; Scurry to Jackson, p. 544; Colton, *Civil War in the Western Territories,* p. 70; Whitford, *Colorado Volunteers,* p. 119; Gaither, "'Pet Lambs' at Glorieta Pass," p. 33.

46. Alberts, *Rebels on the Rio Grande,* p. 85; Colton, *Civil War in the Western Territories,* pp. 71–73; Whitford, *Colorado Volunteers,* pp. 119–22; Thompson, *Sibley,* pp. 289–90.

47. Haas, "Diary of Julius Gieseke," p. 58; Alberts, *Rebels on the Rio Grande,* pp. 86–87; Williams Diary, Mar. 29, 1862; Wright, "Reminiscences," p. 21.

48. Alberts, *Rebels on the Rio Grande,* pp. 87–88; Haas, "Diary of Julius Giesecke," p. 58; Williams Diary, Mar. 30, 1862.

49. As Assistant Adjutant General, Maj. Alexander M. Jackson would have been responsible for addressing the troops; Howell Diary, Mar. 30, 1862.

50. Faulkner, "With Sibley in New Mexico," p. 140.

51. [Davidson], "Reminiscences of the Old Brigade," Mar. 17, 1888.

52. Faulkner, "With Sibley in New Mexico," p. 140; Howell Diary, Mar. 30, Apr. 1, 1862; Hall, *Confederate Army of New Mexico,* pp. 62, 320, 346; McCown to Editor, May 6, 1862, *Bellville Countryman,* June 7, 1862; [Davidson], "Reminiscences of the Old Brigade," Mar. 17, 1888.

53. Sibley to Cooper, p. 541; Thompson, *Sibley,* p. 293.

54. Hunter Diary, Apr. 2–3, 1862.

55. Gaither, "'Pet Lambs' at Glorieta Pass," pp. 35–36.

CHAPTER 11. EMPIRE RETREATING

1. Haas, "Diary of Julius Giesecke," p. 91.

2. Williams Diary, Apr. 3, 1862, p. 222.

3. Modern medical practices prescribe fever patients to be wrapped in cold, moist towels, allowing evaporation to lower the body temperature; flushing wounds with cold, clear, water is also recommended to reduce swelling, clean the wound of bacteria buildup, and to reduce bleeding.

4. Alberts, *Rebels on the Rio Grande,* pp. 88, 94, 97; Haas, "Diary of Julius Geisecke," p. 58; Williams Diary, Apr. 1–3, 1862; [Davidson], "Reminiscences of the Old Brigade," Mar. 15, 1888.

5. Alberts, *Rebels on the Rio Grande,* pp. 91–92; Gracy, "Campaign Letters of Frank Starr," p. 140.

6. Alberts, *Rebels on the Rio Grande,* pp. 91–92; Faulkner, "With Sibley in New Mexico, pp. 140–41.

7. Gracy, "Campaign Letters of Frank Starr," pp. 183–84; Alberts, *Rebels on the Rio Grande,* pp. 90, 101; Hall, "Letter to Nacogdoches," p. 332.

8. Sibley to Cooper, p. 509; Alberts, *Rebels on the Rio Grande,* p. 94.

9. Thompson, *Sibley,* p. 96; Williams Diary, Apr. 4, 7, 1862.

10. Alberts, *Rebels on the Rio Grande,* p. 91.

11. Sibley to Cooper, p. 541; Thompson, *Sibley,* p. 293.

12. Conner, *Colorado Gold Fields,* pp. 144–45.

13. [Davidson], "Reminiscences of the Old Brigade," Mar. 29, 1888.

14. Canby to the Adjutant General of the Army, Apr. 11, 1862, *OR,* 9:550; McCown to Editor; Thompson, *Sibley,* p. 293.

15. Williams Diary, Apr. 6–7, 1862; Alberts, *Rebels on the Rio Grande,* p. 97; Sibley to Cooper, p. 510; Thompson, *Sibley,* p. 293.

16. Alberts, *Rebels on the Rio Grande,* pp. 98, 101; Haas, "Diary of Julius Geisecke," p. 59.

17. Williams Diary, Apr. 3, 1862; Wright, "Reminiscences," pp. 21–23; Hall, *Confederate Army of New Mexico,* p. 222.

18. Hunter Diary, Apr. 10–15, 1862; [Davidson], "Reminiscences of the Old Brigade," May 10, 1888.

19. Hall, *Confederate Army of New Mexico,* pp. 35, 37; Alberts, *Rebels on the Rio Grande,* p. 101; Sibley to Cooper, p. 510.

20. [Davidson], "Reminiscences of the Old Brigade," Mar. 29, 1888.

21. Ibid.

22. Alberts, *Rebels on the Rio Grande,* pp. 101, 112; Sibley to Cooper, pp. 510–11; Hall, *Confederate Army of New Mexico,* p. 35.

23. Alberts, *Rebels on the Rio Grande,* p. 103; McCown to Editor.

24. Alberts, *Rebels on the Rio Grande,* p. 102.

25. [Davidson], "Reminiscences of the Old Brigade," Mar. 29, 1888.

26. Hall, *Confederate Army of New Mexico,* p. 35; Alberts, *Rebels on the Rio Grande,* p. 103; Whitford, *Colorado Volunteers,* p. 130; Canby to Adjutant General, Apr. 23, 1862, *OR,* 9:551.

27. Seat, "Memoirs," p. 100.

28. [Davidson], "Reminiscences of the Old Brigade," Mar. 29, 1888.

29. Ibid.

30. Ibid.

31. Ibid.

32. Ibid.

33. Alberts, *Rebels on the Rio Grande,* p. 105; Haas, "Diary of Julius Giesecke," p. 59; The position held by the Confederates was considered by Canby as "the stongest in New Mexico," aside from Fort Union (Canby to the Adjutant General, p. 551); [Davidson], "Reminiscences of the Old Brigade," Mar. 29, 1888.

34. Alberts, *Rebels on the Rio Grande,* p. 104.

35. [Davidson], "Reminiscences of the Old Brigade," Apr. 8, 1888.

36. Ibid.

37. Alberts, *Rebels on the Rio Grande,* p. 104; see also Sibley to Cooper, p. 510.

38. Alberts, *Rebels on the Rio Grande,* pp. 106–107; Howell Diary, Apr. 15, 1862; Canby to the Adjutant General, p. 551; [Davidson], "Reminiscences of the Old Brigade," Apr. 12, 1888.

39. Howell Diary, Apr. 16–17, 1862; Alberts, *Rebels on the Rio Grande,* p. 107; Canby decided that his troops, who had marched for over a day without rations, were too exhausted to attempt a battle (Canby to Adjutant General, p. 551).

40. [Davidson], "Reminiscences of the Old Brigade," Apr. 12, 1888.

41. Thompson, *Sibley,* p. 309; Hall, *Confederate Army of New Mexico,* p. 36; Sibley to Cooper, p. 511.

42. [Davidson], "Reminiscences of the Old Brigade," Apr. 12, 1888.

43. Ibid.

44. Howell Diary, Apr. 17, 1862; Alberts, *Rebels on the Rio Grande,* p. 109; Sibley to Cooper, p. 511.

45. [Davidson], "Reminiscences of the Old Brigade," Apr. 12, 1888; Howell Diary, Apr. 17, 1862; Alberts, *Rebels on the Rio Grande,* p. 109; Sibley to Cooper, p. 511.

46. Canby to Adjutant General, p. 551.

47. Hunter Diary, Apr. 17–21, 1862.

48. Thompson, *Sibley,* pp. 299–300; Sibley to Cooper, p. 511; Alberts, *Rebels on the Rio Grande,* p. 110.

49. Haas, "Diary of Julius Giesecke," p. 59; Alberts, *Rebels on the Rio Grande,* pp. 111–16; Howell Diary, Apr. 18–24, 1862.

50. Alberts, *Rebels on the Rio Grande,* pp. 111–16.

51. Howell Diary, Apr. 23, 1862; Alberts, *Rebels on the Rio Grande,* pp. 109–10, 112–13, 121.

52. Gracy, "Campaign Letters of Frank Starr," p. 180. Haas, "Diary of Julius Giesecke," p. 60; Howell Diary, Apr. 22, 1862; Alberts, *Rebels on the Rio Grande,* pp. 113–14; James Graydon to Gabriel Paul, May 14, 1862, *OR,* 9:672.

53. Alberts, *Rebels on the Rio Grande,* p. 112; Thompson, *Westward the Texans,* p. 101.

54. *Sacramento Daily Union,* Monday, Aug. 25, 1862.

55. Alberts, *Rebels on the Rio Grande,* p. 114.

56. Howell Diary, Apr. 21, 25, 1862; Haas, "Diary of Julius Giesecke," p. 60; Alberts, *Rebels on the Rio Grande,* pp. 116–17. Napoleon's march over the Alps in the spring of 1796 was an epic of human will over natural adversity. By braving snow-blocked passes thought to be impassible at that time of year, the young Bonaparte was able to steal a march on his Austrian opponents and to make a decisive concentration against their divided forces. Peticolas is certainly alluding to the romantic notions of the brave French soldiers suffering the elements and altitude to bring victory to France.

57. Alberts, *Rebels on the Rio Grande,* p. 117; Howell Diary, Apr. 24, 1862; Haas, "Diary of Julius Giesecke," p. 60.

58. Alberts, *Rebels on the Rio Grande,* p. 117.

59. Howell Diary, Apr. 27, 1862; Alberts, *Rebels on the Rio Grande,* pp. 117–18; Haas, "Diary of Julius Giesecke," p. 60.

60. Collard, "Reminiscences."

61. Ibid.

62. Ibid.

63. Hall, "Court-Martial of Arthur Pendleton Bagby, p. 60–67.

64. Finch, "Sherod Hunter," pp. 179–81; William McLeve, "Reminiscences of a California Volunteer," William McCleve Papers, Bancroft Library, Berkley, California, pp. 3–5.

65. James Reily to Ignacio Pesqueira, Mar. 18, 1862, *OR*, 50, 1:1032–33; Martin Hardwick Hall, "Colonel James Reily's Diplomatic Missions to Chihuahua and Sonora," *New Mexico Historical Review* 31 (July, 1956): 238–39.

66. Finch, "Sherod Hunter," 186–87; Hunt, *Army of the Pacific,* pp. 88–89.

67. Finch, "Sherod Hunter," pp. 187–88; Hunter to Baylor, Apr. 18, 1862, reproduced in ibid., p. 204.

CHAPTER 12. EMPIRE IN RUIN

1. Benjamin Roberts to Lorenzo Thomas, Apr. 23 1862, *OR*, 9:552; Paul to Adjutant General, May 1, 1862, *OR*, 9:553.

2. Thompson, *Sibley,* p. 301; Sibley to Cooper, p. 511; Hall, *Confederate Army of New Mexico*, p. 37.

3. Alberts, *Rebels on the Rio Grande,* p. 122; Howell Diary, Apr. 28, 1862.

4. Alberts, *Rebels on the Rio Grande,* pp. 123, 125.

5. Ibid., p. 118; Gracy, "Campaign Letters of Frank Starr," p. 182; [Davidson], "Reminiscences of the Old Brigade," May 24, 1888.

6. Gracy, "Campaign Letters of Frank Starr," pp. 180, 186.

7. Hall, *Confederate Army of New Mexico,* pp. 212–13, 289–92; Alberts, *Rebels on the Rio Grande,* p. 129.

8. Thompson, *Sibley,* pp. 301–302; Hall, "Letter to Nacogdoches," p. 331.

9. Thompson, *Sibley,* pp. 311–12.

10. Alberts, *Rebels on the Rio Grande,* pp. 131–32; Haas, "Diary of Julius Giesecke," p. 60–61; Howell Diary, May 25, 1862; Gracy, "Campaign Letters of Frank Starr," p. 182.

11. Gracy, "Campaign Letters of Frank Starr," p. 185; Howell Diary, May 8–15, 16, 23, 1862; Haas, "Diary of Julius Giesecke," p. 61.

12. Gracy, "Campaign Letters of Frank Starr," p. 185; Hall, "Letter to Nacogdoches," p. 330.

13. Alberts, *Rebels on the Rio Grande,* pp. 129, 134; Haas, "Diary of Julius Giesecke," p. 61.

14. Hall, "Letter to Nacogdoches," p. 331; Alberts, *Rebels on the Rio Grande,* pp. 128–31; H. H. Sibley to Hamilton P. Bee, May 27, 1862, *OR*, 9:714.

15. Alberts, *Rebels on the Rio Grande,* pp. 128–29; Gracy, "Campaign Letters of Frank Starr," p. 186.

16. Hall, "Letter to Nacogdoches," p. 331; McCown to Editor; Haas, "Diary of Julius Giesecke," pp. 60–61; Alberts, *Rebels on the Rio Grande,* p. 129.

17. Hall, *Confederate Army of New Mexico,* p. 37; Thompson, *Sibley,* p. 302; Sibley to Cooper, p. 511; Roberts to Thomas, p. 553; see also Williams Diary, Apr. 20–May 28, 1862.

18. Alberts, *Rebels on the Rio Grande,* pp. 121, 127; Jacqueline Dorgan Meketa, ed.,

Legacy of Honor: The Life of Rafael Chacón, a Nineteenth-Century New Mexican, pp. 188–89.

19. Gracy, "Campaign Letters of Frank Starr," pp. 182–83; Howell to W. S. Howell, May 2, 1862, Howell Papers.

20. Gracy, "Campaign Letters of Frank Starr," p. 184; McCown to Editor, June 7, 1862.

21. Hall, "Letter to Nacogdoches," p. 331; Gracy, "Campaign Letters of Frank Starr," p. 181.

22. [Houston] *Tri-Weekly Telegraph,* Aug. 27, 1862.

23. Ibid.

24. Ibid.

25. Ibid.

26. Ibid.

27. Sibley to Cooper, pp. 511–12.

28. Ibid., p. 502.

29. The skirmish at Picacho Pass, Apr. 15, 1862, was the most westerly land action of the Civil War.

30. Canby to Adjutant General, p. 551; Roberts to Thomas, p. 553; James H. Carleton to Richard C. Drum, May 25, 1862, ibid., 9:553; Henry W. Halleck to Edwin M. Stanton, Mar. 20, 1862, ibid., 8:627–28; Henry W. Halleck to J. W. Denver, Apr. 5, 1862, ibid., 8:664–65. The regiments promised from Kansas included the First Kansas Infantry, Twelfth and Thirteenth Wisconsin Infantries, Second and Seventh Kansas Cavalries, Carpenter's Wisconsin Battery and Allen's Kansas Battery; reinforcements from California included elements of the First and Fifth California Infantries, First and Second California Cavalries, and Shinn's Light Battery, Third U.S. Artillery.

31. Collard, "Reminiscences," p. 7.

32. Collard, "Reminiscences," p. 8.

33. Collard, "Reminiscences," pp. 8–9; Joseph G. Tilford to A. L. Anderson, May 30, 1862, *OR,* 9:608.

34. Collard, "Reminiscences," pp. 8–9; Tilford to Anderson, p. 608.

35. Collard, "Reminiscences," pp. 5–6.

36. Ibid., p. 7.

37. Ibid., p. 8.

38. Ibid., p. 9; Canby to Adjutant General, May 25, 1862, *OR,* 9:608–609. Canby mentions a firefight between his pickets and Texans on May 23, 1862, eight miles south of Fort Craig, resulting in four Rebel casualties—no known Confederate sources verify this report.

39. Finch, "Sherod Hunter," p. 190–92.

40. Robert E. Lee to Paul O. Hébert, May 31, 1862, *OR,* 9:716; Jefferson Davis to H. H. Sibley, June 7, 1862, *OR,* 9:717–18; Sibley to Hamilton Bee, May 27, 1862, *OR,* 9:714.

41. Sibley to Bee, p. 714.

42. [Davidson], "Reminiscences of the Old Brigade," May 24, 1888.

43. Hall, *Confederate Army of New Mexico,* pp. 38–39; Thompson, *Sibley,* p. 304; D'Hamel, *Adventures of a Tenderfoot,* pp. 17–18.

44. Randolph to Baylor, p. 1108; Baylor to Randolph, June 18, 1862, p. 1108.

45. Hall, *Confederate Army of New Mexico,* pp. 38–39; Thompson, *Sibley,* p. 304; Sibley to Bee, p. 714.

46. Alberts, *Rebels on the Rio Grande,* p. 142.

47. Ibid., p. 145.

48. [Davidson], "Reminiscences of the Old Brigade," May 10, 1888.

49. Jerry Thompson, *Westward the Texans,* pp. 104–106.

50. [Davidson], "Reminiscences of the Old Brigade," May 24, 1888.

51. Thompson, *Westward the Texans,* p. 109.

52. "Special Meeting in Prairie Lea, Caldwell County, Texas, June 1, 1862," *Plum Creek Almanac* 1 (Fall, 1983): 54–57.

53. [Davidson], "Reminiscences of the Old Brigade," May 10, 1888.

54. Thompson, *Westward the Texans,* p. 109; Haas, "Diary of Julius Giesecke," p. 63; Alberts, *Rebels on the Rio Grande,* p. 155.

55. Gracy, "Campaign Letters of Frank Starr, 1861–1862," p. 187.

CHAPTER 13. ECHOES OF EMPIRE

1. Hall, *Confederate Army of New Mexico,* p. 38; Steele to Cooper, July 12, 1862, *OR,* 9:721–22; McCleve, "Reminiscences," pp. 6–8; Curry, *Sun Rising on the West,* pp. 104–105.

2. *Sacremento Daily Union,* Monday, Aug. 25, 1862.

3. William Steele to William Marks and Anton Brewer, June 24, 1862, William Steele "Letters Sent," Record Group 109, United States Archives, Washington, D.C.; Steele to Sibley, June 26, 1862, *OR,* 9:720.

4. Collard, "My War Horse, Pete," p. 3, in "Reminiscences."

5. Ibid.

6. Ibid.

7. Ibid.

8. *Houston Tri-Weekly Telegraph,* Aug. 18, 1862; Hall, "Native Mexican Relations," pp. 176–77; Carleton to Drum, pp. 554–55.

9. Hall, "Native Mexican Relations," pp. 176–77. Hall, *Confederate Army of New Mexico,* pp. 243–47; Henry Connelly to Edward R. S. Canby, June 15, 1862, *OR,* 50, 1:1140.

10. Collard, "My War Horse, Pete." pp. 5–6.

11. Wright, "Reminiscences," pp. 31–32.

12. Ibid.

13. Ibid., p. 36.

14. Collard, "My War Horse, Pete," p. 6.

15. Ibid., p. 7.

16. Ibid.

17. Ibid.

18. Ibid.

19. Ibid.

20. Ibid., pp. 9–10.

21. Ibid., p. 8.

22. Ibid., pp. 10–11.

23. Steele to Cooper, pp. 721–22; James H. Carleton to Commander of Confederate Troops, San Antonio, Tex., Sept. 1, 1862, ibid., 9:580.

24. Williams Diary, Apr. 22–30.

25. Ibid., May 1–June 5.

26. Ibid., June 6–30.

27. Ibid., July 1–Aug. 24.

28. Ibid., Aug. 26–Sept. 3.

29. Hord, "Diary of E. J. Robb," p. 70.

30. Ibid.

31. Ibid., p. 75.

32. Conner, *Colorado Gold Fields,* pp. 132–33.

33. Ibid., p. 138.

34. Denver, Colorado, *Rocky Mountain News,* Aug. 11, 14, 18, 19, and 23.

35. Conner, *Colorado Gold Fields,* pp. 146–47.

36. Ibid., p. 148.

37. See William J. Husaker, "Lansford W. Hastings' Project for the Invasion and Conquest of Arizona and New Mexico for the Southern Confederacy," *Arizona Historical Review* 4 (1931–32), pp. 5–12.

38. See Smith, *Birth of Colorado.*

39. Thompson, *Baylor,* pp. 82–84.

40. Thompson, *Baylor,* pp. 82–84. J. H. Carleton to J. R. West, Nov. 18, 1862, *OR,* 15:599.

41. J. R. West to Ben Cutler, Dec. 28, 1862, *OR,* 50, 2:266–67.

42. Thompson, *Baylor,* pp. 82–84, Baylor, *Baylor,* pp. 13–15.

43. Thompson, *Baylor,* pp. 82–84.

44. Ibid.

45. Thompson, *Sibley,* p. 314.

46. By far the most authoritative work on this subject is L. Boyd Finch, "Arizona in Exile: Confederate Schemes to Recapture the Far Southwest," *The Journal of Arizona History* 33 (Spring, 1992): 57–83.

47. Thompson, *Sibley,* pp. 331–34.

48. Baylor, *Baylor,* p. 16.

49. Thompson, *Sibley,* p. 335.

EPILOGUE

1. Anderson, "Canby's Services," pp. 697–98.

Bibliography

MANUSCRIPTS

Austin, Texas. University of Texas. Eugene C. Barker Texas History Center.
    Baylor Family Papers.
    Burrowes Family Papers.
    E. Jarvis Baker Memoirs.
    Hall Family Papers.
    Henry C. Wright. "Reminiscences of H. C. Wright of Austin."
    Oscar Haas Papers. Joseph Faust Letters.
    Thomas J. Rusk Papers.
    William Randolph Howell Papers.
Austin, Texas. Texas State Library and Archives.
    Holbrook Collection. Ebenezer Hanna Diary.
    Martin Hardwick Hall Papers.
Berkley, California. Bancroft Library.
    William McCleve Papers. "Reminiscences of a California Volunteer."
Columbus, Texas. Shropshire-Upton Confederate Museum.
    John Samuel Shropshire Letters.
El Paso, Texas. William B. Peticolas Collection.
    Alfred B. Peticolas Diary.
Fayetteville, Arkansas. University of Arkansas. Special Collections.
    Benton Bell Seat Memoir.
Fort Worth, Texas. Geraldine Hudson Collection.
    Joseph C. Terrell Letters.
Galveston, Texas. Rosenberg Library. Texas and Local
History Collection.
    Diary of a Union soldier.
    Robert M. Franklin Speech.
    Trueheart Papers.
    William Pitt Ballinger Diary.
Hillsboro, Texas. Hill College. Harold B. Simpson Confederate Research
Center.

Robert Thomas Williams Diary.
Laredo, Texas. Jerry Thompson Collection.
    Edgar A. Treadwell Letter.
    John E. Hart Diary.
Lufkin, Texas.
    Probate Records. William H. Cleaver "Last Will and Testament."
New Orleans, Louisiana. Tulane University. Howard-Tilton Memorial Library.
Special Collections.
    Louisiana Historical Association Collection. J. L. Brent Papers.
    Louisiana Historical Association Collection. C. M. Horton Diary.
    Wharton Collection. Baylor Letters.
New Orleans, Louisiana. Historic New Orleans Collection.
    MS 17. Samuel Gault Diary.
Silver City, New Mexico. Robert F. Collard Collection.
    Felix R Collard. "Reminiscences of a Private, Company
    'G,' 7th Texas Cavalry, Sibley Brigade, C.S.A."
Tyler, Texas. Smith County Archives.
    Ben Johnson Papers.
    Harold J. Hunter Diary.
Waco, Texas. Baylor University. Texas Collection.
    John M. Bronough Papers.
    Moritz Maedgen Papers.

GOVERNMENT DOCUMENTS

Confederate

Compiled Service Records of Confederate Soldiers Who Served in Organizations
    from the State of Texas. Microfilmed records of the Second, Fourth, Fifth,
    Seventh Texas, and Second Arizona Cavalry Regiments, and the Thirteenth
    Texas Cavalry Battalion. Confederate Adjutant General's Office, Record
    Group 109, National Archives, Washington, D.C.
Confederate States of America. Prize Commission Papers. Texas and Local
    History Collection. Rosenberg Library. Galveston, Texas.
Confederate States Ordnance Bureau. *Field Manual for the Use of the Officers
    on Ordnance Duty.* Richmond: Ritchie and Dunnavant, 1862.

United States

Austin, Texas. Texas State Library and Archives. Martin Hall Collection. Post
    Returns of Fort Davis, Texas.
Austin, Texas. Texas State Library and Archives. Martin Hall Collection. Post
    Returns of Fort Stanton, New Mexico Territory.
Official Records of the Union and Confederate Navies in War of Rebellion. 31
    vols. Washington, D.C.: Government Printing Office, 1899–1908.
Texas Legislature. *Senate Journal,* Third Legislature.

The War of the Rebellion: A Compilation of the Official Records of the Union and Confederate Armies. 128 vols., Gettysburg: National Historical Society, 1972.

United States Census Office. *Agriculture of the United States in 1860; Compiled from the Original Returns of the Eighth Census, Under the Direction of the Secretary of the Interior.* Washington, D.C.: Government Printing Office, 1864.

United States Census Office. Eighth Census of the United States, 1860: Harrison, Upshur, Austin, Lavaca, . . . counties, Texas. Population schedules.

BOOKS

Alberts, Don E., ed. *Rebels on the Rio Grande: The Civil War Journal of A. B. Peticolas.* Albuquerque: University of New Mexico Press, 1984.

Anderson, Charles. *Texas, Before, and on the Eve of the Rebellion.* Cincinnati: Peter G. Thompson, 1884.

Austerman, Wayne R. *Sharp's Rifles and Spanish Mules: The San Antonio–El Paso Mail, 1851–1881.* College Station: Texas A&M University Press, 1985.

Barr, Alwyn, ed. *Charles Porter's Account of the Confederate Attempt to Seize Arizona and New Mexico.* Austin: Pemberton Press, 1964.

Baylor, George W. *John Robert Baylor, Confederate Governor of Arizona.* Edited by Odie B. Faulk. Tucson: Arizona Pioneers' Historical Society, 1966.

Bickley, George. *Rules, Regulations and Principles of the K.G.C., issued by Order of the Congress of the K.C.S. and the General President.* New York: Benjamin Urner, 1859.

Billington, Ray. *The Far Western Frontier, 1830–1860.* New York: Harper, 1956.

Binkley, William C. *The Expansionist Movement in Texas, 1836–1850.* New York: Da Capo Press, 1970.

————. *The Texas Revolution.* Baton Rouge: Louisiana State University Press, 1952.

Bowden, J. J. *The Exodus of Federal Forces From Texas.* Austin: Eakin Press, 1986.

Brown, Charles H. *Agents of Manifest Destiny: The Life and Times of the Filibusters.* Chapel Hill: University of North Carolina Press, 1980.

Christian, Asa K. *Mirabeau Buonaparte Lamar.* Austin: Von Boechmann-Jones, 1932.

Colton, Ray C. *The Civil War in the Western Territories: Arizona, Colorado, New Mexico, and Utah.* Norman: University of Oklahoma Press, 1959.

Conner, Daniel Ellis. *A Confederate in the Colorado Gold Fields.* Norman: University of Oklahoma Press, 1970.

Cravens, John Nathan. *James Harper Starr: Financier of the Republic of Texas.* Austin: Daughters of the Republic of Texas, 1950.

Curry, W. Hubert. *Sun Rising on the West: The Saga of Henry Clay and*

Elizabeth Smith. Crosbyton, Tex.: Crosby County Pioneer Memorial, 1979.

Cutrer, Tom W. *Ben McCulloch and the Frontier Military Tradition.* Chapel Hill: University of North Carolina Press, 1993.

D'Hamel, E. B. *The Adventures of a Tenderfoot: History of 2nd Regt. Mounted Rifles and Co. G, 33 Regt. and Capt Coopwood's Spy Co. and 2nd Texas in Texas and New Mexico.* Waco: W. M. Morrison Books, n.d.

De Forest, John William. *A Volunteer's Adventures: A Union Captain's Record of the Civil War.* New Haven: Yale University Press, 1946.

De León, Arnoldo. *They Called Them Greasers: Anglo Attitudes Towards Mexicans in Texas, 1821–1900.* Austin: University of Texas Press, 1983.

DuFour, Charles L. *Gentle Tiger: The Gallant Life of Roberdeau Wheat.* Baton Rouge: Louisiana State University Press, 1957.

Evans, Clement, ed. *Confederate Military History: Library of Confederate States History in Twelve Volumes Written by Distinguished Men of the South.* 12 vols. Atlanta: Confederate Publishing Co., 1899.

Fehrenbach, T. R. *Lone Star: A History of Texas and Texans.* New ed. New York: Wings Books, 1991.

Fifteen Southerners. *Why the South Will Survive.* Athens: University of Georgia Press, 1981.

Fitzpatrick, Charles, and Conrad Crane. *The Prudent Soldier, the Rash Old Fighter, and the Walking Whiskey Keg: The Battle of Val Verde, New Mexico, 13-21 February 1862.* Fort Bliss, Texas: Air Defense Artillery School, 1984.

Flinn, Frank M. *Campaigning with Banks in Louisiana, '63 and '64, and with Sheridan in the Shenandoah Valley in '64 and '65.* Lynn, Mass.: Press of Thomas P. Nichols, 1887.

Foner, Eric. *Free Soil, Free Labor, Free Men: The Ideology of the Republican Party before the Civil War.* New York: Oxford University Press, 1970.

Ford, John S. *Rip Ford's Texas.* Edited by Stephen B. Oates. Austin: University of Texas Press, 1987.

Freeman, Douglas Southall. *Lee's Lieutenants: A Study in Command.* 3 vols. New York: Charles Scribner's Sons, 1944.

Fuller, John D. P. *The Movement for the Acquisition of All of Mexico, 1846–1848.* Baltimore: Johns Hopkins University Press, 1936.

Gambrell, Herbert Pickens. *Mirabeau Buonaparte Lamar: Troubadour and Crusader.* Dallas: Southwest Press, 1934.

Ganaway, Loomis Morton. *New Mexico and the Sectional Controversy.* Albuquerque: University of New Mexico Press, 1943.

Garber, Paul N. *The Gadsden Treaty.* Philadelphia: University of Pennsylvania Press, 1923.

Gerson, Noel. *Sad Swashbuckler: The Life of William Walker.* Nashville, Tenn.: T. Nelson, 1976.

Goetzmann, William. *When the Eagle Screamed: The Romantic Horizon in American Diplomacy 1800–1860.* New York: Wiley, 1966.

Goyne, Minetta Altgelt. *Lone Star and Double Eagle: Civil War Letters of a*

German-Texas Family. Fort Worth: Texas Christian University Press, 1982.

Graebner, Norman A. *Empire on the Pacific: A Study in American Continental Expansion.* New York: Ronald, 1955.

————, ed. *Manifest Destiny.* Indianapolis: Bobbs-Merrill, 1968.

Green, Laurence. *The Filibuster: The Career of William Walker.* New York: Bobbs-Merrill, 1937.

Hall, Martin Hardwick. *Sibley's New Mexico Campaign.* Austin: University of Texas Press, 1960.

————. *The Confederate Army of New Mexico.* Austin: Presidial Press, 1978.

Hardee, William J. *Hardee's Rifle and Light Infantry Tactics, For the Instruction, Exercises and Manuevers of Riflemen and Light Infantry.* New York: J. O. Kane, Publisher, 1862.

Harris, Gertrude. *A Tale of Men Who Knew Not Fear.* San Antonio: Alamo Printing Company, 1935.

Hayes, Charles W. *Galveston: History of the Island and the City.* 2 vols. Austin: Jenkins Garrett Press, 1974.

Haynes, Sam W. *Soldiers of Misfortune: The Somervell and Mier Expeditions.* Austin: University of Texas Press, 1990.

Heartsill, W. W. *Fourteen Hundred and 91 Days in the Confederate Army: A Journal Kept by W. W. Heartsill for Four Years, One Month and One Day, or Camp Life; Day by Day, of the W. P. Lane Rangers From April 19, 1861 to May 20, 1865.* Edited by Bell Irvin Wiley. Wilmington, N.C.: Broadfoot Publishing Company, 1987.

Heitman, Francis B. *Historical Register and Dictionary of the United States Army, from its Organization September 29, 1789 to March 2, 1903.* 3 vols. Washington, D.C.: Government Printing Office, 1903.

Hietala, Thomas R. *Manifest Design: Anxious Aggrandizement in Late Jacksonian America.* Ithaca, N.Y.: Cornell University Press, 1985.

Holmes, Lucile Barbour. *Oaklawn Manor: Ante-bellum Plantation Home.* Franklin, La.: The author, 1980.

Horn, Calvin. *New Mexico's Troubled Years: The Story of the Early Territorial Governors.* Albuquerque, N.M.: Horn and Wallace, 1963.

Hunt, Aurora. *The Army of the Pacific: Its Operations in California, Texas, Arizona, New Mexico, Utah, Nevada, Oregon, Washington, Plains Region, Mexico, etc. 1860–1866.* Glendale, Calif.: Arthur Clark, 1951.

Ickis, Alonzo F. *Bloody Trails along the Rio Grande: A Day-by-Day Diary of Alonzo Ferdinand Ickis.* Edited by Nolie Mumey. Denver: Fred A. Rosenstock, 1958.

Johnson, Robert Underwood, and Clarence Clough Buel, eds. *Battles and Leaders of the Civil War.* New ed. 4 vols. Secaucus, N.J.: Book Sales Inc., 1984.

Josephy, Alvin M., Jr. *The Civil War in the American West.* New York: Alfred A. Knopf, 1991.

Joyce, W. J. *The Life of W. J. Joyce, Written by Himself: The History of a Long, Laborious, and Happy Life of Fifty-Seven Years in the Ministry in Texas—*

From the Sabine to the Rio Grande. San Marcos: San Marcos Printing Company, 1913.

Kendall, George Wilkins. *Narrative of the Texan Santa Fe Expedition*. 2 vols. Austin: The Steck Company, 1935.

Kennedy, Elijah R. *The Contest for California in 1861: How Colonel E. D. Baker Saved the Pacific States to the Union*. Boston: Houghton Mifflin, 1912.

Lamar, Mirabeau B. *Papers*. Edited by C. A. Gulick. 6 vols. Austin: Baldwin, 1921–27.

Lecompte, Janet. *Rebellion in Rio Arriba, 1837*. Albuquerque: University of New Mexico Press, 1985.

Lewis, Oscar. *The War in the Far West: 1861–1865*. Garden City, N.Y.: Doubleday and Company, 1961.

Lowrie, Samuel H. *Culture Conflict in Texas, 1821–1835*. New York: Columbia University Press, 1932.

Lubbock, Francis R. *Six Decades in Texas: The Memoirs of Francis R. Lubbock, Confederate Governor of Texas*. Edited by C. W. Raines. Austin: The Pemberton Press, 1968.

McKee, James, C. *Narrative of the Surrender of a Command of U.S. Forces at Fort Fillmore, New Mexico in July* A.D. *1861*. Boston: John A. Lowell, 1886.

Maketa, Jaqueline Dorgan, ed. *Legacy of Honor: The Life of Rafael Chacón, a Nineteenth-Century New Mexican*. Albuquerque: University of New Mexico Press, 1986.

Mandel, Bernard. *Labor: Free and Slave*. New York: Associated Authors, 1955.

May, Robert E. *John A. Quitman: Old South Crusader*. Baton Rouge: Louisiana State University Press, 1985.

_____. *The Southern Dream of a Caribbean Empire, 1854–1861*. Baton Rouge: Louisiana State University Press, 1973.

Meining, D. W. *Imperial Texas: An Interpretive Essay in Cultural Geography*. Austin: University of Texas Press, 1969.

Merk, Fredrick and Lois Bannister Merk. *Manifest Destiny and Mission in American History: A Reinterpretation*. New York: Alfred A. Knopf, 1963.

Miller, Edmund T. *Financial History of Texas*. Austin: University of Texas Press, 1936.

Morris, Richard B. *Encyclopedia of American History*. New York: Harper & Brothers, 1953.

Nackman, Mark E. *Nation within a Nation: The Rise of Texas Nationalism*. Port Washington, N.Y.: Kennikat Press, 1975.

Nance, Joseph M. *Attack and Counterattack: The Texas-Mexican Frontier, 1842*. Austin: University of Texas Press, 1964.

_____. *After San Jacinto: The Texas-Mexican Frontier, 1836–1841*. Austin: University of Texas Press, 1963.

Neighbours, Kenneth Franklin. *Robert Simpson Neighbors and the Texas Frontier 1836–1859*. Waco, Tex.: Texian Press, 1975.

Noel, Theophilus. *A Campaign From Santa Fe to the Mississippi: Being a*

History of the Old Sibley Brigade From Its First Organization to the Present Time; Its Campaigns in New Mexico, Arizona, Texas, Louisiana and Arkansas in the Years 1861-2-3-4. Edited by Martin Hardwick Hall and Edwin Adams Davis. Houston: Stagecoach Press, 1961.

_____. *Autobiography and Reminiscences of Theophilus Noel.* Chicago: The author, 1904.

O'Neil, James B. *They Die But Once: The Story of a Tejano.* New York: Knight Publications, 1936.

Olmstead, Frederick Law. *The Papers of Frederick Law Olmstead,* edited by Charles Capen McLaughlin. Baltimore: Johns Hopkins University Press, 1981.

Oltorf, Frank Calvert. *The Marlin Compound.* Austin: University of Texas Press, 1968.

Peck, Anne Merriman. *The March of Arizona History.* Tucson: Arizona Silhouettes, 1962.

Phillips, Ulrich B. ed. *The Correspondence of Robert Toombs, Alexander H. Stevens, and Howell Cobb.* New York: Da Capo Press, 1970.

Pletcher, David M. *The Diplomacy of Annexation: Texas, Oregon, and the Mexican War.* Columbia: University of Missouri Press, 1973.

Pomfrey, J. W. *A True Disclosure and Exposition of the Knights of the Golden Circle, including the Secret Sign, Grips, and Charges, of the Three Degrees, as Practised by the Order.* Cincinnati: The author, 1861.

Potter, David M. *The Impending Crisis: 1848–1861.* New York: Harper and Row, 1973.

Procter, Ben. *Not Without Honor: The Life of John H. Reagan.* Austin: University of Texas Press, 1962.

Raphael, Morris. *Battle in the Bayou Country.* Detroit: Harlo, 1984.

Reese, Timothy J. *Syke's Regular Infantry Division, 1861–1864: A History of Regular United States Infantry Operations in the Civil War's Eastern Theater.* Jefferson, N.C.: McFarland and Company, 1990.

Roland, Charles P. *Albert Sidney Johnston: Soldier of Three Republics.* Austin: University of Texas Press, 1964.

Rosengarten, Frederic, Jr. *Freebooters Must Die!: The Life and Death of William Walker, the Most Notorious Filibuster of the Nineteenth Century.* Wayne, Pa.: Haverford House, 1976.

Schwartz, Rosalie. *Across the River to Freedom: U.S. Negroes in Mexico.* El Paso: Texas Western Press, 1975.

Scobee, Barry. *Old Fort Davis.* San Antonio: The Naylor Company, 1947.

Scroggs, William O. *Filibusters and Financiers: The Story of William Walker and His Associates.* New York: Russell and Russell, 1969.

Smith, Cornelius C., Jr. *William Sanders Oury: History-Maker of the Southwest.* Tucson: University of Arizona, 1967.

Smith, Duane A. *The Birth of Colorado: A Civil War Perspective.* Norman: University of Oklahoma Press, 1989.

Smith, Joseph W. *Texan Statecraft, 1836–1845.* San Antonio: Naylor, 1941.

Sonnichsen, C. L. *Roy Bean: Law West of the Pecos*. New York: The MacMillan Company, 1943.

_____. *The Mescalero Apaches*. Norman: University of Oklahoma Press, 1966.

Sprague, J. T. *The Treachery in Texas: The Secession of Texas and the Arrest of the United States Officers and Soldiers Serving in Texas*. New York: New York Historical Society, 1862.

Spurlin, Charles. *West of the Mississippi with Waller's 13th Texas Cavalry Battalion CSA*. Hillsboro, Tex.: Hill Junior College Press, 1971.

Stout, Joseph Allen, Jr. *The Liberators: Filibustering Expeditions into Mexico, 1848–1862, and the Last Thrust of Manifest Destiny*. Los Angeles: Westernlore Press, 1973.

Sweeney, Edwin R. *Cochise: Chiricahua Apache Chief*. Norman: University of Oklahoma Press, 1991.

Taylor, Richard. *Destruction and Reconstruction: Personal Experiences of the Late War*. New York: D. Appleton and Company, 1879.

Tevis, James Henry. *Arizona in the '50s*. Albuquerque: University of New Mexico Press, 1954.

Thompson, Jerry, ed. *Westward the Texans: The Civil War Journal of Private William Randolph Howell*. El Paso: Texas Western Press, 1990.

Thompson, Jerry. *Colonel John Robert Baylor: Texas Indian Fighter and Confederate Soldier*. Hillsboro, Tex.: Hill Junior College Press, 1971.

_____, ed. *From Desert to Bayou: The Civil War Journal and Sketches of Morgan Wolfe Merrick*. El Paso: Texas Western Press, 1991.

_____. *Henry Hopkins Sibley: Confederate General of the West*. Natchitoches, La.: Northwestern State University Press, 1987.

Tyler, Ronnie C. *Santiago Vidaurri and the Southern Confederacy*. Austin: Texas State Historical Association, 1973.

Urwin, Gregory J. W. *The United States Cavalry: An Illustrated History*. [New York: Blandford Press], 1985.

Van Alstyne, Richard. *The Rising American Empire*. New York: Oxford University Press, 1960.

Walker, William. *The War in Nicaragua*. Mobile: S. H. Goetzel and Company, 1860.

Wallace, Edward S. *Destiny and Glory*. New York: Coward-McCann, 1957.

Warner, Ezra. *Generals In Gray: Lives of the Confederate Commanders*. Baton Rouge: Louisiana State University Press, 1959.

Warren, Harry, comp. *Paso del Aguila: A Chronical of Frontier Day on the Texas Border as Recorded in the Memoirs of Jesse Sumpter*. Austin: Encino Press, 1969.

Weaver, Richard M. *The Southern Essays of Richard M. Weaver*. Edited by George M. Curtis, III, and James J. Thompson, Jr. Indianapolis: Liberty Press, 1987.

Weems, John Edward and Jane Weems. *Dream of Empire: A Human History of the Republic of Texas, 1836–1846*. Fort Worth: Texas Christian University Press, 1986.

Weinberg, A. K. *Manifest Destiny: A Study of Nationalist Expansionism in American History.* Baltimore: Johns Hopkins University Press, 1935.

Whitford, William Clarke. *Colorado Volunteers in the Civil War: The New Mexico Campaign in 1862.* Boulder, Colo.: Pruett Press, 1963.

Wilbarger, J. W. *Indian Depredations in Texas: Reliable Accounts of Battle, Wars, Adventures, Forays, Murders, Massacres, etc., etc., Together with Biographical Sketches of Many of the Most Noted Indian Fighters and Frontiersmen of Texas.* Austin: Hutchings Printing House, 1889.

Williams, R. H. *With The Border Ruffians: Memories of the Far West, 1852–1868.* Notes by Arthur J. Mayer and Joseph Snell. Lincoln: University of Nebraska Press, 1982.

Winkler, Ernest W., ed. *Journal of the Secession Convention of Texas.* Austin: University of Texas Press, 1912.

Winters, John D. *The Civil War in Louisiana.* Baton Rouge: Louisiana State University Press, 1963.

Wooster, Ralph A. *The Secession Conventions of the South.* Princeton: Princeton University Press, 1962.

Worcester, Donald E. *The Apaches: Eagles of the Southwest.* Norman: University of Oklahoma Press, 1979.

ARTICLES

Anderson, Hattie M., ed. "With The Confederates in New Mexico During the Civil War: Memoirs of Hank Smith." *Panhandle Plains Historical Review* 2 (1929): 65–97.

Bailey, Lance. "Sibley's Texas Confederate Brigade." *Texas Historian* 43 (May, 1983): 6–10.

Barker, Eugene C. "Land Speculation as a Cause of the Texas Revolution." *Texas Historical Quarterly* 10 (Spring, 1906): 76–95.

Barker, Eugene C. "President Jackson and the Texas Revolution." *American Historical Review* 12 (Winter, 1907): 788–809.

Binkley, William Campbell. "The Last Stage of Texan Military Operations Against Mexico, 1843." *Southwestern Historical Quarterly* 22 (January, 1919): 206–71.

Bridges, C. A. "The Knights of the Golden Circle: A Filibustering Fantasy." *Southwestern Historical Quarterly* 44 (January, 1941): 287–302.

Buenger, Walter L. "Texas and the Riddle of Secession." *Southwestern Historical Quarterly* 87 (October, 1983): 151–82.

Campbell, Randolph. "Texas and the Nashville Convention of 1850." *Southwestern Historical Quarterly* 76 (July, 1972): 1–14.

Carroll, H. Bailey. "Steward A. Miller and the Snively Expedition of 1843." *Southwestern Historical Quarterly* 54 (January, 1951): 275–78.

Crane, Conrad. "A Careful Examination of the Field of Battle: Military Lessons from the Battle of Val Verde." Unpublished paper presented at the Fort Craig

Conference, Socorro, New Mexico, 1989.

Dunn, Roy Sylvan. "The KGC in Texas, 1860–1861." *Southwestern Historical Quarterly* 70 (April, 1967): 543–73.

Eaton, W. Clement. "Frontier Life in Southern Arizona, 1858–1861." *Southwestern Historical Quarterly* 36 (January, 1933): 173–92.

Faulkner, Walter A. ed. "With Sibley in New Mexico: The Journal of William Henry Smith." West Texas Historical Association *Year Book* 27 (October, 1951): 111–42.

Finch, L. Boyd. "Arizona's Governors without Portfolio: A Wonderfully Diverse Lot." *Journal of Arizona History* 26 (Spring, 1985): 77–99.

_____. "Sherod Hunter and the Confederates in Arizona." *Journal of Arizona History* 10 (Autumn, 1969): 137–206.

Fornell, Earl W. "Texans and Filibusters in the 1850s." *Southwestern Historical Quarterly* 59 (April, 1956): 411–28.

Gailey, Harry, Jr. "Sam Houston and the Texas War Fever, March–August, 1842." *Southwestern Historical Quarterly* 62 (July, 1958): 29–44.

Gaither, Donald, ed. "The 'Pet Lambs' at Glorieta Pass: Charles Gardiner called the battle 'the severest stroke the Texans ever received at our hands, in this country,'" *Civil War Times Illustrated* 15 (November, 1976): 30–38.

Goetzmann, W. H. "The United States–Mexican Boundary Survey, 1848–1853." *Southwestern Historical Quarterly* 60 (October, 1958): 164–90.

Goldman, Henry H. "Southern Sympathy in Southern California, 1860–1865." *Journal of the West* 4 (October, 1965): 577–85.

Gracy, David B., ed. "New Mexico Campaign Letters of Frank Starr, 1861–1862." *Texas Military History* 4 (Fall, 1964): 169–88.

Haas, Oscar, trans. "The Diary of Julius Gieseke, 1863–1864." *Military History of Texas and the Southwest* 18 (October, 1988): 65–92.

_____. "The Diary of Julius Gieseke, 1861–1862." *Military History of Texas and the Southwest* 18 (1988): 49–63.

Hall, Martin Hardwick "The Mesilla Times: A Journal of Confederate Arizona." *Arizona and the West* 5 (Winter, 1963): 337–51.

_____. "Albert Sidney Johnston's First Confederate Command." *McNeese Review* 13 (1962): 3–12.

_____. "The Court-Martial of Arthur Pendleton Bagby, C.S.A." *East Texas Historical Journal* 19 (1981): 60–67.

_____. "Native Mexican Relations in Confederate Arizona, 1861–1862." *Journal of Arizona History* 8 (Autumn, 1967): 171–78.

_____. "Negroes with Confederate Troops in West Texas and New Mexico." *Password* 13 (Spring, 1968): 11–12.

_____. "The Skirmish at Mesilla." *Arizona and the West* 1 (Winter, 1958): 343–51.

Hall, Martin Hardwick, ed. "The Taylor Letters: Correspondence from Fort Bliss, 1861." *Military History of Texas and the Southwest* 15 (Fall, 1980): 54–60.

_____, ed. "An Appraisal of the 1862 New Mexico Campaign: A

Confederate Officer's Letter to Nacogdoches." *New Mexico Historical Review* 51 (October, 1976): 329–33.

_____, ed. "The Journal of Ebeneezer Hanna." *Password* 3 (January, 1958): 1–29.

Hicks, Jimmie, ed. "Some Letters Concerning the Knights of the Golden Circle in Texas, 1860–1861." *Southwestern Historical Quarterly* 65 (July, 1961): 80–86.

Hord, Ruth Waldrop, ed. "The Diary of Lieutenant E. J. Robb, C.S.A., from Santa Fe to Fort Lancaster, 1862." *Permian Historical Annual* 18 (December, 1978): 59–79.

Howren, Allen. "Causes and Origin of the Decree of April 6, 1830." *Southwestern Historical Quarterly* 82 (Summer, 1978): 117–42.

Hunter, John Warren. "Fighting With Sibley in New Mexico." *Hunters Magazine* 1 (November, 1910): 1–20.

Husaker, William J. "Lansford W. Hastings' Project for the Invasion and Conquest of Arizona and New Mexico for the Southern Confederacy." *Arizona Historical Review* 4 (1931–32): 5-12.

Johnson, Norman K. "Satanic-looking Colonel John R. Baylor fought Yankees, Indians and one unfortunate newspaper editor." *America's Civil War* 3 (January, 1991): 10–72.

May, Robert E. "Young American Males and Filibustering in the Age of Manifest Destiny: The United States Army as a Cultural Mirror." *Journal of American History* 78 (December, 1991): 846–74.

McClendon, R. E. "Daniel Webster and Mexican Relations: The Santa Fe Prisoners." *Southwestern Historical Quarterly* 36 (January, 1934): 288–311.

Merchant, S. W. "Fighting with Sibley in New Mexico," *Hunter's Magazine* 1 (November, 1910): 10–12.

Middleton, Annie. "Donelson's Mission to Texas in Behalf of Annexation." *Southwestern Historical Quarterly* 24 (July, 1925): 23–67.

Miller, Darlis A. "Hispanos and the Civil War in New Mexico: A Reconsideration." *New Mexico Historical Review* 54 (April, 1979): 105–23.

Moseley, Edward H. "Indians from the Eastern United States and the Defense of Northeastern Mexico," 1855–1864." *Southwestern Social Science Quarterly* 46 (Fall, 1965): 273–80.

Neighbours, Kenneth F. "The Taylor-Neighbors Struggle Over the Upper Rio Grande Region of Texas in 1850." *Southwestern Historical Quarterly* 61 (April, 1958): 431–63.

Oates, Stephen B. "Recruiting Cavalry in Texas." *Southwestern Historical Quarterly* 64 (April, 1961): 463–77.

Park, Joseph F. "The Apaches in Mexican-American Relations, 1843–1861: A Footnote to the Gadsden Treaty." *Arizona and the West* 3 (Summer, 1961): 129–46.

Porter, Kenneth W. "The Seminole in Mexico, 1850–1861." *Hispanic American Historical Review* 31 (Spring, 1951): 1–31.

Pratt, Julius W. "John L. O'Sullivan and Manifest Destiny." *New York History*

14 (Fall, 1933): 213–34.

_____. "The Origin of 'Manifest Destiny'." *American Historical Review* 32 (Winter, 1927): 795–98.

Rippy, J. Fred. "The Negotiation of the Gadsden Treaty." *Southwestern Historical Quarterly* 27 (July, 1923): 435–42.

Sandbo, Ana Irene. "The First Session of the Secession Convention of Texas." *Southwestern Historical Quarterly* 18 (October, 1914): 162–94.

Shearer, Earnest C. "The Carvajal Disturbances." *Southwestern Historical Quarterly* 55 (October, 1951): 201–30.

_____. "The Callahan Expedition, 1855." *Southwestern Historical Quarterly* 54 (April, 1951): 430–51.

Stenberg, Richard R. "Jackson, Anthony Butler, and Texas." *Southwestern Historical Quarterly* 13 (Fall, 1934): 264–86.

_____. "The Texas Schemes of Jackson and Houston." *Southwestern Historical Quarterly* 15 (Fall, 1934): 229–50.

Thompson, Jerry D. "The Civil War Diary of Major Charles Emil Wesche." *Password* 39 (Spring, 1994): 37–47.

Timmons, W. H. "American El Paso: The Formative Years, 1848–1850." *Southwestern Historical Quarterly* 87 (July, 1983): 1–36.

Tittman, Edward D. "Confederate Courts in New Mexico." *New Mexico Historical Review* 3 (October, 1928): 347–56.

Tyler, Ronnie C. "The Callahan Expedition of 1855: Indians or Negroes?" *Southwestern Historical Quarterly* 70 (April, 1967): 574–85.

Urban, C. Stanley. "The Africanization of Cuba Scare, 1853–1855." *Hispanic American Historical Review* 37 (Spring, 1957): 29–45.

Van Alstyne, Richard. "The Signifigance of the Mississippi Valley in American Diplomatic History, 1686–1890." *Mississippi Valley Historical Review* 36 (Spring, 1949): 215–38.

Vevier, Charles. "American Continentalism: An Idea of Expansion." *American Historical Review* 65 (Summer, 1960): 323–25.

Vigness, David M. "A Texas Expedition into Mexico, 1840." *Southwestern Historical Quarterly* 62 (July, 1958): 18–28.

_____. "Relations of the Republic of Texas and the Republic of the Rio Grande." *Southwestern Historical Quarterly* 57 (January, 1955): 312–21.

Werne, Joseph Richard. "Partisan Politics and the Mexican Boundary Survey, 1848–1853." *Southwestern Historical Quarterly* 90 (April, 1987): 329–46.

Wooster, Ralph A. "Texas Military Operations against Mexico, 1842–1843." *Southwestern Historical Quarterly* 68 (April, 1965): 465–84.

Young, Hugh H. "Two Texas Patriots." *Southwestern Historical Quarterly* 44 (July, 1940): 16–32.

Index

177–80, 186–87, 194, 202–204, 209, 214, 218, 237, 244, 246; Eighth Infantry, 38, 99, 188; Fifth Infantry, 68, 165, 177, 205; First Cavalry, 158, 186, 194, 205, 215; First Dragoons, 171; Hall's Battery, 163; McRae's Battery, 177; Regiment of Mounted Rifles, 47, 57, 80, 107; Second Cavalry, 215; Second Dragoons, 44, 54, 76, 97; Seventh Infantry, 70, 165, 171, 175; Tenth Infantry, 165, 171, 175; Third Cavalry, 107–108, 158, 170, 173, 186, 194, 205, 215, 218, 269

Utah, 14, 46, 103, 298
Uvalde, 121

Valencia, N. Mex., 193
Val Verde, 153, 155–58, 162, 164–65, 184–86, 192, 235, 269
Val Verde, Battle of, 178, 185, 201, 203, 234, 239, 241, 246, 254, 257, 265–66, 277, 300
Val Verde Battery, 250, 253, 255, 261, 272
Van Dorn, Earl, 38–41, 43, 70, 72
Vasquez, Rafael, 80
Vicksburg, Miss., 289, 295
Victoria, Tex., 87, 92, 162, 263, 274
Victoria County, 218
Victoria Invincibles, 87–88, 277
Vidaurri, Santiago, 12, 27, 83
violence, 124, 130
Virginia, 53, 83, 87–88, 272, 294–96

Waco, Tex., 91
Wafford, John, 92
wagons, 107–108, 113, 118, 120, 133, 135, 140–41, 148–49, 153, 155, 164, 179, 182–83, 188, 192, 195–96, 202, 224–26, 228, 230, 236, 238, 240–41, 244, 246, 250, 252–53, 255, 259, 275–77, 280, 284, 287, 290–91
Walker, William, 81, 83, 133
Walker County, 99
Wallace, Benjamin Rush, 9
Waller, Edwin, 40, 56–57, 68, 101, 110, 114, 116, 126, 147, 294; slave of, 40
War Between the States, 21–22, 80
Ward's Hotel, 266
War for Southern Independence, 21–22, 80
War of the Reforma, 27

Washington, D.C., 14, 99
water holes, 118, 121
weapons, 96, 107, 140, 163, 166–67, 171, 175, 180, 183, 201, 216, 218, 227, 281
weather, 119, 125, 128–31, 133, 135, 140, 147, 150, 153, 154, 158, 169, 188, 193, 200, 208, 225, 240, 247
Weatherford, 27, 89, 91
West, the, 14, 19, 25, 34, 36, 40, 50, 74, 75, 86, 90, 293–96, 298–300
Western Military Institute, 80
West Point, 44, 48, 80, 97, 99, 178, 299
West Texas, 121, 287
Wheeler, Joseph, 44
Whigs, 78
whiskey, 88, 231. *See also* liquor
White, Ami, 206
White, William P., 65
White's Mill, 206
Whitley, Sharp, 203, 216, 219, 221, 224
Willard's Hotel, 279
Williams, John, 89
Williams, R. H., 17, 23, 27, 29, 36, 38, 83, 85, 118
Williams, Robert Thomas, 89, 93, 123, 288, 289
Williams, Wady T., 237
Willow Bar, 133
Wilson's Creek, Battle of, 178
Wingate, Benjamin, 171, 173, 177
Winn Bridge, Tex., 87
Wisconsin, 288, 300
Woll, Adrian, 25
women, 235
Wood, William, 95, 139
Wood's Battery, 95, 117, 139
Worth County, 8–9, 10
W. P. Lane Rangers, 37
wrestling, 123
Wright, Henry C., 87, 90, 93–94, 121–23, 131, 137–38, 141–42, 153, 192, 222, 227, 232, 239, 267, 281–83, 287
Wulff, A. F., 69

Yost, Samuel, 20

Zuloaga, José María, 191